JOURNAL · OF MORAL THEOLOGY

VOLUME 13, SPECIAL ISSUE 2
OCTOBER 2024

LISTENING PRACTICES
in
GLOBAL CATHOLICISM

EDITED BY
ANNA ROWLANDS
and
ALEXIS ARTAUD DE LA FERRIÈRE

JOURNAL · OF
M · O · R · A L
THEOLOGY

Journal of Moral Theology is published semiannually, with regular issues in January and July. Our mission is to publish scholarly articles in the field of Catholic moral theology, as well as theological treatments of related topics in philosophy, economics, political philosophy, and psychology.

Articles published in the *Journal of Moral Theology* undergo at least two double blind peer reviews. To submit an article for the journal, please visit the "For Authors" page on our website at jmt.scholasticahq.com/for-authors.

Journal of Moral Theology is available full text in the *ATLA Religion Database with ATLASerials®* (RDB®), a product of the American Theological Library Association.
Email: atla@atla.com, www.atla.com.
ISSN 2166-2851 (print)
ISSN 2166-2118 (online)

Journal of Moral Theology is published by The Journal of Moral Theology, Inc.

Copyright © 2024 individual authors and The Journal of Moral Theology, Inc. All rights reserved.
Pickwick Publications, An Imprint of Wipf and Stock Publishers, 199 W. 8th Ave., Suite 3, Eugene, OR 97401
www.wipfandstock.com. ISBN: 979-8-3852-3840-8

JOURNAL · OF
M · O · R · A · L
THEOLOGY

EDITOR EMERITUS
Jason King, *St. Mary's University, San Antonio, TX*

EDITOR
M. Therese Lysaught, *Loyola University Chicago Stritch School of Medicine*

SENIOR EDITOR
William J. Collinge, *Mount St. Mary's University*

ASSOCIATE EDITORS
Mari Rapela Heidt, *Notre Dame of Maryland University*
Alexandre A. Martins, *Marquette University*
Mary M. Doyle Roche, *College of the Holy Cross*
Matthew Shadle, *Window Light*
Kate Ward, *Marquette University*

MANAGING EDITOR
Jean-Pierre Fortin, *St. Michael's College, University of Toronto*

EDITORIAL ASSISANT
Aaron Weisel, *Ave Maria University*

EDITORIAL BOARD
Christina Astorga, *University of Portland*
Jana M. Bennett, *University of Dayton*
James Caccamo, *St. Joseph's University*
Victor Carmona, *University of San Diego*
Carolyn A. Chau, *King's University College at Western University, Ontario*
Stan Chu Ilo, *DePaul University*
Meghan Clark, *St. John's University*
Dana Dillon, *Providence College*
Jorge Jose Ferrer, SJ, *Pontifical Catholic University of Puerto Rico*
Daniel Fleming, *St. Vincent's Health Australia/University of Notre Dame Australia*
Julia A. Fleming, *Creighton University*
Joseph Flipper, *University of Dayton*
Nichole M. Flores, *University of Virginia*
Craig A. Ford, Jr., *St. Norbert College*
Matthew J. Gaudet, *Santa Clara University*
Leo Guardado, *Fordham University*
Andrew Kim, *Marquette University*
Cory Labrecque, *Université Laval*
Amy Levad, *University of St. Thomas, MN*
Leocadie Lushombo, *Santa Clara University*
Christina G. McRorie, *Boston College*
Cory D. Mitchell, *Mercy Health Muskegon*
Suzanne Mulligan, *St. Patrick's Pontifical University, Ireland*
Sheryl Overmyer, *DePaul University*
Anna Perkins, *University of the West Indies*
Bernard G. Prusak, *John Carroll University*
Emily Reimer-Barry, *University of San Diego*
Alessandro Rovati, *Belmont Abbey College*
Tobias Winright, *St. Patrick's Pontifical University, Ireland*

JOURNAL OF MORAL THEOLOGY
VOLUME 13, SPECIAL ISSUE 2
OCTOBER 2024

CONTENTS

INTRODUCTION

Listening Practices in a Synodal Church: Interim Reflections from a Symposium in Rome
Anna Rowlands 1

ORIGINAL ARTICLES

Listening across the Américas: Base Ecclesial Communities and Relational Organizing as Listening Practices for a Synodal Church
Richard L. Wood 10

Beyond Synodal Listening: Theological Action Research and Cultures of Conversation
Clare Watkins 36

French Catholics and Synodality: Spiritual Sensibilities and the Will to Participate or Abstain
Yann Raison de Cleuziou 58

Doing Theology by Listening to Marginalized Voices? Methodological Elements from Encountering Indigenous Families in a Northern Canadian Community
Julian Paparella 83

Listening a Synodal Church into Being: Learning Points from the Methodology of the Synod 2021–2024 and the Asian Experience
Christina Kheng 108

More Than Listening is Needed for Synodality: Observations Based on the Australian Plenary Council and the Church in the New Testament
Peter J. McGregor 137

Joseph-Albert Cardinal Malula and the "Listening Bishop": An Institution to (Re)Discover
    Ignace Ndongala Maduku 160

Academic Listening Practices and Synodality: Reflections from a Study of World Youth Days
    Charles Mercier 179

ROUNDTABLE

Two "Fires" of Leadership: Is it Possible to Listen and Lead Parish Cultural Change?
    Hannah Vaughan-Spruce 195

Sabbath, Contemplative Time, and Liturgical Listening
    Clare E. Wolfteich 206

Listening in Stereo and Communicating in Semaphore: Child Sexual Abuse Survivor-Led Strategies for Culture Change in the Catholic Church
    Alana Harris 217

Asking to Listen: Engaging Social Scientific Methods as a Listening Practice in Global Catholicism
    Tricia C. Bruce 239

Research-Backed Practices to Engage Youth in a Vibrant Catholic Church: The Case for Implementing Sacred Listening Practices
    Josh Packard and Megan Bissell 252

EPILOGUE

Listening and the Moral Life
    Alexis Artaud de la Ferrière 271

Listening Practices in a Synodal Church: Interim Reflections from a Symposium in Rome

Anna Rowlands

Abstract: Listening is at the heart of Pope Francis's synodality project. Where does scholarship addressing themes of listening, encounter, and lived experience of Catholicism sit within this project as both a subject addressed by synodality and critical agent of it? This special issue publishes the outcomes of an eighteen-month project, commissioned by members of the Synod's methodology commission, undertaken independently under university research auspices. The project culminated in a symposium in Rome in March 2023. The project aimed to model a form of academic service to the listening phase of the Synod, rooted in a collaboration between scholars and synodal practitioners; that is, to provide a small-scale contribution of what we have outlined above as somewhat missing in the process so far. This introduction provides background context on the research question and an overview of the articles as well as reflection on the implications of the synodal process for moral theology.

WHEN POPE FRANCIS ANNOUNCED IN MARCH 2020[1] that he was amending the usual formula for the convocation of a Synod of Bishops and convoking the whole Catholic world in a now nearly four-year synodal process, he placed the practice of listening at its heart. The first phase of the synodal process would be devoted solely to an exercise of deep ecclesial listening, with a preference for listening to those living along the various social and ecclesial margins. For some, this was a welcome re-orientation of reform and renewal towards the grassroots, the regions and global peripheries, and the embrace of voices and subjects often neglected in official ecclesial discernment. For others, it was a bewildering notion that risked introducing confusion, seemingly

---

[1] See Francis, "Address to the Faithful of the Diocese of Rome," September 18, 2021, www.vatican.va/content/francesco/en/speeches/2021/september/documents/20210918-fedeli-diocesiroma.html.

placing the primary teaching function of the church in suspended animation, perhaps watering down the proclamatory task of mission. As one bishop said to a synodal meeting during the listening phase, manifesting a genuine anxiety he felt, "Yes, but, I'm a bishop, much of what I hear is in error. When can I *teach* people what is right? That's my role," revealing as much about perceptions of episcopacy as the challenges of synodal listening. Others still were broadly welcoming but worried that the listening task seemed vague, too broad, or that the Synod of Bishops was simply the wrong vehicle for such work.

The contemporary institution of the Synod of Bishops was first mooted at the time of the Second Vatican Council and later adopted by Paul VI as a means to deepen episcopal collegiality and enable an ongoing consultative gathering of bishops to aid the ministry of the Bishop of Rome.[2] Francis has made regular—although not unprecedented (see Pope John II)—use of the synod, in its ordinary, extraordinary, and special forms. John Paul II extensively used special synods focused on specific geographical contexts, convoking 16 synods across the three forms in his twenty-six-year papacy. Francis has called five synods in his ten years of papacy. What is novel about Francis's use of this form is his desire to expand the membership and function of the synod to deepen a synodal renewal of the whole church, viewing growth in synodality as the missionary calling of the church in this generation. He has become convinced, partly based on his experience in Latin America, renewed during the Synod on the Pan-Amazon Region, that the dialogical format of the synod enables a spiritual practice that facilitates encounter, mutual learning, and inspiration guided by the Spirit that can break the church out of a variety of forms of stasis, division, and disagreement. He believes such a practice is a necessary transcendent sign to a world locked in the grip of the same dynamics. In the set of pandemic-era interviews that compose *Let Us Dream*, Francis explains that in synodal listening and speaking, there is the possibility of a moment of "overflow," closer to the emergence of musical harmony or polyphony than cognitive agreement or consensus, a transcendent practice that cannot be rendered in terms of mere agreement or disagreement and which is a sign for our age.[3] For Francis, synodality is proposed as an integral *moral*, social, and ecclesial practice.

We should be clear, then, that in the realm of academic study, critical attention to this call to synodality and listening as a constitutive

---

[2] Holy See Press Office, "Synod of bishops: General Information on the Synod," www.vatican.va/news_services/press/documentazione/documents/sinodo/sinodo_documentazione-generale_en.html.

[3] Pope Francis, *Let Us Dream: The Path to a Better Future*, ed. Austen Ivereigh (New York: Simon and Schuster, 2020).

part of the character of a synodal church cannot be left as a matter of interest for hardcore ecclesiologists alone. Indeed, the very call for synodal renewal includes a call for the renewal of theology as an ecclesial practice and promotes the transgression of overly fixed walls between disciplines of study, encouraging dialogue and collaboration. In this sense, scholars are themselves *subjects* of synodal discussion and addressed by the synod fathers and mothers as ecclesial *agents*, called into a more active collaboration in a field of common, if differentiated, labor.

This attention to the role and service of theology relates to a wider difficulty pinpointed by the synodal process but not yet discussed as self-reflexively as it ought to be by synod members or theologians. Whilst there have been creative methods for engaging bishops in forms of listening and discernment and drawing expanded lay membership into formal participation, many have perceived a lack of such creativity in integrating theologians and theology successfully into the process. The place of theology and the role of those who study, teach, and research in service of synodal renewal are elements that have not been well-calibrated thus far. This continued difficulty expresses itself in a number of ways and has various causes, whose more comprehensive mapping lies beyond the task of this editorial introduction. However, it is perhaps important to note in light of the project that has led to this special issue, that a rich and creative contribution of theologians and other scholars of Catholicism from other disciplines to the process has not been aided by either the tendency of some ecclesiologists to dismiss the listening phase as "mere sociology," nor the failure of the synodal process to draw formally on the expertise of those who study Catholicism from the vantage point of the social sciences, whose methods—despite the cries of mere sociology—have ironically been almost entirely undeployed. If synodality is to become the feature of the Catholic Church in this generation in the way the Pope hopes, the work to engage theology in service of, and as a critical companion to, that task remains only very partially begun.

To state the matter more positively, the ambition and character of the synod is a matter that should interest moral theologians deeply. Certainly, many of the issues raised in the grassroots synodal reports were clearly moral-theological in character. Most obviously, a concern for renewed pastoral and theological attention to questions of sexuality, the body, and gender relations was universally raised across global regions. It is worth noting that a careful reading of the reports sent by the Episcopal Conferences and other groupings in 2022 often asked for better guidance and quality reflection on moral questions, teaching that engaged more adequately the pastoral realities of the church at the local level. Whilst media headlines wanted to press questions of grassroots "demands" for changes in teaching, beneath the headlines were nuanced calls for better quality moral theological reflection that engages, informs, and listens to the exercise of conscience and practice of discernment at the grassroots. Those requests should interest moral theologians greatly. It also seems that the areas where the synod found most difficulty articulating either the grounds for convergence or divergences (the language that shaped the Synthesis Report)[4] concerned moral questions. The Synthesis Report of 2023 is able to frame the agreements and disagreements over questions of women's role and status, but lacks similar framing on other moral matters raised in the local reports and discussed in the small groups of the Synod Assembly, a matter that, despite the fears of some, is less likely to be a deliberate suppression and more a lack of capacity to find shared language to frame the debate in terms that those who disagree can recognise, accept, and vote on. The *lack* in the report exposes an important and serious site of moral theological work on questions of theological anthropology, gender, and sexuality for those interested in and committed to ecclesial service. Read carefully, the report itself calls for this work without quite spelling out why it is so sorely needed.

A different kind of challenge for moral theologians is also raised in the views expressed in the local reports: many laity and clergy feel they lack confidence and literacy in areas of social teaching and perceive a "professionalisation" of ethical questions, in particular, around economy, ecology, political community, dignity, and rights. These are seen as topics to be addressed by bishops, academics, and public figures, with social teaching pitched towards their formation. The importance of moral questions as part of ecumenical and interfaith dialogues was also noted as a priority emerging from the local churches not yet matched in official dialogues or documents.

However, we repeat previous mistakes if we reduce moral theology in the context of the synod to ethical issues alone. The synod is throwing up wider questions of how moral theology is at stake and can serve ecclesial renewal. The relationship between theologians and bishops is revealed as rather distant, if not in many instances and contexts quite broken (with notable positive exceptions); the relationship between the formulation of questions at the grassroots and the dominant questions pursued within academic study is revealed as lacking mediation; the relationship between the spiritual practices of the church and the methods of academic inquiry is revealed as at times

---

[4] XVI Ordinary General Assembly of the Synod of Bishops, First Session (4–29 October 2023), "Synthesis Report: A Synodal Church in Mission," www.synod.va/content/dam/synod/assembly/synthesis/english/2023.10.28-ENG-Synthesis-Report.pdf.

non-existent. Currently, it is a significant limitation of the process that canon lawyers, ecclesiologists, and systematicians have been numerous amongst the synodal "experts," and moral theologians present mainly as small group facilitators.

There are, of course, many notable examples where none of this applies, and many moral theologians are at the forefront of impressive practices of dialogical research, deep listening, and ecclesial service. They are also at the forefront of addressing ethical and moral issues in the secular world from a theological point of view and through creative interfaith exchange the church has been woefully slow to engage in, learn from, or celebrate. Nonetheless, the wider picture still requires sober attention and should prompt reflection and discussion. Above all, the synodal process invites questions about the character of moral theology as service, and the extent to which moral theology is integrated—that is, open to dialogue with the social sciences, willing to engage the pastoral life of the local church, interested in the historical (and contemporary) methods of discernment in the various spiritual traditions of the church, and willing to grapple with ecclesial questions of power, trust, authority, and responsibility.[5] We should note that most of the core questions emerging at the tail end of the synodal process have a simultaneously moral and ecclesiological character: power, trust, authority, co-responsibility, and accountability. At present, there is little recognition at an official level that these questions are inherently moral matters.

This brings us to the articles collected in this volume. These articles emerge from an eighteen-month project, commissioned by members of the synod's methodology commission but undertaken independently under university research auspices. The project culminated in the symposium, "Listening Practices in Global Catholicism," held at Angelicum University, Rome, on March 25–27, 2024, jointly organized by the Centre for Catholic Studies (CCS), the Pontifical University of St. Thomas (Angelicum), and Royal Holloway College University of London, in partnership with the Synod on Synodality Listening Project Steering Committee.

The first two years of grassroots listening produced not only a series of official documents but also questions that exceeded the capacity of the formal synodal process to address. These included wider reflections on how listening forms part of theological praxis, how the social sciences can assist ecclesial listening processes and a fuller expression of synodality in the church. They also respond to the repeated insight that local churches found it especially hard to meet the request that they listen with priority to their peripheries. All reports

---

[5] See, e.g., M. Therese Lysaught, "*Ad (Synodalem) Theologiam (Moralem) Promovendam*," *Journal of Moral Theology* 13, no. 1 (2024): 1–14, doi.org/10.55476/001c.92079.

suggested this had been more challenging than expected. We also commissioned articles reflecting learning from other non-synodal ecclesial listening processes. In this sense, the articles gathered here deal with some of the excess the synod cannot entirely contain, which is fertile ground moral theologians, amongst others, can engage. We invited scholars who have mainly not been part of the official process to offer their expertise and be in dialogue with pastoral practitioners who have been and remain at the heart of facilitating the synodal process of the last four years. For this reason, this volume contains an initial section of more conventionally academic articles, followed by a roundtable of shorter more practice-based articles.

A series of connected themes emerge through the articles published here. The most sustained common insight is that the synodal ambitions to become a listening church expressed by Pope Francis cannot be realised without renewed commitment to building and sustaining authentic pastoral relationships. A disposition towards genuine listening, in which attention is gifted to the other, is the pre-condition of possibility for such relationships. The articles note that the current crisis of trust and authority in the church creates a serious barrier to the practice of this otherwise obvious insight. This barrier paradoxically makes its practice all the more necessary. As Josh Packard and Megan Bissell note succinctly in their roundtable contribution, the church continues to use "high trust tools in a low trust world."[6] It appears not yet cognisant of what has happened culturally to our trust relationships. Using the example of their research with young people, they note that authentic deep relationships, which earn trust through relational ministry that starts with listening, are the clear condition of many for a willingness to engage or re-engage with the church. Writing on the experience of synodality in Asia over the last three years, Christina Kheng notes that the condition for overcoming cultural barriers to open listening lies in the willingness to practice radical welcome "in word and deed," a commitment to active relationship-building focused on practices of communion alongside an openness to leverage current structures and create new ones to facilitate this process. At the heart of this ethic is a commitment to forms of encounter created through listening that create, Kheng writes, "an authentic viewpoint" which is "something emergent rather than

---

[6] Josh Packard and Megan Bissell, "Research Backed Practices to Engage Youth in a Vibrant Catholic Church: The Case for Implementing Sacred Listening Practices," *Journal of Moral Theology* 13, Special Issue 2 (2024): 252–270.

pre-existent, ripening through a process of mutual encounter and communal conversion."[7]

This same theme of rooting listening in authentic pastoral relationships emerges in the articles that focus on the possibilities and challenges of listening at the social peripheries or margins. We noted above that one of the consistent reflections of local communities present in the episcopal conference reports was that listening to persons who live their lives along or within various social peripheries proved far more challenging than they expected, something at once humbling, concerning, and thought-provoking. Drawing on their own research, the contributors to this volume note that such listening is most fruitful and least instrumentalist when it happens from within established, dignified, and sustained social relationships. Richard Wood draws on his own research across different kinds of social movements and organisations to suggest that this has to be a meaningful listening in solidarity in which the moral and social dimensions of relationships are part of the picture.[8] Without commitment to listening in solidarity there is no depth of encounter to structure the act of "listening" to those at the peripheries. He draws on the theology of Pope Francis on "encounter" and "social friendship" to suggest that the very idea of synodality and synodal listening is a moral practice: encounter opens us to the acknowledgement of difference and a necessary tarrying with conflict; it also requires an account of power and its use (and misuse). In his article on Indigenous peoples and the listening church, Julian Paparella talks about the theological disposition that accompanies Wood's more sociological insights.[9] Encounter, which builds and receives the life of communion, is the moral goal of listening to the peripheries. In and through encounters with neighbors, Christ's own presence is manifested. In the practice of listening, this deeper and necessary encounter becomes possible. Correspondingly, without such encounters, synodal renewal remains limited. Although not a point he makes directly, there are interesting parallels in Peter McGregor's article and his treatment of the question of looking and not merely aurally listening for the signs of the Spirit at work, *seeing* through encounter as well as *hearing* what God is doing in history—a New Testament emphasis he finds lacking

---

[7] Christina Kheng, "Listening a Synodal Church into Being: Learning Points from the Methodology of the Synod 2021–2024 and the Asian Experience," *Journal of Moral Theology* 13, Special Issue 2 (2024): 108–136.

[8] Richard L. Wood, "Listening across the Américas: Base Ecclesial Communities and Relational Organizing as Listening Practices for a Synodal Church," *Journal of Moral Theology* 13, Special Issue 2 (2024): 10–35.

[9] Julian Paparella, "Doing Theology by Listening to Marginalized Voices? Methodological Elements from Encountering Indigenous Families in a Northern Canadian Community," *Journal of Moral Theology* 13, Special Issue 2 (2024): 83–107.

in the current synodal formulation.¹⁰ Clare Watkins explores the limitations of the "Conversation in the Spirit" method formalised by the Synod for conversations at the social margins, suggesting the need for reclaiming ordinary conversation in its messy interruptive forms.¹¹

A second important connecting theme across these articles concerns the disposition of the researcher and scholar and the place of their craft and vocation in a synodal church. Charles Mercier offers a beautiful and vivid reflection on conducting empirical research on World Youth Day as a social scientist and historian and the relationship between his formation as scholar and Christian, and capacity to offer a service to a church able to receive and recognise (not exactly a plot spoiler, but that last part proves the more challenging).¹² In several articles there is a rather nice interplay between the question of formation through research, especially but not only empirical research which learns about the faith of others, and the creation of information or knowledge that might aid the church in its own formation and understanding.

A key—and perhaps surprising—connecting theme emerging during this synodal process and across the articles is the question of the renewal of models of leadership in the church, including attention to the ministry of the bishop in a synodal church. Ignace Maduku writes of the example of the so-called "listening bishop" Cardinal Malula in the Democratic Republic of Congo in the late 1970s, and explores the need for renewal in the African Church now, more urban and growing in many contexts, in a model of episcopal leadership oriented towards listening in order to foster a *"consensus ecclesiae."*¹³ Wood's exploration of models of community organising and base ecclesial communities considers briefly the possibility of a model of episcopal decision-making expressive of a genuinely "participative hierarchy."¹⁴ Hannah Vaughan-Spruce's contribution to the round-table also addresses the tensive but potentially fruitful relationship

---

¹⁰ Peter J. McGregor, "More Than Listening is Needed for Synodality: Observations Based on the Australian Plenary Council and the Church in the New Testament," *Journal of Moral Theology* 13, Special Issue 2 (2024): 137–159.

¹¹ Clare Watkins, "Beyond Synodal Listening: Theological Action Research and Cultures of Conversation," *Journal of Moral Theology* 13, Special Issue 2 (2024): 36–57.

¹² Charles Mercier, "Academic Listening Practices and Synodality: Reflections from a Study of World Youth Days," *Journal of Moral Theology* 13, Special Issue 2 (2024): 179–194.

¹³ Ignace Ndongala Maduku, "Joseph-Albert Cardinal Malula and the 'Listening Bishop': An Institution to (Re)Discover," *Journal of Moral Theology* 13, Special Issue 2 (2024): 160–178.

¹⁴ Wood, "Listening across the Américas," 11.

between listening and leadership for intentional change in parishes.[15] Alana Harris's roundtable contribution, which considers a movement that aims to address sexual abuse in the Catholic Church, explores the possible ways leaders can both emerge from within the community of survivors to create forms of political-ecclesial action, liturgy, and public art and protest and draw forth the leadership of bishops as listening leaders.[16]

We hope the reader will discover other overlapping themes and connections as they read these articles. Their single, common interest has been to explore a little more the terrain of listening in the church of today as a moral, ecclesial, and scholarly practice. M

Anna Rowlands, PhD, is the St. Hilda Professor of Catholic Social Thought and Practice at Durham University. She is the founding chair of the UK Centre for Catholic Social Thought and Practice. She is co-editor of the *T&T Clark Reader in Political Theology* (Bloomsbury, 2021), author of *Towards a Politics of Communion* (Bloomsbury, 2021), and co-editor of the *Handbook on Religion and Contemporary Migration* (Oxford University Press, 2024). She is an appointed expert member of the Synod on Synodality and was the project PI for the Listening Practices in Global Catholicism Project (2022–2024).

---

[15] Hannah Vaughan-Spruce, "Two 'Fires' of Leadership: Is It Possible to Listen and Lead Parish Cultural Change?," *Journal of Moral Theology* 13, Special Issue 2 (2024): 195–205.

[16] Alana Harris, "Listening in Stereo and Communicating in Semaphore: Child Sexual Abuse Survivor-led Strategies for Culture Change in the Catholic Church," *Journal of Moral Theology* 13, Special Issue 2 (2024): 217–238.

Listening across the Américas: Base Ecclesial Communities and Relational Organizing as Listening Practices for a Synodal Church

Richard L. Wood[1]

Abstract: Catholicism can draw on existing practices of listening to build a more participative church. This paper analyzes listening practices in Catholic and Catholic-engaged interfaith settings, drawing on the author's long-term ethnographic research: i) four years of weekly participation in meetings of *comunidades eclesiales de base* in Mexico and Central America; ii) two decades of participant-observation in multiracial faith-based community organizing work in low-income communities of the United States; iii) participant observation at the US expression of the *World Meetings of Popular Movements* initiative; and iv) participant-observation at the "Prophetic Communities" gathering of organizers, scholars, and church leaders, focused on synodality and community organizing (San Francisco, CA, in 2023). The essay frames its discussion of listening practices around contemporary ideas regarding *acompañamiento,* solidarity, encounter, and the role of civil society and "public religion" as cultural and institutional underpinnings of democracy. A restructured, more synodal church can enable "ethical democracy" in the future, in part through its practices of liturgy and encounter.

SINCE 2021, THE WORLDWIDE CATHOLIC CHURCH HAS engaged in perhaps the most widespread process of social consultation in human history, at least in its aspiration to hold listening forums within every Catholic parish and institution in every society around the world. This "synodal process" generated significant opposition from sectors of the church more oriented toward hierarchical exercise of authority, as well as legitimate criticisms for shortcomings in how the synodal process was carried out.[2] Nonethe-

---

[1] Profound thanks to Leo Guardado of Fordham University and the many participants in the "Listening Practices in Global Catholicism" conference in Rome (March 2024) for critical feedback and suggestions.
[2] The opposition to Francis's project to construct a more synodal church drew from many sources but has been centered particularly within conservative figures in the American episcopacy including Cardinal Raymond Burke and Vatican allies including former papal nuncio in the US Carlo Maria Viganò. Less virulent opposition has come from a new generation of conservative American Catholic priests; see Ruth Graham,

less, the effort to ground the exercise of legitimate authority via more participative ecclesial processes appears likely to survive into the next papacy. Indeed listening to the experience of the faithful may be vital to recovering institutional credibility and moral authority following the catastrophic sexual abuse scandals, related scandals of episcopal sheltering of pedophiles, and more generally the rising rejection of institutional authority under the pressures of modernism, post-modernism, and libertarian individualism.[3]

Synodality, or the construction of a "listening church," thus seems likely to be a central thrust within global Catholicism into the future. While some hope it leads to internal democracy within church structures, it more likely holds promise to advance a model of "participative hierarchy" that will exist alongside and complement the deep traditions of episcopal authority and apostolic succession that have long been central to Roman Catholicism.[4] If implemented successfully, such participative hierarchy might better root episcopal decision-making in the experience and faith journeys of the People of God in ways that generate greater internalization of Catholic spiritual teaching by lay Catholics *and* wiser discernment among church leaders (lay, religious, priestly, and episcopal), as well as a church better able to take advantage of lay professional expertise on the secular processes involved in running complex organizations and a global institution.

Contrary to common misperceptions, Catholicism does not need to start from scratch in learning how to listen. This paper mines extant practices of listening already widespread in some settings for insights and practical wisdom from which a synodal church of the future can learn. The author's ethnographic research in four settings informs the analysis: i) four years of weekly participation in meetings of *comunidades eclesiales de base* in Mexico and Central America; ii) two decades of participant-observation in multiracial faith-based community organizing work in low-income communities of the United States; iii) participant observation at the US expression of the *World Meetings of Popular Movements* initiative, convened for four days in 2017 by the Vatican's Dicastery for Integral Human Development and the Faith in Action national network in the Central Valley of California; and iv) participant-observation at the "Prophetic Communities" gathering of organizers,

---

"America's New Catholic Priests: Young, Confident, and Conservative," *New York Times* (July 10, 2024).
[3] Michele Dillon, *Postsecular Catholicism: Relevance and Renewal* (New York: Oxford University Press, 2018).
[4] On "participative hierarchy" and its promise for bringing Catholic mobilizing power and moral witness to bear on contemporary societal issues, see Mark R. Warren, *Dry Bones Rattling* (Princeton, NJ: Princeton University Press, 2001).

scholars, and church leaders, focused on synodality and community organizing (San Francisco, CA in 2023). These represent a mixture of *ad extra* (ii and iv) and *ad intra* (i and iii) listening, but all offer lessons for the construction of a more synodal church—in the dual belief that internal ecclesial practices can empower a more effective public Catholicism and that public ecclesial practices can teach new listening skills useful for the internal construction of synodality. I analyze the listening processes in these settings under a conceptual framework rooted in contemporary ideas regarding *acompanimiento,* solidarity, "encounter," and the role of civil society and "public religion" as cultural and institutional underpinnings of democracy.[5] I argue that despite some retrenchment into narrowly hierarchical structures in recent decades, the church preserves vigorous listening practices that can inform restructuring efforts toward a more synodal church, while remaining grounded in deep Catholic tradition via liturgical practices and the practice of encounter. In conclusion, I argue that these dynamics are critical not only for the internal life of the church but also in enabling the church to more vigorously advance "ethical democracy" in the face of authoritarian assaults on democratic institutions worldwide.[6]

VIGNETTES: LISTENING PRACTICES AND RELATIONAL ORGANIZING IN FOUR SETTINGS

Comunidades eclesiales de base: Colonia popular (*pueblo joven, favela*) *in México (1987)*

Deep in a *barranca* on the outskirts of Cuernavaca, México, temporary shacks and simple cement homes sit on a steep slope. On a Saturday afternoon, fifteen people gather in the open air: migrants to the city from rural Guerrero, *campesinos* by origin and now urban

---

[5] Conferencia Episcopal Latinoaméricano y del Caribe (CELAM), "Documento Conclusivo" of the *V Conferencia General del Episcopado Latinoamericano y del Caribe* in Aparecida, Brazil (Bogotá: CELAM, 2007), www.celam.org/aparecida/Espanol.pdf; Pope Francis, *Fratelli Tutti: Encyclical on Fraternity and Social Friendship* (2020), www.vatican.va/content/francesco/en/encyclicals/documents/papa-francesco_20201003_enciclica-fratelli-tutti.html; María Pilar Aquino and Elsa Támez, *Teología Feminista Latinoamericana* (Quito: Abya Yala, 1998); and José Casanova, *Public Religions in the Modern World* (Chicago: The University of Chicago Press, 1994).

[6] Wes Markofski, *Good News for Common Goods: Multicultural Evangelicalism and Ethical Democracy in America* (New York: Oxford University Press, 2023); Richard L. Wood, *Faith in Action: Religion, Race, and Democratic Organizing in America*, Morality and Society Series (Chicago: The University of Chicago Press, 2002); and Richard L. Wood and Brad R. Fulton, *A Shared Future: Faith-Based Organizing for Racial Equity and Ethical Democracy* (Chicago: The University of Chicago Press, 2015).

construction workers, homemakers, road laborers, street vendors, clerical workers, and aspiring students. Many have no more than a sixth-grade education. We greet each other, tiredly but joyfully after a long work week, and gather as *iglesia,* church. For we have been constituted as church: by Vatican II and Medellín, Don Sergio Méndez Arceo as bishop, the *Escuela de Reflexión Popular* under Dutch former priest Gerardo Thiejssen in training CEB *promotores*; ultimately the Gospels, and ourselves in embracing the call to be church.

Sitting in simple chairs, we gather in a rough circle. Doña Marielena, a homemaker who gave birth to her children in their house at the bottom of the ravine, begins with a prayer. We sing in celebration of God's liberating will for humanity and the Spirit's presence in this community. Don Miguel (her husband, a laborer and the other *promotor*) asks a participant to read the first Bible passage for tomorrow's Mass. Santiago reads from the Book of Isaiah, one of the suffering servant passages from the *Biblia Latinoamericana,* with photographs from settings like this around Latin America and annotations helping less-educated people interpret the scriptures within the realities of their own societies: a liberating God, the call to holiness of all people, and God's will for justice in the world.

We take turns reflecting on this passage. Don Miguel encourages those reticent to speak, sometimes sharing his own thoughts. Everyone offers a reflection, some haltingly, others eloquently. The central themes revolve around what a suffering God means for those who struggle for a living, dignity, a voice. They speak of feeling that perhaps God is with them in that struggle. Another theme concerns servanthood: that a God who comes as a suffering servant calls *us* to also serve brothers and sisters, in the simple ways of daily life—and calls governing officials and other elites (including "those living up there" on the flat terrain above in the elegant second homes of Mexico City families) to serve the whole community.

We listen to each other for two hours while Miguel and Marielena occasionally explain subtler facets of the readings (from the psalms, a difficult passage from the Letter of Paul to the Corinthians, and especially Luke 4). We each speak of our own experience in light of those readings, sometimes amid awkward silences, at other times passionately. Then Miguel invites Ofelia, a skeptical young woman, to close with a prayer. She does so simply and directly by asking God to be with us through the challenges of life in the *barranca*. We chat, promise to see each other again, then climb the steep stairs back to homes higher in the ravine, amid the harder facets of life: raised voices of husbands and parents berating their wives or children, and groups of men drunkenly lounging on the stairway. These are realities in any community—just more public here among the poor.

Such are listening practices in a healthy *comunidad eclesial*.[7] But in other CEBs in other parts of town, the *promotores* are not so adept. Too often they dominate meetings, preventing others from speaking. Or, perhaps worse, they intimidate the reticent, shaming them into speaking rather than inviting them by "listening in the Spirit." Such domineering practices are sometimes adopted by *promotores* lacking adequate formation, as they copy the only model of leadership they know: a certain kind of authoritarian *cacique*, "big man," boss, husband, father, or priest who dominates those around him.

This vignette could have come from virtually anywhere in Latin América—this author has witnessed similar dynamics, both positive and authoritarian, in similar settings in Central America, Peru, and the US.

Faith-based Community Organizing (FBCO, 1990s, Work Continues Today): A Multiracial, Working-Class Neighborhood in the United States[8]

Several dozen lay leaders convene one evening in a church basement, recruited from Catholic parishes, historic African American and liberal white Protestant churches, Jewish synagogues, multiracial evangelical churches, and a local Islamic mosque. They come from working-class neighborhoods, poor districts downtown, and comfortable suburbs. Tonight the gathering is in Denver but it could be happening in any US city—faith-based organizing like this occurs in nearly every state, mostly under the auspices of networks called Faith in Action; the Industrial Areas Foundation; Direct Action, Research, and Training (DART); and Gamaliel; or in a more secular mode by People's Action.[9] Together, the group includes many recent

---

[7] For background on the original dynamism of *comunidades eclesiales de base*, best sources are José Marins, *CEBs e pequenas comunidades eclesiais* (Brasília, DF: CNBB, 2009) and José Marins, Teolide María Trevisan, and Carolee Chanona, *Comunidade Eclesial de Base: foco de evangelização e libertação* (São Paulo: Paulinas, 1980).

[8] On faith-based (that is, broad-based, congregation-based, faith-rooted) community organizing, see Aaron Stauffer, *Listening to the Spirit: The Radical Social Gospel, Sacred Value, and Broad-Based Community Organizing* (New York: Oxford University Press, 2024); Brian Stiltner, "Community Organizing for Democratic Renewal: The Significance of Jacques Maritain's Support for Saul Alinsky and His Methods," *Journal of Moral Theology* 13, Special Issue no. 1 (2024): 146–168, doi.org/10.55476/001c.117001; Jack Delehanty and Michelle Oyakawa, "Building a Collective Moral Imaginary: Personalist Culture and Social Performance in Faith-Based Community Organizing," *American Journal of Cultural Sociology* 6 no. 2 (2018): 266–295; and Wood, *Faith in Action*.

[9] Indeed, a quite similar story could be told from settings in El Salvador, Guatemala, Haiti, Rwanda, and Eastern Europe, as well as very recently in Honduras and Ghana,

immigrants (some legal, some undocumented, mostly from Latin America) and is remarkably multiracial (in the reified categories of American culture, perhaps 40–50 percent Latino/Hispanic, 25 percent white, 15 percent African American, others a mix of immigrants from southeast Asia and people from Native American or multiracial backgrounds). That is important today in the severely segregated organizational and political life in the US: among all civic or political settings in the country, perhaps only in the labor movement do people gather in such a multihued setting of different ethnicities and races. The multifaith character of the group also matters greatly, because building bonds across spiritual traditions helps strengthen the social fabric.

We are here to plan a "public action" to persuade the mayor and City Council to commit to a series of measures improving the quality of life in poor, working-class, and middle-class communities across the city. The proposed measures include more effective and less aggressive policing, along with additional funding for public schools. All the leading roles will be played by volunteer leaders from the churches, synagogue, and mosque (and in a few cases from public schools). The ground has been prepared via a "listening campaign"—an organizing process consisting of hundreds or thousands of "one-to-ones" or "relational meetings" between volunteer leaders and organizers and their family members, friends, neighbors, and co-religionists. These sessions are intended to explore concerns, fears, and hopes for their neighborhoods and communities. The issues to be addressed at the public action have emerged from these meetings.

Still more careful listening happens here today: small groups discuss their hopes and fears for the public action next week; first-time leaders describe excitement at being "up-front" and facing a thousand or more people, and their fear of letting the organization and their colleagues down. A key speaker tells the story of her son's mistreatment at the hands of aggressive police officers and negligent school administrators—a powerful story that will highlight and "frame" the public action next week, helping to create moral pressure on political leaders to commit to action on new policy. Organizers help

---

and soon in México: Faith in Action International—the newest effort to take this model globally—now organizes in all those settings. See Victor Thasiah, "Prophetic Pedagogy: Critically Engaging Public Officials in Rwanda," *Studies in World Christianity* 23, no. 3 (2017): 257–280 and Stacy Keogh and Richard L. Wood, "The Rebirth of Catholic Collective Action in Central America," in *Social Compass* 60, no. 2 (2013): 289–307. Gamaliel has organized in South Africa and the IAF has longstanding organizing in the United Kingdom, and more recently in Berlin and Australia; see Luke Bretherton, *Resurrecting Democracy: Faith, Citizenship, and the Politics of a Common Life*, ed. Kenneth Wald, David Leege, and Richard L. Wood (Cambridge: Cambridge University Press, 2015).

craft that story as a structured narrative effective and true. The whole group discusses strategy and the details of turning out participants. A local policing expert describes alternative approaches to law enforcement in low-income neighborhoods. Everyone listens, intent on finding solutions for their communities.

At the end, we pray together for the Spirit to illuminate the minds of elected leaders next week and open their hearts to the stories we will tell and the needs of these communities; and for our own strength and courage in confronting them with our demands for change. A priest finishes our prayer with a closing benediction, offered in a way accessible to Jews, Muslims, Protestants, and the secularly-minded (done in Spanish, translated simultaneously into English by a gifted immigrant translator). We exit late in the evening. The night air is filled with participants' excitement to be taking action together, and we talk animatedly about getting friends and church members to attend next week. The sounds of urban life surround us as we climb into our cars under a night sky, music thumping from passing traffic and police sirens blaring.

US Regional Gathering for World Meetings of Popular Movements (2017): Central Valley of California

The Central Valley of California is one of the world's most fertile agricultural regions. About fifty miles wide, nearly five hundred miles long and lying at the foot of the vast Sierra Nevada with snow-capped peaks rising up to 4,200 meters above sea level, the Valley enjoys remarkably rich soil and abundant water (prior to climate change impacts), allowing it to produce nearly half of the nation's nuts, vegetables, and fruit. It is also the epicenter of vast social inequality: sprawling corporate agribusiness and private landowners control the best land and have historically exploited migrant laborers living in poor conditions and paid well below the standard minimum wage. Although conditions and wages have improved via union and legal battles, migrant workers and other impoverished residents continue to struggle with California's high cost of living, barriers to healthcare, exploitative labor relations, and the dehumanizing sense of being socially invisible.

This was the setting for a Vatican-sponsored gathering of about six hundred leaders from US civil society and grassroots social movements in February 2017, a regional session of the broader "World Meetings of Popular Movements" under Pope Francis's sponsorship (which has held global meetings in Bolivia in 2015 and

Rome in 2014 and 2016).[10] The gatherings are expressions of Catholic social teaching and principles of subsidiarity; they have been denounced by certain nominally Catholic organizations such as The American Society for Tradition, Family, and Property.[11] Each was the occasion for deep listening within the Catholic tradition and in dialogue with other religious and secular organizations. This author was a participant-observer at the gathering in Modesto, sponsored by the Vatican in partnership with Faith in Action and its affiliate PICO-California; the Catholic Campaign for Human Development of the US Conference of Catholic Bishops; and the Catholic Diocese of Stockton (in which Modesto is located).

Participants were young and old and came from diverse backgrounds: from prominent church leaders and leading scholars and writers to highly trained organizers, laborers, and grassroots movement leaders from marginalized communities across the US, Mexico, and Canada. Many participants from this latter group had limited education.

The flow of the event combined three elements: i) short talks by church authorities regarding particular aspects of church teaching and by civil society experts regarding particular issues; ii) listening and reflection sessions in small groups of about twenty-five people, followed by quick report-outs in the full group (and archiving of key points in small group discussions); and iii) shared prayer, singing, and worship.

Church leaders addressing the gathering included four high-ranking prelates: Cardinal Peter Turkson (Ghana), then the head of the Dicastery for Integral Human Development (key sponsor of this event); Archbishop (now-Cardinal) Joseph Tobin (Newark, NJ); Cardinal Blase Cupich (Chicago); Fr. Michael Czerny, then the Vatican's lead person on immigrants and refugees, now the Cardinal head of the Dicastery; Juan Grabois, a longtime pastoral collaborator with Pope Francis from his decades of work in Argentina; Archbishop

---

[10] On the World Meetings, see popularmovements.org/. For an authoritative report on the first gathering, see "The Strength of the Excluded: World Meeting of Popular Movements at the Vatican," by now-Cardinal Michael Czerny, SJ, and Paolo Foglizzo, www.thinkingfaith.org/sites/default/files/pdf/20150129_1.pdf.

[11] On the ASTFP, see www.tfp.org/radical-catholic-movements-gather-modesto-california-must-disrupt/. Such denunciations generally have criticized the inclusion of non-Catholic movements in the World Meetings, as well as the Meetings' focus on issues the objectors view as outside core Catholic tradition. However, in a tradition such as Catholicism that insists (rightly in this author's view) on both i) the relevance of its teachings for all areas of human life, and ii) a public stance in dialogue with the contemporary world, such objections—although frequently raised in the name of "tradition"—reflect narrow sectarian positions within Catholicism and would undercut not only synodality but the broad Catholic tradition itself.

José Gómez of Los Angeles, CA; and two bishops: Oscar Cantú (Las Cruces, NM, on the US-Mexico border and now of San Jose, CA) and Sheldon Fabre (Louisville, KY)—and Pope Francis himself via a video message from Rome.

Other speakers included prominent activist Heather McGhee, who discussed access to housing and work; john powell, who spoke on the dynamics of racism in America and building social belonging across divisions; and Naomi Klein, who led a conversation on the power of movements to change public policy on climate change and environmental protection. Additional, more grassroots leaders spoke on housing access, Indigenous and immigrant rights, and ecological issues disproportionally impacting communities of color. Intense listening occurred to all ecclesial and lay experts, and intense dialogue with some.

The listening-and-reflection sessions were dynamic and efficient, mostly led by skilled lay faith-based community organizers (see vignette 2 above). This researcher participated in many, floating between different small groups to get a broad "flavor" of these discussions. Some broke up into pairs of people to do brief one-to-ones (also called "relational meetings"), others divided into "cohorts" of five to seven people for focused discussion. In either case, they then re-gathered for discussion within the group of about twenty-five, with facilitators keeping those sessions participative and encouraging all to "really hear" each other's stories and points of views, and "really see" one another.

The resulting stories—many describing the high human costs of poverty and exclusion in America—were often passionate and sometimes heart-breaking. Many were told in a tone of anger at injustice, leavened with hope for something better to come. The latter often drew on a sense of God walking with them as they and others in their movements confronted injustices *together*, drawing courage from one another and sustenance from their faith. These were first-person stories of suffering, struggle, and fear; but also of perseverance and hope.

The overall tone and tenor of the event was shaped by Catholic Mass offered each morning in a nearby chapel; public prayer to start each day; and music and enthusiastic singing at various points. Throughout—in keynote talks, small-group reflections, homilies at Mass—*stories* and listening to stories were central to the flow of the gathering.

Listening among Lay Ecclesial Leaders, Movement Organizers, Scholars, and Priests: The Synod on Synodality (San Francisco, February 2023)

The "Prophetic Communities" gathering took place on the campus of the University of San Francisco, a prestigious Jesuit university, and brought together scholars and church leaders with "organic intellectuals" from within labor organizing, immigrant organizing, environmental organizing, faith-based community organizing, and other forms of grassroots democratic work.[12] Most of the latter were professional organizers, many but not all of them lay Catholics. Others were Catholic religious sisters, Catholic clergy, or leaders within another faith tradition or secular democratic culture. The gathering was sponsored by Network: A Social Justice Lobby, the Jesuits West province of the Society of Jesus, and the Inter-Community Peace & Justice Center of Seattle (a collaboration of several women's religious orders).

From the outside, listening in this setting looked much like at the Modesto gathering (vignette 3 above). But in the small groups, the tenor of discussions reflected the high educational status of most participants: some with doctoral degrees in theology, the social sciences, or humanities; some with other advanced theological degrees; some with professional degrees (MD, JD, MBA); others with master's or bachelor's degrees across a variety of disciplines. Certainly some held less formal education, but many of these appeared to come from strong backgrounds in Catholic formation or (like many of those in Modesto) simply brought a great deal of intelligence and experience to the discussions.

As a result, these listening sessions were more conceptual and less story-based than the other settings above. But careful listening was still central. Concerns were a little more arms-length, emphasizing empathy for those suffering injustice and concern for local ecosystems

---

[12] The notion of "organic intellectuals" comes from leftist Italian organizer Antonio Gramsci, who originally based the concept on the interpretive work of common priests in rural Italy and used it to describe the intellectual figures within social movements who interpret history and politics in service to the movement; see Antonio Gramsci, *Prison Notebooks Volumes 1 & 2* (New York: Columbia University Press, 2011). The concept has also been appropriated by right-wing libertarians, both to critique the left—see Bradley Thomas, "Antonio Gramsci: The Godfather of Cultural Marxism," in *FEE Stories* (Foundation for Economic Freedom, 2019)—and describe their own work in social movements. For a good discussion of the concept, see Vicki Birchfield and Annette Freyberg-Inan, "Organic Intellectuals and Counter-Hegemonic Politics in the Age of Globalisation," in *Critical Theories, International Relations, and the Anti-Globalisation Movement*, ed. C. Eschle and B. Maiguashca (New York: Routledge, 2004), 154–173.

impacted by climate change. Participants also discussed their love for the Catholic Church and concern for its current state in the US, with some leaders seemingly determined to narrow its focus to a limited set of personal moral issues rather than its historic broad concern for humanity in its personal, community, and societal complexity.

These sessions were also marked by careful listening, and occasionally by stories told passionately—including personal stories of the efficacy of organizing as a tool for implementing Catholic teaching. Advanced concepts like "subsidiarity" came up repeatedly, a way to argue for laypeople's initiative in reforming the world. Periodically these sessions intended for attentive listening were reduced to intellectual debates between two people, with other marginalized. But that occurred rarely, which was rather remarkable considering the tendency of intellectuals to default into such debates devoid of active listening.

The *substance* of the gathering—called "Prophetic Communities: Organizing as an Expression of Catholic Social Thought"—was successfully synthesized into a document titled "Synodal Synthesis Report."[13] That report was shared with Catholic Church leaders as an input to the overall process of ecclesial listening within the Synod on Synodality—both the official listening by bishops and unofficial listening of the sponsoring religious communities and faith-based organizations.

OVERVIEW: LISTENING AS FAITHFUL WITNESS AND OPTION FOR THE MARGINALIZED

Four vignettes from quite different settings in which the Catholic Church in the Américas has engaged in significant "listening practices" built on relational organizing (these from the US and México but with parallels in the CEBs of Latin América; in the faith-based organizing projects in the UK, Central America, Haiti, Africa, Germany, Eastern Europe, and Australia; and in certain Catholic academic gatherings worldwide that emphasize deep dialogue). Four dynamic ecclesial experiences in which the church already has extensive experience of listening: sometimes to dedicated practicing Catholics, sometimes to secular voices and voices from other religions, and sometimes to persons alienated from their childhood Catholicism.

---

[13] Maureen O'Connell and Joseph Fleming, *Prophetic Communities: Organizing as an Expression of Catholic Social Thought—Synodal Synthesis Report* (San Francisco: University of San Francisco, 2023), issuu.com/ipjc/docs/prophetic_communities-synodal_synthesis_report_202?fr=sY2NlNzY0Nzc5MzA.

Note how all four cases, in different ways, give priority to the voices of those currently marginalized by society (and, in some cases, marginalized within the church as well). The practice of listening and the model of relational organizing have been most systematically developed within faith-based organizing, but all four cases engage in both. Listening has mattered at times throughout church history: in the governance of religious orders and monasteries,[14] settings of spiritual direction and communal life, gatherings of Catholic scholars and ecclesial leaders (though of course in some periods all these have been taken over by models of authority that suppress attentive listening). One insight the church has gained from its long pastoral experience, articulated clearly by Pope Francis in recent years, is that the best listening practices incorporate a kind of faithful witness to the Church's "option for the poor": listening that pays attention to the profound suffering that occurs amid human struggles for dignity and land, housing, and work (the 3Ts in Spanish: "tierra, techo, trabajo"—the central memo of the World Meetings of Popular Movements), but also witnessing the joy and hope marginalized communities experience when they come together in those struggles and find their church sharing in them. That joy and hope has transformed many Catholic leaders in recent decades, and perhaps throughout history, as written about regarding his own life by Pedro Casaldáliga, the 1960s bishop in the Brazilian backcountry.[15] Contemporary Catholic thought broadens this to an "option for the marginalized" more generally, building on the insight that those excluded from power often see dynamics and realities missed by those close to power—in which the "marginalized" include anyone unjustly denied full voice and participation: women in settings where male authority dominates, racialized or indigenized people in settings of white supremacy, poor workers and the unemployed where capitalist interests rule. But people privileged in one setting may be marginalized in another—for example, priests in a diocese run by an autocratic bishop. Crucially, in any of these settings, attentive listening can involve no pollyannish or condescending posture on the part of church leaders; to be authentic, it must represent a church truly attending to the witness of the faithful and in turn truly witnessing their struggles.

At the same time, these practices must not deify the marginalized. In different ways, each of these settings remains open to expert opinion from civil society and authoritative wisdom from the Catholic

---

[14] The word "Listen" is the first word in the Rule of Saint Benedict, which has influenced nearly all subsequent church governance and in some sense all subsequent European history; my thanks to an anonymous reviewer for this connection.

[15] Pedro Casaldáliga, *Yo creo en la justicia y en la esperanza* (Rio de Janeiro: Desclée de Brouwer, 1975).

tradition, seeking insight for constructing meaning and a more humane society wherever it can be found. All are clear: the option for the marginalized does not mean that the marginalized have all the answers or are always right. Also, like all things human, these listening practices can also be abused—either embracing the distortions of power (as noted in vignette 1 above, but potentially true in all of them); by turning the marginalized into objects of idolatry such that *only* their views matter; or turning the option for the poor into a rigid ideology rather than a fundamental resource for listening and decision-making—alongside other resources such as secular expertise, authoritative wisdom, and collective discernment.

But at their best, the listening practices witnessed in these four settings reflect a dual role of the church: on one hand permanently discerning its own way and teaching in light of sacred Scripture, the signs of the times, its own deep traditions, and the best secular knowledge available; on the other hand as a catalyst in civil society: encouraging participation from a variety of stakeholders, soliciting authentic voice from all sources of insight, and proposing solutions to societal challenges.[16] The first dimension of this ecclesial vocation strives to empower the faithful to live the Gospel in their daily lives, families, and communities. The second dimension strives to evangelize the wider structures of society, reforming them in ways that embody the Gospel vision of humanity as beloved community. Through such work, the church strives to broaden and deepen the experience of human dignity here and now, and channel that experience into concrete work to reform society in the service of everyday people—that is, to advance what I have elsewhere called "ethical democracy": a public life that reflects the diversity and pluralism of society; democratic institutions that successfully allow people effective voice and vote in decisions that govern them; economic arrangements that grant all realistic opportunity to a dignified life (typically via economic markets allowed to function but regulated reasonably by public officials); and a culture of accountability that insists on all of that.[17]

By bearing witness to human dignity *and* ethical democracy, these listening practices thus are in continuity with the deep Catholic

---

[16] The dual role of the church laid out here differs from the traditional "listening/teaching church" distinction, in which teaching represents the external ecclesial role striving to instruct the wider society. This traditional framing fails to accurately capture the actual role of the church in the pluralistic setting of the contemporary world, as well as the way internal and external practices can enrich and cross-fertilize one another.

[17] For in-depth discussion of ethical democracy, see Wood, *Faith in Action*; Wood and Fulton, *A Shared Future*; and especially Markofski, *Good News for Common Goods*.

tradition of societal solidarity—and reject both a liberal "therapeutic culture" of narcissistic individualism and the neoliberal economic order that leaves persons to the not-so-tender mercies of libertarian economic markets.

New work by Christian social ethicist Aaron Stauffer analyzes listening practices in faith-based community organizing, finding there:[18] i) a form of practical politics that places sacred values at the center of addressing societal challenges, and ii) a recognition of the sacred value of "the other."[19] Stauffer's core argument—relational organizing represents a form of "social practical reasoning" that when done well constitutes a process of listening to the Spirit—dovetails deeply with the synodal ideal of "listening in the Spirit." Stauffer thus renders an understanding of relational organizing that captures its close relationship to Francis's theological language of "encounter." The following section builds towards a deeper understanding of that connection.

A THEOLOGICAL AND SOCIOLOGICAL FRAMEWORK FOR A LISTENING CHURCH

Given the diversity of these ecclesial listening settings—across decades, geographic settings, classes, and educational levels—how can we synthesize insights for a more deeply listening, synodal church in the vision of Pope Francis? The remainder of this essay reflects analytically on those experiences in a mode simultaneously sociological and theological, striving to offer a framework for understanding what is fundamentally happening in these settings. I will draw on categories of analysis from Catholicism in Latin America, democratic social theory, and Catholic and Protestant political theology. Methodologically, in beginning from experience via the vignettes of Catholic listening practices in (mostly) marginalized communities in Latin America and the US, I broadly follow Gustavo Gutiérrez's approach of critical reflection on praxis in light of the Gospels and Catholic teaching, which in turn has affinities

---

[18] See Aaron Stauffer's *Listening to the Spirit: The Radical Social Gospel, Sacred Value, and Broad-Based Community Organizing* (New York: Oxford University Press, 2024).

[19] Aaron Stauffer's *Listening to the Spirit* arrived to me just as this article was being submitted, so I do not engage with it fully here. Especially valuable are Stauffer's accounts (55–69) of: i) the role of "agitation" within relational meetings and listening campaigns, and ii) the link between relational organizing and liturgy. On the intersection between relational organizing and liturgy, see also Larry Gordon, "Reverence and Democratic Practice," *Journal of Catholic Social Thought* 21, no. 3 (2024): 229–247.

with the inductive methodology of the social gospel tradition in American Christianity.[20]

Although it is impossible to present detailed ethnographic evidence in a short essay, broadly speaking we can say that these listening processes embody a number of core values that have emerged in church teaching in recent decades: solidarity and *acompañamiento*; political work for justice as "the institutional path of charity," linked to commitment to the common good and a politics of the common life; and Catholicism as "public religion."

Perhaps most fundamentally, each of the four settings displays *solidarity in action*: not simply verbal expressions of concern, care, or empathy for those who suffer in the world, but a clarity of commitment and analysis to taking action in solidarity with those suffering injustice or marginalization as a result of the workings of social power. Notably, this solidarity is not "charity": the important and sometimes noble acts of "giving" that almost never change the real situation of the marginalized, and too often condescend to them. Rather, this solidarity gathers the marginalized and those supporting them to reflect on their experience and struggles and begin to transform their world:[21]

> [Solidarity] is above all a question of interdependence, sensed as a system determining relationships in the contemporary world, in its economic, cultural, political, and religious elements, and accepted as a moral category. When interdependence becomes recognized in this way, the correlative response as a moral and social attitude, as a "virtue," is solidarity . . . a firm and persevering determination to commit oneself to the common good. . . . This determination is based on the solid conviction that what is hindering full development is that desire for profit and that thirst for power already mentioned. (Pope John Paul II, *Laborem Exercens*, no. 38)

Solidarity is enacted even when, as in San Francisco above, those gathering come from relatively more privileged backgrounds—scholars, priests, professional organizers—and do so from within

---

[20] See Gustavo Gutiérrez, *A Theology of Liberation: History, Politics, and Salvation*, trans. Caridad Inda and John Eagleson (Maryknoll, NY: Orbis Books, 1973), and *We Drink from Our Own Wells*, trans. Matthew J. O'Connell (Maryknoll, NY: Orbis Books, 2013 [1983]); and Stauffer, *Listening in the Spirit*, 3–16.

[21] The concept of solidarity was central to Pope John Paul II's thinking, forming an important part of at least three major encyclicals: *Laborem Exercens*, www.vatican.va/content/john-paul-ii/en/encyclicals/documents/hf_jp-ii_enc_14091981_laborem-exercens.html); *Sollicitudo Rei Socialis*, www.vatican.va/content/john-paul-ii/en/encyclicals/documents/hf_jp-ii_enc_30121987_sollicitudo-rei-socialis.html; and *Centesimus Annus*, www.vatican.va/content/john-paul-ii/en/encyclicals/documents/hf_jp-ii_enc_01051991_centesimus-annus.html.

social relationships with the marginalized and attempt to embody their views. Such relationships offer at least the possibility of political and ecclesial accountability to the realities of "the underside of history" and an intellectual, theological, ecclesial, and political "view from below" as called for by a careful understanding of the church's "option for the poor."[22] In other words, this is *listening in solidarity*—an important ecclesial learning in the global church developing from decades of rich ecclesial experience of grassroots pastoral work among the poor in Latin America.

Note, too, how all of this draws on and reflects Pope Benedict XVI's emphasis in his encyclical *Caritas in Veritate* (2009) on "the institutional path of charity," i.e., the reform of social structures and policies through institutional action, including politics and economics.[23]

A second crucial theme also originating in the Latin American ecclesial experience emerges from examining these case studies. In each, albeit to differing degrees, ecclesial listening occurs from within a stance of *acompañamiento* ("accompaniment" in English, but it sounds better and carries specific implications in Spanish and Portuguese).[24] This is the church "walking with" the People of God, especially in their marginalization and suffering, and hearing from them about their experience. Again, such *acompañamiento* does not determine the correct solution to every societal problem, but as the church formulates its position regarding such solutions, it refracts the church's vision through the lens of the world of the marginalized to assure that proposed solutions address their concerns and uphold their dignity.

Recent writings in political theology illuminate two additional key dynamics within these four ecclesial listening venues. First, work by

---

[22] On the underside of history, the view from (the societal) "below," and the option for the poor, see Gustavo Gutiérrez, *The Power of the Poor in History* (Eugene, OR: Wipf and Stock, 2004); Simon C. Kim, *An Immigration of Theology: Theology of Context as the Theological Method of Virgilio Elizondo and Gustavo Gutiérrez* (Eugene, OR: Wipf and Stock, 2012); and Marc H. Ellis and Otto Maduro, eds., *Expanding the View: Gustavo Gutiérrez and the Future of Liberation Theology* (Eugene, OR: Wipf and Stock, 2011).

[23] See Daniel K. Finn, ed., *The Moral Dynamics of Economic Life: An Extension and Critique of "Caritas in Veritate"* (New York: Oxford University Press, 2012).

[24] For discussions of accompaniment, see my discussion below (drawing on Roberto S. Goizueta, *Caminemos con Jesús: Toward a Hispanic/Latino Theology of Accompaniment* [Maryknoll, NY: Orbis Books, 1995]) as well as Robert Lassalle-Klein, "Jesus of Galilee and the Crucified People: The Contextual Christology of Jon Sobrino and Ignacio Ellacuría," *Theological Studies* 70, no. 2 (2009): 347–376; and Jon Sobrino, SJ, *Christology at the Crossroads: A Latin American Approach*, trans. John Drury (Eugene, OR: Wipf and Stock, 2002) and *Witnesses to the Kingdom: The Martyrs of El Salvador and the Crucified Peoples* (Maryknoll, NY: Orbis Books, 2015).

Whelan and Tran draws on the writings and public utterances of the early twentieth century sociologist W. E. B. Dubois (US), and the martyred and recently canonized St. Oscar Romero (El Salvador) to elaborate a concept of *coalitional solidarity*.[25] This concept identifies the ways different sectors or layers of society sometimes generate a sufficient sense of shared identity and struggle to deepen democracy by effectively making claims on government or society in the name of the marginalized (for Dubois, the formerly enslaved African Americans who had been promised equal status during the American Civil War but were rapidly re-marginalized by the Jim Crow South and segregated North; for Romero, the Salvadoran *campesinos* driven to the most marginal lands or into landlessness and desperate wage labor).

To various degrees, our four case studies exhibit the church's role in launching processes with promise to advance coalitional solidarity. This is perhaps least developed in the *comunidad ecclesial de base* case from México; there, because all participants (except this researcher) came from almost identical social origins in *mestizo* or Indigenous rural Guerrero state and became urban migrants working in the informal labor sector and shared residence in a marginalized *colonia* in a ravine far from the city center. They are almost the definition of a single-class marginalized community. Thus, it is hard to identify a "coalitional" dimension to their impressive solidarity (except perhaps when this author occasionally brought more elite groups to reflect with and learn from this CEB). But CEBs sometimes generate coalitional solidarity, as when in Nicaragua in the 1970s or Brazil under the dictatorship CEBs sometimes convened laborers, *campesinos*, and sympathetic bourgeoisie (in Brazil, across racial lines) into coalitions that undergirded the struggle against Somoza or the military dictatorship; or when in Peru in recent decades CEBs brought together Indigenous and *mestizo* urban dwellers in *pueblos jóvenes* with middle-class professionals to defend the interests of marginal communities.

Coalitional solidarity is more clearly displayed in the other three cases:

Faith-based community organizing and the labor union movement represent the two fields that most consistently and successfully mobilize people across divides of religion, "race"/ethnicity, immigrant status, and socioeconomic status/class. In a society as segregated as the US—and in which it has become acceptable in some settings to

---

[25] Matthew Whelan and Jonathan Tran, "Looking Up and Looking Out: Du Bois, Romero, and Democratic Solidarity," *Journal of Catholic Social Thought* 21, no. 3 (2024): 246–268.

demonize others on the basis of these categories—this represents an important democratic achievement.[26] The field has become all the more crucial amid the current antidemocratic climate of polarization in the US, since it pulls people into broadly political (but generally non-partisan) settings of public action and into electoral mobilization efforts to defend democratic institutions.

The World Meeting of Popular Movements regional convening likewise drew people across these lines of social difference. Furthermore, it successfully convened a vast range of social movements, from addressing climate change and protecting Indigenous rights to opposing white supremacy, from promoting living wage campaigns, opposing mass incarceration and excessive police force to advocating for public education reform and immigrant rights. Notable in this setting was that organizers did *not* rely on a "rainbow coalition" strategy, whereby organizers imagine that groups will support one another simply out of their mutual interest in gaining power. Instead, the gathering drew on the convenors' rich experience of relational organizing to create processes of listening and reflection, along with moments of shared prayer, singing, and worship. These practices constitute the kind of "bridging cultural practices" that researchers have argued offer the cultural glue that can hold together highly diverse coalitions—i.e., foster coalitional solidarity and allow it to survive through inevitable conflict and periodic political disappointment.[27]

Finally, while the Prophetic Communities synodal gathering in San Francisco was less racially and religiously diverse than the other settings, it still exhibited impressive coalitional solidarity by convening university-based scholars, community-based activists and organizers, and church-based thought leaders—and treating all of them as thought partners in the spirit of Gramsci's organic intellectuals. The gathering began to construct a long-term coalition of democratically-focused thought leaders capable of sustained "thinking with" both the church and democratic movements.

The second insight from political theology illuminated by these four cases arises from recent critiques of the concept of "the common good" that has long undergirded Catholic social teaching across

---

[26] See Wood and Fulton, *A Shared Future*, and Brad R. Fulton and Richard L. Wood, "Interfaith Organizing: Emerging Theological and Organizational Challenges," *International Journal of Public Theology* 6 (2012): 1–23.

[27] Ruth Braunstein, Brad R. Fulton, and Richard L. Wood, "The Role of Bridging Cultural Practices in Racially and Socioeconomically Diverse Civic Organizations," in *American Sociological Review* 79, no. 4 (2014): 705–725, doi:10.1177/0003122414538966.

centuries.[28] Luke Bretherton notes the critique to which any coherent notion of common good has been subjected, due to the postmodern proliferation of different understandings of the good life, community, and the goals toward which humanity can and should aspire.[29] In its place, he suggests a focus on "a politics of the common life" as a way to advance a shared democratic polity in which all can participate and benefit without assuming or imposing any one notion of the good society. A politics of the common good focuses on the substance of issues, about which people are expected to converge on a shared understanding of what is good. A politics of the common life focuses instead on the *process* of reaching provisional agreement: even as people may differ regarding what is ultimately best in society, such a politics strives to formulate provisional steps forward upon which people can agree despite their differences. Jonathan Tran makes a crucial contribution in this direction by articulating a form of anti-racist and intersectional politics rooted not in racial identity but rather in political economy.[30]

The CEB in México might have benefitted from such an understanding: though at times they impressively and intuitively lived out such politics by eschewing political differences in favor of shared political work to get potable water and sewage lines built into their neighborhood, at other times they ran up sharply against their contradictory understandings of the good for their community. Sometimes differences were partisan, at other times they were centered on ideology regarding gender and the family, and at still other times centered on how to treat their aggressively proselytizing Pentecostal neighbors (whom they saw as anti-Catholic, in the sharp religious tensions of the time). Coming from villages in which solidarity was based on shared social status and views on such issues, these recent urban migrants struggled to conceive how they might sustain solidarity amid such sharply differing views. Partly as a result, this CEB sometimes struggled to stay together, periodically dissolving (implicitly, by simply not meeting) and having to re-form. The concept

---

[28] Rhys Williams, "Public Religion and Hegemony: Contesting the Language of the Common Good," in *The Power of Religious Publics*, ed. William Swatos and James K. Wellman (Westport, CT: Praeger, 1999), 169–186.

[29] See Luke Bretherton, *Resurrecting Democracy* and *Christ and the Common Life: Political Theology and the Case for Democracy* (Grand Rapids, MI: Eerdmans, 2015).

[30] See Jonathan Tran, *Asian Americans and the Spirit of Racial Capitalism* (New York: Oxford University Press, 2021). On the common good: I do not advocate shedding the language of "common good" central to Catholic thought and authoritative papal teaching for generations. Rather, supplementing it with a strong commitment to a politics of common life can enable appropriate Catholic advocacy for the common good within polities that disagree deeply on what the common good actually entails.

of a politics of common life, in which neighbors suspend some areas of difference in favor of shared work for a shared future within a common society, might have helped them.

Though the concept of "common good" was often invoked in the other three settings—and I doubt anyone present there had ever heard of "a politics of common life"—these sessions were structured by a common-life politics capable of suspending differences in favor of constructing a shared societal future. Faith-based organizing, the Modesto WMPM gathering, and the synodal gatherings like Prophetic Communities all include people committed to a range of views: political ideologies; racial ideologies; feminist versus patriarchal views on the family and gender relations; gender and sexual identities; and varying commitments to or critiques of "the American dream," free markets, and a host of other potential objects of contention. But the ethos underlying these settings, and the disciplined organizing practices the event organizers strove to adopt, fostered a process of listening to one another that largely suspended ideological contention.

Finally, from democratic theory and the sociology of religion, the concept of "public religion" elaborated by José Casanova provides a framework for seeing the similarities and differences across these four cases.[31] They exemplify what we might call dynamic public Catholicism: groups that bring Catholic ethical and pro-social commitments and orientations into the public sphere. All four cases—whether the particular group is all Catholic (the CEB), heavily Catholic (Prophetic Communities), predominantly Catholic but with large participation from other religious and secular traditions (the WMPM), or extremely religiously diverse (FBCO)—draw inspiration from Catholic traditions dating back to the origins of modern Catholic social teaching in *Rerum Novarum* (1891), historical Catholic labor activists, and Catholic Action and its descendants.

The concept of "the public sphere" requires clarification, as common usage of the phrase has obscured its meaning in ways that undermine its analytic utility. The public sphere is not simply anywhere people gather (sporting events, say). Rather, the public sphere exists wherever people gather to consider together their social situations, public policies, the direction society should go, and how to get there. Sometimes such settings are quite civil; at other times they involve political conflict. Thus, the public sphere has both dialogical (dialogue-based) and agonic (conflict-based) dimension; both are critical for sustaining a robust democratic life.[32]

---

[31] See Casanova, *Public Religions in the Modern World*.
[32] An important distinction between two versions of such conflict: in an *agonic* public setting, rivals compete for influence while treating one another as holding legitimately different positions and respecting the dignity of the other; in an *antagonistic* public

Casanova draws on the political scientist Alfred Stepan to argue that the public sphere exists across three levels of society: the state (all government settings, including the bureaucracies of governing), political society (associations oriented toward influencing or conquering government power but not part of the state—examples include business associations, labor associations, corporate lobbyists, political parties, etc.), and civil society (associations not directly political, but where people engage in discussion of public issues).

An important contribution of public Catholicism to a world where all authority is suspect is that it brings into the public sphere—at all three levels—an appreciation for the legitimate exercise of authority. At its best, and despite appearances to the contrary in some settings, Catholicism is not an authoritarian tradition. Rather, it is an authoritative tradition in the sense that it simultaneously embraces the need for legitimate decision-making power to reside in accountable hands and the need for human persons to hold authority over their own actions and consciences.[33] This allows us to see how all our settings of Catholic listening represent a dynamic form of public Catholicism.

Typically, CEBs exist primarily at the level of civil society. They discuss their communities and reflect on their political realities in light of the Gospel and Catholic teaching. They are not, however, centered on conquering political power. Of course, they can become mobilizing structures for political involvement, but they typically are centered on listening to Scripture and one another while reflecting on the realities within their own communities, and how those realities can be improved.

Faith-based community organizing represents public Catholicism oriented much more strongly toward the political society level of the public sphere: These groups actively seek to shape public policy and political decision-making in the hope of making them conform more closely to the visions of thriving communities carried in Catholic social teaching, the Jewish ethical tradition, African-American "social Christianity," the Protestant "social Gospel," Islamic jurisprudence, and democratic humanism. They strive to remain non-partisan, though that has become more difficult today in highly polarized or authoritarian settings, including the US and El Salvador. They thus fall at the boundary between civil and political society, "reaching up" to

---

setting, at least one rival treats the other as an illegitimate political actor and seeks to undermine their public dignity. Dialogue and agonic public spheres form the foundation of political democracies; antagonistic public settings can undermine and ultimately destroy democracy, especially in the hands of authoritarians and autocrats.
[33] See Dillon, *Postliberal Catholicism*, and Jerome P. Baggett, *Sense of the Faithful: How American Catholics Live Their Faith* (New York: Oxford University Press, 2008).

pressure political society and the state to better deliver on the promises of democracy for marginalized communities.

The WMPM and Prophetic Communities gatherings lay somewhere between those two orientations: clearly hoping to create conditions for more vigorous Catholic engagement in the public arena, working solidly in civil society but with hopes of shaping Catholicism to have a broader and deeper influence on political society and public issues broadly understood. In both these settings, we also see the authoritative dimension of Catholicism reflected: both academic experts and church leaders are accorded respect and voice to offer authoritative knowledge (from academic expertise) and authoritative guidance (from senior leaders of the ecclesial community). Thus, a listening church is neither a "democratic" church in the political sense nor a rudderless collectivity; it is the Body of Christ in listening mode, with ecclesial leaders discerning the church's future in dialogue with the faithful.

SUMMARY DISCUSSION: LISTENING AS ACCOMPANIMENT AND ENCOUNTER

Theologian Roberto Goizueta draws on liberationist theological insights to develop a "theology of accompaniment" rooted in the realities of Hispanics/Latinos living in the US.[34] Noting the minority status and generally low economic status of Hispanics in the US (though with *much* variation, including significant wealth), he argues for such a theology to start from the "underside of history" as seen in the powerlessness, oppression, and societal neglect that confront low-income Hispanic communities. This draws on and reflects the deep commitments developed by Latin American theologians in recent decades, as well as the discussion above regarding public Catholicism.

But Goizueta makes an additional move important for our contemporary moment of sheer crassness and ugliness in public life within many societies around the globe. Against a narrow and ideologically-hued concept of "social justice" sometimes invoked by sectors of the contemporary political left or political right and used as a bludgeon with which to beat up one's opponents (as much as they might deserve that for the injustices they perpetuate), Goizueta argues for a commitment to "beauty *and* justice" as the proper standard against which to assess anything claiming to represent a social justice movement and an embodiment of the Gospel-mandated preferential option for the poor. That is, any movement claiming to represent Gospel values and the ethic of Jesus must proceed in ways that assert social power to back Christianity's demand for social justice, and must

---

[34] Goizueta, *Caminemos con Jesus*.

also embody human relations centered on beauty and human dignity, rather than *simply* the drive for power.

In the Catholic tradition, such a stance must ultimately be embodied in liturgy—that is, in the Mass and other settings in which the Catholic community comes together as the People of God. Good liturgy draws together, in a setting shaped by beautiful architecture and music, the broad experience of the faithful living in the world—personal, familial, social, political, and economic—and offers all that up in the context of God's love for humanity and creation. Through encounter with the Word (both scriptural and homiletic) and the sacraments (most paradigmatically the Eucharist), the faithful reflect on their experience, come to construct and understand its deeper meanings, and allow it to be valued and/or judged in light of values that transcend their own experience. From that dynamic arises both the spiritual journey of the faithful and the sense of holiness that infuses good liturgy.[35]

Finally, the most crucial theological category for interpreting the centrality of the listening practices analyzed here comes from Pope Francis. In several of his authoritative statements regarding the church's way of proceeding amidst the deep divisions of contemporary life, he invokes the language of "encounter" to signify two or more persons meeting in a way that embodies "human fraternity" and "social friendship" (see *Fratelli Tutti*, nos. 5, 6, 99, 154, 232). Broadly speaking, encounter relates to two strands of philosophical, social, and political thought.[36] The first, represented in thinking from Cicero to Max Weber and Isaiah Berlin, recognizes the inevitability of conflict in human relationships and the challenge of channeling it in peaceful directions. The second, most prominently from Hans-Georg Gadamer and Martin Buber, approaches dialogue not merely or primarily as a rational exchange of arguments but also as an encounter of whole persons embedded in different histories and cultures. While Gadamer envisions the possibility of a kind of synthesis—a "fusion of horizons"—Buber draws on the Jewish tradition to emphasize the integrity of the other ("Thou") in their transcendent individuality and thus separateness. Francis appears to draw on these lines of thought,

---

[35] On faith-based community organizing, its core listening practices, and their relationship to liturgy, see Larry Gordon, "Reverence and Democratic Practice." Space limitations preclude addressing the ways in which liturgy can instead reinforce the extant workings of societal power by some groups against others—itself an important topic.

[36] This paragraph draws extensively from Thomas Banchoff, "Catholic Social Teaching: Journeying Together," *The Tablet* (September 23, 2023): 4–5 and "Abrahamic Dialogue in the Shadow of War," *Commonweal* (February 16, 2024), www.commonwealmagazine.org/interfaith-dialogue-israel-hamas-francis-abraham-al-azhar.

refracted through his Jesuit formation in the way of proceeding of Ignatius of Loyola. Encounter also can represent a deeper, more realistic and experiential alternative to Jurgen Habermas's concept of "ideal speech situation," which underlies much thinking regarding the democratic public sphere and theory in the last forty years.[37] In all these dimensions, Francis's concept of encounter can offer theological grounding for our analysis of listening.

In Francis's thinking, a culture of encounter is a social and political space in which we fully acknowledge human differences and the inevitable conflicts they entail, yet nevertheless seek to develop points of agreement, pursue common projects, and learn from others' experience. Francis first called for a culture of encounter as archbishop of Buenos Aires (1998–2013), in a city and country marked by deep social and political divisions. From there the concept became central in the Latin American bishops meetings at Aparecida, Brazil in 2007 and ultimately in Francis's authoritative papal writing: his 2020 encyclical *Fratelli Tutti* mentions "encounter" forty-nine times and "culture of encounter" seven times. He writes, "To speak of a 'culture of encounter' means that we, as a people, should be passionate about meeting others, seeking points of contact, building bridges, planning a project that includes everyone" (no. 216).

To see the listening practices of CEBs, faith-based organizing, and the other sites analyzed here as versions of encounter challenges participants to deepen even the careful listening practices they have developed until now, engaging them with a renewed sense of the humanity of the other person and their distinct background and experience. It also challenges those who train faith-based organizers or CEB *animadores* and *promotores* to form these future artisans of ecclesial listening processes in ways attuned to a culture of encounter.

Francis also describes the ethos such encounters can embody, and links them to spiritual experience:

> Today more than ever we need men and women who, on the basis of their experience of accompanying others, are familiar with processes which call for prudence, understanding, patience, and docility to the Spirit. . . . We need to practice the art of listening, which is more than simply hearing. Listening . . . is an openness of heart which makes possible that closeness without which genuine spiritual encounter cannot occur. (no. 171)

---

[37] Key conceptual resources include "Rethinking the Public Sphere: A Contribution to the Critique of Actually Existing Democracy," in *Habermas and the Public Sphere*, ed. Craig Calhoun (Cambridge, MA: MIT Press, 1992), and Wendy Brown, *In the Ruins of Neoliberalism: The Rise of Anti-Democratic Politics in the West* (New York: Columbia University Press, 2019).

Thus, understanding and engaging in the kinds of listening practices analyzed here will require new learning—even *metanoia*—on the part of all of us responsible for formation of future Catholic leaders, whether in university, ecclesial, or other settings. The ongoing synodal process that will form the future of the church can learn from its long experience in CEBs, faith-based organizing, and the other case studies examined here how to listen to *all dimensions* of the world's joys and struggles. Ministry must certainly address the individual sinfulness, brokenness, and lack of meaning in contemporary lives, but must also engage with the social factors that constrain people's lives and sometimes drive individual failings. A synodal church can learn to draw on its prior experience to truly "hear" the political and economic struggles that make contemporary life so difficult for many and accompany people in their efforts to address those challenges.

CONCLUSION: LISTENING TO FORM MISSIONARY DISCIPLES

This article calls for more dynamic forms of public Catholicism rooted in the kinds of listening practices seen in the four case studies— embracing both a deep Catholic ethic of human dignity and solidarity as well as the legitimacy of ecclesial, intellectual, and civil authority that serves human communities and ethical democracy. Such arrangements might begin to constitute something like the politics of a common life and ethical democracy discussed above.

The church serves the world in myriad ways, not least through shaping human actors capable of reforming cultural, political, and economic institutions so that they better serve humanity. The types of listening practices analyzed here offer promise for the church's ever more vigorous involvement in shaping a humane world. But ultimately their more fundamental purpose lies in shaping a church that thrives into the future. For both roles, the church needs to form "missionary disciples" (*Evangelii Gaudium*, nos. 24, 40, 120–121): fully humanized persons capable of renewing both church and world, illuminated by the Gospel and the rich Catholic intellectual tradition.

Such missionary disciples must surely embody the theological virtues of faith, hope, and love. But they must just as surely embody what Saint John Paul II called the modern Christian virtue of solidarity—a "firm and persevering determination to commit oneself to the common good" (*Laborem Exercens*, no. 38)—and carry that virtue into the world as missionary disciples. They will do so more truly to the extent that they are formed by a church that embodies solidarity in her action in the world, politics of the common life, and listening to the faithful.

Richard L. Wood is president of the Institute for Advanced Catholic Studies at the University of Southern California and professor of sociology at the University of New Mexico. He is the author of scholarly articles and book chapters on the sociology of religion, social movements, public Catholicism, and democratic theory, many of which focus on faith-based community organizing. He is the author of *Faith in Action: Religion, Race, and Democratic Organizing in America* (2002) and, with co-author Brad R. Fulton, *A Shared Future: Faith-Based Organizing for Racial Equity and Ethical Democracy* (2015), both with The University of Chicago Press. He serves as co-editor of the book series *Cambridge Studies in Social Theory, Religion, and Politics* at Cambridge University Press.

Beyond Synodal Listening: Theological Action Research and Cultures of Conversation

Clare Watkins

Abstract: In the contemporary Catholic Church's engagement with synodality *listening* has become the dominant emphasis; methods for "spiritual conversation" are designed to give priority to listening—to one another and, fundamentally, the Holy Spirit. This paper offers some critiques of this emphasis and seeks to explore *conversation* as the synodal fundamental. Conversation overly controlled by listening is, I argue, susceptible to subtle and unhelpful power dynamics. "Ordinary conversation"—interruptive, informal, spontaneous, and not always polite—has its own theological significance and must also find its place in a truly synodal church. Drawing on extensive experience of theological action research and insights from systems theory, the paper sets out why such "ordinary conversation," distinct from what might be seen as "formal listening," is ecclesiologically essential for a full realisation of church. By way of conclusion, key themes are identified whose development is needed for the further enrichment of synodal processes through attention to ordinary conversation.

SINCE 2021, CATHOLIC COMMUNITIES ACROSS THE GLOBE have been invited in a formal way,[1] at Pope Francis's behest, to become increasingly involved in processes of "synodality."[2] These processes have culminated in two international synodal assemblies in Rome, in October 2023 and 2024, where bishops and other clerics are joined by lay women and men, all with equal voting and speaking rights. These assemblies have been organised to be deeply conversational and shaped around prayer and refection, as

---

[1] The language and theology of synodality as a "walking together" was a growing theme in Pope Francis's teaching from earlier in his pontificate, as he found expression for a vision of a less bureaucratic, discerning, and communal church. Much of this is reflected in the 2018 document of the International Theological Commission (ITC) *Synodality in the Life and Mission of the Church*, work for which began as early as 2014, just the year after Pope Francis's election: www.vatican.va/roman_curia/congregations/cfaith/cti_documents/rc_cti_20180302_sinodalita_en.html.

[2] For the Vatican's own website supporting synodality see www.synod.va/en.html.

delegates work together on submissions sent to Rome by every region of the world, drawn from local submissions based on the reflections and concerns of Catholic laity and, in the best cases, those to whom they relate in the wider world.[3] As the working document (*Instrumentum Laboris*) for the second of these synodal sessions is published, with its focus on "How to be a missionary synodal Church,"[4] we are already seeing a wide range of organisational, educational, and pastoral practices for renewal being contemplated.

However, whatever decisions and further work may arise from this Roman Synod, the effectiveness of those synods depends on a necessary consideration and practice of "synodality" on the ground which the renewal of the Catholic Church in mission and life in the Spirit requires going forward. Synodality is not a short-term, consultative process. Rather, it is "the specific *modus vivendi et operandi* of the Church, the People of God."[5] This wider living and practice of synodality is the particular concern of this article.

Many pages have been written on what is meant by "synodality,"[6] and there is too much to be said on the subject to include in this article.[7] For the reader for whom this may be a new or less clear idea, I begin with a brief outline of the most salient characteristics of synodality. The most recent document, the 2024 *Instrumentum Laboris*, partly in

---

[3] Processes developed varied not only from nation to nation, but also from diocese to diocese. In my own context—England and Wales—parish listening groups, with open agendas, were encouraged, and written submissions then made, often in response to some preset themes, then sent to Diocesan Synodal Teams. These teams then synthesized these submissions so as to contribute to a document drawn together by the Bishops' Conference's Synod team, which then was incorporated into the European Continental Level Document for the Synod in Rome 2024.

[4] *How To Be a Synodal Church On Mission? Five Perspectives for Theological Exploration in View of the Second Session of the XVI Ordinary General Assembly of the Synod of Bishops*, www.synod.va/en/resources/documents/documents-for-the-second-phase/towards-the-2024-assembly/how-to-be-a-synodal-Church-on-mission.html.

[5] ITC, *Synodality in the Life and Mission of the Church*, no. 6, quoted in the *Preparatory Document*, no. 10. *Preparatory Document*, 2021: www.synod.va/content/dam/synod/common/preparatory-document/pdf-desktop/en_prepa_desktop.pdf.

[6] The complex and sometimes disputed nature of the term is reflected in the way in which, following the 2023 Synod assembly in Rome, calls have been made for greater attention to be given the term, and its theological as well as practical meaning. This has been picked up in the 2024 Synod's *Instrumentum Laboris*, nos. 5–9.

[7] As well as the excellent materials on the School for Synodality website (www.schoolforsynodality.org.uk) and the Vatican's synod site, I would draw attention to: Jos Moons, "A Comprehensive Introduction to Synodality: Reconfiguring Ecclesiology and Ecclesial Practice," *Roczniki Teologiczne* 69, no. 2 (2022): 73–93; Massimo Faggioli, "From Collegiality to Synodality: Promise and Limits of Francis's 'Listening Primacy,'" *Irish Theological Quarterly* 85, no. 4 (2020): 352–369; Rafael Luciani, *Synodality: A New Way of Proceeding in the Church* (Mahwah, NJ: Paulist, 2022); Stephen McKinney, Thomas O'Loughlin, and Beata Toth, eds., *Synodality and the Recovery of Vatican II: A New Way for Catholics* (Dublin: Messenger, 2024).

recognition of a perceived lack of clarity concerning the term, helpfully cites the *Synthesis Report* from the 2023 Synod assembly thus:

> Synodality can be understood as Christians walking together in communion with Christ toward the Kingdom along with the whole of humanity. Its orientation is towards mission, and its practice involves gathering in assembly at each level of ecclesial life. It involves a reciprocal listening dialogue, community discernment, and creation of consensus as an expression that renders Christ present in the Holy Spirit, each taking decisions in accordance with their responsibilities.[8]

The vision here is one of the church, *at every level*, becoming a participating and discerning communion, and so being able to follow in the ways the Spirit is calling us to be in and for God's world. More than this, as frequently emphasised in official documents throughout the synodal process, this participation and discerning together is not just for those actively and visibly "in" the church, but needs to include *all*—with a special place for the voices of those marginalised or living with poverty of one kind or another. Informed by such a spirit of total inclusion, church communities are called to practise and learn what it is to walk and discern together through patterning our lives by attentive listening, shared celebration, speaking out in courage, with honesty and love whatever is in our hearts (*parrhesia*), and sensitivity and obedience to the Spirit's promptings. All this requires a profound personal and communal formation, and outward-looking engagement with all in society, especially the poor and marginalised.[9]

As with all great theological and especially ecclesiological visions, the challenge that meets us head on is that of *how* such discernment, attentiveness, and obedience to the Spirit is to be practised. I write this article from a position of theological and vocational commitment to and enthusiasm for synodality, as described in these texts, whilst reflecting more critically on my own, albeit limited, experience of what this has meant in practice for what I would argue is the majority of Catholic lay people.

It is helpful to acknowledge my own position in relation to these practices of synodality. My interest in and experience of synodal practices is rooted not only in a longstanding theological concern for Catholic ecclesiology and, especially, the theology of lay living, but also in participating at parish level in such practices. As an academic theologian, I have reflected on both the practice and underpinning

---

[8] *Synthesis Report* 1h, www.synod.va/content/dam/synod/assembly/synthesis/english/2023.10.28-ENG-Synthesis-Report.pdf.
[9] See the "Ten Thematic Nuclei" presented in the *Preparatory Document*, no. 30.

understandings of synodality, which has also led to my being involved in national and European-wide gatherings; as a parishioner of a small, rural parish in the East of England, I have had a small leadership role in instigating and helping resource a variety of synodal practices in response to the requests from Rome and the Bishops' Conference of England and Wales. As a member of the theological advisory group for the UK-based School for Synodality,[10] I have also been glad to hear firsthand of the great promise of synodal practices for parish and diocesan renewal, whilst also being able to develop some critical responses to how the practices are, and are not, effective, helpful, and truly transformative. Significantly, for what is to follow, I have also become increasingly aware of the ways in which my academic research, using theological action research methods and methodology, shines a light on synodal experiences, which both illuminates more sharply, and casts shadows.[11] I begin, then, with some reflections on particular dominant practices of synodality, that valorise *listening*, before going on to reflect on how this might be more properly and helpfully complexified by, first, theological action research methods and experience and, secondly, the insights of complexity theories of organisation. To conclude, I argue for a greater emphasis on speech and conversation, identified as "ordinary conversation," and a greater reserve in the prominence of "formal listening" practices in synodal processes. I suggest that it is ordinary conversation, rather than formal listening and the "spiritual conversations" it often advocates, which better embodies the vision of synodality with which the contemporary Catholic Church is working and reflects our longer traditions around discernment, the search for what is true, and following the Spirit.

SYNODAL PRACTICES AND THE (OVER)VALORISATION OF "LISTENING"

In the previous paragraph, I differentiated between "ordinary conversation," for which I want to argue, and "formal listening," which I associated with "spiritual conversation" or, as this practice is also known, "conversations in the spirit." Whilst there are various accounts of what these spiritual conversations involve, a clear and highly influential one is helpfully and accessibly described on the

---

[10] See footnote 7 above.

[11] As a co-originator of theological action research, I have been part of its development since the beginning. See, in particular, Helen Cameron, Deborah Bhatti, Catherine Duce, James Sweeney, and Clare Watkins, *Talking about God in Practice: Theological Action Research and Practical Theology* (London: SCM, 2010); and Clare Watkins, *Disclosing Church: Generating Ecclesiology through Conversations in Practice* (London: Routledge, 2020).

School of Synodality website.¹² Here, as the Vatican Synodality website describes,¹³ a method of spiritual conversation in three "rounds," each followed by a time of silent contemplation and prayer is employed. A first round allows each member of the group to say, in turn, what is in their heart and has come to them in the recommended time of prayerful preparation for the spiritual conversation. In the second round, following the time of silence, each is called upon to respond to what they have heard in the first round, identifying what seems to them an important insight for the group. This is where discernment of the Spirit's guiding of the group begins to take place. Following a second time of silence, the third round follows a similar pattern of turn-taking in sharing insights and reflections, and the group moves towards noting what is surfacing in their time together. These surfaced themes inform a final review of the spiritual conversation, in which significant themes or directions are identified upon which they want to report more widely. Throughout this process which lasts about two hours, the emphasis is on *listening*—to each other and the Spirit— and responding. There is no direct engagement in discussion, debate, or questioning between group members, as discernment is seen to be primarily taking place in listening. This is not, in my experience, "conversation" in any ordinary sense.

There is a great deal to be said for this practice of spiritual conversation and its formal listening emphasis, and I have no doubt of its value in particular circumstances and groups. However, both my experiences of it at a variety of ecclesial levels, and deepening theological enquiry of it, have left me with the rather provocative question: Is it possible that there has just been too much emphasis on "listening" in this synodal process? To be clear, I, along with the majority of those committed to synodality as a way of being church, would instinctively answer: "Of course not!" The careful, loving work of attending to the voices of all, and especially of those less heard, often silenced in and by church and society, is a central call to which we must respond. It is one of the great tragedies of church life that this listening has been so rare a practice among us.¹⁴ In my questioning of the formal listening advocated by spiritual conversation, I am not in

---

¹² See www.schoolforsynodality.org.uk/our-resources/conversations-in-the-spirit-a-how-to-guide.

¹³ There is recommendation for this way of working also given on the Vatican's own synodality site: www.synod.va/content/dam/synod/common/phases/en/EN_Step_6_Spiritual-Conversation.pdf. This is slightly less accessible, and also—interestingly— leads with a stronger emphasis on the dispositions required for discerning conversation, before offering a form of spiritual conversation method as a *possible* way to proceed.

¹⁴ This lack of listening is amply illustrated by *The Cross of the Moment* report into clergy sexual abuse in the Catholic Church of England and Wales: www.durham.ac.uk/research/institutes-and-centres/catholic-studies/research/boundary-breaking-/.

any way trying to undermine this essential call to listening—especially listening to those less-heard, marginalised voices, among whom, I suggest, the Holy Spirit speaks in especially powerful and necessary ways.

Yet I am raising questions about the dominance of listening and its character in our practices for a synodal church. One way of construing what follows is as a critique of what seem to be growing assumptions about "methods" for listening epitomised by the spiritual conversation model just described. My critique reflects a desire to reset our accounts and practices of synodality in the more complex and varied practices of "journeying together"[15]—practices which need to involve the open and courageous speech of *parrhesia*[16] every bit as much as listening, and to remember consistently the practical toil of accompanying each other in the mundane sufferings and joys of living life. We need to recall that in the *Preparatory Document* for the synodal process of 2021–2024, "listening" is listed as the second of *ten* "thematic nuclei" for the process, and described as "a first step." First steps are foundational. But I would argue that we run the risk of making the foundation of listening so valorised that we rob it of its full, complex, and somewhat messy context of that journeying together also characterised by speech, disagreement, practice, relationship, spiritual discipline, shared worship, outreach, work for social justice, ecumenism, and the quotidian practices of household living.[17] In this, I am suggesting a shift of emphasis from listening and spiritual conversation towards ordinary conversation, which has its own culture of listening and attention (and their lack). Any reification of listening, with its accompanying establishing of "methods" and formats, risks specialising "listening" in ways which, paradoxically, disempower the ordinary conversations, shared lives, and journeying together, which are the true matter and properly messy context for God's conversing with women and men.

The theological importance of such human and often stumbling ordinary conversation pre-dates the current call to synodality and, I would argue, finds particular place in the Second Vatican Council's

---

[15] *For a Synodal Church: Communion, Participation, and Mission. Preparatory Document for Synod 2021–2023*, Synod of Bishops 2021, 1, www.synod.va/content/dam/synod/common/preparatory-document/pdf-desktop/en_prepa_desktop.pdf.

[16] "Speaking of all things," with courage, "integrating freedom, truth and charity" (*Preparatory Document*, no. 30). This multifaceted complexity is also reflected in the "ingredients for synodal process" set out in section 4.5 of the *Vademecum for the Synod on Synodality*, Synod of Bishops 2021, www.synod.va/content/dam/synod/common/vademecum/en_vade.pdf. I note especially here the ingredients of informal conversation, shared activity, and non-verbal expressions. The 2014 ITC document on synodality concludes with a rallying call not around listening, but *parrhesia*.

[17] See *Preparatory Document*, no. 30.

account of church. Beyond the specifically ecclesial, there is a fundamental sense that through such conversation human beings work together to discern truth, in matters of faith, but also in all matters of authentic discovery. As the Declaration on Religious Liberty, *Dignitatis Humanae*, describes it:

> Truth, however, is to be sought after in a manner proper to the dignity of the human person and his social nature. The inquiry is to be free, carried on with the aid of teaching or instruction, communication, and dialogue, in the course of which men [sic] explain to one another the truth they have discovered, or think they have discovered, in order thus to assist one another in the quest for truth.[18]

The discerning of truth through ordinary conversation where both true and less than true understandings are shared is a human call rooted in the heart of what it is to be a person, based in the human dignity of all women, men, and children. This commitment to multifaceted conversation, with all the implied and inevitable tensions and misunderstanding typical of its ordinariness is, further, given a prominent place in Catholic fundamental theology, as the "development" or "progress" (*processio*) of revelation more specifically in the life of the church is described at the Second Vatican Council:

> This tradition which comes from the Apostles develops in the Church with the help of the Holy Spirit. For there is a growth in the understanding of the realities and the words which have been handed down. This happens through the contemplation and study made by believers, who treasure these things in their hearts (see Luke, 2:19, 51) through a penetrating understanding of the spiritual realities which they experience, and through the preaching of those who have received through Episcopal succession the sure gift of truth.[19]

This dynamic sense of the "development" or "progress" (*processio*) of revelation taken together with the accounts of church and mission in *Lumen Gentium* and *Gaudium et Spes* have suggested to me an understanding of Vatican II ecclesiology in which contro-versing, conversation, and communication are essential.[20] Conversing, discussing together, sharing our diversity of insights is fundamental to the church being what she is truly called to be, in and for the world: a

---

[18] Vatican II, "Declaration on Religious Liberty" (*Dignitatis Humanae*), no. 3.
[19] Vatican II, "Dogmatic Constitution on Divine Revelation" (*Dei Verbum*), no. 8.
[20] This is argued in Clare Watkins, *Laity and Communication: Some Implications of Organization Theory for the Ecclesiology of Vatican II* (PhD diss., Cambridge University, 1990), www.repository.cam.ac.uk/handle/1810/250979.

witness to "the living tradition" of God's loving of and reaching out to all in our world.

This desire to rediscover ordinary conversation as the beating heart of Christian life and mission is not, however, merely an "academic," or abstracted concern. Rather, the argument set out in this article is motivated by my growing concern for the very practical need to make listening, discernment, conversation-in-the-Spirit, *parrhesia*, participation, and so forth more mundane, quotidian, and ordinary. We know that the current systems, methods, and roadmaps for these synodal gifts have been of extremely limited impact in terms of numbers of church people involved; if we take seriously that central call to include those "protagonists of the church"[21] marginalised and variously impoverished in our societies, then these limitations are thrown into even sharper relief. Our well-intentioned ordering, systematising, and quasi-professionalising of formal listening through spiritual conversation models may well be part of the problem here.

Let me illustrate something of my problem with formal listening and the method for spiritual conversation described earlier, through two experiences of my own. These practical experiences, and others like them, have often felt, to me, as a disappointing mismatch for the deeper theological account of conversation implied in Vatican II's ecclesiology and missiology. One experience concerned a continental level event which employed the method of spiritual conversation in small groups described above: following prayer, each of us spoke in turn what was in our heart; a time of quiet followed, after which each could comment on what they had heard, and so on. Insights were then gathered from this careful and prayerful process. Careful, prayerful—and, in my experience, strangely and adversely *controlled*. So, when—on occasion—conversation became fuelled with flashes of excitement, when words from different contributors began to fuel each other to new ideas, challenging, developing, confusing, misinterpreting, realising, laughing . . . all this was quickly closed down with the reminder that our time together was not about discussion. It was not, in fact, about anything I much recognised as natural, human meaning-making through the clumsy and joyful adventure of open and trusting ordinary conversation. Given the inclusive intention of synodality, a question arose for me: Is this carefully curated spiritual conversation the kind of conversation I would want to invite my less church-y friends, family, and colleagues, into? This is an important question, as it seems to me that the authentic vision of synodality and its discerning processes depends on including just such people.

---

[21] *Synthesis Report, XVI Ordinary General Assembly of the Synod of Bishops, First Session*, Synod of Bishops 2023, no. 4, www.synod.va/content/dam/synod/assembly/synthesis/english/2023.10.28-ENG-Synthesis-Report_IMP.pdf.

My sense that the carefully curated nature of the spiritual conversation in this first example might also—somewhat paradoxically—result in some subtle but significantly problematic power dynamics was further suggested by a second experience. This time I was taking on the role of facilitating a reflective conversation as an intentional response to the early stages of the synodal process. The participants in the conversation were all experienced and qualified counsellors, working in a Catholic charity. As such, attentive listening in a context of pastoral care and discernment was, at least potentially, something in which they were especially experienced. They did, of course, know, in both theory and practice, a great deal about listening and felt assured they thereby not only were well-equipped for the synodal process, but also had a good deal of wisdom to offer that process—and they were right. However, as our work together developed, I had to reflect on my own growing unease around how listening was being understood in our conversations. As counsellors the participants were experienced in a very particular therapeutic form of listening, characterised by a clear asymmetry of client and counsellor. The listening in which they were expert is not part of a conversation in any ordinary sense, but is, rather, the caring and expert exercise of a professional skill set, so as to enable the thinking-through of the speaker. Vulnerabilities are not equal; and whilst love, care, and attentiveness were quite rightly recognised as part of this work, shaping a true Christian vocation, this seemed to me a different kind of listening from that which—*ordinarily*—we would want to characterise our church relationships or, indeed, any of our close relationships. Listening—like loving—necessarily takes different forms in different contexts, of course; and I question whether the complexity of the variety of listening, speaking, conversation, and journeying has yet been even partially understood in our synodal processes. However, what the experience working with Catholic counsellors led me to think about more deeply was whether, in formalising our ecclesial practices of listening, we were more indebted to the professional models of listening, such as found in counselling, or spiritual direction—with all their asymmetries and complexities of power and projection—than to a theological and humanly embodied experience of ordinary, loving conversation in which listening is practised, largely imperfectly, in more contextual, intuitive, and so, potentially, symmetrical ways.

I have spent considerable time describing the emphasis on formal listening and spiritual conversation methods in the current practices of synodality and raising critical questions about them. I suggest that these are, on their own, inadequate for embodying the rich theological insights of both Pope Francis's vision for a synodal church, and the fundamental theology and epistemology of the second Vatican

Council upon which it is built. In particular, as these methods of formal listening and spiritual conversation gain currency, there remain un-examined questions as to whose articulation they enable, and whose they might disable, as specific cultures of speech and silence mix with subtle and pervasive asymmetries of power in the relation between those who are listened *to,* those who listen, and those who choreograph the listening and its articulated outcomes. There is another essay to be written specifically about these questions of power and the need to recognise them in synodal processes. In this article, I want to keep the focus on de-emphasising the formal listening of spiritual conversation, and centering, instead, ordinary conversation for our journeying together. With this purpose in mind, in the next two sections, I turn to explore how synodality might be alternatively informed and enriched by insights from the two areas of thought and practice named at the start: theological action research and organisational studies.

CONVERSATION AND/AS LEARNING: INSIGHTS FROM THEOLOGICAL ACTION RESEARCH WORK

In wishing to highlight the importance of *ordinary conversation*, I am informed by my own research practices, both in terms of methods and content. The last two decades have seen the development of a participative qualitative practical research methodology—theological action research—of which I am a co-originator.[22] This methodology

---

[22] For an early overview see Cameron, Bhatti, Duce, Sweeney, and Watkins, *Talking about God in Practice*. This work has been developed further in a range of papers, and most notably in Watkins, *Disclosing Church*. For additional perspectives on theological action research see Clare Watkins, "Practising Ecclesiology: From Product to Process: Developing Ecclesiology as a Non-Correlative Process and Practice through the Theological Action Research Framework of Theology in Four Voices," *Ecclesial Practices* 2, no. 1 (2015): 23–39; Tone Stangeland Kaufman and Jonas Ideström, "Why Matter Matters in Theological Action Research: Attending to the Voices of Tradition," *International Journal of Practical Theology* 22, no. 1 (2018): 84–102; James Butler, "Prayer as a Research Practice? What Corporate Practices of Prayer Disclose about Theological Action Research," *Ecclesial Practices* 7, no. 2 (2020): 241–257; James Butler, "'Denomination Doesn't Matter'? A Proposal for a Receptive Ecumenical Missiology from a Theological Action Research Project on Methodists and Catholics Engaging Together in Social Action," *Ecclesial Practices* 10, no. 2 (2023): 165–181; Helen Cameron and Andrew Rogers, "Theological Action Research in Conversation with Contextual Biblical Interpretation," in *Challenging Contextuality: Bibles and Biblical Scholarship in Context*, ed. Louise J. Lawrence, Peter-Ben Smit, Hannah M. Strømmen, and Charlene van der Walt (Oxford: Oxford University Press, 2024), 129–146, doi.org/10.1093/9780191982415.003.0008; and Daniel P. Rhodes, "Theology as Social Activity: Theological Action Research and Teaching the Knowledge of

draws on participative action research,[23] both in terms of methods and epistemology, but reshapes this in terms of a "whole theology" approach,[24] which names, surfaces, and integrates the proper variety of specifically theological sources and authorities (loci of revelation), as understood in, for example, Catholic fundamental theology, and—differently—the Wesleyan Quadrilateral.[25] For theological action research, the practices of quotidian faith life and language are recognised as properly and fundamentally theological—as "bearers of theology" in their own right. As such, they are held in ongoing, mutually critical conversation with the more established and already discerned theological voices of normative Christian teaching and formal, academic theological accounts.[26] The methods for such a whole theology include a variety of qualitative research methods which enable thick description of and practitioner testimonies to practices to be expressed in forms which enable wider reflection. This data is, significantly, *discerned* (as distinct from "analysed") not only through attentive reading and thematic surfacing but, most crucially, through reflective but free-flowing—so in that sense "ordinary"—conversation between academics and practitioners.[27]

Whilst this is not the place to explore this methodology and its concomitant epistemology in any further detail, for the purposes of this paper I would draw attention to two significant points regarding listening, conversation, and discernment which arise in its practice. The first of these concerns the ways in which theological action research both roots its theological claims in a vision of whole theology, itself built on a "conversation" between different "voices" or authorities within theology, and resolutely refuses to allow such conversation to be simply abstracted. Thus, the authoritative sources for theological action research are understood as "four voices of theology"—the operant (embodied in practices), espoused (articulated by practitioners), normative (received and established traditions), and formal (academic)—drawn into an interpenetrating and mutually (in)forming conversation. The image of "conversation" is, of course, not strange to interdisciplinary theology and especially current within practical theology. In the same way, the influential British practical theologian Stephen Pattison famously described the discipline of

---

Christian Ethics and Practical Ministry," *Scottish Journal of Theology* 73, no. 4 (2020): 340–357.
[23] For a helpful introduction see Alice McIntyre, *Participatory Action Research: Qualitative Research Methods* (Thousand Oaks, CA: Sage, 2008).
[24] Watkins, *Disclosing Church*, 239–249.
[25] Watkins, *Disclosing Church*, 39–53.
[26] This is referred to as the "Four Voices of Theology." See Watkins, *Disclosing Church*, chapter 4.
[27] An account of this process can be found in Watkins, *Disclosing Church*, 17–23.

practical theology in terms of a conversation between theology, practice, and experience.[28] Superficially, this seems to accord with theological action research's commitment to understanding and listening to theology in the "four voices" just outlined.

However, as Pattison himself observes in a later article,[29] in framing theological conversation in this way we run the risk of formalising and abstracting what are, in every case, practically, contextually, and personally embedded accounts of theological realities. These "voices of theology" named in theological action research form merely a shorthand for the deeply human and embodied accounts of how God is at work in the world, and how we try to make sense of our encounters with God's presence in Spirit and Word. Fundamentally, the conversations which form the dynamics of divine revelation, and must thus shape our best attempts at any whole theology, are not conversations between abstract ideas or codified traditions, but rather between real, imperfect, and not entirely articulate human beings.[30]

This brings us to a second learning point from theological action research concerning conversation: the way in which the embodied theologies of practice (the operant and espoused voices) are gathered and discerned through multilayered conversational practices. In order to give form and expression to the operant theology (embodied in practices and daily life), theological action research employs a range of qualitative data gathering. Commonly this will involve open or semi-structured interviews and focus groups, but will also draw on more image-led, or creative expressions, as well as the attention to practice of participant observation and other ethnographic methods. The core practice which informs all these methods, although in different ways, is that of conversation: between participants in focus groups and participatory events and, in a particular way, in the form of interview we employ which emphasises the interviewer following the energy of the (asymmetrical) conversation, rather than imposing a predetermined structure of questions, and so aiming to keep it as close to ordinary conversation as possible.

Whilst such an approach to qualitative data gathering is not unique, its conversational emphasis is taken further in the way in which all resulting data—whether in the form of transcripts or non-verbal

---

[28] James Woodward and Stephen Pattison, *The Blackwell Reader in Pastoral and Practical Theology* (Oxford: Blackwell, 2000).
[29] Stephen Pattison, "Conversations in Practical Theology," *Practical Theology* 13, nos. 1–2 (2020): 87–94.
[30] This is emphasised in Watkins, *Disclosing Church*, 29 as something of critical reflection on the variety of ways in which the four voices of theology have been employed since they were introduced in the 2010 volume, *Talking about God in Practice*.

expression—is read and discerned by reflector groups, both from the more academic research perspective, and that of the practitioner participants themselves. Here it is the conversation among the reflectors, framed by prayer and personal reading of the data and enabled by the building up of a trusting relationship through the research process, that are crucial. Data is not thematised by the attentive coding work of any individual, but rather read, prayed over, and reflected on in conversations between diverse individuals. The thematic emphases of any one person are thus affirmed, re-shaped, and challenged by the reading and perceptions of others in the reflector team, and slowly a shared reading emerges of what we are seeing *together* in the practices and accounts explored. In our writing up of these conversations, it is important that the differences in view, the disagreements and tensions, are clearly expressed, resisting the research temptation to smooth over such matters, so as to arrive to clear results or recommendations.

In all these processes, attentiveness to what is heard and observed, and deep and prayerful listening, are fundamental. In training theological action research reflectors and participants, this listening is emphasised, both as a practice of care for the other person and, most crucially, a call to attentiveness to the Holy Spirit. Listening is crucial. However, this pneumatological imperative necessarily complexifies listening, and our methods contextualise it in messy, erring, humanly ordinary conversation. For, as we know, the Holy Spirit is not simply to be perceived through majority views and themes; nor, in general, does the Spirit speak through the most practised, articulate, or eager to share. We may even ask whether we can assume that the Spirit always works through the most "prayerful" or "virtuous"—even if we were able to identify such people. Here, in our characterful and open conversations, listening is practised, but in more mundane and obviously fallible ways than those suggested in the methods of spiritual conversation.

However, the methodology of theological action research is pertinent to this article's argument. Over the past six years, I have overseen an extensive theological action research project exploring faith learning, focussing (as guided by the funders) on Methodist sites of learning in the UK.[31] This work is currently being extended into a

---

[31] This research was funded by the Susanna Wesley Foundation, and carried out by Clare Watkins (Principal Investigator) and James Butler (Post-Doctoral Researcher). For an overview of this project see www.susannawesleyfoundation.org/faith-learning-and-churches/. Some of the learning from the project has been made available for a practitioner and ministry audience through the online journal of Church Mission Society, *Anvil*: www.churchmissionsociety.org/anvil-journal-theology-and-mission/learning-faith-anvil-vol-39-issue-2/.

new project, more ecumenical in scope, working with Christian groups "on the margins" of both church and/or society, so as to deepen understanding of how faith is handed on, learned, and grown in such "edgy" places.[32] In both projects, we have been repeatedly struck by the central place conversation holds in the faith life and learning of so-called "ordinary" Christians, and those coming to faith in the more fragmented realities of social and ecclesial margins. If there is one, simple conclusion I would draw from this work, it is that *conversation-in-ordinary* is the single most important way in which people learn, grow in, and come to faith. Such an apparently simple finding does, however, carry with it some complicating factors, both for conversation as an ecclesial practice and so, necessarily, for understanding listening practices as a Christian calling.

One such factor becomes clear when we think further about what ordinary conversation describes. In our research, the term grew in meaning, as we recognised the places of growing in faith in terms of apparently mundane "chats" between people: the brief but regular conversations between dog walkers; the way things might "pop up" unexpectedly over a cup of tea in a neighbour's kitchen; the occasional word, daily, at the school gate; the comments, banter, and exchanges at the pub. All these appeared throughout our research not only as the necessary precursors to any "deep conversation" when such might be needed, but also as loci where faith itself was nurtured, and stimulated to develop fresh expression. Such conversations-in-ordinary are, by their very nature, unmanaged and unmanageable. It was consistently clear that the group conversations organised in intentional adult faith learning, for example, were—whilst valuable—not only the preserve of a minority but generally less impactful than the day-to-day conversations "in the wild" participants experienced. These unplanned chats are fragmentary, interrupted, and interrupting by nature: they are also significantly free from the shaping, and often unacknowledged, power of those clergy and educational professionals who sought to emphasise courses and preaching as primary places for Chistian learning. It was in such unmanaged and unmanageable fragmented places that, again and again, our participants recorded some of their most significant faith learning. As reflectors on the research data, it was here that we felt drawn to understand better how the Holy Spirit leads the vast majority of people more deeply into life in Christ.[33]

---

[32] This research is jointly funded by St. Peter's Saltley Trust and the Susanna Wesley Foundation, and carried out by Clare Watkins (Principal Investigator), James Butler (Post-Doctoral Researcher), and Ian Jones (Director, Saltley Trust).

[33] Some initial insights drawn from this research can be found in "Learning Faith: Reflections from Researching Everyday Faith," *Anvil: Journal of Theology and Mission* 39, no. 2 (2023), www.churchmissionsociety.org/anvil-journal-theology-

What might this mean for properly complexifying our listening practices? First, it suggests that we need to be listening to what is at work in the ordinary places of the lay living of faith. The identity of the "we" here then becomes important: this is not so much about "expert listeners" gathering up the words and experiences of "ordinary" lay people. It is rather more about we as a whole church developing, recognising, and celebrating, wherever they occur, the quotidian practices of ordinary conversation, and its attendant, ordinary listening and response. These gifts are at work *already* among God's people; this is not about adding training courses, toolkits, and skill sets. Rather, this is about nurturing what is already at play, as women, men, and children develop their existing gifts of listening and speaking in daily, muddled-up, but graced, conversation.

The emphasis in all I have tried to draw out in talking of theological action research work here has been, quite intentionally, on ordinary conversation among people in quotidian, interrupted contexts of living and loving. It can be seen how very different this is from the disciplined methods of spiritual conversation. This leads me to suggest that—whilst helpful, and perhaps essential, as *part* of church and indeed wider faith practice—these latter intentional practices of formal listening and carefully curated speaking do not, and cannot, reflect the realities of that conversing of the whole People of God where faith, hope, and love are coming alive, albeit in fragmentary, obscured, and seemingly time-inefficient ways. There are, in fact, both practical theological and powerful pneumatological reasons for privileging this chaotic ordinary over the more controlled and disciplined, to which this article can only allude briefly, but in light of my introductory remarks calling for fuller appreciation of a variety and complexity of practice around synodality and its calling to listening *and* speech, to conversation, formal, informal, and non-verbal, it can perhaps already be seen how these research learnings suggest to me a different account of the place of listening in our faith, and more specifically, discernment practices.

CONVERSATION AND HUMAN SOCIALITY: LEARNING FROM SOCIAL SCIENCE ACCOUNTS

A second area of learning and enrichment for synodal processes comes, for me, from the social sciences and, in particular, social science accounts of human organisation, in which the importance of conversation as generator of knowledge (of various kinds), practice,

---

and-mission/learning-faith-anvil-vol-39-issue-2/. The research and its insights are to be published in Clare Watkins and James Butler, *Christian Faith and Christian Learning: A Theological Action Research Account* (London: Routledge, 2025).

and change is increasingly acknowledged. To some of these I now turn.

I am thinking here of the ways in which complexity theory and related theories of emergence have begun to transform not only theories of human organisation, but practices related to human sociality and organisational change.[34] These theories aim to move us away from our embedded thinking around order/stability versus disorder/instability, and focus instead on the ways in which human social reality is constantly emergent, caught up in a dynamic of being and coming to be. As people formed by the dominant epistemologies of modernity, we are used to thinking of process leading to product, activity leading to conclusion or achievement, conversation leading to decision. Indeed, I would suggest that such dominant ways of thinking have tended to shape a more methods-driven account of formal listening practices in our responding to the call to synodality. Within a complexity approach to organisations, and especially to organisational change, it is the less-managed, informal conversation which provides the fundamental locus for insight and authentic culture change. It is in the apparent aimlessness of human activity, relationship, and daily living that authentic forms of human sociality and knowing *emerge*. The undirected, unmanaged processes of human interaction, including conversation, are *self-organising*, and generative of forms of life and more or less explicit epistemologies. Organisations must attend to this embedded human dynamic if authentic change and sustainable organisational life is to be enabled.

An example might helpfully illustrate what I am describing here. Patricia Shaw's admirably readable and practical study of complexity and emergence, offers a number of real-life accounts of how such theories play out in practice.[35] In one such account she relates a conversation with a senior leader—"John"—looking for her help with "changing the culture" of his organisation. John is in business mode and looking for a meeting where they can plan a strategy and series of facilitated events that can effect this desired change. Both he and Shaw are only too familiar with these kinds of organisational processes; it is just a matter of tailoring these tried and trusted methods to the current situation. However, Shaw is becoming less sure that these ways of going about things should be so trusted. She writes tellingly of the crucial turn in her conversation with John:

---

[34] I am especially indebted in what follows to the work of Patricia Shaw, *Changing Conversations in Organizations: A Complexity Approach to Change* (London: Routledge, 2002).

[35] See note 22 above.

> I say I would be happy to come and talk with him and suggest we include others in the meeting so that we can discuss what people are making of what has happened. At first John hesitates, wouldn't it be better for us to meet first before involving anyone else, so that he can brief me and we can sketch our approach? I ask what makes him hesitate about going straight into a more inclusive conversation that would engage more viewpoints, interests, and ideas about what is going on and what needs to change? There is a pause, and I say that I am increasingly doubtful about "culture change" programmes in situations like this. Yes, says John, we've already had countless change programmes. . . . I can sense a difference in his voice, he sounds less business-like, less rehearsed.[36]

There are a number of things going on in this account, not least of all issues of power and keeping control that lie just beneath the surface, as John hesitates to let go of the tried and tested (but ineffective), and trust something he will be less able to manage. For our purposes, what is significant is the way in which Shaw's refusal to fold the conversation along the usual crease-lines here, and her questioning of the very premise of what is being asked, relaxes the conversation, albeit through a few moments of discomfort. As the rehearsed expectations and performances give way, a more honest, person-to-person communication is opened up. It is from there that they are able to work with (as it turned out) a rather ad hoc, self-selecting group whose un-choreographed, agenda-free, and largely unmanaged conversation opens up new ways of working and being together. The conversation embodies the self-organising principle of complexity theory, allowing a new culture to emerge from existing realities.

For Shaw, attention to conversation in human sociality becomes crucial. This is not about organising, facilitating, or managing carefully curated conversation, but rather about opening spaces for conversations to find their own participants, dynamics, and topics. Such conversation is expressly not a management issue, although at key points managers and organisational leaders do well to respond to the fruits of such conversation. Rather, it is understood as "an everyday art form by which we make ourselves together."[37] Such ordinary talking and listening constitutes social organising, as it tutors people in how we are to live together in the in-between-ness and paradox of ordinary, unplanned conversation so as to let shared meaning and action emerge.

All this discussion is drawn, of course, from social sciences, and so stops short of giving any account of how such processes might inform us of God's action and speaking in our conversing, and how it

---

[36] Shaw, *Changing Conversations*, 23–24.
[37] Shaw, *Changing Conversations*, 27.

is to be discerned. Nonetheless, there are well-established theological reasons to suggest that these same patterns and dynamics might characterise the manner in which God makes Godself known in our life in the Spirit together. What Shaw, and the complexity and emergence theories upon which she draws, enable us to articulate more clearly is the deeply human, proper place of paradox and the unresolved in our knowing and acting. As she describes it herself: "I am interested in a logic that is always dissolving categories and staying in the tension of the paradoxes inevitably created by thinking within the movement of sense-making itself."[38]

We can read these complexity and emergence theories as one genuine account of how human beings learn and share learning, and how we then grow socially into a body from such conversational learning. In a longer essay, I would want to set out the ways in which different kinds of human and human-divine conversation have held a significant place in the Christian tradition and can be interestingly identified and reflected on in the scriptures. Here I will more simply introduce the idea for which I would argue: these contemporary accounts of human sociality and practical wisdom emerging from unmanaged conversation have significant resonances with the ways in which the longer Christian tradition has understood theology and, indeed, the self-revelation of God in human lives. Theology—the faith practice of seeking deeper understanding of God—is itself a wondering, communal conversing over hundreds of generations, and the theologian is the one who, in a variety of ways, takes part in this unresolved sense-making. Conversation can be presented, then, as the primary way of human learning, social life, and meaning making, and so as one proper and essential locus for encounter with the Spirit and God's guiding Word. Centering conversation in this way, especially in its more informal, unmanaged, uncurated forms, suggests a context for an ordinary but essential listening practice—in which listening is intractably and precariously caught up in, and interwoven between, the humour, misunderstanding, interruptions, fragmentations, and emerging wisdom of people's affectively-led talk with one another, their ordinary conversation.

FROM THE FORMAL LISTENING OF SPIRITUAL CONVERSATIONS TO THE SPIRITUALITY OF ORDINARY CONVERSATIONS

In this article, I have made a preliminary case for arguing that there has been an over-valorisation of listening in present Catholic practices of synodality, which has taken an especially unhelpful form through

---

[38] Shaw, *Changing Conversations*, 30.

the dominance of methods for formal listening processes. Spiritual conversation is one such method which I have suggested is inadequate, on its own, for the inclusivity and complexity of that journeying together in all the diversity and unevenness of life synodality calls for. In particular, I have argued that such formalised listening practices run the risk of a paradoxical tendency to limit precisely those ordinary conversations contemporary practical theological research and the human sciences would recognise as essential and normal means by which God's grace is encountered and ways of loving and living discerned. Ordinary, interruptive human conversing, with all its misunderstandings, humour, missteps, and passions—held in trusting and purposeful relationships—is *the* way in which we all learn and grow in faith. Our homes, friendships, work and church lives, and most intimate relationships embody this truth for each of us; and it is perhaps to these slightly messy and difficult-to-control places that we need to look and from which we need to learn, if we are truly to become an attentive, communicative, conversing church in and for the world. What I have presented is as much a provocation to further ordinary conversation on these themes, as an argument in itself. As this provocation comes to its end, and opens a beginning, I hope, to further sharing of perspectives and questioning, I want to suggest that we might helpfully turn, as a synodal church, to what might be learned of conversation and discernment from Christian tradition.

Notably, we might do well to consider the ways in which the centering of ordinary conversation, with its "messy" contextualisation of listening, is a feature of both Scripture and the longer, especially premodern, theological tradition. Within patristic and early medieval writing, there is an interweaving of the proper intellectual task of theology, and that particular kind of *conversatio* which is prayer, conversing with God.[39] Here many of us would readily bring to mind the writings of Anselm and the *Confessions* of Augustine. The apophatic theological traditions of Eastern Christianity, typified by Denys the Areopagite, also commingle the ecstatic language of prayer and conversing with God, and the work of theology. Indeed, despite the modern reader's tendency to read Thomas Aquinas in a rather analytical mode, it is clear here, too, that the critical to-and-fro of pedagogical *conversation* lies at the heart of his *Summa Theologiae*.[40]

---

[39] See Ashley Cocksworth, *Prayer: A Guide for the Perplexed* (London: Bloomsbury, 2018), 35–40.

[40] This is well and extensively discussed by Jennifer Jackson in *Conversation, Friendship, and Transformation: Contemporary and Medieval Voices in a Theology of Discourse* (Abingdon: Taylor & Francis, 2016). I have also been impacted in this account by Victor White's *Holy Teaching: The Idea of Theology According to St. Thomas Aquinas* (London: Blackfriars, 1958).

St. Thomas's own account of learning, whilst emphasising divine agency as the only teacher, places the so-called teacher and the learner in a conversation of shared discernment of the truth of God.[41] Here the *conversatio* of prayer, fundamental to the patristic and medieval accounts of theologising, is understood, further, to be interwoven into that natural and everyday mystery of human conversation, through which we all fundamentally learn and make (or perhaps better, discern) meaning.

Referencing these aspects of our premodern tradition, cannot lead to a simple mapping of what is described there onto our contemporary practices and thinking. The lines of continuity and fruitful recognition of the perdurance of these themes into our own context are there to be drawn, but they must be the subject of a much longer study. For now, I mention these themes simply to underline two things: first, the proper place human conversation has held in the tradition as a key way of faith seeking understanding, theological meaning-making; and, second, the ways in which conversation *with* God, and *inclusive of* God's presence and agency, is recognised as an essential part of such conversation and locus of revelation. The key to unravelling this dynamic further, to aid our own understanding and practice of such conversation today, lies, I believe, in our deepening awareness of the place conversation—of a muddled, misunderstanding, thoroughly human kind—holds within Scripture, and especially in the Gospels. Indeed, we are reminded of just this in the way in which the *Preparatory Document* for the Synods 2021–2023 reflects on two significant biblical narratives: that of the "Council of Jerusalem" (Acts 15), and of the more diffuse Gospel image of "the crowd" that surrounds Jesus.[42] Especially in the latter (although reading Acts 15 in light of Galatians suggests something similar concerning that story) we see something of the importance of the informal, affectively-driven, impromptu, and often humanly unsatisfactory conversations that form a major part of the fabric of the story of Jesus's life, death, and resurrection. The *Preparatory Document* reminds us of Jesus's uncompromising openness to those in the crowd, as "the widest possible audience" and his acceptance "as interlocutors [of] all who emerge from the crowd."[43] It is especially those cast out from their communities and seemingly separated from God to whom he attends;

---

[41] See Aquinas, *De Veritate*, q. 11. On the contemporary significance of this see Clare Watkins, "The Faith-Full Intellect: Catholic Traditions and Instincts about the Human Person and Their Significance for Teaching and Learning," in *Christian Faith, Formation, and Education*, ed. Ros Stuart-Buttle and John Shortt (London: Palgrave Macmillan, 2018), 61–78; Vivian Boland, *St. Thomas Aquinas*, Bloomsbury Library of Educational Thought (London: Bloomsbury, 2007).

[42] *Preparatory Document,* nos. 16–24.

[43] *Preparatory Document,* no. 18.

and, thus attending, Jesus specifically calls them into conversation with him, allowing profoundly transformative conversing which is, nonetheless, frequently characterised by misunderstanding and tension. Here the mystery of human-divine conversation as the heart of divine revelation and the person's coming to deeper relationship in God is spelt out in day-to-day narratives, transformed by the presence of the incarnate Word, Jesus.

The truth of this necessary centrality for ordinary conversation in Christian life and learning can be especially felt when we recall that, in the current call to synodality, what is involved is nothing less than a change *in all we do*. The *Vademecum* puts it like this:

> This kind of discernment is not only a one-time exercise, but ultimately a way of life, grounded in Christ, following the lead of the Holy Spirit, living for the greater glory of God. Communal discernment helps to build flourishing and resilient communities for the mission of the Church today. Discernment is a grace from God, but it requires our human involvement in simple ways: *praying, reflecting, paying attention to one's inner disposition, listening and talking to one another in an authentic, meaningful, and welcoming way.*[44]

The question as to how our listening practices, and spiritual conversations can really become "a way of life" is so pressing—a question which, I argue, can only be inadequately responded to by formal models of such conversing. Perhaps, in devising our (in many ways excellent) "models" we have failed to see and recognise what has been there—"in the wild"—all along.

In an ecumenical synodal event in which I was privileged to take part, I remember especially one contribution in our group's (formal and disciplined) listening exercise. This is (more or less) what was said in that place of attentiveness: "We should never use the word 'synodality' without also referring to the word 'economics.'" What was being raised was an essential and critical question about whether the synodal practices we are beginning to formalise could really take account of the realities of the lives of the majority for whom the sheer economic pressures of getting on with life were all but overwhelming. For any of our supposed models of listening, the great challenge and, indeed, ultimate test of their spiritual authenticity, must surely be how far they are embodied in the daily lives of *all* the baptised. This cannot, I think, simply be a matter of getting more than the usual ten percent or so of people to sign up to the quasi-professionally designed "models" for listening and conversational practices. Rather, more

---

[44] *Vademecum* no. 2.2 [emphases, added].

radically, it requires a recognition of the *already existing*, although often unnamed and unrecognised, realities of faith conversation going on in fragmentary and quotidian ways in the daily lives of millions of "ordinary" people. Here, as my own participative research constantly reminds me (often inconveniently), the Holy Spirit is working and enabling that mysterious and perennial *conversatio* which is the living power of God's Word among us. If this *conversatio* is to become, through our synodal efforts, a more celebrated and effective authority in the church—as I hope and pray it will—then we will need to attend more to the ordinary conversations than to any of our more particular disciplined and curated models of listening and speech in which it is only ever going to be the minority who are heard. Ⓜ

Clare Watkins is professor of Christian theology: faith and practice at the University of Roehampton, and research professor at Durham University. A Roman Catholic, laywoman theologian, committed to teaching and research in the areas of ecclesiology, sacramental, and practical theology, Clare has a particular concern for working in ways that contribute to the integration of academic theology and faith practice. A co-originator of "theological action research," Clare is now director of the Theology and Action Research Network, director of the UK Network of Catholic Practice-Engaged Theologians, and principal investigator on a theological action research project exploring the realities of faith learning particularly in contexts often considered "marginal." She has worked with a wide range of church providers of adult formation, as well as with agencies of the Catholic Bishops' Conference of England and Wales, and international ecumenical bodies. Her latest book, *Disclosing Church: An Ecclesiology Learned through Conversations in Practice* (Routledge, 2020) develops these varied concerns. *Christian Faith and Christian Learning: A Theological Action Research Account*, a book co-authored with James Butler, based on their theological action research project exploring faith and learning in British Methodism, is to be published by Routledge in 2025.

French Catholics and Synodality: Spiritual Sensibilities and the Will to Participate or Abstain

Yann Raison du Cleuziou

Abstract: Using the situation of French Catholicism as a starting point, this article shows how sociologists of Catholicism have continued to refine the methods and categories used to construct the representation of Catholicism and understand the expectations of Catholics. The most recent surveys are based on an in-depth analysis of how Catholics think about "their church," and identify what is causing the crisis within it. They are of particular interest in understanding why some practicing Catholics, especially younger ones, have shown little interest in the Synod on Synodality scheduled by Pope Francis. In fact, sociological surveys help us understand how the synodal process, through its procedure and legitimization, encourages the participation of certain sensibilities and discourages others. Sociological analysis also enables us to identify resources for overcoming this resistance, developing listening among Catholics and working towards the authentically ecclesial character of synodality. In conclusion, the article argues that the contribution of the social sciences should be taken into account in the development of consultation techniques and ecclesial governance.

T HE IMPLEMENTATION OF THE SYNOD OF BISHOPS ON SYNODALITY launched by Pope Francis in 2021 requires tackling five delicate questions:

1. How do you develop a participatory process in an institution that has long encouraged docility among its members? It is not enough to create participatory procedures for Catholics to take them up. In the same way that universal suffrage is not enough to make every citizen a voter, not every Catholic will necessarily take part in synod consultations.
2. Trends in the political sociology of contemporary democracies show that there is nothing random about people's willingness to take part in politics. Social elites and activists readily consider

themselves competent and participate more than the working classes.[1] Why should the church escape this oligarchic trend?
3. Given these potential biases, how can we guarantee the authority of synod consultations or decisions without checking that they are representative?
4. How can this representativeness be created without agreement on the criteria for relevant representation of Catholics?
5. How can this representation be made legitimate and fruitful without valuing pluralism and developing a culture of listening among Catholics?

The social sciences are essential to thinking about these issues of participation and representation.[2] In France, for example, sociology has played an important role in the understanding Catholics have developed of their diversity of opinion and place in society. In the absence of representative institutions, sociology has taken on, almost single-handedly, the task of objectifying the reality of Catholic practices and opinions, particularly the cleavages and power relations that bring them together or divide them.

Sociological controversy has been a privileged forum for describing and raising awareness of intra-ecclesial power relations. The way in which Catholics identify and distinguish themselves depends in part on the categories of sociological description. The typologies developed by sociologists to describe Catholics therefore have as much a descriptive role as an ecclesiological one. Indeed, their influence can be decisive in the visibility or invisibility of Catholic practices and opinions and the problematisation of the attitude ecclesial authorities should adopt towards them.

In this article, I will first show how the thinking of sociologists of Catholicism has continued to shape the methods and categories intended to construct the representation of Catholicism and understand the ways in which Catholics participate in or abstain from ecclesial arrangements. I will then take a closer look at the results of a multi-year survey, designed to listen to French Catholics and the resulting representation of Catholicism. I will then show how this survey approach helps us understand differing attitudes to synodal participation among Catholics in France, particularly attitudes of resistance. Finally, based on the survey data, I will suggest ways of developing a culture of listening conducive to synodal mobilisation.

---

[1] A classic text on this point: Daniel Gaxie, *Le Cens caché. Inégalités culturelles et ségrégation politique* (Paris: Seuil, 1978).
[2] Loïc Blondiaux and Jean-Michel Fourniau, "Un bilan des recherches sur la participation du public en démocratie : beaucoup de bruit pour rien ?," *Participations* 1 (2011): 8–35, doi.org/10.3917/parti.001.0008.

REPRESENTING AND ANALYSING THE PARTICIPATION OF CATHOLICS: SOCIOLOGICAL QUESTIONS

The category of layperson is hardly ever used in the sociology of Catholicism. The relationship of lay people with the church is analysed using other descriptive categories. In the Catholic Church, Sunday worship is a canonical obligation (Can. 1246–1247), and for this reason Gabriel Le Bras and Fernand Boulard, the founders of the sociology of Catholicism in France, used it as a criterion of integration into Catholicism. Le Bras and Boulard distinguish between the zealous (Mass attendance several times a week), the *messalisants* (Mass attendance every Sunday), the seasonal conformists (Mass attendance for major seasonal festivals), and the detached (Mass attendance for individual rites of passage).[3] In Fernand Boulard's famous map of religious practice in France, the "lands of Christianity" are those where practice is unanimous and the "lands of mission" where practice is in the minority.[4] The frequency of Mass attendance is thus a measure of both Christianisation and de-Christianisation.

This sociological description has contributed to pastoral discussions and action being structured by the opposition between practising and non-practising Catholics, identified as a problem to be resolved. The parish was at the heart of this debate and, in order to mobilise non-practising Catholics, new churches had to be built in the new districts or the priest had to be freed from existing tasks to enable him to better reach the people where they were, in the factories in particular.[5] This first system of representation was based on a close link between sociological and pastoral approaches. Priests often conducted sociological surveys and then interpreted them.[6] From their viewpoint, observing the rhythm of Mass attendance was the relevant indicator of the intensity of faith. This did not make it easier to listen to Catholics, and sociologists gradually began to break away from pastoral work by challenging clergy's prejudices about "working-class" people, whom it was argued, were less de-Christianised than they appear.[7]

---

[3] Gabriel Le Bras, *Etudes de sociologie religieuse,* tome 2 : De la morphologie à la typologie (Paris: PUF, 1956).
[4] Fernand Boulard, *Premiers itinéraires en sociologie religieuse* (Paris: Les éditions ouvrières—économie et humanisme, 1954).
[5] Olivier Chatelan, *L'Église et la ville : le diocèse de Lyon à l'épreuve de l'urbanisation 1954–1975* (Paris: L'Harmattan, 2012).
[6] Alain Chenu, "Les enquêteurs du dimanche. Revisiter les statistiques françaises de pratique du catholicisme (1930–1980)," *Histoire & mesure* 26, no. 2 (2011): 177–221, doi.org/10.4000/histoiremesure.4261.
[7] François-André Isambert, *Christianisme et classe ouvrière. Jalons pour une étude de sociologie historique* (Tournai: Casterman, 1961), 17.

From the 1960s onwards, the criterion of Mass attendance was called into question because it was suspected of confusing faith with religion. Gabriel Le Bras himself came to condemn this founding presupposition of the analysis of dechristianisation.[8] The high rate of Sunday observance in the past was suspected of masking the superficiality of faith and only testifying to the strength of social conformism. The figure of the Catholic Action activist, not only a practising Catholic but also a Catholic committed to transforming society, has become the model for authentic participation in the church's mission. After May 1968, despite the fact that many activists distanced themselves from Sunday observance, they retained their aura of exemplarity. In this period, Michel de Certeau observed that "more and more Christians are less practising the more they believe."[9] The Mass as a norm of participation was seen as disqualified. Émile Poulat suggested updating the methods used in the sociology of Catholicism, because while the frequency of religious practice is a measure of religious integration, the same cannot be said for faith.[10] Danièle Hervieu-Léger confirms that "a whole population of very committed Catholics" might be missed by a census based on Mass attendance.[11] Sociology therefore helps us listen to Catholics who feel the Mass does not nourish authentic Christian life.

This new stage of sociological questioning has contributed to pastoral debates being structured around the issue of reducing the distance between intermittent consumers of Catholic ritual and Catholic activists. But the promotion of activists as role models is extremely elitist. As Michel Brion showed in 1972, while 97% of French people are baptised, only 0.6% can be identified as catholic activists.[12] As a result, when priests cast suspicion on parents who ask their babies to be baptised or children who make their solemn communion, accusing them of conformism, they are acting as if all French people could adhere to an extremely elitist way of being Catholic. The sociologist Henri Mendras considers this pastoral approach to be perilous: "Wanting to transform the *credentes* into *perfecti* and, if we don't succeed, abandoning them to their fate, to look after only the latter, inevitably leads to transforming the Church

---

[8] Gabriel Le Bras, "Déchristianisation : mot fallacieux," *Cahiers d'histoire publiés par les universités de Clermont-Lyon-Grenoble*, tome IX (Grenoble: Imprimerie Allier, 1964), 92.
[9] Michel de Certeau and Jean-Marie Domenach, *Le christianisme éclaté* (Paris: Seuil, 1974), 11.
[10] Emile Poulat, "Trois problèmes pour la sociologie du catholicisme," *Social Compass* 16, no. 4 (1969): 471–483, doi.org/10.1177/003776866901600404.
[11] Danièle Hervieu-Léger, *Vers un nouveau christianisme ? Introduction à la sociologie du christianisme occidental* (Paris: Cerf, 1986), 24.
[12] Michel Brion, *La religion vécue des Français* (Paris: Cerf, 1972), 89.

into a sect."[13] The Dominican friar and sociologist Serge Bonnet denounced the contempt for the ritualism of the working classes that lay behind the elitist apology of the activists of the Catholic Action movements.[14] In *Prières secrètes des Français d'aujourd'hui* (1976), Bonnet describes the prayers of Catholics from modest backgrounds whose religious needs are still expressed through ritual devotions, whose aim is to banish misfortune (illness, unemployment, divorce, etc.) from everyday life.[15] For Bonnet, the contempt and ignorance of what can be authentically spiritual in popular devotions shows that the clergy is more interested in restoring its legitimacy with the new avant-garde cultural elites than with the people.

During the 1970s, the internal divisions within Catholicism were reflected in the growing use of adjectives to describe the various antagonistic currents: progressive, traditionalist, and so forth. To analyse the dimensions of this Catholic civil society, asserting itself by demanding or rejecting reforms, sociologists of Catholicism constructed typologies based on the paradigm that had replaced de-Christianisation: modernisation. For Émile Poulat, the observation of representations of modernity in the church made it possible to identify three positions that structure the divisions between Catholics: liberalism, intransigentism, and integralism.[16] Jean-Marie Donegani and Guy Lescanne took their analysis of Catholic divisions of modernity a step further, distinguishing four attitudes: integralism, stability, innovation, and secularity.[17] Then, in *La liberté de choisir* (1993), Jean-Marie Donegani refined this system of representation and replaced integralism with *christianitude*.[18] This typology, based on numerous interviews, helps pacify the expression of differences between Catholics by showing that this pluralism is irreversible because it is the translation of the process of modernisation of society within Catholicism. But there is a limit to this analysis, insofar as it classifies Catholics according to their acceptance or rejection of the "sense of history" modernity appears to represent. The different forms of participation that result from these positions are implicitly classified on a time scale as more or less promising for the future. This tends to

---

[13] Henri Mendras, *La seconde révolution française 1965–1984* (Paris: Gallimard, 1988), 119.
[14] Serge Bonnet, *À hue et à dia. Les avatars du cléricalisme sous la Ve République* (Paris: Cerf, 1973).
[15] Serge Bonnet, *Prières secrètes des Français d'aujourd'hui* (Paris: Cerf, 1976).
[16] Emile Poulat, *Modernistica, horizons, physionomies, débats* (Paris: Nouvelles éditions latines, 1982).
[17] Jean-Marie Donegani and Guy Lescanne, *Catholicismes de France* (Paris: Desclée de Brouwer, 1986).
[18] Jean-Marie Donegani, *La liberté de choisir. Pluralisme religieux et pluralisme politique dans le catholicisme contemporain* (Paris: Presses de la FNSP, 1993).

present the more "intransigent" currents as remnants of the past doomed in the long term; and yet they are organised for persistence, had the support of Popes John Paul II and Benedict XVI, and have an alternative vision of the future.[19]

Modernity as a global macro-sociological process is also becoming the main key to analysing religious detachment, because of the individualism of which it is the matrix. Danièle Hervieu-Léger's research explores the various effects of this deregulation of the frameworks of religious subjectivation: "In modernity, to be religious is not so much to know that one is engendered as to want to be engendered."[20] Her typology of the "pilgrim" and the "convert" sums up the issues at stake in a religious demand now rooted in the logic of self-construction and emancipated from the constraints of inherited belonging and hierarchically imposed disciplines.[21] This insistence has led to "God-seekers" being seen as former or future Catholics whose expectations must be listened to, and surveys have been undertaken to this end.[22]

In the early 2000s, a new turning point in the sociology of French Catholicism began with renewed attention on the Catholic institution, no doubt due to the pontificates of John Paul II and Benedict XVI. The reshaping of the exercise of authority and the relationship with established rules and roles are now back at the heart of the analysis of religious change.[23] Renewed interest in the priesthood, liturgy, parishes, and the relationship between Catholics and social issues is leading to new conceptualisations of internal conflict independent of the question of modernity.[24] Clergy and Catholic activists in parishes and dioceses are once again the focus of attention. Philippe Portier has suggested interpreting the polarities of their confrontation as an opposition between "identity" and "openness."[25] Jacques Lagroye's approach to these polarities is based on the concept of regimes of truth developed by Michel Foucault. This concept refers to the set of procedures and devices an individual must comply with in order to be

---

[19] Laurent Frölich, *Les catholiques intransigeants en France* (Paris: L'Harmattan, 2002).
[20] Danièle Hervieu-Léger, *La religion pour mémoire* (Paris: Cerf, 1993), 245.
[21] Danièle Hervieu-Léger, *Le pèlerin et converti. La religion en mouvement* (Paris: Flammarion, 1999).
[22] Jean-François Barbier-Bouvet, *Les nouveaux aventuriers de la spiritualité : enquête sur une soif d'aujourd'hui* (Montreal: Mediaspaul, 2015).
[23] Céline Beraud, *Prêtres, diacres, laïcs. Révolution silencieuse dans le catholicisme français* (Paris: PUF, 2007).
[24] Céline Beraud, Frédéric Gugelot, and Isabelle Saint-Martin, eds., *Catholicismes en tension* (Paris: EHESS, 2012).
[25] Philippe Portier, "Pluralité et unité dans le catholicisme français," in *Catholicismes en tension*, 19–36.

"true," to be "in the truth."[26] Lagroye describes the confrontation between Catholics on the basis of their competing conceptions of the institutional form the expression of faith should take, distinguishing between a "system of certainties" and a "system of testimonies."[27] On the one hand, there is a relationship with God which, through the mediation of natural law, theological knowledge, and religious and natural authorities (the role of the "fathers"), is imposed and must be accepted with confidence and self-surrender. On the other hand, the relationship with God is experienced in the horizontality of an exchange, the risk of equality of speech, and a welcoming of differences. The divine absolute then emerges from the shared recognition of the value of personal witness as a method of identifying what is emancipating in life.

This analysis draws attention back to what happens in liturgies, discussion groups, parishes, and Catholic movements. However, these two conceptual approaches, which illustrate the institutionalist turn in the sociology of Catholicism, have little empirical basis and are not based on any methodical listening to Catholics. The spokespersons of the various Catholic movements and communities are too often taken as the only references, to the detriment of the Catholic "base." Yet the rare ethnological approaches to the ordinary reality of Catholicism have shown the fruitful nature of the researcher's involvement in the field.[28] A return to this kind of listening was becoming necessary in order to properly update the representation of Catholics and the understanding of the driving forces behind their relationship with the church.

In 1980, François-André Isambert proposed an approach to the crisis of Catholicism free of any reference to the paradigm of modernity. In his view, this crisis can be identified with a "conflict of interpretation, even schism, over the origin and nature of the crisis itself."[29] Jacques Lagroye updated this position when he wrote that, for the sociologist, the crisis is above all a collective representation of reality that objectifies the truth system of those who share it.[30] Following this orientation, the description of the internal divisions within Catholicism can no longer be derived from a contextualisation or scholarly paradigm; we need to listen to Catholics to discover what

---

[26] Michel Foucault, *Le gouvernement des vivants,* Cours au collège de France, 1979–1980 (Paris: EHESS-Gallimard-Seuil, 2012), 91–110.

[27] Jacques Lagroye, *La vérité dans l'Église catholique. Restauration et contestation d'un régime de vérité* (Paris: Belin, 2006).

[28] Albert Piette, *La religion de près. L'activité religieuse en train de se faire* (Paris: Métailié, 1999).

[29] François-André Isambert, "Le sociologue, le prêtre, et le fidèle," in *La sagesse et le désordre*, ed. H. Mendras (Paris: Gallimard, 1980), 219.

[30] Lagroye, *La vérité,* 25.

their representation of the context in which "their Church" operates is, how they identify with it and rank what is in crisis or imagine solutions. Then, based on what they have to say, we need to reconstruct the concepts necessary for a more general understanding of Catholicism. To this end, a vast qualitative survey of Catholics was undertaken, presented in more detail in the following section.

QUALITATIVE SURVEY OF THE RELATIONSHIP BETWEEN COMMITTED CATHOLICS AND "THEIR" CHURCH

Starting in 2009, the organization Confrontations—association d'intellectuels chrétiens undertook a major survey to make the voice of Catholics heard.[31] I took part in drawing up the survey, collecting the data and analysing it. It is based on 177 semi-structured interviews conducted between 2010 and 2013. The targeted respondents are committed Catholics, i.e., people who have precise opinions on the vocation of their church, the definition of legitimate Catholic practices, and who undertake to a greater or lesser extent to disseminate them. Committed Catholics are divided because they defend various and sometimes antagonistic definitions of the faith and practices on which Catholic membership is based. While they all consider themselves faithful, the foundations to which their loyalty refers are multiple. To understand the tensions and dynamics that run through Catholicism, we need to look at the different foundations of faith invoked.

In analyzing the results of the survey, a certain number of patterns could be identified in the respondents' comments: relatively standardised and therefore predictable arguments about Jesus, the relationship with the ecclesiastical institution, and its future. Most of the time, these comments were made by respondents with similar religious backgrounds. This plurality of paths and expectations can be interpreted on the basis of two major variables. The first is the relationship with God. This can be either more or less informal (reading the Gospels; meeting "witnesses"; feeling God in front of a landscape; fraternal experience) or more or less cultic, and therefore

---

[31] Confrontations was founded in 1979 by leading figures such as René Rémond, Marcel Merle, and Renaud Sainsaulieu, following the dissolution of the Centre catholique des intellectuels français, to provide a forum for research based on the Christian faith but independent of the ecclesiastical hierarchy. Interviews and survey conducted by a team comprising Françoise Parmentier, Catherine Grémion, Christian Manuel, Geneviève Dahan-Selzer, Hervé Legrand, and Yann Raison du Cleuziou. The survey was published in Yann Raison du Cleuziou, *Qui sont les cathos aujourd'hui* (Paris: Desclée de Brouwer, 2014). For more information on Confrontations, see www.confrontations.fr/.

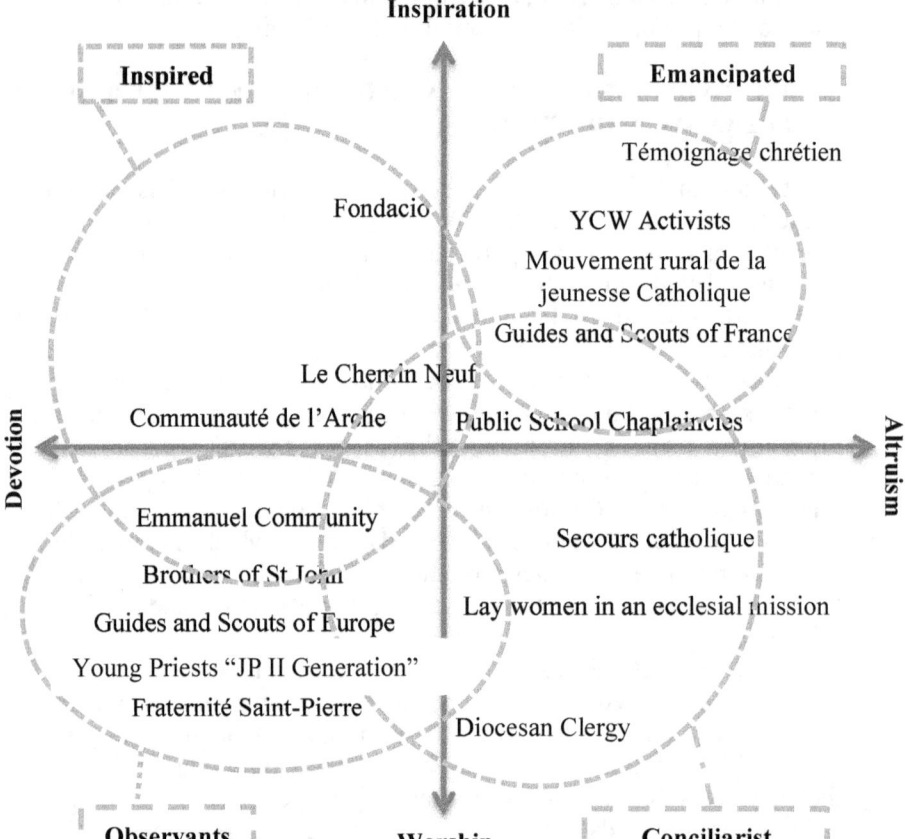

involving codified forms (participating in the Mass, receiving the sacraments). The second is putting faith into action. This can take the form of altruism (donations, mutual aid, street outreach, visits to lonely people, political or charitable involvement) or devotions (rosaries, fasting, prayers, Eucharistic adoration). Of course, these four dimensions are not mutually exclusive. Devotion does not exclude altruism, and the spiritual experience of looking at a landscape is not antagonistic to the feeling of intimacy experienced with Jesus during the Eucharist. But when you listen to and observe Catholics, it quickly becomes apparent that they will emphasise one of these dimensions to a greater or lesser extent, and this is what enables them to be distinguished.

On the basis of these two variables, it is therefore possible to construct a typology of four Catholic cultures.[32] There are, of course, many intermediate positions, and these families of sensibility overlap and are not mutually exclusive. A typology does not exhaust the complexity of the facts studied; it offers a synthetic representation of collective trends in order to make reality thinkable through comparison.

The right-hand side of the graph shows the altruism pole. It is subdivided into two types. The first nebula, most represented in the sample, is that of the self-professed conciliarists. I call them thus not because they are the only ones to respect the Second Vatican Council, but unlike other Catholics, they make it a central part of their identity. There is a generation effect here. This group was enthusiastic about the Council when it occurred, and it has left a lasting impression on them. When they talk about their faith, they invoke a certain figure of Christ. For them, Jesus is the one who includes the excluded, who transgresses the social order of his time to show God's mercy: he heals lepers, forgives the adulterous woman, talks to a Samaritan woman. Following this example, being Catholic means taking care to include those excluded from the social order: adopting a posture of welcome and compassion towards them; fighting against discrimination. The reference to Matthew 25 is recurrent: we must see the face of God in the stranger.

The conciliarists are faithful to Sunday Mass. They like this moment to be a time of welcome and communion where everyone can find their place: adults and children, men and women, remarried divorcees and homosexuals, French and foreigners. They do their utmost to ensure that the liturgy manifests this horizontal communion. Their attitudes show this attention. They like to greet their neighbour in the pew at the start of Mass; they appreciate the gesture of the rite of peace; they recommend joining hands to say the Our Father. They like priests who are like them: fraternal and who do not hesitate to deviate from certain rules to welcome those who have difficulty finding their place in the church. They identify well with Pope Francis's image of the church as "field hospital." They are also very committed to altruism and are active in *Secours catholique* (Caritas), etc. They are also very involved in diocesan and parish structures. They regret that the church can appear so intransigent and believe many French people would renew their ties with the church if it focused less on questions of sexual morality. For them, Catholics are not a minority in French society. Rather, they are a suffering majority. If the French are to reconnect with the church of their childhood and family traditions, Catholics must adopt a stance of compassion and

---

[32] See Yann Raison du Cleuziou, *Qui sont les cathos aujourd'hui*.

fraternisation towards them. Pope Francis is setting an example through his words and actions. In their view, he has already broken down many of the prejudices that previously kept French people away from the church.

In the altruistic pole, there are also Catholics much less attached to forms of worship than the conciliarists: these are the emancipated. At the heart of the faith, they claim is Christ the Liberator. For them, Jesus is the one who frees human persons from that which makes them lose their dignity. Jesus fights against injustice and invites people to assume their freedom in service to their neighbour. To be faithful to him is to be fully responsible for one's life, be aware of the collective consequences of one's actions, and be involved in social and political struggles against injustice. These emancipated people have no taste for Sunday Mass, which they find obsolete in relation to contemporary culture. They prefer Masses within their movement when they are the culmination of a collective process, during high points at Lourdes or the *Frat*.[33] Moreover, for them, what is at stake during these major celebrations is often less about their relationship with God than living together, their relationship with the group of which they are members. You can see this in their attitudes. Their bodies are restless, they comment, chat, and move about. The pleasure of being together comes first. Their relationship with God is more likely to involve reflective activities: sharing workshops, Bible groups, team life reviews, Taizé retreats, or personal reading of a Gospel. They expect the priest to be a big brother, an elder in the faith or companion on the road who can stimulate their reflection and sharpen their critical thinking about their commitments and way of life. Following the example of Jesus, they seek a word that liberates and want to be actors in the emancipation of their contemporaries.

Receptive to the institutional framework of the church, emancipated Catholics are critical of all aspects of the magisterium that play into the hands of conservatism. They regret that the church is too often confused with a certain bourgeois class and focuses on sexual morality to the detriment of social and environmental issues. Highly committed, they favour militancy in non-confessional organisations: environmental or third-world NGOs; associations for popular education or socio-cultural development. However, they also join conciliarists among the volunteers of *Secours catholique*. Like the

---

[33] The *Frat* is a pilgrimage organised for the Pentecost in Jambville or Lourdes for young Christians aged 13 to 18 from the Ile-de-France region. It brings together young people from parishes, chaplaincies, schools, movements, and communities for three to five days. This major gathering, both spiritual and festive, is an ideal way for the church in France to improve its image and reach out to young people who rarely attend Mass.

conciliarists, they believe that the decline in religious practice is mainly the consequence of the conservative evolution of the church encouraged by Popes John Paul II and Benedict XVI. They are much more in line with Pope Francis. In their view, Catholics will regain a grip on society when they position themselves as selfless servants of human progress. They believe personal responsibility and commitment to social transformation must be the two fundamental attitudes of Catholics in society.

The second pole is made up of Catholics who favour devotions as a way of putting their faith into practice. Of course, this is not exclusive of altruism, but in the interviews, they emphasise this first dimension more than the second. The largest group in this cluster is made up of observant Catholics. They mobilise a figure of Christ quite distinct from the conciliarists and the emancipated, although of course there is always some overlap between profiles. For them, Jesus is the Son of God, who died on the cross and rose from the dead to offer salvation to humanity. To be faithful to him is to seek to be worthy of this salvation through personal and ascetic effort of rectification; it is always better to conform to the path of holiness recommended by the church. They see observance of the rules as a way of emptying oneself in order to be filled with God. Mass and the sacraments are central for them. They are very assiduous and make weekly Mass attendance the essential criterion for identifying Catholics. They like solemn Masses where divine transcendence is manifested through a certain hieraticism: incense, deep silence after communion, Latin hymns, or prayers. They like priests who take great care with the liturgy and preach Catholic doctrine with rigour. Their respect for God and deference to the forms of worship are shown by their bodies: disciplined, kneeling at the moment of consecration and possibly just before communion, on the lips for many. They love devotions, especially those that require them to put ordinary social life at a distance in order to have better access to God: adoration, retreats, pilgrimages, personal silent prayer time, and the rosary.

These Catholics form a family environment and often come together in parishes of affinity, where Masses are celebrated by priests of their own persuasion. They frequent the new congregations that emerged in the 1970s, whether in the charismatic (Emmanuel, Beatitudes), neo-classical (Brothers of St. John, Saint Martin's Community) or traditionalist (Fraternité Saint-Pierre, Christ the King Sovereign Priest) movements. Despite the differences in liturgical sensibility, the milieu of observants creates a continuum between these movements. It is not uncommon for traditionalists, neo-classicalists, and charismatics to come together at various festivals in Paray-le-Monial. They can also be found in scouting movements (Scouts d'Europe; Scouts unitaires de France), in movements for the defence of the family (AFC, Alliance Vita), and are very involved in educational issues (Fondation pour l'école).

Observant Catholics see society as decadent, and they expect the church to affirm the truth of which it is the bearer in and out of season, without fear or half-heartedness, especially the defence of human life from conception to natural death. Concerned about the collapse of religious practice and the decline in vocations, they see this as the consequence of the church's slackening of doctrine and liturgy in the 1960s and 1970s. Many of those interviewed spoke of the perverse effects of the *spiritualité de l'enfouissement* (a term suggesting a spirituality both embedded and concealed) and of a humanist drift on the part of Catholic activists, who had substituted service of neighbour for a relationship with God. They feel Catholics are now in the minority, that they must unabashedly assert their identity in society and take back control of the transmission of faith. Many of the people surveyed said they had received a "soft" catechism centred on generosity but lacking theological consistency.

The second nebula of the devotional pole is made up of the inspired. This group is made up of Catholics usually described as "charismatic." The figure of Christ they use to explain their faith is very personal. For them, Jesus is a person they met in a moment of conversion. Someone they know intimately and with whom they maintain an almost perpetual dialogue. To be faithful to him is to be ever more fully converted, to let Jesus into every aspect of their lives. Their faith is a love story, a path to happiness. Most of the time, the inspired have grown up in a Catholic family, even practised; but one day they had an experience, an "encounter with Jesus" after which their previous life of faith seemed artificial to them. So they are often reaffiliated.

They form communities of converts. They are not to be found everywhere, but mainly within their communities or the parishes entrusted to them. They appreciate community Masses (more than parish or Sunday Masses) where times of collective worship alternate with moments of solitary meditation. This is reflected in their bodily attitude, which is very mobile: their bodies sway collectively in rhythm during hymns; at other times, they are individually prostrate face down in meditation. They like priests in their image, converts who bear witness to an encounter. If they are on the side of devotions, it is because they appreciate vigils of praise, adoration, and pilgrimages like the observant. Some groups, such as the Emmanuel Community,[34] are at the intersection of these two sensibilities.

---

[34] The Emmanuel community is an international public association of the faithful of pontifical right, born from a prayer group founded in 1972. The spirituality offered to members is based in particular on Eucharistic adoration, compassion, and evangelisation.

The inspired interpret the decline of the church as a consequence of the superficiality of the faith of Catholics. They expect the church to have a more spiritual face, for Catholics to be genuine converts inhabited by the presence of God. The crisis in Catholicism is therefore an opportunity for them. It is a timely opportunity for Catholics to break out of the habits they have inherited, convert, and live up to their faith by bearing public witness to their encounter with Christ.

These different Catholic sensibilities translate into spiritual and institutional expectations. They structure specific modes of participation and commitment, and therefore also of abstention and disengagement. As we have shown elsewhere, detachment from the practice of Mass can be observed in all Catholic sensibilities, albeit in different proportions. Religious abstention as much as commitment depends on the spiritual, cultural, and social factors specific to each sensibility.[35] The same Mass will satisfy the observant and exasperate the conciliar, stimulating the practice of the former and abstention of the latter. The opportunities for participation in the life of the ecclesial institution, depending on the way they are offered, will also be more or less congruent with the sensibilities of Catholics and more or less welcomed for this reason. Thus, it is not surprising to find that some are more involved in the charity sector and others in the school sector. The successes and failures of the synodal consultations can also be interpreted in light of the different motivations behind the commitment of Catholics.

Through community life, it associates lay people, consecrated persons, and priests with the mission of the church while remaining at the heart of society. See emmanuel.info/.

[35] Yann Raison du Cleuziou, "Décrire les formes de l'engagement catholique : une typologie et une cartographie à partir de données qualitatives et quantitatives," in *Appartenances et ruptures. Le rapport des baptisés à l'institution ecclésiale catholique aujourd'hui. Perspectives comparatives,* ed. A. Ky-Zerbo (Paris: Cerf, 2020), 305–334.

Summary of Catholic Sensibility Cultures[36]

	Observants	Inspired	Emancipated	Conciliars
Faith Matrix	Jesus the Savior	Jesus love	Jesus the Liberator	Jesus the Brother
Form of Loyalty	Rectification	Conversion	Accountability	Compassion
Expectation of Mass	Sacred	Celebration	Reflection	Communion
Disappointment with the Mass	Secularization	Superficiality	Nerdiness	Clericalism
Reference Group	A "milieu of families"	Community	Movement	Territorial parish
Methods of Evangelization	Family transmission and self-assertion	Personal conversion and public testimony	Solidarity with the poor and fight for social transformation	Compassion and brotherhood with all men
Conception of the Church	Beacon of light in the darkness	Community of converts	Counterweight denouncing the injustices of established order	"Field hospital"

THE DIFFICULTIES OF PARTICIPATION IN A DIVIDED ECCLESIAL CONTEXT

Questioned on the occasion of the first session of the synod on synodality, the French cardinal Jean-Marc Aveline expressed his enthusiasm but also "apprehension": "Because I saw in my country that not everyone had embarked on the synodal process."[37] This observation is not isolated among the bishops. In France, participation by 25–40 year-olds was very low, and many parishes did not participate, with parish priests scorning the organisation of the consultation. In some diocesan summaries, there is a potential distortion between the results of the consultation and the opinion of practising Catholics.[38] The preamble to the national summary of the local phase of the synod makes a statement that puts the value of the results into perspective:

> The synodal process has given rise to generous participation in many places, with the feeling that we are living through a promising experience, a communal process of listening and discernment. This

---

[36] These are described in Raison de Cleuziou, *Qui sont les cathos aujourd'hui*.
[37] See www.rcf.fr/articles/actualite/ce-synode-qui-ne-fait-pas-lunanimite.
[38] Synod 2021–2023, Summary of the diocese of Vannes, www.vannes.catholique.fr/.

consultation has also met with resistance of various kinds. Firstly, the difficulty of hearing the voices of the most vulnerable; secondly, the difficulty of reaching out to and mobilising young people and young adults; thirdly, the fear among some Catholics that this process would be used to impose changes on the Church to which they are attached; and finally, the difficulty for many priests in recognising the value of this synod.[39]

In a context of profound decline in religious practice, the fact that the voice of young people and young adults is being neglected is worrying insofar as the future of the church depends, in part, on the perpetuation of their membership. While the French bishops questioned possible methodological problems, sociology can also contribute hypotheses.[40] The qualitative survey of committed Catholics conducted by Confrontations has been followed up by three quantitative surveys. Without presenting all the results, they provide useful information for understanding resistance to the synodal process.

Firstly, the Bayard-Ipsos survey of June 2016, based on a panel of 1,007 respondents representative of committed Catholics, aimed to quantify the universes of sensibility and assess the dynamics of their perpetuation.[41] The survey shows that while the trend towards religious detachment cuts across the observant, conciliar, inspired, and emancipated, the proportions are not the same. The general trend is that the more Mass attendance is seen as a duty based on an ascetic logic, with submission to this discipline allowing people to empty themselves in order to be filled with God, the more robust and lasting is the integration into Catholicism. Conversely, if weekly attendance at Mass is not valued, practising Catholic grandparents tend to have non-practising Catholic children, who in turn have non-Christian children. Within three generations, the family is dechristianised. Of course, this summarises a more complex process, but the trend in the balance of power within Catholicism depends on this central dynamic.

From one generation to the next, observant and inspired Catholics gain in importance and influence within French Catholicism. On the other hand, conciliar and emancipated Catholics, while dominant among older Catholics, are becoming increasingly rare among younger Catholics. Elsewhere, we have described this dynamic as

---

[39] See Église.catholique.fr/synode-des-eveques-2024-sur-la-synodalite/quest-ce-que-le-synode-des-eveques-sur-la-synodalite-2021-2024/527445-collecte-nationale-des-syntheses-locales-sur-le-synode-2023-sur-la-synodalite/.
[40] Interview with Msgr. Laurent Ulrich by Philippe de Saint-Pierre, KTO, July 1, 2022, dioceseparis.fr/interview-de-mgr-laurent-ulrich-58659.html.
[41] *La Croix*, "Le vrai visage des catholiques," January 12, 2017, 2–5; *Pèlerin*, "Qui sont vraiment les catholiques," January 12, 2017, 18–32. For an in-depth presentation, see Yann Raison du Cleuziou, "Décrire les formes de l'engagement catholique."

counter-revolutionary insofar as change in Catholicism today depends on currents whose religious and political value system is more conservative: paradoxically, they are changing the church by resisting change.[42]

In May 2023, the survey carried out in partnership with *La Croix* using the database of those registered for the World Youth Day in Lisbon confirms this.[43] Of course, WYD registrants should not be confused with young Catholics as a whole, but they tend to represent those who are best integrated religiously, both because they are in contact with the church and their families are prepared to allocate a budget for their religious education. This integration is also measured, of course, by the impact of Mass on their religious socialisation. Eighty per cent of them come from regular church-going families, 12% from irregular families, and 3% from non-Catholic families. In terms of attendance, 24% go to Mass several times a week, 51% every Sunday, 16% several times a month, 6% for the main seasonal festivals and 2% for large gatherings.

Their expectations about Mass are marked by observant and inspired sensibilities: for 47% it is a moment of intimate encounter with Jesus and spiritual renewal; for 24% the celebration of a sacred mystery; for 15% a moment of collective celebration and reflection; for 14% a moment of communion between all participants that builds the church. The same trend can be seen in the positive attitude towards Latin Masses: 8% say it is their favourite Mass; 11% like it as much as the French Mass; 19% find it an occasional source of inspiration; 40% do not think it meets their expectations but have nothing against it; 12% think it is an unnecessary step backwards; 10% do not know about it.

Lastly, the fact that they are rooted in observant and inspired sensibilities is reflected in the way they see their relationship with society: 58% see the church as a beacon that shows the way in darkness; 22% as a community of converts that must bear witness to their encounter with Jesus; 12% as an emancipation movement fighting against injustice; 7% as a "field hospital" open to those wounded by life. These young Catholics already have experience of militant commitment, mainly on issues relating to the "defence of life" and bioethics (67%), with social and ecological issues attracting less

---

[42] Yann Raison du Cleuziou, *Une contre-révolution catholique. Aux origines de La Manif pour tous* (Paris: Seuil, 2019).

[43] Online questionnaire sent by the Conférence des évêques de France, the Emmanuel, Chemin Neuf, and Saint Martin communities to their subscribers (30,164) from May 7 to 11, 2023. 4,028 respondents with complete validated answers. 3,111 respondents processed, after applying quotas based on gender and region (Paris/Province). I would like to take this opportunity to thank Yvonne Herbin for her very efficient processing of the survey data.

support (17%). While young people's distrust of societal developments is quite clear, they are confident in church authorities despite the sexual abuse crisis: 81% have confidence in bishops, although only 23% have "a great deal" of confidence. 35% believe sexual abuse is the result of deviant personalities, and only 8% believe it is the result of clericalism. Only a minority of these young people are in favour of changes in the church: 14% are in favour of opening up the priesthood to women, 12% are in favour of their access to the diaconate, 63% are opposed to these reforms.

A survey of French seminarians in December 2024 confirms these analyses.[44] Among them, 72% come from families where Mass is attended on a weekly basis. Their religious socialisation is marked by the family as the main vehicle for transmitting the faith, followed by parishes. They have a militant profile and 46% have taken part in actions to defend life. Nearly 68% attended a charismatic community and 47% a traditionalist community during their religious training. They have a classical understanding of the priesthood, with the Curé d'Ars being the most frequently cited figure of reference. For 72%, the celebration of the sacraments is at the heart of their mission. Their conception of Mass is in line with that of observant and inspired people: 52% see it as a sacred mystery and experience of transcendence, and 39% see it as a moment of intimate encounter with Jesus. Only 14% consider the Latin Mass to be an unnecessary step backwards, and although only 7% consider it to be their favourite form of liturgy, most seminarians consider its continuation to be legitimate and are open to it. Clothing style also reflects this orientation: 48% of seminarians are in favour of wearing the cassock on a regular basis and 25% on an occasional basis. Finally, their vision of the church once again reflects the process of internal desecularisation described earlier: 48% see the church as a lighthouse that must show the way in darkness; 33% as a community of converts who bear witness to their encounter with Jesus; 22% as a "field hospital" that takes in those wounded by life; 1% as an emancipation movement that must fight against inequality. Quite logically, these seminarians are not particularly keen on reform, and their views on the place of women in the church illustrate this: 34% consider that women have enough recognition in the church; 38% think they could obtain more recognition and exercise roles of authority, but without changing access to the diaconate or priesthood; only 3% are in favour of changes of this kind. As can be imagined, their reception of synodality is very cautious: 46% see it as an apprenticeship in collective listening, whose

---

[44] *La Croix*, Cemoleme, Conférence des évêques de France survey of French seminarians subject to the ratio, 434 respondents, a response rate of 64%, December 2024.

benefits and limits will have to be assessed; 16% see it as a method that risks opening the way to alignment with societal demands; 7% see it as a complicated and uncertain decision-making process; 22% see it as the most appropriate form of church governance, towards which we should be moving.

These surveys show the extent to which the church is caught up in a dynamic of internal de-secularisation: as society becomes more secularised, Catholicism recomposes itself around those who remain. However, they are more often than not the bearers of a conservative and fundamentalist conception of the faith and see themselves as a counter-culture challenging the dominant social values.[45] For older generations of Catholics, this development is often seen as a "step backwards," whereas it is fully a manifestation of contemporary culture. The context between the younger and older generations is very different, which increases the gap between their mentalities and the theological orientation of their aspirations.

Older people are both in the majority in a Catholicism where the age pyramid is reversed, and marked by the Catholicism in which they have lived, still the social majority. They find it hard to understand young Catholics who live in a world very different from their own. This is because they are both a minority as young people in Catholicism and a minority as Catholics in society. The 2018 EVS survey shows that only 15% of 18–29 year-olds are now declared Catholics, compared with 13% who are declared Muslims.[46] The majority experience leads to a search for the perpetuation of a consensus with society, while the minority experience leads to resistance to erasure. The internal transformations of Catholicism, like the overall religious changes in French society, are widening the gap of incomprehension between generations.

This generational tension is directly relevant to resistance to synodal consultation. In fact, my experience of Catholics in the field leads me to hypothesise that the synodal consultation is not experienced by the younger generation of observant Catholics as an ecclesial process that commits them, but as a particular process attached to the reform agenda of conciliar Catholics. This is because the synodal consultation is supported first and foremost by diocesan structures dominated by older Catholics often inspired by conciliar views. Secondly, the synod process itself is underpinned by a media or militant narrative about the changes needed in the church, at odds

---

[45] Yann Raison du Cleuziou, "Les droites, le changement, et le sacré," in *À la droite du Père. Les catholiques et les droites de 1945 à nos jours*, ed. Y. Raison du Cleuziou and F. Michel (Paris: Seuil, 2022), 613–650.

[46] Pierre Bréchon, Frédéric Gonthier, and Sandrine Astor, eds., *La France des valeurs. Quarante ans d'évolutions* (Grenoble: PUG, 2019).

with the more conservative young people, whose obsession is rather with the perpetuation of a church that seems to them to be threatened by the advanced secularisation of society. Furthermore, as classic political science research has shown, participation always depends on a feeling of competence and collective dynamic. By analogy, the spiritual value system and religious socialisation have a direct impact on ecclesial participation. The observant matrix is based on a more vertical representation of the church, so knowledge belongs to priests and lay people are more in a position of waiting, whereas in the conciliar matrix, the conviction of belonging to the "People of God" gives a feeling of competence and encourages participation. As for the effects of socialisation, it would be enough to compare education in decision-making among the Guides and Scouts of France with what is practised among the Guides and Scouts of Europe to give an example of the strong differences between these worlds. On the one hand, collective deliberation in the service of the collective project; on the other, the hierarchical authority of the leader and trusting dedication of each individual within the limits of the competence they have been delegated. It is not surprising, moreover, that the Guides and Scouts of France, or the Catholic Action movements trained in the practice of enquiry, are over-represented in the synodal consultations.

Finally, over and above this organisational ethos, we need to understand that reticence can run very deep because it sometimes touches on the inner workings of the experience of God. The very method that emphasises the horizontal nature of exchanges as an experience of the Holy Spirit is in line with the sensibilities of the conciliar and emancipated movements. On the contrary, it offends the hieratic dimension of the relationship with God, which corresponds better to the experience of the observant and inspired. While for some, the synod is the culmination of a spiritual experience, for others, it is more of a distraction from what is essential: the appropriation of the church's teaching and personal conversion.

HISTORICAL CONDITIONS AND RIVALRY BETWEEN CATHOLICS

The sociological approach is not only useful for mapping potential resistance to synodal consultation, it can also provide resources for overcoming these obstacles and fostering a culture of listening among Catholics.

All too often, Catholic pluralism is interpreted as a mechanical effect of the individualism that characterises modern societies. Religious convictions are then seen as opinions that can be amended and brought together through collective deliberation. Discussion would then suffice to resolve conflict. Based on my investigations, it seems to me that this interpretation is not heuristic.

The diversification of forms of belonging to the church is a reflection of the acceleration of social change over the last two centuries or so. Put to the test by social, technical, and political transformations, the church has multiplied its doctrinal, organisational, and spiritual responses in order to keep a grip on customs that no longer offer anything more than a shifting and fragile foundation. The pastoral reorientations required to constantly adapt have created cultural strata among Catholics. The variations in sensibility among Catholics are not random, but correspond to social, generational, or organisational anchors that find their coherence in a moment of diagnosis and ecclesial tactics in the face of change. These moments of mobilisation become habitus and are then transmitted from one generation to the next in the form of a regime of truth in which the relationships to the world, God, and personal experience are closely intertwined in an unsurpassable figure of "truth."

The qualitative survey, based on life stories told in the course of interviews, makes it possible to guess approximately the moment when the structuring background of imaginations and habitus is created.

Among observants, the system of truth that structures the evaluation of manifestations of authentic Catholic fidelity tends to be rooted in the Catholic intransigence developed in the nineteenth century in reaction to the consequences of the French Revolution on morals. They were attached to a conception of the social order embedded in a natural order itself dependent on a divine order. Hierarchy, vocation, duty of state, obedience, and observance make acceptance of the limited nature of each person's place and role a condition for participation in the divine order. Observants take from the Gospels elements that legitimise a certain stance of opposition to dominant social values. The norms of worship marginalised by post-conciliar pastoral practice retain an ascetic value in their eyes, because conforming to them remains the condition for access to God. While they welcomed the Second Vatican Council, they moderated its implementation by maintaining the framework that had previously structured Catholic mentalities.

The emancipated inherited the culture of Catholic Action and the spirituality of the laity, which began to assert itself in the 1930s and enjoyed the support of Pius XI. This spirituality had a puritanical dimension. Forms of worship were devalued because of the dualism between ordinary life and the life of faith they seemed to organise. For these Catholics, faith is true when integral, i.e., when it reconfigures the relationship with work and, more generally, the whole of ordinary life. Its translation must be a commitment to the fight against injustice. Religious forms that detract from the transformation of society would only be the mask of a compromise with the established order.

The conciliar regime of truth is rooted in the 1950s and 1960s. At its heart is the enthusiasm for the future that runs through this period. Humanity was progressing and with confidence had to take the risk of abandoning certain heritages. The deepening of individual autonomy, listening to deep individual desires, is being reclassified as a way of restoring authenticity in our relationship with ourselves, the world, and God. This enthusiasm for change is based on the experience of a time when the hopes of the church and social expectations seem to converge. The Second Vatican Council and the theology of the "signs of the times" make meeting the "other" and listening to the "calls of the world" an actualised theophany of the "All Other." The reconciliation between church and world was perceived in a time so close that there remains a strong nostalgia for this aborted possibility.

The inspired inherit an evangelical matrix structured by conversion and rebirth. For them, a life of faith is only true when founded on the experience of a "personal encounter with Jesus." They are the heirs of the 1970s when, on the fringes of the church, interest in charismatic evangelism as experienced in the Pentecostal currents of Protestantism intersected with initiation experiences that brought esoteric currents into the circle of the awakened, and techniques of the body that spread with Asian spirituality. They found in individual virtuosity, stimulated within the collective framework of community utopias, a lever for transforming church and world.

Like the nave of a church, which often bears the mark of different architectural styles and successive devotions, the "People of God" has a historical dimension. The internal divisions within Catholicism can therefore be thought of as sedimentations of regimes of truth linked to periods and militant segments of Catholicism. They reflect varying ways of problematising the use of faith in the construction of the self and in relations between church and society. The divisions within Catholicism are frozen conflicts, legacies of a forgotten history.

If these moments, which have become regimes of truth and habitus, are juxtaposed rather than succeeding one another, it is because of the crisis of history which, from the 1970s onwards, manifested itself with the end of the great teleologies.[47] The present is now less tense between past and future than fragmented between so many rival conceptions of the past and future. We must not forget that these Catholic cultures are all evolving and interacting with contemporary culture, even those most resistant to secular culture. They are all expressions of a past and a possible future. We need to get away from the dichotomy between traditionalism and progressivism, because all

---

[47] François Hartog, "Towards a New Historical Condition," *Le Débat* 188 (2016), 169–180, doi.org/10.1007/978-3-476-05460-9_18; François Hartog, *Régimes d'historicité. Présentisme et expériences du temps* (Paris: Seuil, 2003).

these worlds of sensibility are rooted in tradition, carry their vision of the conditions for authentic progress in the faith, and produce contemporary experience.

The importance of systems of truth that structure oppositions between Catholics can be measured by the difficulty they have in admitting pluralism in their midst. They all use their conception of truth to evaluate the practice of others. The consequence of this reasoning is always the same: they can find no better model than themselves. The form they seek and respect is never anything other than that which objectifies their conception of the truth of religious practices.

This parameter is all the more powerful because anchored in the body through the learning and repetition that build the habitus of Catholics. Through this incorporated sensibility, the feeling of sacramentality is imposed as a dimension of reality itself and not as the imprint of their own history.[48] Catholics find it difficult to measure the historicity of their relationship with and the forms that allow access to God. As a result, they tend to confuse their sense of sacramentality with the very object of their faith. Their convictions and the relativity of their historical conditioning are made sacred, which makes debate all the more difficult.

These historical and cultural influences make it difficult to regulate Catholicism. The experience of a fragmented time explains the hesitant nature of recourse to the authority of the Second Vatican Council to regulate the Catholic body and reorient it in a unitary manner. Caught up in the accelerating pace of Western society, the Council's doctrinal concretion has lost its capacity to be authoritative over time, becoming just another moment in time. The authority of the priest is undergoing the same historicization, i.e., relativisation. Priests need to realise that their sensibilities, just like those of their parishioners, are conditioned by the truth of the moment. The man of God is not immune to history, and ignoring this condemns him to imposing his sensibility and roots as the only legitimate ones, or even, through the sacramental significance of his actions, to having them identified as ahistorical norms. This can only exacerbate the faithful's frustrated or wounded feelings of sacramentality.[49] The same applies

---

[48] Yann Raison du Cleuziou, "L'attente et la règle. Quelques éléments de réflexion sur le lien entre le sentiment de sacramentalité et les régimes de vérité dans le catholicisme contemporain," in *Du bon usage des normes en liturgie. Approche théologique et spirituelle après Vatican II*, ed. H. Bricout (Paris: Cerf, 2020), 35–49.
[49] To appreciate this, we need only look back at the controversies that arose from the refusal to baptise young children or the abolition of solemn communion in the 1970s. See Serge Bonnet, *Défense du catholicisme populaire* (Paris: Cerf, 2015).

to the synodal process. Its style and expectations will mobilise some and repel others.

Awareness of the long-term effects of sedimentation should lead ecclesiastical authorities to exercise caution. Learning to be authentically aware of historicity, and therefore of the relativity of forms of faith or affiliation, is the condition for real and sincere listening between Catholics. Furthermore, within liturgical or synodal arrangements, it is reasonable to articulate as far as possible, and not to oppose, the different existing expectations and resulting feelings of sacramentality. The communion, transcendence, conversion, and commitment to justice that differentiate Catholic sensibilities can be combined and restore to the tradition actualised in each liturgy the depth and breadth of what Catholicism really is as a complex historical dynamic. Catholics will be better disposed to listen to each other when they accept each other as different moments in the same history, heirs to pastoral responses that at one time the church gave to social change, sedimented experiences also summoned by the need to provide a new response in a new moment.

CONCLUSION

Sociological research practices and conceptualisations have made it possible to construct a representation of the "People of God." Sociology has helped this faceless, voiceless reality, which has no established representation within the church, to become representable and audible. Sociology has also enabled this representation to be adjusted to the changes sociologists were able to record when clergy still only saw "deviance" in relation to canonical norms.

The synodal construction of a representation of expectations in the church can prove problematic and encourage the domination of one sensibility or generation over another. Sociology remains an indispensable complement for objectivising and analysing the structuring of cleavages that run through the church. This contextualisation provides a healthy relativisation that pacifies oppositions by defusing some of their emotional or even religious charge, as the experience of God merges with historically situated practices and frameworks of thought.

I think it would be useful not to make the synodal process too sacred. Ritualised recourse to the Holy Spirit can give a strong charge to what is going on and create fears because God is put in the balance of the exchanges.[50] The social sciences can be useful in secularising

---

[50] See Francis, "Address at the Opening Session of the XVIᵉ Ordinary General Assembly of the Synod of Bishops," October 4, 2023,

the process. It may seem shocking, but understanding the historical or cultural relativity of each person's Christianity can encourage people to move towards a more "distanced" interpretation of their experience of the Gospel message, and contribute to a common move towards bringing it up to date. This process will be all the easier if its horizon—adapting the church's governance and ministries to contemporary issues—is assumed to be exclusively historical: the need of the moment. Desacralising the process helps to play down the stakes, because other synods and councils will one day be necessary. It is simply a question of assuming the present condition of the church by deploying this presence with all the relevance necessary to respond to the needs of our contemporaries.

On the other hand, sacralising the outcome of a synod, identifying its result with the expression of the Holy Spirit, without having worked upstream to develop a culture of participation or reflected on how to guarantee representativeness, can only contribute to sacralising the particular opinion of those predisposed to participate to the detriment of others. The sacralisation of the synod, its often quasi-sacramental presentation, the visible process conditioning a relationship with the invisible, can exert a double exclusion: those not represented are now religiously deviant if they do not accept the conclusions of the synod. The reference to the Holy Spirit is then simply a means of legitimising an exercise of domination. M

Yann Raison du Cleuziou is professor of political science at the University of Bordeaux. His research focuses on the history and political sociology of French Catholicism. He is particularly interested in the interplay between religious and political changes. Latest publications: *A la droite du Père, les catholiques et les droites de 1945 à nos jours* (Seuil, 2022) edited with Florian Michel; *Une contre-révolution catholique. Aux origines de La Manif pour tous* (Seuil, 2019); *De la contemplation à la contestation. La politisation des dominicains de la Province de France (Années 1940–1980)* (Belin, 2016).

---

www.vatican.va/content/francesco/en/speeches/2023/october/documents/20231004-apertura-sinodo.html.

Doing Theology by Listening to Marginalized Voices? Methodological Elements from Encountering Indigenous Families in a Northern Canadian Community

Julian Paparella[1]

Abstract: Based on the experience of encountering Indigenous families in a northern Canadian community, this article draws methodological elements for doing theology by listening to people who suffer marginalization. Firstly, I situate *listening to marginalized voices* as an act of receiving Vatican II and a way of putting into practice Pope Francis's call for a church that goes out to be evangelized on a path of encounter and dialogue. Secondly, I question the terminology used in referring to those who are marginalized and revisit the centre-periphery paradigm from a theological perspective, in favour of the disruptive movement of bringing the peripheries to the centre, in resonance with Matthew 25. Finally, I draw lessons from the experience of listening to Indigenous families in the Canadian north, on the journey towards a theology that listens to the voice of God in those who are marginalized.

THERE IS A RISING ASPIRATION EMERGING IN THE CATHOLIC Church today to inform our theology with voices that have been marginalized, and thus to do theology starting from the "existential peripheries."[2] This intuition finds fertile ground in the pontificate of Pope Francis, which constitutes a new stage in the reception of Vatican II. This article begins by briefly situating the theme of listening to marginalized voices in the teachings of the Council and examining its articulation in Francis's magisterium. I subsequently question the terminology used in referring to those who are marginalized and revisit the centre-periphery paradigm from a

---

[1] I would like to thank M. Therese Lysaught, Alexis Artaud de La Ferrière, Brigitte Cholvy, Marion Lugagne Delpon, and the anonymous reviewers of this article for their helpful feedback.

[2] A worldwide research project has been undertaken by the Dicastery for Promoting Integral Human Development entitled "Doing Theology from the Existential Peripheries," for which the final reports from each continent were published in October 2022, migrants-refugees.va/resource-center/publications/.

theological perspective. I then delve into the particular experience of listening to Indigenous families in the context of Canada and inquiring as to what can be learned from these encounters to renew theology in the church. The question I seek to respond to is: *What does the experience of encountering Indigenous families in Canada contribute to developing ways of doing theology by listening to people whose voices are marginalized?*

I approach this question as a non-Indigenous Canadian from a Catholic perspective, specializing in theology regarding families. My aim is not to elaborate a systematic theology of the family in the context of a given Indigenous community, and certainly not for Indigenous peoples in general. Rather, it is to begin gleaning lessons from conversations that open up new perspectives and horizons both for informing theology regarding families and doing theology by listening to Indigenous persons. In the wake of the papal apology issued for the residential school system, in response to Call to Action no. 58 of the Final Report of the Truth and Reconciliation Commission of Canada, this approach hopes to contribute to the work laid out in the subsequent Calls to Action. Calls to Action nos. 59 and 60 call upon churches to raise awareness among their congregations and clergy regarding the involvement of Christian churches in colonization, in particular the history and legacy of residential schools, and their responsibility on the path of reconciliation.[3]

In this article, I will speak about doing theology as a way of living out the call for the Church to listen to people who have been marginalized—whether by society, the church, or both. This includes but is not limited to those who find themselves in a situation of poverty from a socio-economic perspective. In referring to marginalized persons, Pope Francis has spoken in terms of "the peripheries." This term has its usefulness but also its limitations. It is associated with the centre-periphery model developed as a way of understanding dynamics

---

[3] Call to Action no. 59 calls upon churches in Canada to "develop ongoing education strategies to ensure that their respective congregations learn about their church's role in colonization, the history and legacy of residential schools, and why apologies to former residential school students, their families, and communities were necessary." Call to Action no. 60 calls upon Christian academic institutes and schools of theology to "develop and teach curriculum for all student clergy, and all clergy and staff who work in Aboriginal communities, on the need to respect Indigenous spirituality in its own right, the history and legacy of residential schools and the roles of the church parties in that system, the history and legacy of religious conflict in Aboriginal families and communities, and the responsibility that churches have to mitigate such conflicts and prevent spiritual violence." Truth and Reconciliation Commission of Canada (TRC), *Honouring the Truth, Reconciling for the Future: Summary of the Final Report of the Truth and Reconciliation Commission of Canada*, 2015, 224, 232, ehprnh2mwo3.exactdn.com/wp-content/uploads/2021/01/Executive_Summary_English_Web.pdf.

of inequality in the world. On the one hand, "periphery" can be seen as a horizontal, not a vertical term: it does not designate higher or lower, better or worse, but rather further or closer. On the other hand, it is a rather static term, designating some as being on the peripheries and others at the centre without suggesting mobility between the two. It is not enough to speak of people "on the margins" as if they were meant to be there. This would only normalize the inequalities they face, as if there was no need to do anything about it. Unfortunately, any way of referring to those who experience inequality and injustice runs the risk of being reductive.

In this article, I will speak mostly in terms of those who are "marginalized," making every effort to avoid any essentialization or romanticization of the real people I am speaking about. It is noteworthy that both Indigenous scholarship[4] and documents of the Government of Canada[5] utilize the language of marginalization with reference to the situation of Indigenous peoples. To speak of "being marginalized" denotes a condition imposed on someone by another. It is not a judgment on the marginalized person, but rather a critique of the system and structures that have marginalized him or her. Ultimately, these terms pale in comparison to the real people to whom they seek to refer, whose dignity defies and exceeds any term used to speak to their condition in life. No generic term can speak satisfactorily about the realities of peoples' lives, though we must always be in search of the most respectful language. The tension here is to find ways of naming the situations of suffering, injustice, and inequality people face, while at the same time using terminology that does not inflict further suffering, injustice, or inequality. The aim is not simply to speak of those who are "marginalized," but to do so in

---

[4] See Wellesley Institute, "Towards Understanding and Supporting Marginalized Children and Youth in Ontario: The Case of Growing Up Indigenous," June 2019, wellesleyinstitute.com/wp-content/uploads/2019/06/Towards-Understanding-and-Supporting-Marginalized-Children-and-Youth-in-Ontario-The-Case-of-Growing-Up-Indigenous.pdf; Terry Moore, "Aboriginal Agency and Marginalisation in Australian Society," *Social Inclusion* 2, no. 3 (2014): 124–135; Jo-Anne Fiske, "Boundary Crossings: Power and Marginalization in the Formation of Canadian Aboriginal Women's Identities," *Marginalised Peoples* 14, no. 2 (2006): 247–258; Mylène Jaccoud and Renée Brassard, "The Marginalization of Aboriginal Women in Montreal," in *Not Strangers in These Parts: Urban Aboriginal Peoples*, ed. David Newhouse and Evelyn Peters (Ottawa: Policy Research Initiative, 2003), 131–146.

[5] See Government of Canada—Department of Justice, "Socio-economic Marginalization," in "Understanding the Overrepresentation of Indigenous People in the Criminal Justice System," June 11, 2024, justice.gc.ca/socjs-esjp/en/ind-aut/uo-cs; Government of Canada—Indigenous Services Canada, "An Update on the Socio-Economic Gaps between Indigenous Peoples and the non-Indigenous Population in Canada: Highlights from the 2021 Census," October 25, 2023, sac-isc.gc.ca/eng/1690909773300/1690909797208.

view of their *de*-marginalization, bringing those on the peripheries to the centre.

LISTENING TO THE MARGINALIZED AS AN ACT OF RECEIVING THE COUNCIL

The impetus to listen to marginalized voices resonates strongly with certain key emphases present in the teachings of Vatican II. The first paragraph of *Gaudium et Spes* emblematically expresses the desire for the church to resonate with the men and women of our time, based on the conviction that "nothing genuinely human fails to raise an echo" in the hearts of the followers of Christ (no. 1). This calls for a theology that takes seriously and exemplifies in its way of proceeding the close solidarity of the church with men and women today—and *especially those who suffer in any way*—listening to and identifying with their "joys and hopes, griefs and anxieties" (no. 1). In what could be seen as a prefiguration of synodality, the Pastoral Constitution goes on to affirm: "With the help of the Holy Spirit, it is the task of the entire People of God, especially pastors and theologians, to hear, distinguish, and interpret the many voices of our age, and to judge them in the light of the divine word, so that revealed truth can always be more deeply penetrated, better understood, and set forth to greater advantage" (no. 44). In this light, the act of listening is not a mere sociological exercise, but a matter of delving more deeply into the truth of the Gospel so that it may be better understood and presented in each culture and era.

In the midst of the Council, Yves Congar posited that the church was "called to find a new style of being present in the world."[6] Congar proposed a church "imbued with the evangelical ideal of poverty" in order to overcome tendencies to "betray the spirit of the Gospel" on the one hand, and "isolate and put up barriers" between the church and the people on the other hand.[7] What Congar saw as the most promising path to this poor and servant church capable of embracing the Gospel was "a true dialogue between the Church and the world," including a dialogue between "the periphery and the centre," based on his conviction that the church becomes itself only in realizing the truth of its relationship with others.[8]

In this light, listening to those who are marginalized can be considered an act of receiving Vatican II insofar as it puts into practice certain fundamental principles that emerge from the Council. Based on the writings of Jesuit historian John O'Malley, Laurent Villemin

---

[6] Yves Congar, *Pour une Église servante et pauvre* (Paris: Cerf, [1963] 2014), 109.
[7] Congar, *Pour une Église servante et pauvre*, 109, 112.
[8] Congar, *Pour une Église servante et pauvre*, 114.

pointed out three transversal questions that span the Council's teachings: the way the church manages change; the relationship between the centre and the periphery; and the Council's *modus operandi* or "style."⁹ All three relate, more or less directly, to listening to people on the margins, which can be seen as a way of navigating a change of era, a path for recalibrating the relationship between centre and periphery, as well as a *mise en oeuvre* of the style of Vatican II.

In terms of the Council's *style*, three traits could be delineated that underpin the church's call to listen to people on the peripheries. The first is the *listening attitude* of the church. This is established perhaps most firmly in the preamble of *Dei Verbum*: the church *listens* to the Word of God so that the Gospel message of salvation might be heard by all (no. 1). The mission of proclamation is grounded first and foremost in the ongoing act of *listening*. In this sense, a posture of listening can be understood as an act of receiving the Council. The church listens above all to the Word of God, but it must also listen to the multiplicity of voices it is called to interpret. In the language of Francis's pontificate, this includes hearing the cry of the poor, as well as of the earth (*Laudato Si'*, no. 49). It is interesting to ask what resonance exists between the Word of God and these many voices in the world. Pope Francis has characterized Vatican II as "a re-reading of the Gospel in light of contemporary culture," affirming that "the dynamic of reading the Gospel, actualizing its message for today—which was typical of Vatican II—is absolutely irreversible."¹⁰ Francis sees Vatican II as operating a dialogue between the Gospel and contemporary culture, in other words, between the Word of God and the many voices of the age. Perhaps in light of the Council, we could see the place of the church as being precisely at the crux of that dialogue.

A second trait of the Council's style that promotes the call to listen to the marginalized is *concern for people living in poverty*. The Council Fathers were aware of the poverty afflicting countless people around the globe, and the conciliar documents witness lucidly to their solicitude for people facing poverty and hardship. The socio-economic principles enumerated in *Gaudium et Spes* carry a strong exhortation for individuals and nations to come to the aid of those in need: "Since there are so many people prostrate with hunger in the world, this sacred council urges all, both individuals and governments, to remember the aphorism of the Fathers, 'Feed the man dying of hunger, because if you have not fed him, you have killed him'" (no. 69).

---

⁹ See Laurent Villemin, *L'Eglise à la rencontre de l'autre* (Paris: Cerf, 2022), 108.
¹⁰ Francis, "Interview with Antonio Spadaro, SJ," September 21, 2013, www.vatican.va/content/francesco/en/speeches/2013/september/documents/papa-francesco_20130921_intervista-spadaro.html.

Indeed, for certain Council Fathers, this was such a central concern that they committed to personally living in a spirit of poverty by signing the *Pact of the Catacombs*.

A third trait of the Council's style that undergirds listening to the peripheries is the *dynamism of going out*. The decree *Ad Gentes* on the mission activity of the church affirms that "The pilgrim Church by its very nature is missionary" (no. 2). Richard Gaillardetz has referred to the missiological vision of Vatican II as that of a "centrifugal Church."[11] This *exocentric* vision of the church corresponds with the double principle announced in *Dei Verbum*: that the Church *listens* to the divine Word so that it may be *heard* by all. The church does not own the Word of God. Rather, the church must continually *receive the Gospel* in order to go out to discover how it resonates in the lives of men and women of every time and place.

STARTING FROM THE MARGINS TO BE EVANGELIZED AS A CHURCH

These conciliar principles find new expression in Francis's emphasis on *going out to the margins*—a leitmotif of his pontificate from the outset. In the General Congregations that preceded his election as pope, then-Cardinal Bergoglio stated: "The Church is called to come out from itself and to go to the peripheries, not only geographical, but also existential: those of the mystery of sin, of suffering, of injustice, those of ignorance and of the absence of faith, those of thought, those of every form of misery."[12] These words clearly indicate the dynamism of a *church that goes out*, which Francis would further develop in his programmatic exhortation *Evangelii Gaudium*.

As indicated in *Fratelli Tutti*, Francis sees the peripheries as being both the destination of the church's *going out* as well as the starting point for beginning anew (nos. 215, 235). Going out to encounter the peripheries is a fundamental *gesture* of Francis's pontificate, and the dynamic that he aspires to for the entire church. The question then becomes, *why* start from the peripheries? Several key elements of response are found in Francis's articulation of the church's preferential option for the poor.

> They have much to teach us. Not only do they share in the *sensus fidei*, but in their difficulties they know the suffering Christ. We need to let ourselves be evangelized by them. The new evangelization is an

---

[11] Richard R. Gaillardetz, *An Unfinished Council: Vatican II, Pope Francis, and the Renewal of Catholicism* (Collegeville, MN: Liturgical Press, 2015), 116.

[12] These words were received by Cardinal Jaime Ortega of Havana, in the form of handwritten notes.

invitation to acknowledge the saving power at work in their lives and put them at the centre of the church's pilgrim way. We are called to find Christ in them, to lend our voice to their causes, but also to be their friends, listen to them, speak for them and to embrace the mysterious wisdom God wishes to share with us through them (*Evangelii Gaudium*, no. 198).

If theology today aspires to *listen to marginalized voices*, this paragraph provides a convincing reason *why* to do so. Here, Pope Francis introduces a notion to which the church's theology and pastoral practice are not necessarily accustomed, namely: being evangelized by those who are marginalized. Oftentimes throughout history, the church has gone out to evangelize. Yet how often does the church go out *to be evangelized*? According to Francis, this is not only as a call or invitation for the church in our day but rather a *need*. At first glance, going out to the peripheries could be seen as a response to the needs of the people living there. Yet here Francis situates the need in the other direction. It is the church who needs to receive from those often seen as being "in need." A key Francis identifies for letting this need be met is the call to *listen to them*, which in turn corresponds to his conviction that "they have much to teach us." Francis frames this assertion in profoundly theological terms. Listening to marginalized people goes hand in hand with the call to "find Christ in them." Learning from them responds to the invitation to "embrace the mysterious wisdom God wishes to share with us through them." The church is called "to put them at the centre of its pilgrim way," recognizing God's "saving power at work in their lives." Through this Christological and theological underpinning, it becomes clear that listening to people on the peripheries is a way of hearing God's mysterious wisdom and getting in touch with the salvation he is working out.

The need to listen to marginalized voices could be framed as a gauge of listening to everyone. This is logical in theory: if we listen to those who for various reasons find themselves far from "the centre," then we ought to be able to listen to everyone in between. Yet there is a double risk here. On the one hand, listening is reduced to a mere democratic exercise. On the other hand, seeing listening to marginalized persons as a way of listening to everyone makes them a mere stepping stone in order to listen to all, rather than a privileged locus in their own right. The most recent Assembly of the Synod framed the special need to listen to those on the margins as a step forward on the path toward healing, repentance, justice, and reconciliation with them: "The Church needs to listen with special attention and sensitivity to the voices of victims and survivors of sexual, spiritual, economic, institutional, power, and conscience abuse by clergy members or persons with Church appointments. Authentic listening is a fundamental element of the path to healing, repentance, justice, and reconciliation."[13] Moreover, those gathered in the Synodal Assembly emphasized their attentiveness to the cry of those who are suffering around the world, asking themselves how the church can contribute to pursuing paths of reconciliation, hope, justice, and peace: "The cry of those who are poor resounded among us, of those forced to migrate and of those suffering violence and the devastating consequences of climate change. . . . We have all, at all times, taken this cry into our hearts and prayers, wondering how our Churches can foster paths of reconciliation, hope, justice, and peace."[14]

QUESTIONING THE RAPPORT BETWEEN THE MARGINS AND THE CENTRE IN LIGHT OF THE GOSPEL

When referring to real people who face difficult situations, it is essential to question the terminology we employ. Terms such as "margins," "peripheries," and "the poor" all have their limitations. They can come across as demeaning, patronizing, or reductive. Indigenous scholar Margaret Kovach speaks of the need to avoid the "tattooing of lack."[15] Kovach warns against seeing Indigenous individuals or communities in terms of what they *do not have*—what they lack. It is critical to find the most adequate way of speaking of people who experience marginalization without reducing or relegating them to categories that either romanticize their existence or stigmatize them further. For example, the Assembly of the Synod that took place in 2023 spoke in terms of "people in poverty" instead of "the poor," conscious of the "many faces" of those who experience its diverse forms, and spoke explicitly of the "constant risk, one to be carefully avoided, of viewing those living in poverty in terms of 'them' and 'us,' as 'objects' of the Church's charity."[16]

The centre-periphery model is part of the dependency theory that sought to explain a lack of economic development in Latin America in the 1960s, according to which resources flow from less wealthy countries "on the periphery" to more wealthy nations "at the

---

[13] XVI Ordinary General Assembly of the Synod of Bishops, *"A Synodal Church in Mission": Synthesis Report from the First Session*, no. 16f, October 28, 2023, synod.va/content/dam/synod/assembly/synthesis/english/2023.10.28-ENG-Synthesis-Report.pdf.
[14] Synod of Bishops, *Synthesis Report from the First Session*, Introduction.
[15] Margaret Kovach, *Indigenous Methodologies: Characteristics, Conversations, and Contexts*, 2nd ed. (Toronto: University of Toronto Press, 2021 [2009]), 238.
[16] Synod of Bishops, *Synthesis Report from the First Session*, no. 4.

centre."[17] In this sense, powerful centres in global capitalism maintain their dominance at the expense of less powerful regions, kept on the peripheries of the system that thrives on their inequality. In recent decades, scholars in various fields have sought to revisit and rethink the centre-periphery paradigm. There have been efforts to "reconceptualize multi-layered relationships" and "question existing hierarchies and focusing in particular on perspectives from 'lesser' states and cultures."[18] Efforts to remap the centre-periphery dichotomy have sought a multifaceted approach that embraces complexity, fluidity, and dynamic exchange between different parties. It also opens the possibility of networks and liminal spaces that foster more equitable and reciprocal relationships.[19]

From a social perspective, the peripheries can be associated with those who are marginalized, pushed to the edges of society. Theologically, we could conceive of the peripheries as those who are afflicted, as in the biblical term *anawim*, which signifies the "little ones" of God. This "littleness" may sound disparaging or infantilizing. Yet it is to be interpreted as meaning that those who are "little" in the eyes of the world are in fact great in the eyes of God. Thus, from a Christian point of view, the "peripheries" are in reality the *centre* in God's eyes. Scripture reveals time and again how the centre of God's attention is not those who are economically or politically powerful, but those who on the outskirts both of society and the dominant religious communities of the day. Jesus's ministry manifests a clear orientation towards "the lame, the mute, the blind, the maimed," whom he heals with compassion (Matthew 15:30). In the logic of the Gospel, the margins are not forsaken; rather, they are privileged *loci* of God's engagement with humanity, where healing and redemption are at hand.

The logic of the Gospel thus implies remapping the configuration of the centre and peripheries, so that the peripheries may constitute the centre of the church's attention and action. It is in these terms that Pope Francis has spoken of social transformation: "When I speak of change, I don't just mean that we have to take better care of this or that group of people. I mean that those people who are now on the edges become the protagonists of social change. That's what's in my

---

[17] See Claudio Katz, *Dependency Theory after Fifty Years: The Continuing Relevance of Latin American Critical Thought*, trans. Stanley Malinowitz (Leiden: Brill, 2022).
[18] Ulrich Tiedau, "Re-Mapping Centre and Periphery: Concluding Thoughts," in *Re-Mapping Centre and Periphery: Asymmetrical Encounters in European and Global Contexts*, ed. Tessa Hauswedell, Axel Koerner, and Ulrich Tiedau (London: UCL, 2019), 189.
[19] Jordan Kellman, "Beyond Centre and Periphery: New Currents in French and Francophone Atlantic Studies," *Atlantic Studies* 10, no. 1 (2013): 4, doi.org/10.1080/14788810.2013.769793.

heart."[20] It is not a mere matter of charity towards those who have less, but a question of disrupting systems and structures that foment inequality, discrimination, oppression, and injustice.

THE CASE OF LISTENING TO INDIGENOUS FAMILIES IN CANADA

For generations, Indigenous peoples in Canada have suffered from the marginalization that has resulted from colonization at the hands of government, churches, and society at large. As Indigenous writer Patty Krawec recounts, the ravenous hunger of "big brother" the white man sought to make Indigenous peoples vanish from the lands of their ancestors: "From the very beginning, the newcomers worked to destroy Indigenous people. Their aim included destroying our beliefs about ourselves and our relationship with the seen and unseen world and replacing them with European Christian beliefs."[21] Like projects of settler colonialism across the globe, it was an attempt to "destroy in order to replace."[22] Colonization sought to erase the identities, cultures, and histories of Indigenous peoples in Canada. In residential schools, Indigenous children were given numbers rather than names. Their languages were forbidden, and their stories not heard. Their culture and way of life were seen as an obstacle to eradicate on the path of "settling" Canada.

As a non-Indigenous person, I am an outsider within Indigenous communities. My position in Canada is that of a newcomer whose family came to the country last century, a drop in the bucket compared to the immemorial Indigenous generations that have inhabited these lands for millennia. This double status—newcomer and outsider—requires an epistemologically and personally humble approach. An example of studying families from a marginalized cultural group to which one does not belong is found in the work of Lisa Sowle Cahill. Cahill sought to glean lessons from African American families to renew the Christian vision of the family in today's society. Cahill stated her purpose as follows:

> I do not aim to treat theories of the black family in America comprehensively nor claim anything like a full and true appreciation of the realities behind the theories that I do treat. I certainly do not presume to speak for African Americans in relation to family matters.

---

[20] Pope Francis and Austen Ivereigh, *Let Us Dream: The Path to a Better Future* (New York: Simon & Schuster, 2020), 18.
[21] Patty Krawec, *Becoming Kin: An Indigenous Call to Unforgetting the Past and Reimagining Our Future* (Minneapolis, MN: Broadleaf, 2022), 41–44.
[22] Patrick Wolfe, "Settler Colonialism and the Elimination of the Native," *Journal of Genocide Research* 8, no. 4 (2006): 387–409.

My aim is, rather to begin to absorb the lessons about family life that African American experience can teach those of us who come from other segments of America and who tend to approach the situations of families in this country primarily from the standpoint of the "traditional," middle-class nuclear family, relatively privileged by class and socioeconomic standing.[23]

As a white woman, Cahill did not try to offer a comprehensive black theology nor claim expertise in African American culture or history; rather she sought to integrate the experience and perspective of African American family life to more fully understand the family from a Christian point of view. Like Cahill, I am not a member of the community whose perspective I seek to learn from. My research seeks to *start* absorbing lessons about family life the experiences of Indigenous persons can teach those of us who come from other segments of Canadian society, and indeed other parts of the world, enlarging the cultural horizons of Catholic theology regarding families.

Significant research has been done on Indigenous families in other domains, such as law, social work, and family studies, but relatively little in theology. The aim here is not simply to take families into account or study them from afar, but to encounter them personally as the basis for doing theology. What is more, Catholic theology on families has often focused heavily on a Western understanding of family, rather than engaging with the vast array of family models in diverse cultures. Researching Indigenous peoples in Canada, one becomes quickly aware of the crucial importance of *family*. On the one hand, family is the foundation for the kinship relationships that characterize Indigenous life. On the other hand, the long history of colonization in Canada has had a particularly devastating impact on Indigenous families, whose effects continue to this day. In many ways, the situation of Indigenous peoples in Canada today is deeply connected with the systematic rupture of families through the residential school system.

In theological terms, the past and present marginalization of Indigenous peoples in Canada constitutes a "sign of the times"[24] that demands our attention. In Canadian society at large, and specifically

---

[23] Lisa Sowle Cahill, *Family: A Christian Social Perspective* (Minneapolis, MN: Fortress, 2000), 112.
[24] Here we speak of "sign of the times" as that which cannot be ignored without jeopardizing the credibility of our witness to the Gospel, and thus where God awaits the church in the present. See Massimo Faggioli, "Reading the Signs of the Times through a Hermeneutics of Recognition: *Gaudium et Spes* and Its Meaning for a Learning Church," *Horizons* 43 (2016): 338.

in the Catholic Church, there is a growing awareness of the wounds suffered by the Indigenous peoples in Canada, particularly as a result of the residential school system: a government-mandated, church-administered policy in which children were removed from their families in a project of forced cultural assimilation,[25] whose express aim was to "kill the Indian in the child."[26] In 2015, the Final Report of the Truth and Reconciliation Commission of Canada stated that "the establishment and operation of residential schools were a central element of [Canada's Aboriginal policy for over a century], which can best be described as 'cultural genocide.'"[27] Returning from his visit to Canada in 2022, Pope Francis likewise characterized the experience of the residential school system—"taking away children, changing culture, changing mentality, changing traditions, changing a race"—as "genocide."[28] In the face of this tragic situation, the church is gradually recognizing its need to repent and be converted. The residential school system intentionally destroyed the bonds that characterize Indigenous kinship to eradicate Indigenous cultures, languages, and spiritualities. Removing children from their parents has led to intergenerational trauma, creating a context in which residential school survivors may have struggled to raise their own children since they themselves did not receive the parenting they needed as children. In many ways, the situation of Indigenous peoples in Canada today is intimately related to the harm inflicted on family life over generations. The church is slowly realizing that it cannot remain unmoved in the face of the suffering it has imparted to Indigenous families.

---

[25] "These residential schools were created for the purpose of separating Aboriginal children from their families, in order to minimize and weaken family ties and cultural linkages, and to indoctrinate children into a new culture—the culture of the legally dominant Euro-Christian Canadian society" (TRC, *Summary of the Final Report*, v.)
[26] TRC, *Summary of the Final Report*, 130; 369; 375; 376.
[27] TRC, *Summary of the Final Report*, 1.
[28] See Francis, "Apostolic Journey to Canada (24–30 July 2022): Press Conference on the Return Flight to Rome," July 29, 2022, vatican.va/content/francesco/en/speeches/2022/july/documents/20220729-voloritorno-canada.html. Moreover, "Many Catholics are calling on Church leaders to take more decisive action with Indigenous peoples to assist in the healing of those wounded by the Church, particularly by the Indian Residential School system and its legacy. There is also a general desire to listen to, and walk with, Indigenous Peoples (the theme of the Summer 2022 visit of Pope Francis to Canada's Indigenous Peoples is 'Walking Together'). Many expressed a desire for the Church to walk in greater humility, in a restored relationship with Indigenous Peoples and with all of creation." See Canadian Conference of Catholic Bishops, *Synod on Synodality: National Synthesis for Canada*, no. 8, August 31, 2022, cccb.ca/wp-content/uploads/2022/09/Synod-on-Synodality-EN-2022-08-31.pdf. This is accompanied by a wider awareness in the church of the importance of Indigenous people, particularly evident in the Synod on the Amazon in 2019 and the Apostolic Exhortation *Querida Amazonia* that followed.

Amidst this complex situation, Catholic theology regarding families has much to learn from listening to Indigenous families in Canada. The effects of colonization and the residential school system on families were unfortunately understated in the public addresses and apologies offered by Pope Francis during the penitential pilgrimage to Canada in 2022. Indigenous families were critically attacked by the colonial project of forced assimilation and cultural genocide in which the church was a key actor. On the path of truth and reconciliation, the church must recognize its role in the intergenerational trauma Indigenous families have inherited from the past, raise awareness of the realities they face in the present, and support their journey of healing into the future.

LEARNING FROM EXPERIENCE IN A NORTHERN CANADIAN COMMUNITY

The experience of listening to Indigenous families in a community in the Canadian north took place in the wake of the historic visit of Pope Francis to Canada from July 24–29, 2022, for a penitential pilgrimage of healing and reconciliation with Indigenous peoples. The visit was a response to Call to Action no. 58 of the Final Report of the *Truth and Reconciliation Commission*, which called upon the Pope to come and apologize for residential schools on Canadian soil. News of the discovery of unmarked graves in Kamloops and elsewhere in 2021 redoubled the cry for the Pope to apologize in Canada. In spring 2022, an Indigenous delegation of First Nations, Métis, and Inuit went to the Vatican to share their stories and witness with Pope Francis. After meeting in private with each group, he asked them for forgiveness during a public audience.[29] A few months later, the Pope reiterated his apology at the site of the former residential school in Maskwacis, Alberta. There were mixed reactions to the Pope's visit and criticism over certain "missed opportunities," such as ambiguity about the church's *institutional* responsibility for residential schools, no explicit reference to *sexual abuse* suffered in the schools, and absence of Indigenous cultures and languages in the *liturgies* celebrated over the course of the visit. In spite of some disappointment over the more formal aspects of the visit, the informal moments were perhaps more transformative, both for the Pope and those he met with. Fr. Daryold Winkler, an Indigenous Catholic priest, recounted that: "The Pope met

---

[29] "For the deplorable conduct of those members of the Catholic Church, I ask for God's forgiveness and I want to say to you with all my heart: I am very sorry. And I join my brothers, the Canadian bishops, in asking your pardon." Pope Francis, "Meeting with Representatives of Indigenous Peoples in Canada," April 1, 2022, vatican.va/content/francesco/en/speeches/2022/april/documents/20220401-popoli-indigeni-canada.html.

with survivors and really listened to them. He listened without barriers. Most of the work of reconciliation took place behind the scenes and was not witnessed by the public. He took extra time to listen fully, careful not to interrupt the survivors' stories, which sometimes made him late for other engagements."[30] Jane Barter has characterized this as the "patient work of listening" by which "a shared horizon of meaning can emerge."[31] Barter summarized Francis's action as follows, which offers a template for non-Indigenous people in walking with Indigenous: "The Pope invites the Indigenous peoples of Canada to permit him to accompany them on this journey (*ashtêhtew*) in lamenting the wounds of the body of Christ among Indigenous peoples and seeking their healing."[32] However, as Jeremy Bergen has noted, "The Pope will not remain in Canada to implement follow-up actions; these will largely be the responsibility of the church in Canada."[33]

The varied responses to Francis's visit reflected the diversity of Indigenous peoples in Canada. The three main groups of Indigenous peoples in Canada are the First Nations, Métis, and Inuit. Together, they comprise approximately 1.8 million people or 5 percent of the Canadian population. Among First Nations, there are over 630 communities, representing over fifty nations and fifty Indigenous languages.[34] As Indigenous writers Bob and Cynthia F. Joseph note: "Indigenous communities in Canada are made up of people from many different cultures and languages. A generic or homogeneous 'Indigenous People of Canada' does not exist. . . . However, the cultural diversity among the Indigenous population is often overlooked or not realized."[35]

During the two summers that followed Francis's visit to Canada, I had the privilege of being welcomed in a Dene community in the Canadian north as part of a program working to raise awareness and build relationships between Indigenous and non-Indigenous on the

---

[30] Doris M. Kieser and Jane Barter, "Missed Opportunities and Hope for Healing: Reflections of an Indigenous Catholic Priest—Interview with Fr. Daryold Winkler," *Journal of Moral Theology* 12, no. 1 (2023): 78, doi.org/10.55476/001c.66253.

[31] Jane Barter, "Walking Apart and Walking Together: Indigenous Public Reception of the Papal Visit," *Journal of Moral Theology* 12, no. 1 (2023): 83, doi.org/10.55476/001c.66237.

[32] Barter, "Walking Apart and Walking Together," 86.

[33] Jeremy M. Bergen, "Papal Apologies for Residential Schools and the Stories They Tell," *Journal of Moral Theology* 12, no. 1 (2023): 51, doi.org/10.55476/001c.66235.

[34] See Government of Canada—Crown-Indigenous Relations and Northern Affairs Canada, "Indigenous Peoples and Communities," June 13, 2024, rcaanc-cirnac.gc.ca/eng/1100100013785/1529102490303.

[35] Bob Joseph and Cynthia F. Joseph, *Indigenous Relations: Insights, Tips & Suggestions to Make Reconciliation a Reality* (Saanichton, BC: Indigenous Relations, 2019), 12.

path of reconciliation.[36] I found it to be an arduous context, both geographically and socially, where suffering, hardship, and death are part of daily life. As in other remote Indigenous communities, there are alarming rates of suicide, particularly among young people.[37] I also recognized many of the other key issues that affect Indigenous communities in Canada, such as a shorter life expectancy, more limited access to education and health care, and difficulties in finding employment.[38] This particular community was never home to a residential school but it did have a so-called Indian Day School that operated from the 1940s to the 1980s. Families speak of how they suffer from substance abuse and domestic violence. I found it to be a community in which spirituality plays a central role in daily life, with a strong emphasis on prayer and trust in God. Among the younger generations, there has been disillusionment with the church in the wake of revelations of unmarked graves in 2021, which has stung the wounds inflicted across generations by the residential school system.

The primary objective of my time in the community was simply to be with the people and listen to them. Part of this listening took the form of a research project that aims to inform Catholic theology by learning from Indigenous perspectives and experiences regarding family life.[39] As I got to know people, I would ask if they would be interested in being interviewed. The aim was not so much to seek a representative sample, but rather to listen to those I encountered about the joys and challenges their family had experienced. This research in

---

[36] To protect the confidentiality of the research participants in the community, its precise location is not disclosed in this article. The risk associated with personal data, such as family experiences and religious beliefs, being attributed to the participant seems to outweigh the possible benefit of mentioning the name of the community.

[37] See Statistics Canada, "Suicide among First Nations People, Métis, and Inuit (2011–2016): Findings from the 2011 Canadian Census Health and Environment Cohort (CanCHEC)," June 28, 2019, statcan.gc.ca/n1/en/pub/99-011-x/99-011-x2019001-eng.pdf?st=RS2r9P2u; T. Kue Young, Boris Revich, and Leena Soininen, "Suicide in Circumpolar Regions: An Introduction and Overview," *International Journal of Circumpolar Health* 74 (2015): 1–8, doi.org/10.3402/ijch.v74.27349.

[38] See Joseph and Joseph, *Indigenous Relations*, 36–38.

[39] The research project was ethically reviewed and approved by competent authorities of the Pontifical John Paul II Theological Institute for Marriage and Family Sciences in Rome and by KU Leuven in Belgium, the universities with which the researcher is associated. However, since the research context is located in Canada, special attention was paid to the guidelines laid out in the *Tri-Council Policy Statement: Ethical Conduct for Research Involving Humans* (TCPS 2), which "provides ethics guidance that applies to all research involving human participants—including their data and/or biological materials—conducted under the auspices of an institution eligible for funding by the federal Agencies (CIHR, NSERC, SSHRC)." While the research does not fall under the jurisdiction of a Canadian academic institution, the researcher nevertheless completed the CORE-2022 course, including Module 9 on research with Indigenous persons.

no way intends to portray "the Indigenous family" as if the vast diversity of Indigenous families could be essentialized or rarefied as a singular object of study. Rather, the motivation is to listen to Indigenous individuals about their personal experience, so as to receive their words and break down the ignorance of Indigenous perspectives among non-Indigenous. My hope is that this contributes, even in some small, modest way, to the shared journey of reconciliation between Indigenous and non-Indigenous in Canada. Overall, I was privileged to interview forty persons—of whom thirty-eight were from the local Dene community and two others were cultural mediators—spanning over thirty hours of interview in total and 250 pages of written transcript. On a human level, it was clear from the outset that the "encounter" had primacy over the "interview" itself. My priority was to spend time with people and get to know one another. Only after interacting with a person informally on one or more occasions would I ask if he or she would be interested in doing an interview.

The present article does not analyse the thematic content of the interviews. Rather, I will draw some lessons from the *experience of listening* to Indigenous families in a community in the Canadian north that may be helpful in doing theology by listening to people who suffer marginalization. Doing theology in this way is a two-fold path of letting what we have heard *inform* our theology and at the same time letting the experience of listening itself *form* our way of doing theology. The following eight points serve as elements of response to the question: *What does the experience of encountering Indigenous families in Canada contribute to developing ways of doing theology by listening to people living on the existential margins?*

Entering Another's World as a Guest

This attitude is almost natural when one travels thousands of kilometres to arrive in an unfamiliar, isolated community. However, it can also be a disposition to cultivate more generally in approaches to theology that seek to listen. This calls for reflection on not only *how* we listen to people but also *where* we listen to them. Do we meet them "on their turf" or on ours? Of course, this question not only applies to the physical location of where the encounter takes place. It is most importantly a style and posture to adopt wherever we might be. Especially when it comes to asking questions that touch upon a person's life story, it is of the utmost importance to "take off our sandals" as we realize that we are standing on sacred ground. This also underlines the importance of welcome. It is the hospitality of the local community that enables the relationship to develop and makes the research possible. In a spirit of mutuality, this calls for being hospitable in return, welcoming the words and experiences that community members have to share.

I have realized that this calls for adapting myself to encounter the other person on his or her terms. This can also mean shifting the research methodology according to the concrete conditions, leaving space for methods to be prudently and discerningly adapted. Ultimately, I experienced this as a certain emptying of myself; not pretending to be someone I am not, but rather making room for others.

Trust Develops by Being There and Sharing Life

As Indigenous supporter Clare Land has observed, "The first aspect of working with Indigenous people is to try to build trust."[40] The first interview I conducted in the community began by cutting wood. Without saying a word, it was as if the person was asking me, "Are you willing to walk the mile with me?" As we began the interview, it started raining. So, there we sat, out in the rain, as the man responded to my questions and shared his story. After some twenty minutes, he invited me under a tarp next to his tent, where our interview continued. The longest interview took place after sharing a family meal together. I was grateful to be invited as a guest around the kitchen table. The interview that ensued out on the porch of the home lasted over two and a half hours.

In both cases, I dare to think that the experience of having *been there*, of having shared an experience together, was the key to these two men opening up and having so much to share with me, as someone whom they felt was genuinely interested in listening to what they had to say. The point is not to be with people and share life in order to "win the prize" of an interview. Rather, it is to see trust as an indispensable condition for authentic listening. In an organic and unforced way, trust develops as we spend time together and share ordinary experiences of life with one another. Trust is especially crucial when one is an outsider in a community that has suffered injustice and inequality at the hands of outsiders. Ethical research protocols also help to cultivate trust, including confidentiality, informed consent, and clearly stating the scope and purpose of the research.

Of utmost importance is the climate of the interview and the interaction between the interviewer and interviewee, fostering a rapport of trust, respect, cultural sensitivity, and authentic care and concern. A key disposition of the interviewer is that of a student who wishes to learn from what the interviewees have to share. This requires an attitude of openness and the suspension of preconceived notions as

---

[40] Clare Land, *Decolonizing Solidarity: Dilemmas and Directions for Supporters of Indigenous Struggles* (London: Zed, 2015), 147.

much as possible, while at the same time being aware, and not naïve, regarding one's own cultural lens.

Letting Ourselves Be Surprised by the Faith of Others

Given the significant influence of the Missionary Oblates of Mary Immaculate (OMI) in this area for over a century, the community remains largely Roman Catholic. The sole place of worship in the community is a Catholic church. I had not expected that the community would be so strikingly marked by Catholicism. Arriving in the community I had assumed there would be a strong rejection of Catholicism given the church's role in Canada's colonial past and the residential school system. The range of attitudes of Indigenous in Canada towards the Christian faith and church institutions is but one example of the vast diversity across Indigenous communities.

In the case of this community, public places such as the airport, the health clinic, the band hall, the convenience store, and the local lodge are adorned with images of the Blessed Virgin Mary. The devotion of the people is evident in the way they pray the Rosary before Mass, the heart with which they sing hymns in their own Dene language, and their undying trust in God no matter the hardships they face. Of course, this would not necessarily be the case for all Dene communities, as Indigenous peoples have varied and complex relationships with Christianity. While some Indigenous are fervent Christians, others understandably contest the influence of Christianity in favour of the resurgence of Indigenous spiritualities. In many cases, people practice both Indigenous and Christian spiritual traditions, bringing together these two identities in various "hybrid" forms.[41]

Communities characterized by popular piety can sometimes challenge those who have received a theological formation. It can be easy to forget that throughout his ministry Jesus was often amazed by the faith of others. Christ was not struck by the eloquence or sophistication of people's faith, but rather its audacity, simplicity, and sincerity. Perhaps theology today is called to be surprised by the faith of others, welcoming it as a precious gift touched by the spark of divine wisdom.

Especially in a context of evident interculturality, in which differences can seem like a source of division or separation, I came to see that recognizing each other as brothers and sisters in Christ can be a way of finding common ground to journey together, enriched by the diverse ways faith is lived out and expressed.

---

[41] See *Native and Christian: Indigenous Voices on Religious Identity in the United States and Canada*, ed. James Treat (New York: Routledge, 1996).

Wrestling with Our Complicity and Letting Our Views Be Shifted

Against the backdrop of colonization in Canada and the church's role therein, I have come to bear a sense of complicity with the structural causes underlying much of the suffering Indigenous persons experience. In this regard, the words of Clare Land offer an important orientation: "The challenge is to admit it, to resist it, to undo it, yet also to see how it provides us with opportunities to resist the workings of colonialism. These aspects of reckoning with complicity are nonetheless based on the realization that complicity is inescapable. This is a contradiction that must be factored in and reflected upon continuously."[42]

Of course, doing research with Indigenous peoples, and listening to the peripheries in general, runs the risk of a kind of *transactionalism*, in which we go out to receive something we need or want from others. Another way of seeing this would be *extraction*, whereby the researcher goes to "extract" data for the sake of his or her own research without considering any possible benefit for the community, as occurs with natural resources in many contexts of colonization throughout history and to this day. This would only exacerbate existing inequalities. Avoiding this risk requires being aware of it and reflecting upon how to mitigate it on an ongoing basis. Key remedies in this regard, so it seems, are reciprocity and relationship.

These relationships can open us to a new awareness that brings us to question and shift our conceptions of faith and society. For me, the experience in the north brought me to revisit my vision of God, my country, the church and its mission, and the relationship between Indigenous and non-Indigenous in Canada. I was struck to the heart as I learned anew how God scorns triumphalist missionary conquest, and acts rather through closeness with people who suffer, in order to redeem what they are going through. I saw before my eyes the ongoing effects of the settler colonialism that is the spine of the nation called Canada. This has made me turn my attention and focus my energy on the situation of Indigenous peoples in Canada and working towards right relationship with them as a non-Indigenous person.

Experiencing the "Mystique" of Living Together as a Path of Reciprocity

Even over a limited period of time, the experience of *living together* with others offers a unique richness to the atmosphere in

---

[42] Land, *Decolonizing Solidarity*, 229.

which research unfolds. When working across cultures, there is a risk of perpetuating an excessive and unhelpful division between "us" and "them." This can be accentuated by a "folkloric" approach to interculturality, fascinated by various cultural aspects without genuinely encountering the *persons* who are part of that culture and understanding their situation. According to Clare Land, overcoming cultural distance "is not directed to denying differences"; rather, it is a question of "reconstructing the interests of members of dominant groups" to reach "different modes of relating: modes marked by a greater sense of mutuality."[43] Everyday moments of living life together and enjoying one another's company can help nourish the sense of reciprocity. During my time in the community, this included such simple activities as going fishing, playing Monopoly, and drinking Kool Aid together.

Sitting with the Pain of the Other and Sharing in Their Grief

On numerous occasions during interviews, painful experiences were recounted. The lesson learned in the Canadian north was to simply be there, showing solidarity through our attentive and supportive presence. Those moments give the impression of being in touch with the suffering of Christ. It is an experience of *compassion* in the etymological sense of the word: being with the suffering of another. This is the experience of Mary and her *stabat* at the foot of the Cross. We could ask ourselves, to what extent does "remaining with" or "abiding in" Jesus involve staying with the suffering of others, not to idealize or perpetuate it, but to be present to it as a way of journeying forward together, following the dynamic of the parable of the Good Samaritan. It is a call to realize how Christ suffers with and in those who are suffering. We, like Mary, have the opportunity to be there with him, standing in the hope that there will be redemption. I realize my own poverty when I recognize that I cannot "solve" anything. Yet I find meaning in letting someone else's poverty meet my own. There lies a space for discovering Christ who makes himself poor with us.

Being Clear about Our Intentions

I have grappled with the question of *why* I am doing this research. I am confronted with the need to clarify my intentions for myself and others. It is important that the people I conduct interviews with are conscious of my intentions. The key ethical requirement in this regard

---

[43] Land, *Decolonizing Solidarity*, 226.

is that of *informed consent*. Here, being "informed" includes being aware of who I am as a researcher and what the research will be used for. Māori scholar Linda Tuhiwai Smith refers to this as "positioning," which she explains as follows: "Given the history of unethical and exploitative research on Indigenous peoples, it is important for a researcher to be clear and open about who they are and what they are seeking and to locate themselves in context. The basic questions to answer are 'Where are you from?' 'What brings you here?' 'How long do you intend staying?'"[44] This calls for ongoing critical reflection on my own intentions, as well as on my positioning and relationships with the community in which the research takes place.

Returning to the Essential

Listening to men and women in the community, I was often struck by how their words and way of being have the power to bring us quietly back to the essentials. On the walls of their homes, many have sayings such as "Family is everything" or "Here we love," surrounded by photos of their loved ones and family members across multiple generations. I saw these as signs of the central role of family in the lives of individuals.

This is also evident in the ways funerals take place in the community. The entire community stops in this shared moment of grieving: the local store is closed, and the attention of the whole community turns to supporting one another amidst the loss they share. Amidst such suffering and difficulties, many aspects of their life point to a keen awareness of what is most important, what really matters. In this regard, they have much to teach us so that we too can learn from them how to be more focused on the essential.

In spiritual terms, "returning back to the essential" could be seen as a path of *conversion*, coming back to what truly matters in God's eyes, to the source of life and meaning to which God draws us and where he awaits us. In theological terms, this return to the essential could be seen as a dynamic of *ressourcement*, rediscovering the sources of faith and the church to inspire a new fidelity to the Gospel and shed new light on the priorities and orientations of our mission in the world today.

---

[44] Linda Tuhiwai Smith, *Decolonizing Methodologies: Research and Indigenous Peoples*, 3rd ed. (London: Zed, 2021).

EMERGING QUESTIONS AND NEXT STEPS FOR THEOLOGY ON THE PATH OF DECOLONIZATION

This singular experience of listening does not pretend to be a perfect exemplar, but rather one modest attempt to listen to people in one Indigenous community as part of the ongoing learning process of the entire church. In seeking right relationships between Indigenous and non-Indigenous in Canada, it is clear that reconciliation without decolonization is ineffective and insincere. The colonial project in Canada hinged upon the marginalization of Indigenous peoples across the country. Overcoming such systemic marginalization demands systemic change. This is true of Canadian society at large, but also of churches in Canada. Christian communities that take reconciliation seriously cannot avoid decolonizing their practices and theology. As Jane Barter has noted, "To be sure, theology provides the hidden concepts that underwrite the colonial project . . . yet it also provides the resources for interruptions to historicist fatalism."[45] Whereas theology was previously an instrument justifying various tenets of colonialism, today it has a role to play in disrupting the patterns of injustice, inequality, and discrimination engrained in the history of Canada and harming Indigenous peoples across the country to this day. Doing theology in a decolonial key raises a number of questions for further reflection, including the following.

1. How could Indigenous methodologies and epistemologies be integrated into theological inquiry and discourse? For example, doing research in a way that embraces Indigenous worldviews and ways of knowing. It can be a challenge for non-Indigenous researchers to embrace Indigenous perspectives in their work on and with Indigenous persons. A key here would be to closely collaborate with Indigenous persons throughout the successive stages of the research process.
2. How can the protagonism of Indigenous persons and communities be fostered in theology? In addition to *listening*, what are other ways of involving Indigenous as more active protagonists of theological analysis and reflection in a synodal style? This raises the question of expanding and diversifying the *subjects* of theology—*for* whom and *by* whom.[46] The question is thus how to effectively do theology *with them*, as subjects and not merely objects of theological research. It is not only a question of whom

---

[45] Jane Barter, "God Keep Our Land? Unsettling Christian Theology," *Toronto Journal of Theology* 38, no. 2 (2022): 173, doi.org/10.3138/tjt.2022-0028.
[46] Cf. Gilles Routhier, "La naissance d'une théologie pratique et pastorale. Dans le sillon du concile Vatican II et l'interrogation actuelle sur les 'sujets' de la théologie," *Recherches de Science Religieuse* 107, no. 3 (2019): 478, doi.org/10.3917/rsr.193.0463.

theology seeks to address but who it involves in the various stages of its development, reflection, and articulation.
3. In encountering Indigenous peoples, how can research avoid falling into the trap of scientific "extraction," collecting data for academic objectives with little relevance for the participants? The *community dimension* of research—done not only *on* a community but *with* and *within* a community—emerges as a helpful aspect to foster. This could include, for example, involving participants in interpreting the research, finding ways to share results with them and receive feedback, both to verify the contents and deepen the ongoing encounter with them. Reflection can also be dedicated to finding ways of benefiting those involved in the research, without ever having the pretension of fixing problems or finding permanent solutions.

MATTHEW 25 AS PARADIGM FOR THE CHURCH'S RELATIONSHIP WITH INDIGENOUS PEOPLES IN CANADA

Lilla Watson, an Australian Aboriginal, had the following message for non-Indigenous who seek to support Indigenous peoples and their causes: "If you have come to help me, you are wasting your time. If you have come because your liberation is bound up with mine, then let us work together."[47] Jesus's account of the Final Judgment in Matthew 25 makes it clear that our liberation is indeed "bound up" with one another. As such, the Gospel passage constitutes a powerful paradigm for considering the church's relationship with Indigenous peoples in Canada. These words of Christ are a call to action against the backdrop of eternity. They open up a horizon for considering the ultimate meaning of reconciliation between Indigenous and non-Indigenous in Canada and beyond. It is chilling to think of this biblical scene in light of the colonial project of forced assimilation and cultural genocide in which the church participated: *"Whatever you did to the least of these brothers and sisters of mine, you did it to me."* As we have seen above, "the least" is certainly not a satisfying way to identify any particular group or individual. However, the phrase does not intend to be pejorative. Jesus's words do not imprison anyone in a position of being "lesser." Rather, they are a poignant wake-up call, intended to change the point of view of the listener: those who may be considered "least" from a human perspective are those with whom God most closely identifies. What has the church done to those

---

[47] Lilla Watson, "Recognition of Indigenous Terms of Reference," Keynote Address at "A Contribution to Change: Cooperation Out of Conflict Conference: Celebrating Difference, Embracing Equality," Hobart, Tasmania, September 21–24, 2004. Watson identifies this slogan as a collective statement from activists working in Brisbane in the 1970s.

considered "least of Christ's brothers and sisters" among Indigenous peoples in Canada? What is the church doing today?

In the face of settler colonialism in Canada, God identifies personally with each man, woman, and child who has suffered because of the residential school system and its devastating consequences. God grieves the ongoing suffering of countless Indigenous families who bear the wounds of intergenerational trauma, made manifest in substance abuse, domestic violence, and suicide. Amidst these tragic struggles, God dares to open a horizon of eternal hope. The church is called to conversion from colonialism of the past and the indifference of the present to a future of being with God in our Indigenous brothers and sisters.

Whereas the church contributed to silencing Indigenous cultures, languages, and spiritualities, it is now time for the church to open the ears of its heart to listen deeply. What it hears will inevitably entail disrupting the existing rapports that perpetuate colonial inequalities, keeping certain people at "the centre" of church and society while leaving others marginalized.

If God identifies personally with those who are marginalized, then efforts to listen to them, hear their voices and stories, learn from their wisdom and experiences, are in fact pathways of listening to God. For those who practice theology, the question is thus: do we listen to those whose voices are marginalized? And if not, are we in fact leaving God's voice on the margins?

The horizon of the Final Judgment sheds light on the ultimate meaning of listening to marginalized voices. Doing theology by listening to marginalized voices is a step towards a church that lets itself be continually converted by Christ, who speaks in those whose voices often go unheard. The Final Judgment makes clear what is at stake in the daunting task of listening carefully to our brothers and sisters who are marginalized. God waits on the margins, seeking our solidarity. Duane Gastant Aucoin of the Tlingit Nation in the Yukon fittingly captures the journey of redemption that Indigenous and non-Indigenous can walk together with God: "Just as God brought good out of the evil done to His Son after they crucified Him, by raising Him up from the dead, so too we must work with God and with each other to bring good out of the evil done to our people. So that we as a whole may be given new life and rise up from the tomb in which we have been placed, stronger and more alive than before."[48]

---

[48] Cited in Brian McDonough, "The Truth and Reconciliation Commission of Canada," in *The Church and Indigenous Peoples in the Americas: Between Reconciliation and Decolonization*, ed. Michel Andraos (Eugene, OR: Cascade, 2019), 71.

Julian Paparella is a doctoral researcher at the Pontifical John Paul II Theological Institute for Marriage and Family Sciences in Rome and at KU Leuven in Belgium. Originally from Canada, Julian has studied biology and catholic studies at McGill University, as well as theology at the Institut Catholique de Paris. Julian was an auditor at the Synod of Bishops on Young People in 2018 and collaborated with the Commission on Methodology for the Synod on Synodality. Julian's research focuses on what the church and theology can learn by listening to Indigenous families in Canada.

Listening a Synodal Church into Being: Learning Points from the Methodology of the Synod 2021–2024 and the Asian Experience

Christina Kheng

Abstract: This article examines the multiple dimensions of listening entailed in the Synod on Synodality and highlights some challenges posed by the context of Asia. It then examines the outcomes of the synod consultation on the Asian continent and identifies key elements which enabled fruitful listening experience despite the anticipated barriers. These elements include a concerted stance of radical welcome in word and deed, the building of relationships along with structures, the integration of theology "from above" and "from below" through a pilgrim hermeneutic, and the use of consultation methods that embodied a spirituality of communion. The article discusses these elements alongside theological scholarship and church teachings on synodal processes, *sensus fidei*, and theological method. As such, its elucidation of these elements could help encourage synodal listening in practically effective and theologically relevant ways. It is hoped that this might in turn support future efforts to harness the *sensus fidei* and promote a more synodal way of being church and doing theology.

THE SYNOD ON SYNODALITY IN THE CATHOLIC CHURCH HAS been unprecedented in many ways. Among its notable features is an emphasis on listening, underscored in official documents, press statements, speeches, and publicity materials to an extent that listening has become synonymous with the synod. Yet the notion of listening in this synod is not a straightforward one. There are complexities and challenges inherent in the desired form of listening prescribed for the synod. Concrete experiences of implementing the synod process have also produced several unexpected outcomes and provide valuable learning points with regard to methodologies and practices for a synodal church.

In this article, I will discuss the listening intended in this synod, the anticipated challenges of implementation especially in the Asian context, and the results produced by the process. I will then propose a pneumatological key to view these experiences and elaborate on lessons that can be reaped for a method of fruitful listening in the church and beyond.

Personally, I have been closely involved in designing and accompanying the work at the universal church level as well as within Asia. The approach I take in this study is one that leverages my direct experiences as well as examines the global synod process that has occurred to-date, alongside data from the Asian churches. In particular, I will revisit and highlight direct testimonies from synod reports of local churches, which are a rich and relatively untapped source of data from the field. These serve as valuable windows into the realities of local contexts as well as into the reception of the synod process on the ground and the impact of certain ways of proceeding.[1] I will present this data in dialogue with church teachings and recent theological scholarship on synodal listening and the *sensus fidei* so that insights about contextually-effective methods of listening in synergy with the developing faith tradition can be reaped. Some areas for further theological and pastoral research will also be highlighted. As the synod on synodality proceeds towards the implementation phase, I hope this study will contribute to the strengthening of synodality on the ground especially in Asia so that the hopes and dreams enkindled by this process among the people will be fulfilled.

THE SYNOD ON SYNODALITY AND ITS MULTIPLE DIMENSIONS OF LISTENING

A fundamentally new approach towards the Synod of Bishops in the Catholic Church was first signified in early 2021 when a decision was announced to postpone the synod assembly for a year from October 2022 to October 2023. According to the press statement from the Synod Office, this was to enable the adoption of a "new method" envisaged to "make possible a true listening to the People of God to ensure the participation of all."[2] Concretely, this comprised a multi-phase, iterative, and lengthier process that required dedicated efforts at the diocesan, continental, and universal levels. Citing *Episcopalis Communio*, the Press Statement called for "mutual listening to the Holy Spirit at every level of the Church's life" including "all of the baptised, who are the subject of the *sensus fidei*, infallible *in credendo*."[3] Cardinal Mario Grech, in one of his first interviews as the newly-appointed General Secretary of the Synod, remarked that these changes were made because "the time was ripe for a wider participation of the People of God in a decision-making process that

---

[1] For a methodological discussion on the use of these synod reports, see Appendix.
[2] Holy See Press Office, "Note of the Synod of Bishops," May 21, 2021, press.vatican.va/content/salastampa/en/bollettino/pubblico/2021/05/21/210521b.html#.
[3] Holy See Press Office, "Note of the Synod of Bishops," May 21, 2021.

affects the whole Church and everyone in the Church."[4] Some months later, Pope Francis reiterated these views in his address to the Diocese of Rome and emphasized that "the exercise of the *sensus* fidei . . . is not about garnering opinions, not a survey, but a matter of listening to the Holy Spirit."[5]

All these remarks highlight an inherent complexity in the notion of listening in the synod. At least three dimensions of listening can be identified, each having a distinct nature and requiring distinct capabilities. First, every participant in the synod process "listens" to, or more accurately, takes note of personal intuitions, feelings, experiences, and viewpoints in response to the synod questions, in accord with the nature of the *sensus fidei* as a "vital instinct" or "spontaneous and natural knowledge" as described by the International Theological Commission (ITC).[6] Second, participants share their responses with one another and listen attentively to each other. Third, they endeavor to listen collectively to the Holy Spirit through these conversations. There is thus a simultaneous exercise of the corporeal, mental, affective, social, and spiritual senses. The Synod Office has used the term "discernment" in relation to the consultation processes.[7] It also called upon bishops in each episcopal conference to gather together after the local consultations and "listen to what the Spirit has inspired in the churches entrusted to them."[8] The latter point introduces a fourth dimension of listening, done at a meta-level by bishops in assembly, reflecting on the outcomes of local church conversations in which they themselves might have taken part. In fact, the actual practice of the synod process saw many layers of meta-level listening whereby group reports were brought together and collectively reflected upon to arrive at a synthesis. Within local churches, there were often successive tiers of meta-level listening from small neighborhood communities to residential zones, parishes, regional districts, and dioceses.

This communal, layered, and multi-dimensional nature of listening distinguishes the present synod from prior endeavors to tap the *sensus fidei*. In earlier centuries, the task mainly comprised inquiring and

---

[4] Cardinal Mario Grech, cited in Andrea Tornielli, "Synod on Rome on Synodality Postponed to 2023," *Vatican News*, May 21, 2021, republished in English in *Exaudi Catholic News*, www.exaudi.org/cardinal-grech-explores-new-synodal-process/.

[5] Pope Francis, "Address to the Faithful of the Diocese of Rome," September 18, 2021, www.vatican.va/content/francesco/en/speeches/2021/september/documents/20210918-fedeli-diocesiroma.html.

[6] International Theological Commission, *Sensus Fidei in the Life of the Church* (Vatican City: Vatican Press, 2014), nos. 54 and 49.

[7] Holy See Press Office, "Note of the Synod of Bishops," May 21, 2021.

[8] Holy See Press Office, "Note of the Synod of Bishops," May 21, 2021.

ascertaining what the faithful already believed and practiced.[9] In recent synods, consultation took the form of gathering feedback and experiences from relevant groups of people. The present synod, however, calls for the whole church to enter a concerted and coordinated process of communal discernment so as to find out what the Holy Spirit is asking of it. The attendant listening even extends to those normally seen as being outside the church, including people of other faiths, secular groups, and local communities, with special attention to those on the margins of society. This represents yet another dimension of listening in which the faithful are reminded to "not neglect all those 'intuitions' found where we would least expect them."[10] It is an attentive listening to the signs of the times. As expansive and demanding as this is, the objective of the synod goes even further. The *Vademecum* for the synod highlights that "the whole Synodal Process aims at fostering a lived experience of discernment, participation, and co-responsibility, where a diversity of gifts is brought together for the Church's mission in the world."[11] In other words, communal discernment, with its attendant listening, is not simply a means to an end. The goal is for people to have a concrete experience of synodality through the very process of listening. For the first time, the theme of the synod is to be directly experienced and not just talked about. This collective experience is then envisaged to shed new light on synodality and how the church is called to live it more faithfully. Herein lies a final dimension of listening, which might be expressed as "listening to the listening." The whole experience is observed and reflected upon by the community in order to gain awareness about itself, to see where the Holy Spirit is leading, and thus respond accordingly. This signifies a dynamic approach to ecclesiology as a living tradition which moves forward through an active and participative listening praxis.

    The desired ways of proceeding in the synod find resonance in recent theological scholarship on synodal listening, discernment, and the *sensus fidei*. For instance, Ormond Rush highlights the ecclesiological reversal made by the Second Vatican Council in prioritizing the baptismal dignity and co-responsibility of all the People of God, prior to any distinction in ecclesial office or functions. He also underscores the Council's teaching on the *sensus fidei* bestowed on all the faithful by the Holy Spirit. Hence, listening to

---

[9] Some examples are given in ITC, *Sensus Fidei*, chap. 1, no. 2.
[10] Pope Francis, "Address to the Faithful of the Diocese of Rome."
[11] Secretary General of the Synod of Bishops, *Vademecum for the Synod on Synodality* (VD) (Vatican City: Synod Office, 2021), no. 1.3.

"what the Lord asks of His Church today" involves everyone.[12] Likewise, Hervé Legrand highlights that "if [the church] is the temple of the Holy Spirit, this means that the whole range of the gifts of the Spirit, in their diversity, can only be found in the whole of the people of God, and since no one Christian, and no one Church, has a monopoly of these, that implies a system of listening to each other and co-responsibility."[13] More specifically, Dario Vitali emphasizes the need for reciprocal listening between the Magisterium and the People of God as a whole, in light of the *sensus fidei*.[14] Elaborating on communal discernment as the means for such reciprocal listening, Jos Moons highlights the necessity of "speaking out" in terms of sharing "what one believes to be the Spirit's inspiration" based on prayer and "thinking before speaking," among other factors.[15] He also underscores the disposition of mutual listening with genuine interest to hear what the Holy Spirit is revealing in the conversation.[16] Similarly, Amanda Osheim emphasizes the importance of "prayer, dialogue, and self-reflection" as well as mutual listening.[17] These views resonate with the first three levels of listening envisaged in the synod as discussed above. Myriam Wijlens recalls Vatican II's affirmation that "the church exists in and from the local churches" and that "circularity between the different entities" including the local, regional, and universal churches would be mutually enriching.[18] Thus, fruitful reception of the Spirit's inspiration necessitates several rounds of meta-level listening as planned in the current synod, attending reverently to every grassroots community, to "neighbouring dioceses,"[19] and the wider church. Wijlens also alludes to the action-research method in the synod and remarks that "the object is at the same time the method .... Hence, the church convoked in synod may

---

[12] Ormond Rush, "Inverting the Pyramid: The *Sensus Fidelium* in a Synodal Church," *Theological Studies* 78, no. 2 (2017): 321, doi: 10.1177/0040563917698561.

[13] Hervé Legrand, "Synodality is a Matter of Practice: A Plea for Learning," *Concilium* 2 (2021): 120–121.

[14] Dario Vitali, "The Circularity between *Sensus fidei* and Magisterium as a Criterion for the Exercise of Synodality in the Church," in *For a Missionary Reform of the Church*, ed. Antonio Spadaro and Carlos M. Galli (Mahwah, NJ: Paulist, 2017), 196–217.

[15] Jos Moons, "A Comprehensive Introduction to Synodality: Reconfiguring Ecclesiology and Ecclesial Practice," *Roczniki Teologiczne* 69, no. 2 (2022): 86, doi.org/10.18290/rt22692.5.

[16] Moons, "Comprehensive Introduction to Synodality," 87–88.

[17] Amanda C. Oshiem, "Stepping Toward a Synodal Church," *Theological Studies* 80, no. 2 (2019): 374, doi: 10.1177/0040563919836225.

[18] Myriam Wijlens, "The Church of God is Convoked in Synod: Theological and Canonical Challenges Concerning the 2021–2023 Synod," *Centro Pro Unione Bulletin* 99 (Fall 2021): 95–96.

[19] Wijlens, "The Church of God is Convoked in Synod," 96.

reap some of the fruits of a synodal conversion as all engage in experiencing it, reflecting upon it and sharing what they have learned."[20] This underscores the importance of "listening to the listening" as highlighted above.

CHALLENGES IN THE CONTEXT OF ASIA

The goals of the synod, noble as they are, face many challenges in the Asian context. A relatively large proportion of people struggle with daily instabilities from poverty, conflict, and systemic oppression. These stark realities, alongside geographical remoteness, deep-seated social prejudices, and a plurality of local languages present formidable barriers to the synodal process. Moreover, a hierarchical culture prevails in many Asian societies, where listening is more often associated with unquestioning obedience to seniors, elders, and those in authority. A reversal in the direction of listening would not find easy reception on either side. As noted in the Central Asia synod report, "Our people are not accustomed to engage in any sort of explicit 'synodality' or to evaluate in open discussion the workings or intentions of those charged with authority within society, the family, or religion."[21] Similarly, Pakistan highlighted that "priests and heads of commissions used to normalize their people's perspective with the purpose to create harmony" and hence, they were more accustomed to speaking and intervening rather than listening.[22] Even among equals, speaking frankly with *parrhesia* or voicing disagreement and contrary opinions are behaviors which many Asians, being relatively reserved, tend to avoid. The synod report from Japan noted that "it is very difficult to gather the voices of people who even if they come to church do not want to speak."[23]

---

[20] Wijlens, "The Church of God is Convoked in Synod," 87.
[21] Catholic Bishops' Conference of Central Asia (CECAC), "Synthesis Report: Synod of Bishops 2021–2023," 32, FABC Papers no. 176, www.fabc.org/document/fabc-papers-176/. The synod reports from most episcopal conferences in Asia are available publicly on the website of the Federation of Asian Bishops' Conferences (FABC) at www.fabc.org/document-library/. Quotations from the local churches cited in this article are taken from these synod reports unless stated otherwise.
[22] Pakistan Catholic Bishops' Conference (PCBC), "Synthesis Report: Synod of Bishops 2021–2023," 46, FABC Papers no. 178, www.fabc.org/document/fabc-papers-178/.
[23] Catholic Bishops' Conference of Japan (CBCJ), "Synthesis Report: Synod of Bishops 2021–2023," 18, FABC Papers no. 177, www.fabc.org/document/fabc-papers-177/. At this juncture, two important qualifiers regarding my comments on cultures in Asia need to be made. First, there is always the risk of stereotyping whenever cultural traits are being discussed. A systematic ethnographic study would identify and explore such traits more comprehensively especially with regard to whether they facilitate or inhibit synodality. However, that is beyond the scope of this

Besides listening and speaking, the very notion of participating in a synod consultation is foreign to many of the laity. A devotional approach to religion prevails in much of Asia where co-responsibility for mission and ecclesial life is not widely understood or exercised. As noted in the Malaysian report, "Some negative comments and lukewarm reception may have been due to a lack of knowledge and understanding on the synod, synodal process, functions of the parish, diocese, and the wider church."[24] Additionally, the practice of discernment, whether personal or communal, is not widely known, let alone understood or exercised. Consequently, there is a general lack of prior experience to tap on. This is exacerbated by the fact that some ecclesial structures for consultation have not fostered genuine participation or effected real change. The report from Sri Lanka noted that "there are efficient pastoral structures like parish pastoral councils, already within the Church, for the people to speak out and express themselves. Yet the laity finds it difficult to speak out." As a result, an attitude of skepticism has settled in many places. As highlighted in the Korean report, "At the very beginning, the main obstacle to be overcome was passive attitude. This was especially shown in those dioceses where they hardly experienced meaningful changes through their own synod."[25]

RESULTS OF THE PROCESS

Despite these challenges, the synod process showed some notable positive outcomes in Asia. All seventeen episcopal conferences in the

---

essay. For the time being, I have drawn upon direct quotes from the synod reports of the local churches themselves. To some extent, these indicate how they see their own cultural and ecclesial tendencies in relation to various aspects of synodality. Second, I acknowledge that general characterizations do not do justice to the diversity of social and ecclesial cultures across Asia and even within each local community. Nevertheless, I am of the view that such diversity need not preclude attempts to identify some commonalities, at least provisionally and broadly, as starting points for pastoral collaboration and theological networking at the continental level, increasingly called for in the church's synodal process. A similar approach has been taken by the FABC in its recent major documents. See "Journeying Together as the Peoples of Asia: FABC 50 Bangkok Document," March 15, 2023; "Final Document of the Asian Continental Assembly on Synodality," March 16, 2023; "The Asian Face of Synodality," August 2024, www.fabc.org/document-library/. Going forward, further research can be done on cultural distinctions and similarities so as to aid our walking together as church.

[24] Catholic Bishops' Conference of Malaysia-Singapore-Brunei (CBCMSB), "Synthesis Report: Synod of Bishops 2021–2023," 5, FABC Papers no. 178, www.fabc.org/document/fabc-papers-178/.

[25] Catholic Bishops' Conference of Korea (CBCK), "Synthesis Report: Synod of Bishops 2021–2023," 31, FABC Papers no. 177, www.fabc.org/document/fabc-papers-177/.

Federation of Asian Bishops' Conferences (FABC) organized synod teams and carried out consultations more or less in the manner proposed by the *Vademecum*. Although participation rates varied, the overall reception surpassed the expectations of most synod teams. An observer from Malaysia remarked that the response "demonstrated a kind of groundswell never seen before."[26] Throughout the Asian churches, one of the most prominent reactions encountered was that of enthusiasm. Timor Leste reported that "through consultations from the bottom, we discovered the enthusiasm and the spirit of participation of the faithful which were really very gratifying."[27] Similarly, the report from Indonesia remarked that "the enthusiasm of the faithful to participate is very high; they really appreciated the synod process because they felt heard and welcome."[28] A similar enthusiasm was seen in the many ground-up and spontaneous initiatives to create, produce, and share materials that aided and accompanied the synod process. These ranged from graphical explanations, videos, songs, and toolkits designed by diverse individuals, to dedicated web portals and formation resources provided by institutions and pastoral centers. Observing these pro-active initiatives, the Asian continental synthesis team expressed its view that "the general sense of concern for the church as demonstrated in the participation of all in this process reflects a natural or organic inclination to authentic synodality."[29] I would add further, as a personal viewpoint from my own observation of these unfolding events, that it seemed something latent in the hearts of people was awakened and brought to life.

Another relatively unexpected outcome in Asia was the openness and honesty with which people spoke. This enabled the listening process to gather not only positive experiences in the church but also experiences of pain and sorrow. Viewpoints that were mutually contrasting could also be surfaced. It was particularly remarkable that many of the laity spoke frankly about problems in the church, including their difficult experiences with clergy and other pastoral leaders. Participants were candid in calling out shortcomings in transparency, accountability, pastoral care, and competence on the part of those holding ministerial positions. The report from Myanmar,

---

[26] Clarence Devadass, "Towards a Synodal Church: Asian Models and Initiatives—Malaysia & Singapore," in *Towards a Synodal Church: Moving Forward*, vol. 1, ed. S. G. Kochuthara and J. J. Kochumuttom (Bengaluru, India: Dharmaram, 2023), 363.
[27] Catholic Bishops' Conference of Timor Leste (CET), "Synthesis Report: Synod of Bishops 2021–2023," 41, FABC Papers no. 179, www.fabc.org/document/fabc-papers-179/.
[28] Konferensi Waligereja Indonesia (KWI), "Synthesis Report: Synod of Bishops 2021–2023," 3, FABC Papers no. 177, www.fabc.org/document/fabc-papers-177/.
[29] FABC, "Asian Continental Assembly," no. 46.

for instance, remarked that "people reacted negatively to the homilies with emphasis on the sins and failures of the people who are taking part in the liturgy instead of on the joy of being children of God."[30] These spontaneous views of the faithful are valuable in potentially indicating the *sensus fidei* regarding a more evangelical way of proceeding in ministry. Minority voices were also heard and frank testimonies about their experiences of discrimination were expressed. For instance, the Vietnam church highlighted that "expatriates and domestic migrants feel isolated and abandoned due to a lack of social and pastoral care, even sometimes have feelings of not being welcome or excluded."[31] The report from Laos echoes the sentiment expressed by many of the other Asian churches: "The process of consultation . . . produced unexpected fruits: the people of God expressed themselves; they shared their joys, their hopes, their concerns, as well as many criticisms. . . . That Laotian Christians have dared to share what they think and hope testifies to their maturity and their capacity to accept changes that will be beneficial to the local Church."[32]

All around Asia, the synod experience generated fresh insights about synodality and the way of being church. What is significant is that such insights frequently came hand-in-hand with strong expressions of joy and consolation. As reported in Vietnam, "They experienced great joy when participating in the consultation process because of many reasons: (1) feeling a 'new fresh wind' blowing into the life of the Church; (2) having the opportunity to listen to the Church's teachings and to have their voices heard; (3) experiencing more clearly to be living members of Christ's Church."[33] In India, a synod facilitator remarked that "it is heartwarming to know that several women cried when asked to share, as this was the first time it had happened in the Church."[34] As a result, the Indian synod report noted that "the most significant experience was that all those who participated in the consultation realized their communion with one

---

[30] Catholic Bishops' Conference of Myanmar (CBCM), "Synthesis Report: Synod of Bishops 2021–2023," 28, FABC Papers no. 178, www.fabc.org/document/fabc-papers-178/.
[31] Catholic Bishops' Conference of Vietnam (CBCV), "Published National Syntheses," www.synod.org.pl/vietnam-catholic-bishops-conference-of-vietnam/.
[32] Catholic Bishops' Conference of Laos and Cambodia, "Synthesis Report: Synod of Bishops 2021–2023," 59, FABC Papers no. 177, www.fabc.org/document/fabc-papers-177/.
[33] CBCV, "Published National Syntheses."
[34] "Delhi Archdiocese's Synodal Sessions Help Focus 'Unnoticed Persons,'" *Matters India*, May 4, 2022, mattersindia.com/2022/05/delhi-archdioceses-synodal-sessions-help-focus-unnoticed-persons/.

another."³⁵ In many countries, this realization was accompanied by an increased desire to engage those not present and include people at the peripheries. In particular, participants were able to identify the marginal groups in their own contexts neglected by the local church, beyond the examples given in the official synod guiding documents.

A palpable transformation was observed in some churches. In Korea, for example, it was reported that "the greatest fruit was that many of the People of God in Korea participated in the synodal path, deepened communion and experienced the synodal Church. In result, the Catholic Church in Korea saw the stronger will and hope to carry out her mission emerging."³⁶ Concrete improvements in various aspects of ecclesial life also took place, such as in the Philippines, which reported that "many remarked how the consultations positively affected the celebration of the liturgies" and that the synodal process "has succeeded in pushing them (the dioceses) to finally implement the abolition of the *arancel* system."³⁷ According to the synod reports, some people who have left the church also started coming back after the synod consultation. Hence, more than a participatory exercise to experience synodality as originally envisaged, there seems to have been some signs of communal conversion. As expressed by the Taiwanese team, "This synthesis report is not an end, but the beginning of a new way of dialogue for a synodal Church in Taiwan."³⁸

SENSUS FIDEI AND THE DYNAMIC PROCESS OF CONVERSION: A PNEUMATOLOGICAL KEY

The responses described in the Asian reports bear some semblance to the ITC's description of dispositions for authentic manifestations of the *sensus fidei*.³⁹ These include statements in the reports about participants' openness, enthusiasm, solicitude for the church, desire for unity, fidelity to the tradition of church teachings, willingness to engage in the process with faith and reason, and most of all joy, which seemed akin to that of "the person who has found the treasure of

---

[35] Conference of Catholic Bishops of India (CCBI), "Synthesis Report: Synod of Bishops 2021–2023," 47, FABC Papers no. 176, www.fabc.org/document/fabc-papers-176/.
[36] CBCK, "Synthesis Report," 31.
[37] Catholic Bishops' Conference of the Philippines (CBCP), "Synthesis Report: Synod of Bishops 2021–2023," 56. 72, FABC Papers no. 178, www.fabc.org/document/fabc-papers-178/. The *arancel* system in the Philippines refers to the local church fee-based system for administration of the sacraments. These fees have sometimes caused church sacraments to be beyond the reach of the poor.
[38] Chinese Regional Bishops' Conference, "Synthesis Reports: Synod of Bishops 2021–2023," 5, FABC Papers no. 179, www.fabc.org/document/fabc-papers-179/.
[39] ITC, *Sensus Fidei*, nos. 87–105.

salvation."[40] In studying these responses, the Asian continental synthesis team expressed its view that much of the people's feedback and desires, whether associated with consolations or desolations, conveyed "a deep love for the Church."[41] I venture that a sense of *sentire cum ecclesia* was perhaps engendered to some extent and this enabled people to speak freely out of faith and love. What is even more significant are the signs that point to the transformative action of the Holy Spirit in participating communities, creating a synodal church and fostering conversion in the course of the listening process. The Korean report, for instance, recounted that participants began with skepticism, but "in the process of gathering, listening, and discernment, the people in many communities shared their experience of faith, listened to one another, and finally confessed that they gradually and strongly recognized the presence of the Holy Spirit among them."[42] Similarly, despite the initial hesitation, Japan reported that "in the process of gathering opinions, there was a growing understanding that it is important for all who have received the blessing of baptism to walk together, sharing and discerning the guidance of the Holy Spirit who calls them. . . . Each believer realized the importance of regularly sharing their 'feelings for the Church.'"[43]

These testimonies of transformation have significant implications for the listening process in the synod. They show that an authentic viewpoint is something emergent rather than pre-existent, ripening through a process of mutual engagement and communal conversion. What each participant brings initially to the table might contain either a seed of insight or even something contrary to the *sensus fidei fidelis* since, as the ITC points out, a variety of opinions can exist in the "mental universe" of believers which influence and sometimes distort their intuitions of the *sensus fidei*.[44] A communal discernment process with its accompanying conversion can enable a refined viewpoint to emerge which more authentically manifests the inspirations of the Holy Spirit since it comes from believers who have grown together in faith, hope, and love. In fact, from the results encountered, it can be said that the answer to the synod question of what steps the Holy Spirit is calling the church to take in order to grow in synodality lies in the very processes participants have been undergoing. It is thus useful to examine the whole synod process thus far to identify those elements which have helped to foster a fruitful experience of communal discernment and synodal conversion, especially in light of the barriers

---

[40] ITC, *Sensus Fidei*, no. 102.
[41] FABC, "Asian Continental Assembly," no. 50.
[42] CBCK, "Synthesis Report," 31.
[43] CBCJ, "Synthesis Report," 17.
[44] ITC, *Sensus Fidei*, no. 55.

anticipated in the Asian context. This would then illuminate how methodological principles outlined by theological scholarship could be translated into concrete pastoral practice. No doubt cause and effect can neither be correlated definitively nor even measured in religious matters, especially when the Holy Spirit is considered to be the main agent. Nevertheless, the following section presents some elements which have been relatively prominent in this synod and more evidently made an impact on the participants and outcome.

KEY ELEMENTS ENABLING A FRUITFUL LISTENING PROCESS

The main factors that have helped to enhance the effectiveness of the listening phase in the synod process can be traced to four key elements. These include a stance of radical welcome communicated consistently in word and deed, the building of relationships along with structures, the integration of theology "from above" and "from below" through a pilgrim hermeneutic, and the use of consultation methods that embody a spirituality of communion.

A Stance of Radical Welcome Communicated Consistently in Word and Deed

In line with the synod's inclusive approach, a message that has been communicated resoundingly about the listening process is that all are welcome and no one should be left out. This has been reiterated in synod documents and publicity materials, in media statements from synod officials, and especially in speeches from Pope Francis.[45] One

---

[45] The Holy Father underscored this point in his homilies and messages throughout the synod process. Among the most prominent quotes is his emphasis that "*La Chiesa delle porte aperte a tutti, tutti, tutti!* (The doors of the Church are open to everyone, everyone, everyone!)" Pope Francis, "Homily at the Opening Mass of the Ordinary General Assembly of the Synod of Bishops," October 4, 2023, www.vatican.va/content/francesco/en/homilies/2023/documents/20231004-omelia-nuovi-cardinali.html. On this point, there is some notable divergence in the theological scholarship. For instance, echoing Pope Francis, Jean-François Chiron emphasizes the authoritative voice of the poor by virtue of their connaturality with the suffering Christ while Declan Marmion points out that "the Church has much to learn from the experience of its sceptical." (Jean-François Chiron, "*Sensus Fidei* et vision de l'Église chez le Pape François," *Recherches de Science Religieuse* 104 [2016]: 187–205; Declan Marmion, "A Church that Listens: Synodality in the Life and Mission of the Church," *New Blackfriars* 120, no. 1100 [July 2021]: 450, doi:10.1111/nbfr.12609). In contrast, other scholars underscore the importance of holiness, alignment with the faith tradition, and involvement in the church as among the necessary qualities for exercising the *sensus fidei*. (For example, see Bernhard Blankenhorn, "The *Sensus Fidei* and Synodality: Theological Epistemology and the *Munus Propheticum*," *The Thomist* 87 [2023]: 311–338 and Moons, "Comprehensive Introduction to Synodality," 84.) It would appear that the Synod Office has adopted

integral aspect of this inclusiveness and radical welcome is the encouragement to speak with freedom, honesty, and confidence since every voice matters, especially those from the margins. In my view, such an inclusive stance is not only consonant with the dignity and uniqueness of every human person as upheld in Catholic anthropology but also recognizes the possibility, as highlighted by the ITC, that the "minority" and "little ones" can sometimes give better witness to the true faith.[46] Consequently, it was deliberately stressed in the *Vademecum* that "we must personally reach out to the peripheries, to those who have left the Church, those who rarely or never practice their faith, those who experience poverty or marginalization, refugees, the excluded, the voiceless, etc."[47] The *Vademecum* also emphasized that minority or divergent viewpoints should be included in the final consultation report. The communications team of the Synod Office reinforced this message by using its newsletters and social media platforms to feature outreach efforts to often-marginalized groups such as the differently-abled, migrants, and LGBTQ+ community. Moreover, in keeping with a welcoming image, many of its communications and publicity materials were also unprecedented in their user-friendly and visual appeal.

All these initiatives at the global level seemed to have been effective in prompting local churches to be more mindful about inclusiveness and welcome and helped counter to a certain extent the stigma that had prevented engagement or even explicit acknowledgement of certain groups. As a result, many synod teams in Asia went the extra mile to widen participation. The India report, for example, highlighted that "the dedication of the organising teams was commendable, some making long journeys into remote villages and working within the time that the people could offer."[48] Similarly, the Korea report noted that "some dioceses were outstanding in putting special efforts to listen to the voice of those on the peripheries such as the lukewarm Catholics, the people with special needs, migrants, refugees, sexual minority, North Korean defectors as well as . . . believers of other religions and other denominations and the civil society."[49] These gestures made a difference to the targeted participants, especially those who felt included for the first time, as

---

the former stance, in line with the approach of Pope Francis, consistent with his ongoing emphasis on the peripheries.
[46] ITC, *Sensus Fidei*, no. 118ii.
[47] Secretary General of the Synod of Bishops, *Vademecum*, no. 4.1.
[48] CCBI, "Synthesis Report," 36.
[49] CBCK, "Synthesis Report," 30.

testified in the India report that "the efforts by the Synod teams of lay faithful, religious, and priests touched the hearts of those they met."[50]

A stance of radical welcome necessitates additional effort to adapt the listening process to certain segments of the population. In the Asian context, this often meant translating synod materials into a myriad of local languages by carefully exploring and employing terms that ensured the right reception in each culture. The questions were also adapted to be relevant to the context and capacity of each target group. Some synod teams made further adjustments to suit people's livelihoods, especially when these inhibited their presence in the church community. In these cases, listening often took more time to develop. As reported in Pakistan, "It was difficult to engage people who are not regular to go to Church, therefore, meetings were conducted with brick kiln workers, farmers, and other neglected groups. After regular contacts and series of consultations, they shared information, their problems and expectations to the Church."[51] The Philippines also reported that "one parish reimbursed the sectors' forgone day's labor since they lost their income when they attended the consultations."[52] Sometimes, additional adjustments had to be made to ensure conditions for speaking freely. For instance, the India report pointed out that "special efforts to encourage candid feedback were made in certain cultural contexts like organising women-only consultation groups."[53] Moreover, in Asian cultures where relationality is highly emphasized, a personal and informal approach also proves effective. In this regard, a respondent in the Philippines who considered himself an "inactive Catholic" gave the following testimony: "I was invited by a friend who is dear to me and was paying respect to an invitation, so I attended. It was memorable when we were sharing experiences. . . . It makes me more eager to know more about God and read more about God's words."[54] Complementing this personal face-to-face approach, the synod process included online channels of outreach such as the Digital Synod, which successfully connected with many who had left the church or tended to be on the peripheries. All these outcomes show that when global and local gestures are mutually reinforcing in conveying a clear stance of radical welcome in word and deed—not unlike the example shown by Christ

---

[50] CCBI, "Synthesis Report," 36.
[51] PCBC, "Synthesis Report," 42.
[52] CBCP, "Synthesis Report," 55.
[53] CCBI, "Synthesis Report," 36.
[54] Cited in Rechilda Estores, "Philippines: A Catholic Parish Journeys Together, Living Synodality," *Vatican News*, October 19, 2022, www.vaticannews.va/en/church/news/ 2022-10/philippines-catholic-parish-journeys-together-living-synodality.html.

in the gospels—they can foster the participation of those who would otherwise be left out in the listening exercise.

Building Relationships along with Structures

A second element which can be seen to contribute significantly towards a fruitful listening process is the building of relationships along with structures. For the first time, the synod comprised a three-tier listening phase corresponding to the local, continental, and universal levels alongside concurrent consultations in trans-geographical associations such as religious and lay communities, Vatican dicasteries, and institutes of higher learning. These multiple loci of listening are not mere structures for organizational efficacy. Rather, they resonate with theological and social markers of identity, belonging, and mission. Moreover, as highlighted by Vatican II and elaborated in the theological literature, the church is fully present in each local church with its unique contexts. Hence, the structure of the consultation process enabled the synod to obtain diverse perspectives from multiple domains. Reports were also synthesized and re-circulated so that communities could respond further and deepen the reflection from their own contexts. This enabled the whole church from the grassroots to the provincial, continental, and universal levels to be in mutual dialogue. Circularity was also seen in synod assembly meetings, where plenary and small group sessions alternated in conversation, reflection, feedback, and refinement of syntheses. Similarly, communities at the parochial level came together in progressive stages. Although these iterations entailed additional effort and might have seemed repetitive at times, they fostered greater dialogue and resulted in a more coherent yet polyhedrally-enriched output while also facilitating concrete experiences of synodality. As highlighted in the Asian continental report, "What the DCS (Document for the Continental Stage) has been able to do is be the catalyst for more profound spiritual conversations. In many places, it was indeed experienced as a moment of living synodality in the Church through a process of shared identity and shared responsibility."[55] To this I would add that the synod's way of promoting circularity has given flesh to the theological concept of existential "perichoresis" among the local, universal, and all other levels of the church.[56]

In the process of consultation, existing structures were utilized while new ones were also formed. Some dioceses leveraged their official pastoral committees, while others assembled new teams

---

[55] FABC, *Asian Continental Assembly*, no. 45.
[56] International Theological Commission, *Synodality in the Life and Mission of the Church* (Vatican City: Vatican Press, 2018), no. 60.

specifically for the synod. An appendix to the Philippines report highlighted that "most synodal teams created committees that attended to various concerns: program, communications, spirituality, synthesis drafters, content, facilitators, respondents, IT logistics, secretariat work, documentation, etc."[57] This detailed glimpse into the granular realities of operating more synodally brings to life theological principles about identifying, activating, and coordinating diverse charisms. Alongside structures, there were also unprecedented efforts in relationship-building and personal outreach. For instance, the Synod Secretariat conducted frequent meetings with episcopal conferences and other groups to clarify the method, encourage participation, promote mutual learning, share best practices, and exchange updates. There were also multiple channels for raising questions and giving feedback. Many synod teams expressed their appreciation for the closer communication and greater openness on the part of the Synod Secretariat. Within each locality, peer accompaniment was promoted through the initiatives of episcopal conference and diocesan coordinators. This inter-parochial interaction was novel for some teams and provided a concrete experience of walking together beyond parochial silos. In this regard, Indonesia reported that "the virtual consultation process between diocesan contact persons is very helpful. . . . The process of journeying together and inspiring each other, guiding each other is very pronounced at this stage."[58] Likewise, the continental assemblies catalyzed new collaborative structures, friendships, and a greater sense of belonging.

In line with relationship-building, deliberate efforts to be more flexible and transparent could be observed throughout the synod process. The Synod Office made several adjustments in extending deadlines and modifying the process in response to feedback from the ground. There has also been unprecedented transparency in the publication of reports, processes of syntheses, composition of various official teams, and rationale for various decisions taken. Senior officials at the Synod Office made personal visits to local churches and regions around the world throughout the process. These initiatives helped to build trust and demonstrate the spirit of synodality. For Asian churches, such role modelling by the centers of authority is often influential. In the words of the Timor Leste report, "The hierarchy of the Church must approach and actively create a climate of trust so that the faithful can participate more actively in the Church's mission."[59]

---

[57] CBCP, "*Salubong* (Welcoming Encounter): The Philippine Catholic Church Synodal Report," Attachment 1, 11, August 15, 2022, www.synodphilippines.com/wp-content/uploads/2022/08/Philippines_National-Synodal-Report.pdf.
[58] KWI, "Synthesis Report," 3.
[59] CET, "Synthesis Report," 43–44.

The report also noted that people at the grassroots called for "the hierarchy of the Church to, not only [meet] the representatives in the councils, but also listen to all members, . . . opening up themselves to the local problems that the members of the community and society may have."[60] This feedback from the people resonates with the ITC's emphasis that "it is always within the communion life of the Church that the magisterium exercises its essential ministry of oversight" even as it has final responsibility for confirming the *sensus fidei*.[61] Thus, authentic encounter and genuine human relationships, rather than faceless bureaucracies, are what make structures for listening effective.[62]

Integrating Theology "from above" and "from below" through a Pilgrim Hermeneutic[63]

Though the synod guidelines emphasized a disposition of radical openness in listening to what the Holy Spirit was asking of the church, the process did not begin with a blank slate. Existing church teachings on synodality had been conveyed to participants as an integral part of the process especially through the Preparatory Document and *Vademecum*. A plethora of formation activities were also initiated by dioceses, educational institutions, pastoral centers, and individuals around the world. Notably, the questions for reflection provided in the official materials were in themselves instructive on synodality. Along with the main question for consultation, ten areas were elaborated upon, each with specific accents that helped unpack the composite notion of synodality. The questions also called for drawing upon real life experiences, reflecting on them more deeply, and conversing about them with one another. Hence, the underlying pedagogy of the questions was as formative about synodality as the religious teachings

---

[60] CET, "Synthesis Report," 44.
[61] ITC, *Sensus Fidei*, no. 77.
[62] The need for effective structures alongside a genuine relational spirit has been highlighted in the theological literature. For example, see Rush, "Inverting the Pyramid," 322–323; Wijlens, "The Church of God is Convoked in Synod," 88–89; and Rafael Luciani, *Synodality: A New Way of Proceeding in the Church* (New York: Paulist, 2022), 44. The present synod has now brought to life this theoretical principle by providing the opportunity for synod teams at all levels to experience it firsthand and reflect on the experience.
[63] The terms "from above" and "from below" have been used in varied ways in relation to theologizing. In this article, I use the term "theology from above" to imply an approach to theological reflection which takes as its starting point the existing body of religious doctrine and tradition. These serve as the predominant and orienting point of reference. Conversely, "theology from below" begins with experience and context, and tends to privilege these perspectives in theological reflection. For a brief discussion on these approaches, see Rajesh Kavalackal, "New Paradigms for an Integral Theological Education Today," *Asian Horizons* 12, no. 4 (Dec 2018): 638.

that accompanied them. For those conducting the listening exercise, the *Vademecum* offered detailed steps designed to model a synodal approach, such as in the diverse composition of local synod teams and the encouragement of trans-parochial collaboration. Overall, there was a deliberate effort to be more instructive in the local phase. This enabled people to organize and participate in the listening exercise more meaningfully. As highlighted in the Myanmar report, "Our people have never heard of synodality as a nature of the Church until the opening of this Synod."[64] Similarly, Japan reported that the consultation process fostered a growing understanding of synodality which was "the result of efforts by the Synod Secretariat in each diocese to create and explain various useful materials."[65] These testimonies attest to the view underscored by the ITC that theology has an essential role in formation "to explicate the Church's faith" as passed on in Scripture and Tradition so that the *sensus fidei* will be more authentically manifested.[66]

At the same time, the synod process made room for theology "from below." Without this emergence of theological reflection from experience, the listening exercise would have been futile and the church's teachings on synodality would lack the opportunity to grow as a living tradition. Hence, most of the official guidelines stressed openness and adaptation to contextual realities in the synod consultation process, and allowing for creativity. The reflection questions themselves sought local stories and perspectives, and encouraged participants to draw upon their own experiences. As a result, new contextual and cultural perspectives on synodality were reaped. For instance, the Philippines report highlighted that "the synodal journey has brought out the innate synodality in the Filipino culture. Indigenous symbols and images help explore the depth of communion, participation, and mission in Filipino culture."[67] New accents and dimensions of synodality initially not featured in the official guiding documents also emerged from the consultations in Asia. These included the family as a locus of synodality, the importance of basic ecclesial communities, the complexity of interfaith relations, the richness of Indigenous communities, and the centrality of inculturation. Such fruits are evidence that effective space had been created for the emergence of new perspectives or particular accents that can potentially enrich the church's understanding of synodality. On a global level, the *Vademecum* encouraged direct

---

[64] CBCM, "Synthesis Report," 36.
[65] CBCJ, "Synthesis Report," 19.
[66] International Theological Commission, *Theology Today: Perspectives, Principles, and Criteria* (Vatican City: Vatican Press, 2012), no. 35.
[67] CBCP, "Synthesis Report," 71–72.

quotes in the synod reports so as to convey participants' voices more vividly. The DCS similarly preserved the integrity of viewpoints from ecclesial grassroots. Likewise, the *Instrumentum Laboris* for the October 2023 synod assembly presented provisional conclusions and questions that emerged from the listening process. These approaches are consonant with the theological view that "the concrete reality of the existential situations" of believers, especially the laity, enriches their experiences and makes an indispensable contribution towards refinement of church teaching.[68]

Resonating with this view, Rush highlights that "the people of God's intuition in the contexts of today regarding faith and morals should be a primary consideration in the process of the hierarchy's teaching."[69] Similarly, Wijlens points out that "the living faith is an important witness and source of faith and thus a *locus theologicus*."[70] At the same time, Moons stresses that "this does not discard other essential faith convictions, such as God's self-revelation in Christ."[71] The views of these scholars thus indicate the need to bring theology "from below" and "from above" together in an integral path. Luciani expresses this integration well when he notes that "it is in that communal interaction [of "all ecclesial subjects"] that the contents of faith are discerned and reinterpreted in the light of tradition and with the help of theological reflection from a particular context, thus producing something new."[72] The synod experience has shown that navigating this path has not been without challenges. The Philippines report, for instance, noted that "it was also important to reorient the facilitators about their listening role since they were used to lecturing."[73] In Malaysia, it was highlighted that "two polarities emerged, one side citing that the church was too hierarchical and rigid, and needed more flexibility; while the other side wanted to see more reverence and tradition brought back to church as they felt too much accommodation was made to modernism."[74] At the global synod assembly in October 2023, scriptural and theological inputs as well as sharing of experiences were all integral parts of the meeting and reflection materials. Yet some participants felt that too much attention was given to current experiences at the expense of church traditions and teachings while others felt that there was not enough consideration of experiences, especially of people at the peripheries. Indeed, even

---

[68] ITC, *Sensus Fidei*, no. 59.
[69] Rush, "Inverting the Pyramid," 312.
[70] Wijlens, "The Church of God is Convoked in Synod," 94.
[71] Moons, "Comprehensive Introduction to Synodality," 79.
[72] Luciani, *Synodality*, 95–96.
[73] CBCP, "Synthesis Report," 62.
[74] CBCMSB, "Synthesis Report," 11.

though Vatican II had underscored the developmental nature of the church's understanding of divine revelation and the dynamic interaction of Scripture, Tradition, and lived experience as integral poles of revelation, there will never be precise formulae for the relative proportion of each pole. Consequently, conflicts will continue to occur and are perhaps even necessary for the church to navigate the right balance.

In my view, a fruitful way of proceeding could be to adopt a "pilgrim hermeneutic" as offered by Pope Francis.[75] This implies seeing and interpreting with the lenses of one travelling along the path of history, mindful of being always at the crossroads of past and present, known and unknown. Guided by an ultimate horizon, such a wayfarer "is always journeying" through an evolving context, striving to be faithful to the tradition "begun in the Acts of the Apostles" while also being open to newness.[76] Thus, each step is taken with humility and strives towards integrity between the past, present, and desired future as authentically as possible, even amidst risk-taking and learning from trial and error. The Pope highlights that this way of proceeding can be fostered "by praying and opening our eyes to everything around us; by practicing a life of fidelity to the Gospel; by seeking answers in God's revelation."[77] I would add that a pilgrim hermeneutic also bears in mind that divine mystery is inexhaustible and can never be fully penetrated, even as the Christ event constitutes God's definitive revelation. Echoing this, Catherine Clifford highlights Pope Francis's stance on the development of doctrine, noting that "Francis makes clear that while Christ has revealed God's saving love for us once and for all, the church can never exhaust its understanding of this unfathomable mystery. Indeed, its understanding of revelation can grow and mature" and the church can "learn to 'interpret better' what it has received."[78]

The crucial task, in my view, is that amidst a diversity of experiences, cultural and scientific developments, signs of the times, and even interpretations of the faith tradition, the church needs to rediscover the kernel of its beliefs whenever new questions are faced. To this end, the ITC highlights that the *sensus fidei* illuminates "the core of the faith" and "what is essential for an authentic Catholic faith."[79] At the same time, the *sensus fidei* enables the believer to identify those aspects of religious practice or teaching that are

---

[75] Pope Francis, "Address to the Faithful of the Diocese of Rome."
[76] Pope Francis, "Address to the Faithful of the Diocese of Rome."
[77] Pope Francis, "Address to the Faithful of the Diocese of Rome."
[78] Catherine Clifford, "The 'Hierarchy' of Truths in a New Context," *Theological Studies* 85, no. 1 (2024): 32, doi: 10.1177/00405639231225145.
[79] ITC, *Sensus Fidei*, no. 64.

incidental or "indifferent"[80] and thus adaptable to specific contexts so that the core message of the Gospel can be lived more fully. As conveyed in Luke's account of the Council of Jerusalem in Acts 15:6–21, this "core of the faith" is not a doctrinal formula that can be applied mechanically to every new situation, as though an algorithm could replace the role of a discerning community. Rather, it is a living insight rediscovered anew and developing from the community's sincere effort to acknowledge present tensions, create spaces for genuine listening and dialogue, grow in understanding of the historical tradition, and seek ongoing conversion towards a *sentire cum ecclesia* which fosters, in due course, a consensus inspired by the same Spirit of God.[81]

Consultation Methods that Embody a Spirituality of Communion

Finally, one of the most impactful factors that have enabled the listening process to be fruitful is the method of consultation recommended in this synod. Its essential elements include encounter, equality in participation, authenticity in contribution, spiritual depth, holistic epistemology, and collective emergence. As such, it promotes a "spirituality of communion" that undergirds the dispositions for authentic manifestation of the *sensus fidei*.[82] This method has proven effective in facilitating the multiple dimensions of listening as discussed above. In fact, an observer from Asia noted that "the synodal process was a breakthrough because for the first time, though the methodologies may have varied slightly, the entire diocese and also the Conference of Bishops had a method to create a 'safe space' for faith and life conversations."[83] Given the positive reception, it is useful here to elaborate on the key elements of this method.

First, to promote meaningful encounter, the *Vademecum* called for interpersonal and communal meetings as the preferred form of

---

[80] ITC, *Sensus Fidei*, no. 64.
[81] Rush alludes to such a process when he offers the model of a "hermeneutical circle" comprising iterative acts of understanding, interpretation, and application. In this cyclical pattern, a faith community makes sense of the present by drawing upon the past and in doing so emerges with a new view and understanding of the past itself. (Ormond Rush, "*Sensus Fidei*: Faith 'Making Sense' of Revelation," *Theological Studies* 62, no. 2 [2001]: 233.) Likewise, Luciani points out that it is the communal discernment undertaken by all the faithful in their diverse charisms that "mediates the correct comprehension of the *depositum fidei* ("the body of revealed truth in the Scriptures and Tradition") according to each time and epoch" (Luciani, *Synodality*, 94). Thus, the foundations of the faith tradition are not static formulae but a living insight.
[82] See ITC, *Synodality*, no. 108.
[83] Devadass, "Towards a Synodal Church," 364.

consultation over individual surveys and contributions.[84] Diversity of group composition was also encouraged, thus enabling participants to discover the realities of those with whom they seldom interacted. In the Asian context where informal social bonding is often an important precedent to focused conversation, many synod teams integrated communal moments of conviviality into the consultations. For instance, the Philippines highlighted that "food and fellowship were always part of the experience. From the initial gathering to every consultation in the parishes and chapels, there was *'salu-salo'* (sharing of food)."[85] Along with the principle of encounter, the consultation method emphasized equality in participation through conversation tools that ensured each person an equal turn to speak and express himself or herself as freely as possible, as well as to hear and respond to others. A facilitator was usually involved, who had to be skilled at creating a conducive group atmosphere, encouraging observance of the adopted conversation rules, and countering any unevenness in power and seniority which might affect participation. Consequently, many participants in the synod process have been able to speak with *parrhesia*. As observed in Thailand, where deference to elders and seniors is deeply entrenched, "the atmosphere of the meetings opened wide and fostered direct dialogue and sharing. It made everyone, especially the youth, to be able to open up and have courage to express themselves with different opinions."[86] In turn, this enabled the "mutual exchange of gifts" so integral to synodality.[87] Just as important was the fostering of authentic contributions in which, after proper preparation, participants shared genuinely from their own experiences. Since "faith, not opinion, is the necessary focus of attention" in the *sensus fidei*,[88] the required preparations centered around prayer and reflection with the suggested materials, supported by formation where necessary on the topic at hand.

Closely related to this, another central element in the consultation method was spiritual depth. As reported in Korea, "An emphasis on listening, discernment, and prayer in silence allowed the diocesan synodal path to be experienced as spiritual process, not merely as a

---

[84] Secretary General of the Synod of Bishops, *Vademecum*, no. 5.1.
[85] CBCP, "Synthesis Report," 56.
[86] Catholic Bishops' Conference of Thailand, "Synthesis Report: Synod of Bishops 2021–2023," 22, FABC Papers no. 179, www.fabc.org/document/fabc-papers-179/.
[87] ITC, *Synodality*, no. 76. Resonating with this, Gilles Routhier remarks that "synodality presupposes an effort, for everyone must pull their weight, demonstrate solidarity, and have desire to end up with consensus, a shared conviction. It presupposes the desire to collaborate, to accept and agree, to give and receive" ("Synodality as a Constitutive Dimension of the Church and an Expression of the Gospel," *Concilium* 2 [2021]: 95).
[88] ITC, *Sensus Fidei*, no. 118i.

series of meetings, discussion, and preparation of the synthesis."[89] The synod guiding documents frequently stressed the importance of prayer and interior attentiveness in personal preparation as well as in communal dialogue. Ample suggestions for liturgies and scriptural reflections were also provided throughout the synod process. At all levels of assemblies, regular moments of prayer and silence have become a distinct feature of the synod. The global assembly even included a retreat, a pilgrimage, and special events of prayer in addition to the regular Eucharistic celebration and other liturgies at the meeting. All these helped participants grow in union with the Divine Presence as they shared and discerned. The measures taken gave concrete form to Richard Gaillardetz's apt description that a synodal church "transcends itself in a posture of openness and receptivity to God's self-disclosure" and that "the whole Christian people are enjoined to listen for God's Word."[90] Listening to what the Holy Spirit was asking of the church also meant starting the process not with predetermined conclusions but open-ended questions and a disposition of radical trust in God's accompaniment. At the same time, spiritual depth implies a heart of charity that listens with love and compassion towards one's conversation partners.

Another element integral to the consultation method was a holistic epistemology. This meant that participants listened and expressed themselves not just through literal means and at the level of the intellect but also in ways that engaged their feelings and interior movements. The synod documents suggested some non-literal ways for participants to articulate their intuitions and viewpoints, such as the use of images, symbols, stories, and various forms of art. Conversation groups were also prompted to note the deeper sentiments, affectivities, and energies palpable in the course of their dialogue, and to include these in their report. In particular, moments of consolation and desolation in the group were valued as important cues in recognizing the issues that needed attention. As remarked by the synthesis team in the Asian continental report, "Listening to all and feeling the pulse of the participants aided the discernment process in the writing of the Final Document."[91] The ITC describes the *sensus fidei* as "a knowledge by empathy, or a knowledge of the heart."[92] Hence, it is "akin rather to a natural, immediate, and spontaneous reaction" and might be "compared to an instinct because it is not

---

[89] CBCK, "Synthesis Report," 31.
[90] Richard Gaillardetz, "The Synodal Shape of Church Ministry and Order," *Concilium* 2 (2021): 99.
[91] FABC, "Asian Continental Assembly," no. 32.
[92] ITC, *Sensus Fidei*, no. 50.

primarily the result of rational deliberation."[93] Rather than intellectual discourse, the *sensus fidei* might be manifested as an "accent, desire, or attitude" or through "symbolic or mystical language."[94] In the Philippines, participants were asked to use Indigenous cultural symbols to grasp and convey what synodality meant for them.[95] Elsewhere, various actions done spontaneously by participants such as sharing resources with one another or going the extra mile to visit people in remote areas could be seen as ways in which they expressed spontaneously and non-linguistically what they intuited about synodality. Similarly, having firsthand experience of the consultation process instead of just reading or hearing about it was essential in enabling people to better understand synodality. At the same time, intellect and reason remained indispensable because they enabled participants to examine and evaluate their experiences and form new insights.

The relevance of a holistic epistemology in discernment has been noted by various theological and pastoral scholars. For instance, Moons asserts that "the affective domain has revelatory value," while Rush points out that "the *sensus fidelium* interprets revelation and expresses its insight more on the level of love. Thus, the contribution of the *sensus fidelium* is not to be found in neat, systematic theological precision."[96] Commenting on the Holy Spirit's movements in human interiority, Ladislas Orsy explains that "we discover such knowledge by experiencing peace, gladness, joy, and encouragement in God's presence. Such psychological signs are certainly not the logical outcome of a reasoning process."[97] Going forward, perhaps more theological and empirical study are needed on the epistemological aspect of the *sensus fidei*, including the association, if any, between the fruitful presence of the Holy Spirit (Galatians 5:22–23) and the movements of human affectivity and interiority.[98] For now, what this

---

[93] ITC, *Sensus Fidei*, nos. 54 and 49.
[94] ITC, *Sensus Fidei*, nos. 82i and 82iii.
[95] Subsequently, these symbols were discussed in the group dialogue between participants and the synod teams, and their meanings were communicated in written form in the final text of the synod report.
[96] Jos Moons, "Synodality and Discernment: The Affective Reconfiguration of the Church," *Studia Canonica* 56, no. 2 (2022), 391; Rush, "Inverting the Pyramid," 322.
[97] Ladislas Orsy, *Discernment: Theology and Practice, Communal and Personal* (Collegeville, MN: Liturgical Press, 2020), 9.
[98] Certain spiritual traditions within the church have attended to this matter in varying degrees. For instance, Ignatius of Loyola describes spiritual movements of consolation and desolation as indicators of the influence of the spirits (nos. 313–336 in *The Spiritual Exercises of St. Ignatius: Based on Studies in the Language of the Autograph*, trans. Louis Puhl [Chicago: Loyola University Press, 1951]). However, these insights have yet to be comprehensively explored and systematized in the corpus of mainstream Catholic teaching. Contemporary scholar Beáta Tóth has noted the "bi-

synod has helped underscore was that synodal listening is exercised not just with scientific intellect but also with the affective sensitivity of a contemplative heart which hears "the sometimes silent cry that goes up from the People of God."[99]

A final element in the consultation method was collective emergence. The synod guiding documents highlighted that it was not enough for participants to simply share their individual responses and listen to each other attentively. Thereafter, they needed to note the reactions, themes, directions, or even new questions that emerged from the sharing and listening. These might pertain to viewpoints that had wide resonance within the group, as well as those in mutual conflict or which aroused curiosity and tension. Further exploration, reflection, and dialogue by group members in a prayerful manner then enabled more evolved insights to be formed. The aim was to advance in collective understanding and gradually recognize what the Holy Spirit might be revealing to the group as a whole. Such a way of engendering the collective emergence through iterative stages of conversation often led to a widening of each participant's perspectives, a maturation of viewpoints in the group, and even conversion of heart. It can be said that the final output is a new creation which emerges from a generative listening methodology showing that "the whole is greater than the part, but it is also greater than the sum of its parts."[100] Similarly, the synod guiding documents highlighted that group reports were not to be synthesized by simply summarizing what each group had said but by prayerfully discerning the themes and movements that emerged collectively. This discernment involved listening not only to the answers obtained from the listening process but also "listening to the listening," which meant observing the process and noticing significant aspects of the experience, including the moments of consolation and desolation in the group. For this reason, both the DCS and the *Instrumentum Laboris* began by highlighting key observations about the experiences of the synod process around the world as these were also indications of what the Holy Spirit was generating in the church. In my view, the endeavor to identify the collective emergence is possibly the most challenging aspect of the consultation method because it requires an honest exchange of viewpoints, exploration of divergences and disagree-

---

polar anthropological scheme" espoused in the ITC document on the *sensus fidei* and calls for more focused efforts to construct an adequate epistemological framework in relation to the *sensus fidei*. See Beáta Tóth, "Knowledge of the Heart: Notes on the Definition of the *Sensus Fidei* in the Personal Life of the Believer," *New Blackfriars* 104, no. 1110 (2023): 204, doi:10.1111/nbfr.12788.

[99] ITC, *Synodality*, no. 114.

[100] Pope Francis, Apostolic Exhortation on the Proclamation of the Gospel in Today's World (*Evangelii Gaudium*) (Vatican City: Vatican Press, 2013), no. 235.

ments, openness to tensions, willingness to learn and change assumptions when needed, and patience to give time for insights to ripen. As the Asian continental report remarked, "The process of having the synodal conversations as requested has sometimes been painful and unsettling, while at the same time, making us vulnerable to each other."[101] Nevertheless, such processes potentially create, in the words of the ITC, "a vital field where conflicts, tensions, and opposites can reach a pluriform unity which generates new life."[102] In this regard, collective emergence is the touchstone of synodality.[103]

A particular format of dialogue found to incorporate many of the above elements is Conversation in the Spirit. Participants at the local, continental, and universal levels have found it effective in enabling a synodal listening experience. As reported in the Philippines, "Although diverse in personalities and backgrounds—socio-political, cultural, and religious, as well as different in theological mindsets—the spiritual conversations brought forth joyful as well as painful realizations about our church's life and mission."[104] Similarly, Pakistan highlighted that "the joy of experience lay in experiencing how the Holy Spirit is poured out on each person and encountered in spiritual conversation. Listening and speaking to each other under guidance of the Holy Spirit proved joyful, liberating, and encouraging."[105]

CONCLUSION

The Synod on Synodality has sought to discern what the Holy Spirit was asking of the church with regard to communion, participation, and mission. Based on the testimonies of many participants in the consultation phase, it might be said that the answer is to be found not at the end of the synod process itself but in the very way the church has been living it these recent years. The approaches adopted in listening reflect a transformation in the church to some extent, and elucidate key elements that make for fruitful communion, participation, and mission. As such, a synodal church could be described as one which demonstrates a stance of radical welcome in word and deed, builds relationships along with structures, integrates

---

[101] FABC, "Asian Continental Assembly," no. 43.
[102] ITC, *Synodality*, no. 111.
[103] Luciani alludes to this when he writes that "while expressing and living Christianity, the faithful will become aware of the great multitude of actors that sustain the ecclesial structures, people who are diverse in terms of gender, experience, training, and culture. The complex interactions among them will give birth to a new sense of faith" (*Synodality*, 96).
[104] CBCP, "Synthesis Report," 57.
[105] PCBC, "Synthesis Report," 44.

theology from above and below through a pilgrim hermeneutic, and adopts consultation methods that embody a spirituality of communion. Indeed, the method is the message. Through appropriate adaptations to local contexts as seen in Asia, these ways of proceeding have helped foster a disposition of *sentire cum ecclesia* and enabled church teachings on synodality and the *sensus fidei* to be not only put into practice but also developed further with the benefit of present experience. Some of the key elements might also be illuminative for dialogue in polarized societies and evangelization through mutual listening. Admittedly, what has been achieved to-date in the Synod on Synodality is far from perfect. Several conflicts remain unresolved and many people at the grassroots level have yet to engage or even feel included. As anticipated at the beginning, this will all take time because "listening is the true pastoral conversion of the Church."[106] Nevertheless, from the joy and fruits experienced by many people around the world so far, there are signs of hope that we are slowly but surely listening a synodal church into being. 🅼

APPENDIX: METHODOLOGICAL NOTE ON THE USE OF DATA FROM LOCAL CHURCH SYNOD REPORTS

This essay draws primarily from the final reports reviewed and approved by the college of bishops in each episcopal conference and submitted to the Synod Secretariat. As mentioned in the above discussion, these reports were cumulatively synthesized through successive rounds of meta-level listening from the grassroots to the country level. The *Vademecum* stressed that synthesis teams "should read all the submissions in a spirit of prayer" and "the team meetings themselves should be synodal and spiritually discerning, listening to the living voice of the People of God across the diocese under the guidance of the Holy Spirit."[107] In other words, the primary method of synthesis, including report-writing, was to be that of communal discernment. As further recommended by the *Vademecum*, synodal assemblies were also held at the diocesan level so that grassroots representatives could discuss and validate the final diocesan report. Some episcopal conferences and dioceses circulated their reports for verification. Nevertheless, there are obvious gaps in these processes. Not all dioceses held assemblies or circulated their final reports. More fundamentally, there were few or no formal audits, quantitative surveys, participant observations, or ethnographic interviews to verify independently the degree to which successive levels of syntheses

---

[106] Cardinal Mario Grech, cited in Andrea Tornielli, "Synod of Rome on Synodality Postponed to 2023."
[107] Secretary General of the Synod of Bishops, *Vademecum*, Appendix D.

represented the views of participants in a fair and accurate manner. Neither was it possible to verify the extent to which the syntheses resulted from prayerful listening to the Holy Spirit and genuine communal discernment. Nevertheless, the synod reports still represent an unprecedented source of data from this first attempt by the Catholic Church to undertake a comprehensive global consultation. Some resonances are also evident between the final reports and testimonies given via other platforms by those directly involved at the grassroots level.[108] Going forward, there is much potential for further research, especially in how social science methodologies and independent sources of verification could complement the religious, personal, and spiritual nature of synodal listening, communal discernment, and the *sensus fidei*.

Another issue pertains to how the contents of the synod reports have been appropriated in my research for this article. Most of the synthesis teams in Asia followed the format and content structure suggested by the *Vademecum* for the final reports, which included a description and reflection on the consultation experience, key points which have "strong resonance" among participants, points "particularly significant, surprising, or unexpected," and minority viewpoints that were noteworthy.[109] I have compared the contents of all the Asian episcopal conference reports to ensure, as far as possible, that the points highlighted in this essay represent a fair view of the local churches as conveyed in the reports. Besides noting what the synthesis teams have themselves highlighted as significant, I have also attempted to note relative proportions of the text occupied by various viewpoints, their repetition or corroboration in similar statements, and inclusion in summaries and conclusions. Additionally, some comparisons were made with the reading done by others at the global and Asian continental levels.[110] Hence, the points highlighted in this essay reflect the main thrusts of the reports. Nevertheless, there is potential for further research in terms of a more systematic textual analysis or even thematic studies focusing on various issues raised.

---

[108] For example, see Shaji George Kochuthara and Joby Jose Kochumuttom, eds., *Towards a Synodal Church: Moving Forward* (Bengaluru: Dharmaram, 2023), Parts V–VI.

[109] Secretary General of the Synod of Bishops, *Vademecum*, Appendix D.

[110] For instance, see Secretaria Generalis Synodi, *Working Document for the Continental Stage*, Vatican City, October 24, 2022; and FABC, "Asian Continental Assembly."

Christina Kheng is from Singapore and teaches theology and pastoral ministry at the East Asian Pastoral Institute in Manila. She has been a member of the Methodology Commission for the Synod on Synodality 2021–2024, which produced the *Vademecum* and guided synod teams at various levels. She was also a member of the global synthesis team which worked on the Document for the Continental Stage. In Asia, Christina was a moderator and speaker at the Asian continental synod assembly. She currently serves as a non-voting expert (facilitator) at the synod assembly in Rome held in October 2023 and 2024. Christina holds a PhD in Theology from the Australian Catholic University and a Master in Public Administration from the John F. Kennedy School of Government, Harvard University. Her research focuses on foundations for interdisciplinary method in church-society dialogue.

More Than Listening is Needed for Synodality: Observations Based on the Australian Plenary Council and the Church in the New Testament

Peter J. McGregor

Abstract: This essay will examine how the Australian Plenary Council and the church revealed in the New Testament can help us come to a deeper understanding of the nature and practice of synodality. The first part will look at how the Plenary Council was envisaged as a response to the call for synodality, the preparations for the Council, the composition of its membership, and the foci of the Council's deliberations, so as to make suggestions about how a Synod could be organised and conducted. This could be called an investigation into the "body" of synodality. The second part will examine the church in the New Testament from the perspective of being in both *koinonia* and *homothumadon*, in the hope that such an investigation can help us develop a synodal process which, through both "listening" and "looking," can come as close as possible to consensus. This could be called an investigation into the "soul" of synodality.

I n response to Pope Francis's call for greater synodality in the church, during 2021 and 2022 the Catholic Church in Australia held a Plenary Council. As well as bishops, the 277 members of the Council included people nominated by dioceses, eparchies, ordinariates, leaders of religious congregations, some church ministries, and a personal prelature. Six themes guided the deliberations of the Council: the need for a church that is 1) missionary and evangelising; 2) inclusive, participatory, and synodal; 3) prayerful and Eucharistic; 4) humble, healing, and merciful; 5) a joyful, hope–filled, and servant community; 6) open to conversion, renewal, and reform. Both Pope Francis and those who prepared the Council stressed the need to listen to the Holy Spirit through listening to each other.[1]

---

[1] For more on synodality and the Australian Plenary Council, see Timothy Costelloe, "Plenary Council Closing Mass," *Australasian Catholic Record* 100, no. 1 (2023): 38–41; Bruce Duncan, "The Australian Plenary Council: A Bold Beginning with Much Further to Go," *Australasian Catholic Record* 100, no. 2 (2023): 149–159; Denis Edwards, "The Spirit of God and the Plenary Council," *Australasian Catholic Record* 95, no. 4 (2018): 387–398; Richard Lennan, "The Plenary Council as a

However, in this essay it will be argued that there were some deficiencies in the preparation for and implementation of the Council. One was an approach to the selection of Council members that led to the practical exclusion of many potential members who were not "administrative" or "curial" Catholics. Another was the over representation of members of the clergy and religious congregations. A third was an almost exclusive focus in Council deliberations about "what is going wrong with the church" to the exclusion of discussion about "what is going right with the church." In response, this essay, drawing on the experience of the Australian Plenary Council, and the witness of the New Testament church, will present possible solutions to these deficiencies, including how more of those who could be described as "entrepreneurial" and "ordinary" Catholics might be included in any synodal process, and how there could be greater emphasis on "affirmations" of and "testimonies" to how the Holy Spirit is already at work in the church.

The issue of "representation" is a significant concern in the first part of this essay. However, I wish to make clear that I am not advocating proportional representation of any kind. The church is not governed after the fashion of a representative democracy. Nor am I calling for any kind of "quota" system. Furthermore, I am not advocating any usurpation of episcopal responsibilities. The final decisions of a plenary council or synod lie with their serving episcopal members. All other members are there to serve as something like "consultants," with bishops remaining free to make their own decisions. Rather, my motives are to ensure that bishops may receive input from as diverse a range of "voices" as possible, as well as a concern that some "voices" were muted in or absent from the Australian Plenary Council.

The essay will be divided into two parts. The first will examine how the Australian Plenary Council was envisaged as a response to the call for synodality, the preparations for the Council, the composition of its membership, and the foci of the Council's deliberations, to make suggestions about how a Synod could be better organised and conducted. This could be called an investigation into the "body" of synodality. The second will examine the church in the New Testament from the perspective of being in both *koinonia* and

---

Practice of Theology," *Australasian Catholic Record* 100, no. 1 (2023): 3–24; Richard Lennan, Ormond Rush, Gerard Kelly, and James McEvoy, "Theological Reflections on the First Assembly of the Plenary Council," *Australasian Catholic Record* 99, no. 2 (2022): 131–145; Peter John McGregor, "Synodality and the Australian Plenary Council: Listening to and Looking at Those Who Are Living in the Spirit," *Irish Theological Quarterly* 86, no. 1 (2021): 21–38; Nigel Zimmermann, "A Test Case in Synodality: Australia's Fifth Plenary Council in Light of the Thought of Eric Mascall," *Australasian Catholic Record* 100, no. 1 (2023): 25–37.

homothumadon, in the hope that such an investigation can help us develop a synodal process which, through both "listening" and "looking," can come as close as possible to consensus. This could be called an investigation into the "soul" of synodality.

THE AUSTRALIAN PLENARY COUNCIL

The Council as a Response to the Call for Synodality

Pope Francis has pointed out that the very word "synod" is derived from the Greek *syn hodos*, which means "to travel together." He defines a synodal church as

> a Church which listens, which realizes that listening "is more than simply hearing." It is a mutual listening in which everyone has something to learn. The faithful people, the college of bishops, the Bishop of Rome: all listening to each other, and all listening to the Holy Spirit, the "Spirit of truth" (John 14:17), in order to know what he "says to the Churches" (Rev 2:7).[2]

In response to this call for synodality, Archbishop Mark Coleridge of Brisbane unveiled plans to hold a Plenary Council of the entire Catholic Church in Australia.[3] The Archbishop saw the Council as an exercise in the kind of synodality of which the Pope speaks. In defining the nature of this synodality, both the Pope and the Archbishop stressed the need for the bishops and all the faithful to listen to the Holy Spirit and each other. It is the burden of this essay to show that while such "listening" is necessary, it is not sufficient. Although "listening" is an essential prerequisite for success, for true synodality to occur we must also be "looking," to see what the Holy Spirit is already "doing" in the church.

Preparations for the Council

In preparation for the Australian Plenary Council, about 222,000 people participated in "listening and dialogue encounters," and 17,457

---

[2] Francis, "Address at the Ceremony Commemorating the 50th Anniversary of the Institution of the Synod of Bishops," Vatican City, October 17, 2015, w2.vatican.va/content/francesco/en/speeches/2015/october/documents/papa-francesco_20151017_50-anniversario-sinodo.html.
[3] Mark Bowling, "Brisbane Archbishop Calls for First Synod for Entire Catholic Church in Australia since 1937," *The Catholic Leader*, August 17, 2016, catholicleader.com.au/news/brisbane-archbishop-calls-for-first-synod-for-entire-catholic-church-in-australia-since-1937.

submissions were made.[4] From this, six national themes for discernment were identified. The themes were: how is God calling us to be a Christ–centred church in Australia that is:

1. Missionary and evangelising;
2. Inclusive, participatory, and synodal;
3. Prayerful and Eucharistic;
4. Humble, healing, and merciful;
5. A joyful, hope–filled, and servant community;
6. Open to conversion, renewal, and reform.[5]

All this reveals that great efforts were put by the Church in Australia into preparing for the Plenary Council.

My experience of the Council was limited to reading about it in the Catholic and secular press, post-conciliar discussions with people who were members of the Council, and personal participation in a preparatory group composed of representatives of various movements and organisations within the Archdiocese of Sydney. I was a representative of a Public Association of Christ's Faithful, a new ecclesial movement called the Emmanuel Community.[6] From my experience, I can say that almost all the preparatory group's focus was on what the participants perceived as being wrong with the church in Australia. The lesson I took from this is that, in attempting to discern what "the Spirit is saying to the Churches," a more balanced approach is needed, one that tries to look at the whole picture of what is happening in the church. So, the submission made to the Council by the Community to which I belong, authored by me but approved by the local board of the Community, while it included under the headings of "priestly," "prophetic," and "royal" a total of eighty concrete proposals for change, also made thirty-eight "affirmations of existing realities in the church in Australia." It tried to also look at what was "going right" with the church in Australia.

---

[4] Plenary Council, "Listening and Dialogue," plenarycouncil.catholic.org.au/listening-and-dialogue/. The number of participants in the "listening and dialogue encounters" is equal to about 4 percent of the total Catholic population of Australia. Also, it is equal to about 53 percent of regular Mass attendees in Australia. See *National Centre for Pastoral Research*, "The Australian Catholic Mass Attendance Report 2021," 6, ncpr.catholic.org.au/wp-content/uploads/2024/05/Mass-attendance-in-Australia-2021-FINAL.pdf.

[5] "Plenary Council Themes," plenarycouncil.catholic.org.au/themes/about-the-themes/.

[6] "Emmanuel Community Homepage," emmanuel.info/en/.

The Composition of the Council's Membership

The 2021–2022 Australian Plenary Council was the fifth one held in my country.[7] The fourth Council was held in 1937. This fourth Council was attended by 85 people: the papal nuncio, 31 Australian and New Zealander bishops, and 53 priests, amongst whom were theologians, advisors to bishops, and superiors of religious congregations. In contrast, the second assembly of the fifth Council had 277 members: 40 active bishops, 4 emeritus bishops, 102 priests, of whom 19 represented religious congregations, 1 deacon, 24 religious sisters, 4 religious brothers, and 102 laypeople. Members were drawn from 28 Australian Dioceses, 6 Eastern Rite Catholic Churches, the Military Ordinariate, the Anglican Ordinariate, the personal prelature of Opus Dei, religious congregations, church ministries, seminaries, and various institutions. Representatives from each diocese included the diocesan bishop or bishops, priests, the single deacon, religious, and lay people. Clerical members numbered 147, 19 of whom were present as representatives of religious congregations, while religious brothers and sisters numbered 28. Laypeople numbered 102, coincidentally, the same number as priests, but this was split between 34 laymen and 68 laywomen. Finally, six national Catholic ministries were represented by eight laypeople.

What the composition of the Council's membership shows is that, although there was great innovation since the 1937 Council through the inclusion of religious brothers and sisters and lay people as members, the Council was still very clerically and religiously "top heavy." I wish to make five points about this aspect of the Council's membership.

First, clergy other than active bishops, that is, emeritus bishops, priests, and the single deacon, accounted for 38.5 percent of the Council's membership, while laypeople for 37 percent. I suggest that the inclusion of roughly the same number of priests as laypeople was not conducive to overcoming a "clerical" mindset. Here, part of the problem is that, according to current canon law, those who must be called as delegates to a plenary council, besides bishops, include vicars general, episcopal vicars, heads of seminaries and theological institutions, and leaders of religious congregations.[8] In the case of the

---

[7] For information about the Plenary Council, including the composition of its membership, see Plenary Council, plenarycouncil.catholic.org.au.
[8] *The Code of Canon Law*, c. 443, www.vatican.va/archive/cod-iuris-canonici/eng/documents/cic_lib2-cann431-459_en.html#CHAPTER_IV.

Australian Plenary Council, this added up to 180 of the 277 delegates.[9] In my opinion, there needs to be greater provision for non–clerical membership of a plenary council so as to obtain a more balanced picture of the needs of the church. To do this, it would not be necessary to change canon law. Rather, the number of extra delegates could be increased.

Second, representatives of religious congregations accounted for 16 percent of the Council's membership, but members of religious congregations currently make up only 0.1 percent of the Australian Catholic population.[10] Even when measured against the current Mass–going Australian Catholic population, they still make up only 1 percent of that population.[11] This highlights an overrepresentation of members of religious congregations at the Council. Furthermore, on current trends, the great majority of religious congregations in Australia are in what appears to be an irreversible decline. By the middle of this century, we can conjecture that many of them will no longer exist. The reasons for this decline are debatable, but I suggest that, in view of the future composition of church membership and ministry, this provided a reason for increasing lay representation at the expense of religious representation.

Third, although there was an overrepresentation of religious congregations, there was no official representation from the new ecclesial movements. Historically, this would be like holding a church synod in the thirteenth century and inviting the Benedictine, Carthusian, Cistercian, and Premonstratensian monks, but not inviting the Augustinian, Carmelite, Dominican, and Franciscan friars. There were no representatives from movements like the Charismatic Renewal, Communion and Liberation, or the Neocatechumenal Way.

Fourth, the most under–represented group of Catholics at the Council was not laypeople in general but laymen. The president of the Plenary Council stated that

> Bishops were mindful of the large number of clerics who must be called by virtue of their role. There were also many males who will represent religious orders. It was therefore important to prioritise lay people—and especially lay women—in the list of those local delegates who were

---

[9] Australian Catholic Bishops Conference, "Delegates Named for Celebration of Plenary Council," March 23, 2020," ampjp.org.au/wp-content/uploads/2020/03/2020-03-23-Plenary-Council-Delegate-Announcement.pdf.
[10] Australian Catholic Bishops Conference, *Official Directory of the Catholic Church in Australia: 2022–2023* (Strathfield, NSW: St. Pauls, 2023), 761–762.
[11] *National Centre for Pastoral Research*, "The Australian Catholic Mass Attendance Report 2021," 6.

chosen. . . . We are pleased that we were able to . . . lift the proportion of lay people and the proportion of women in the overall delegate list.[12]

Although commendable, the problem with this approach is that it overlooks the fact that the experiences, perspectives, and needs of Catholic men, and indeed, women, are not identical. Those of a young married man with small children can be very different from those of a religious man in a monastic community. Catholic men are young and old; ordained, married, single, religiously consecrated, and widowed; with children and childless; employed, unemployed, and retired; and so on.

Laymen make up roughly half the Catholic population of Australia, and even if one only looks at the Mass–going population, they still make up about 44 percent.[13] Yet, at the Plenary Council, there were exactly twice as many laywomen as laymen. Ten dioceses and two eparchies sent no laymen. An argument could be made that, given the church in the Western world has a problem with attracting male participation, the perspectives of a greater variety of laymen could have contributed substantially to the success of the Council.

The final point has to do with the six national Catholic organisations: the Association of Ministerial Public Juridic Persons (representing major Catholic health, aged and community care, and educational organisations), the St. Vincent de Paul Society, Catholic Health Australia, Catholic Social Services Australia, the National Catholic Education Commission, and the National Aboriginal and Torres Strait Islander Catholic Council. These are ministries of mercy, education, and social justice, and their inclusion was justified, but there was no representation from evangelistic ministries. There were no ministries such as the National Centre for Evangelisation or Charis Australia.[14] A second problem is the absence of Public Associations of Christ's Faithful. These are organisations the church recognises as contributing to its mission in the world, for example, Focolare and the Legion of Mary. Yet these kinds of organisations had no official representation at the Council.

Besides looking at the composition of the membership of the Council from the perspectives of ordination, sex, and ministry, its composition can also be analysed in at least two other ways:

---

[12] See Australian Catholic Bishops Conference Media Blog, "Delegates Named for Celebration of Plenary Council," mediablog.catholic.org.au/delegates-named-for-celebration-of-plenary-council/.

[13] *National Centre for Pastoral Research*, "The Australian Catholic Mass Attendance Report 2021," 10.

[14] Charis Australia represents the Catholic Charismatic Renewal. It is part of an international movement which seeks "to promote and encourage the grace of baptism in the Spirit in the Catholic Church." See www.charisaustralia.org.au.

availability, and what I call a curial/entrepreneurial dichotomy. By "availability" I mean the ability to attend the Council. The first assembly of the Council met for eight days in Perth, WA, while the second met for seven in Sydney, NSW. Given that Australia is a large country, many Council members would have needed extra days to travel to and from the Council. The total time commitment for some members may have been as many as nineteen days. Furthermore, this does not include time spent in preparation for the Council. For anyone in full–time secular employment, being a member of the Council may not have been possible given the loss of income, or the difficulties involved in taking leave from work. This also may have been a contributing factor to the underrepresentation of laymen.

The second point concerns the prominence of what I call "curial" Catholics, and the absence of what I call "entrepreneurial" or "freelance" Catholics, albeit in "good ecclesial standing," from membership in the Council. An analysis of its membership reveals that many members of the Council "work for the church": vicars general, episcopal vicars, heads of religious congregations, and employees of diocesan or other church institutions, in other words, Catholics involved in managerial or administrative roles within church institutions. Here, a few examples of diocesan representation may be helpful:

- The diocese of Broken Bay (215,000 Catholics): the bishop, the vicar general, the diocesan director of the confraternity of Christian doctrine, the director of Catholic schools, and the national director of missions of Couples for Christ Australia.
- The diocese of Sale (125,000 Catholics): the bishop, the vicar general, the episcopal vicar, a religious pastoral associate, and two lay parishioners.
- The Archdiocese of Sydney (595,000 Catholics): the archbishop, three auxiliary bishops, one emeritus bishop, the vicar general, four episcopal vicars, the juridical vicar, two seminary rectors, the deputy and vice deputy chancellor of a Catholic university, three heads of theological institutions or faculties, one professor of canon law, a lay member of the archdiocese's Catholic youth office, a lay member of the archdiocese's office of the episcopal vicar for formation, a lay person involved in "freelance" Catholic marriage and family ministry, and one other layperson.
- The diocese of Wollongong (190,000 Catholics): the bishop, the vicar general, two episcopal vicars, and three lay parishioners.

Besides bearing witness to the prominence of "curial" Catholics, and hence the danger of a "managerial" or "administrative" mindset becoming dominant, these examples show that largely missing from membership were Catholics who developed their own ministries on their own initiative or participate in such ministries. Here, I think examples of such ministries may be helpful:

- In 2003, a small group of laymen, both married and single, established MenALIVE, a national Catholic ministry to men, in order to address the question "Where are all the men in the church?" Since then, the ministry has run more than 450 events in twenty-six dioceses throughout Australia and New Zealand for more than twenty-five thousand men.[15]
- Established in 2010 by a married Catholic layman, Parousia Media seeks to evangelise and catechise Catholics through podcasts, a YouTube channel, and social media platforms. It has an online ecommerce store with over three thousand Catholic resources such as CDs, DVDs, books, Bible studies, and so on. It hosts live events, international speaking tours, courses, Bible studies, and an online Catholic Adult Education certificate program.[16]
- The Youth Mission Team was founded by the Disciples of Jesus Community. Since 1986 it has been presenting the Gospel to Catholic high school students through presentations and retreats on knowing God, self–image, relationships, social justice, and leadership, reaching about sixteen thousand students per year.[17]
- NET (National Evangelisation Teams) Ministries were introduced from the USA to Australia. Since 1988 they have ministered to about five hundred thousand young Catholics in schools, parishes, and universities.[18]
- The Culture Project was established by a group of young Catholic friends. Since 2014, it has worked with many thousands of young Catholics at national conferences, youth groups, schools, and public events, presenting them with the Gospel of their inherent human dignity as children of God.[19]
- SmartLoving was established in Sydney in 1992, initially running weekend marriage retreats integrating the insights of the Theology of the Body with contemporary relationship research. Over thirty years, it has evolved to take advantage of new technologies and is now a global provider of marriage catechumenate resources serving around five thousand engaged couples annually, and thousands more in other stages.

This list is by no means exhaustive. Yet, of these listed ministries, only the last one had any representation at the Council. The insights Catholics like these could have brought to contemporary engagement in the life and mission of the church were missing.

---

[15] "MenALIVE," www.menalive.org.au.
[16] "Parousia Media," www.parousiamedia.com.
[17] "Youth Mission Team Australia," www.ymt.com.au/.
[18] "NET Ministries Australia," netministries.com.au/about-2/.
[19] "The Culture Project," www.thecultureproject.com.au/.

There is one more point I would have liked to but was unable to investigate because of a lack of data. This was the question of how many members of the Plenary Council were chosen, apart from those whose presence was mandated by canon law. When I made enquiries with those responsible for the national organisation of the Council, I was told I would need to make those enquiries with individual dioceses. So, I do not know how many of the members of the Council were selected. Were there requests for volunteers? Were there interviews before committees? Were there exercises in episcopal fiat? This leads into the question of how "representative" the membership of the Council was in terms of presenting the real concerns of "ordinary" Catholics.

Foci of the Council's Deliberations

The foci of the deliberations of the Council can be summarised in eight points.[20]

1. Reconciliation with indigenous Australians,
2. Responding to the sexual abuse of minors,
3. Promoting the mission of the church,
4. Promoting the participation of women in the church,
5. Overcoming "clericalism" and promoting synodality,
6. Promoting care for God's creation,
7. Promoting the liturgical and sacramental life of the church, and
8. Promoting formation and leadership for mission and ministry.

While these foci were valid and, indeed, necessary, a perusal of the motions voted on at the Council reveals that one thing they all have in common is a focus on "problems," that is, the rectification of deficiencies in the life and mission of the church.[21] The fundamental deficiency of the deliberations at the Council is not what was discussed and listened to, but what was not.

One significant problem not addressed has already been mentioned: the crisis of participation in the life and mission of the church by laymen. Ironically, although the laywomen who participate in some way in the life and mission of the Australian Church outnumber laymen by a factor of about six to four, a substantial amount of the Council's time was spent on the discussion of the needs of the former, in fact, more time than on any of the other foci, but none

---

[20] See Plenary Council, "Motions and Voting," plenarycouncil.catholic.org.au/motions-and-voting/.
[21] See Plenary Council, "Motions and Voting."

whatsoever on the needs of the latter. In this instance, it could be said that one group on the social periphery of the church is laymen.

Furthermore, there was also no discussion of something I have already mentioned, the "successes" of the church, the positive initiatives and developments. To use a military analogy, if a breakthrough is made in an offensive, a wise commander will seek to exploit it. It is just as important for the life and mission of the church to discuss where the Holy Spirit is making such "breakthroughs" as it is to shore up weak points in its "defence."

For example, there was no discussion of the growing engagement of Australian Catholics in the new evangelisation; nor the growth and ministry of new ecclesial movements and "entrepreneurial" initiatives; nor the growth in adult catechumens and candidates being received into the church each Easter; nor of the growth of certain devotions, such as adoration of the Blessed Sacrament, and Divine Mercy; nor the explosion of youth and young adult ministries in Australia since the 2008 World Youth Day in Sydney; nor the establishment of new and growing religious congregations and monasteries. In other words, we needed to hear more "affirmations."

LEARNING FROM THE *KOINONIA* AND *HOMOTHUMADON* OF THE CHURCH IN THE NEW TESTAMENT

This essay argues that while listening to the Holy Spirit is necessary, it is not sufficient. We need to broaden the meaning of the term "listening" since, whatever the Holy Father means by "listening," the way in which it generally has been understood has been univocal.[22] It is not enough just to "listen" to what the Holy Spirit may be "saying" through the *sensus fidelium*. The Plenary Council in Australia heard many diverse and even contradictory opinions. How can we discern the voice of the Holy Spirit? Is it just a matter of listening to the opinions of a majority, the most articulate and persuasive, or those with whom we agree? We need to do more than say that we need to listen in order to hear what the Holy Spirit is saying. We need some criteria for discernment.[23] In order to discern what the Holy Spirit is saying we also need to expand our notion of listening to "looking" at what the Holy Spirit is "doing" in the local churches, especially as it

---

[22] For an exception to this general trend, see Edwards, "The Spirit of God and the Plenary Council," 391–392.

[23] With the notable exception of Edwards, thus far, the kinds of discernment being promoted for the Plenary Council have been the kinds suitable for an individual discerning God's will in his or her own life, or general references to reading the "signs of the times." See "Plenary Council 2020: Discernment," plenarycouncil.catholic.org.au/listening-and-discernment/. See also Edwards, "The Spirit of God and the Plenary Council," 397–398.

is revealed in and through those who individually, but even more importantly, corporately, are "living" in the Spirit. As the prophet Isaiah tells us: "Behold, I am doing a new thing; now it springs forth, do you not perceive it? I will make a way in the wilderness and rivers in the desert" (Isa 43:19 ESV). Where is the way that God is making, the rivers he is causing to flow?

For synodal deliberations to be fruitful, it is highly desirable that those engaged in them will arrive at positions as close to consensus as possible. So, to indicate what we should be looking for, where the Holy Spirit is at work, and who is responding to this work, this essay will examine two fundamental realities witnessed to in the New Testament: being in *koinonia* and being *homothumadon*. One should not only look at how the Holy Spirit works in our hearts as individuals. One should also look at how the Holy Spirit brings about *koinonia* (communion) between us and makes us *homothumadon* (of one accord). We could call this an investigation into the "soul" or "spirit" of synodality. What are the spiritual "pre–requisites" for Christians to be able to authentically listen to each other? What spiritual "qualities" do they need to possess? To put things more simply, how can synodality be carried out in a way that answers the prayer of Jesus:

> I do not pray for these only, but also for those who believe in me through their word, that they may all be one; even as you, Father, are in me, and I in you, that they also may be in us, so that the world may believe that you have sent me. The glory which you have given me I have given to them, that they may be one even as we are one, I in them and you in me, that they may become perfectly one, so that the world may know that you have sent me and have loved them even as you have loved me. (John 17:20–23)

Koinonia

The term *koinonia* occurs nineteen times in the New Testament, and is variously translated in the Revised Standard Version either as "fellowship" (Acts 2:42, 1 Cor 1:9, 2 Cor 13:14, Gal 2:9, 1 John 1:3–7), "participation" (1 Cor 10:16, Phil 2:1), "partnership" (2 Cor 6:14, Phil 1:5), "contribution" (Rom 15:26, 2 Cor 9:13), or "share/sharing" (Phil 3:10, Phlm 6, Heb 13:16). In the King James Version, it is sometimes rendered as "communion" (1 Cor 10:16, 2 Cor 6:14, 13:14).[24]

---

[24] For a detailed account of the various ways in which the term is used in the New Testament, see Frederick William Danker, ed., *A Greek–English Lexicon of the New Testament and other Early Christian Literature*, 3rd edition (Chicago: The University of Chicago Press, 2000), 552–553.

It is common to associate *koinonia* with a description of the relationship between Christians. Thus, Paul recounts how James, Cephas, and John gave him and Barnabas the right hand of fellowship (Gal 2:9–19), while Luke tells us that the first Christians devoted themselves to the apostles' teaching and fellowship (Acts 2:42). Finally, in the First Letter of John we are told that the author's intention in proclaiming the Gospel to his readers is that they may have fellowship with him (1 John 1:3).

Notwithstanding the use of the term in this sense, what might be called a human or horizontal sense, the term *koinonia* is more commonly used with reference to the relation of Christians to the Son, the Father and the Son, and the Holy Spirit. So, Christians have been "called into the fellowship of his Son, Jesus Christ our Lord" (1 Cor 1:9). This fellowship includes a participation in the sufferings of Christ (Phil 3:10), and in the body and blood of Christ (1 Cor 10:16). Furthermore, this fellowship includes partnership in the Gospel of Christ (Phil 1:5) and a sharing of faith in Christ between Christians (Phlm 6). This fellowship with the Son is also with the Father (cf. 1 John 1:3), and in the Holy Spirit (2 Cor 13:14, Phil 2:1). It is fellowship with light, not darkness; righteousness, not iniquity (2 Cor 6:14). Indeed, this fellowship with light flows from the fellowship Christians have with God; only through this fellowship are Christians able to have fellowship with one another (1 John 1:3–7). Finally, *koinonia* is used in the sense of "contribution." This contribution is for "the poor among the saints" (Rom 15:26, cf. 2 Cor 8:1–4, 9:11–14), as well as generously sharing what one has with others (Heb 13:16).

Based on this brief survey, four points will be made about the nature of *koinonia*. The first is that *koinonia* is, first and foremost, with the Father, Son, and Holy Spirit. We could call this Trinitarian *koinonia*. The classic expression of this is found at the conclusion of the second letter to the Corinthians: "The grace of the Lord Jesus Christ and the love of God and the fellowship of the Holy Spirit be with you all."

The second is that this *koinonia* with these three is referred to in specific ways. First, it is *koinonia* "in" the Holy Spirit (2 Cor 13:14, Phil 2:1). What is to be "in" the Holy Spirit like? The witness of the New Testament is that the gift of the Holy Spirit enables us to experience God's love being poured into our hearts (Rom 5:5). He is the Spirit of sonship, enabling us to cry out, "Abba, Father" (Rom 8:10, Gal 4:6). He bears witness to us that we are children of God (Rom 8:16). Only through the Spirit can we confess that "Jesus is Lord" (1 Cor 12:3). Our minds are renewed by the Spirit, giving us the mind of Christ (Rom 8:5, 12:2, 1 Cor 2:15–16, Eph 4:23). We are guided by the Spirit into all truth (John 16:3). We can worship God in the Spirit (Eph 6:18, Phil 3:3, Jude 1:20). The Spirit enables us to pray as we ought (Rom 8:26–27). He is a guarantee in our hearts who convinces us of the truth of the Gospel and enables us to know that God is dwelling in us (2 Cor 1:22, 5:5, 1 Thess 1:5, 1 John 3:24, 4:13, 5:7–8). He grants spiritual gifts to us to build up the Body of Christ (1 Cor 12:1–13). Through him we can understand "spiritual truths," and the gifts God has bestowed upon us (1 Cor 2:12–15, Eph 1:17, Heb 6:4). The Spirit works miracles among us (1 Cor 2:4, Gal 3:5, Heb 2:4). We are led by and walk in the Spirit (Rom 8:14, Gal 5:16–18). In the power of the Holy Spirit, we can put to death the deeds of the flesh (Rom 8:2–15, Gal 5:5–25). If we do so we will bear the fruit of the Spirit; love, joy, peace, patience, kindness, goodness, faithfulness, gentleness, and self–control (Gal 6:22, Rom 12:11, 15:13, 1 Thess 1:6, 2 Tim 1:7). When we experience these things in ourselves and see them in each other, we can be confident that we can listen to each other "in the Spirit." The "spirit" of synodality is the Holy Spirit.

Likewise, it is *koinonia* "in" Christ. Being in the Spirit means also being in Christ. Indeed, whenever the term "Christ" is used the Holy Spirit is implied. There is no Christ without the Holy Spirit. It is through the Spirit that the secret and hidden wisdom of God is revealed to us (1 Cor 2:7–10). What those who crucified Christ did not know, "What no eye has seen, nor ear heard, nor the heart of man conceived, what God has prepared for those who love him, God has revealed to us through the Spirit" (1 Cor 2:9–10). The Spirit reveals what Jesus calls the "mysteries of the Kingdom of God" (Matt 13:11, Mark 4:11, Luke 8:10) and Paul calls the "mystery of Christ" (Eph 3:4; Col 2:2, 4:3). And not only of Christ, but of Christ in us (cf. Col 1:27), God's will to unite all things in Christ (Eph 1:9–10), the Gospel (Eph 6:19), faith (1 Tim 3:9), our godliness (1 Tim 3:16), lawlessness (2 Thess 2:7), and resurrection on the last day (1 Cor 15:51–52). Things unaided human reason could never uncover have now been unveiled to us in the Spirit. Not only have they been revealed to us, but with this unveiling the Spirit also gives us the mind of Christ so that we can understand what has been revealed. Christ is in us, and we are in Christ, so now we "have all the riches of assured understanding and the knowledge of God's mystery, of Christ, in whom are hidden all the treasures of wisdom and knowledge" (Col 2:2–3). And we do not just *have* wisdom, for since Christ *is* the wisdom of God (1 Cor 1:24), we who have "become" Christ (Gal 2:20) have now "become" the wisdom of God. Thus, "He [God] is the source of [our] life in Christ Jesus, whom God made our wisdom" (1 Cor 1:30). If we are "in" Christ we will receive wisdom from listening to the Holy Spirit in ourselves and others.

This *koinonia* is not just "in" Christ, it is more specifically "in" his sufferings and his body and blood. Regarding the first, in some way we must all be able to testify to our participation in Christ's sufferings.

We must be patient in tribulation and bless those who persecute us (Rom 12:12, 14). We must, to some degree, embrace being afflicted, perplexed, persecuted, and struck down (2 Cor 4:8–9). We must carry in ourselves the death of Jesus, so that the life of Jesus may also be manifested in us (2 Cor 4:10). Yet this participation in the sufferings of Christ is not yet sufficient. We must also participate in the sufferings of our brothers and sisters in Christ. For their sufferings too are the sufferings of Christ. Moreover, "if one member suffers, all suffer together" (1 Cor 12:26) since we are all "members of one another" (Rom 12:5, cf. Eph 4:25). Not only are we to "rejoice with those who rejoice," we must "weep with those who weep" (Rom 12:15).

We could call our *koinonia* in the body and blood of Christ our Eucharistic *koinonia*. This *koinonia* "discerns the body" (1 Cor 11:29). To what "body" does Paul refer? Paul has been referring to the body and blood of the Lord (1 Cor 11:23–26). He goes on to say that whoever "eats the bread and drinks the cup of the Lord in an unworthy manner will be guilty of profaning the body and blood of the Lord. Let a man examine himself, and so eat of the bread and drink of the cup. For anyone who eats and drinks without discerning the body eats and drinks judgement upon himself" (1 Cor 11:27–29). The fact that Paul says, "discerning the body," not "discerning the body and blood," shows that the body to which he is referring is the one body of Christ to which he referred earlier with the words, "because there is one bread, we who are many are one body, for we all partake of the one bread" (1 Cor 10:17). We profane the body and blood of the Lord when we come to the Eucharistic table with divisions among ourselves (1 Cor 11:18–19). When we do this, we despise the church of God (1 Cor 11:22). The most despicable way in which we can do this is to "humiliate those who have nothing" (1 Cor 11:22). This includes not just the materially poor, but those educationally poor. Indeed, the two usually go together. The contemporary scribes (theologians) and Pharisees (religious leaders) need to make sure that we do not despise the "little ones" (Matt 18:10) and treat them as an ignorant rabble (John 7:49). Having a doctorate in philosophy or sacred theology, teaching at a Catholic institute of higher education, heading an office in a diocesan curia, or occupying an episcopal see, in other words, being one of the supposedly "wise and understanding," puts one in danger of mistaking knowledge for genuine wisdom, and hence despising the "babes" (Matt 11:25, Luke 10:21).

Our *koinonia* in Christ is also in the proclamation of the Gospel (Phil 1:5) and the sharing of our faith with each other (Phlm 6). Those who desire a synodal church must evangelise together and seek to build up the faith of their brothers and sisters in Christ. In *Evangelii*

Nuntiandi, Paul VI told us that the church exists to evangelise.[25] Francis now tells us, "The world in which we live, and which we are called to love and serve, even with its contradictions, demands that the Church strengthen cooperation in all areas of her mission. It is precisely this path of *synodality* which God expects of the Church of the third millennium."[26] It is essential to realise that when Pope Francis speaks of "mission" he takes his cue from *Evangelii Nuntiandi*. This document, more than any other, has shaped his understanding of evangelisation. In *Evangelii Gaudium*, Francis refers to *Evangelii Nuntiandi* no less than thirteen times. Elsewhere, he has called it "a very full text that has lost nothing of its timeliness," "that basic point of reference which remains relevant," and "to my mind the greatest pastoral document that has ever been written to this day."[27]

When it comes to sharing our faith with each other, this is necessary because we all suffer in many ways. We suffer from the effects of our own sins, the sins of others, and the trials God permits. Sharing our faith with each other is a way of building up each other in hope and love. At the beginning of 1 Corinthians 14, after he has told us that the greatest of the theological virtues is love, Paul writes, "Make love your aim, and earnestly desire the spiritual gifts, especially that you may prophesy" (1 Cor 14:1). He then goes on to say that "he who prophesies speaks to men for their upbuilding and encouragement and consolation. . . . [H]e who prophesies edifies the church" (1 Cor 14:3–4). In sharing our faith with each other we are acting towards each other in a prophetic way.

Upbuilding, encouraging, and consoling are promoted by Paul throughout his letters. He tells the Thessalonian Christians to "encourage one another and build one another up, just as you are doing" (1 Thess 5:11) and "comfort one another with these words [about the final resurrection]" (1 Thess 4:18). Paul speaks very beautifully about encouragement. Encouragement must be in love (Phil 2:1). He encourages like a father (1 Thess 2:11). He speaks of hearts being encouraged (Eph 6:22, Col 2:2, 4:8, 1 Thess 5:14). We

---

[25] Paul VI, *Evangelii Nuntiandi*, no. 14, www.vatican.va/content/paul-vi/en/apost_exhortations/documents/hf_p-vi_exh_19751208_evangelii-nuntiandi.html.

[26] Francis, "Address at the Ceremony Commemorating the 50th Anniversary of the Institution of the Synod of Bishops."

[27] Francis, "Address to Members of the 13th Ordinary Council of the General Secretary of the Synod of Bishops," June 13, 2013, w2.vatican.va/content/francesco/en/speeches/2013/june/documents/papa-francesco_20130613_xiii-consiglio-sinodovescovi.html; "Meeting with the Bishops of Brazil," July 28, 2013, w2.vatican.va/content/francesco/en/speeches/2013/july/documents/papa-francesco_20130727_gmgepiscopato-brasile.html; and "Address to the Participants in the Pilgrimage from the Diocese of Brescia," June 22, 2013, w2.vatican.va/content/francesco/en/speeches/2013/june/documents/papa-francesco_20130622_pellegrinaggio-diocesi-brescia.html.

can mutually encourage each other with our faith (Rom 1:12). Consolation is a particular concern of Paul in 2 Corinthians. Because we have been comforted by God, we are able to comfort anyone being afflicted (2 Cor 1:4). If we share in the suffering of Christ, we will also share in his comfort (2 Cor 1:5). Even if we share in the suffering of those who proclaim the Gospel, we will also share in their comfort (2 Cor 1:7).

The love we are meant to have for each other is not a "cold" love that abstractly works for the good of the other. Rather, in a synodal situation, we can fulfil Peter's exhortation to supplement "our faith with virtue, and virtue with knowledge, and knowledge with self–control, and self–control with steadfastness, and steadfastness with godliness, and godliness with brotherly affection, and brotherly affection with love" (2 Pet 1:5–7). These will keep our synodality from being "ineffective and unfruitful" (2 Pet 1:8). As Paul said to the Corinthian Christians, we must be able to say to our co–workers in synodality, "our mouth is open to you . . . our heart is wide" (2 Cor 6:11). As he said to the Christians of Philippi, we must be able to say to each other "how I yearn for you all with the affection of Christ Jesus" (Phil 1:8).

In 1 John 1:3 we are told that we can have *koinonia* "with" the Father as well as the Son. This *koinonia* is the work of the Holy Spirit. The most thorough exposition of this *koinonia* does not actually use the term. Rather, the term used is *menó*, to stay, abide, or remain. The Father and the Son send the Holy Spirit upon us (John 15:16–27). The Spirit remains with us just as he did with Jesus (John 1:33). When the Spirit remains with us, the Father and the Son abide in us (John 15). Through the Father's gift of the indwelling Holy Spirit, the Spirit of sonship, the Spirit of his Son, with Jesus we are able to cry out "Abba! Father!" (Rom 8:15, Gal 4:6).

The third point is that *koinonia* with brothers and sisters is always mediated via the apostles. We should note that all three references to *koinonia* between believers have what might be called an "apostolic" context. They refer to relations between or with apostles or "apostolic men." In 1 John 1:3, the apostle tells his readers that what "we [the apostles] have seen and heard we proclaim also to you, so that you may have fellowship with us; and our fellowship is with the Father and his Son Jesus Christ." In other words, the *koinonia* of believers is via the *koinonia* the apostles have amongst themselves, and with the Father and the Son. In Galatians 2:9–10 it is between Paul and Barnabas on the one hand, and the three "of repute" on the other. The more the successors of the apostles are in *koinonia* with each other the more we will have authentic synodality. Furthermore, in Acts 2:42, being in *koinonia* is inseparable from "continuing steadfastly in the teaching of the apostles." It is also inseparable from liturgical worship, that is, the breaking of bread and prayers. There is no reference to *koinonia* between Christians in isolation from *koinonia* with the apostles.

The last point is regarding *koinonia* being used in the sense of "contribution" and "sharing." This is the conclusive test for the presence of genuine *koinonia*. The generous sharing of our material possessions with each other, especially with brothers and sisters in Christ who are in real want, is the metallurgical assay of the purity of our *koinonia*. It is not enough for us to offer each other the right hand of fellowship and agree on our missionary strategy (Gal 2:9). We must also remember the poor and be eager to do so (Gal 2:10; see also Rom 12:13, 15:25–26, 1 Cor 16:1, 2 Cor 8–9). It is not enough for us to "continually offer up a sacrifice of praise to God, that is, the fruit of lips that acknowledge his name" (Heb 13:15). We must also "not neglect to do good and to share what [we] have, for such sacrifices are pleasing to God" (Heb 13:16). We must not be like Laodicean Christians who said to themselves, "I am rich, I have prospered, I need nothing; not knowing that [they were] wretched, pitiable, poor, blind, and naked" (Rev 3:17). Rather, we must be like the Macedonian Christians who, although they were afflicted and extremely poor, also had an abundance of joy, and "overflowed in a wealth of liberality, [giving] according to their means . . . and beyond their means, of their own free will, begging . . . for the favour of taking part in the relief of the saints" (2 Cor 8:2–4).

All these forms of *koinonia* are interrelated. Like the relationship between virtue and vice, strength in one will strengthen others, and weakness in one will weaken others. So, we cannot be content as long as even one is weak. As we grow in each one the centripetal force of *koinonia* will bring us closer and closer together with the Triune God and each other.

Homothumadon

The term *homothumadon* offers us a way of looking at relationships in the church and with God from the perspective of coming to a consensus. As such, it is of vital importance for the exercise of authentic synodality. We could say it is one of the fruits of *koinonia*. The term is used eleven times in the New Testament, ten of which are in the Acts of the Apostles.[28] It is translated as "of one accord," and/or as "with one mind" or "of one mind." However, these translations do not capture the full meaning of the term. Its root, *thymos*, expresses an outburst of passion. Theologically, it is defined

---

[28] See Acts 1:14, 2:46, 4:24, 5:12, 7:57, 8:6, 12:20, 15:25, 18:12, 19:29, Rom 15:6.

as "with one mind" and "with one emotion." Lexically, it is translated as "same soul" or "same heart," indicating not just intellectual unanimity but also emotional harmony. In other words, it could also be translated as "with or of one heart."[29]

In the Acts of the Apostles, four references to being *homothumadon* concern the relationships between the first Christians (Acts 1:14, 2:46, 4:24, 5:12). In the first three of these, it refers to them being of one accord in prayer; in the cenacle, the temple, and the house where the friends of Peter and John were staying. A reference in Romans also refers to Christians being of one accord in prayer (Rom 15:6). In Acts 15:24–25 it refers to the one accord eventually established, in the face of initial discord, at the Jerusalem assembly of the apostles, elders, and whole church.

From these instances two main points can be made. First, there is reference to what might be called a synodal *homothumadon* made manifest at the Jerusalem assembly. The purpose of this Council was to settle a soteriological argument; whether believers need to be circumcised and keep the law of Moses in order to be saved (Acts 15:1, 5).[30] We are told that the apostles and elders gathered to consider the matter. After much debate Peter testified that, in response to his preaching of the Gospel to the Gentiles, God gave to these Gentiles the same Holy Spirit he had given to Jewish believers, thus making no distinction between the two groups, but cleansing the hearts of the Gentiles through faith, just as he had done to Jews. Peter states that "we [Jews] believe that we shall be saved through the grace of the Lord Jesus, just as they will" (Acts 15:11). After listening to the account of Paul and Barnabas of the signs and wonders God had worked through them among the Gentiles, James declared his judgement that Gentile converts should not be burdened beyond a few things that will make it easier for Jewish believers to relate to them (Acts 15:21). Then we are told that "it seemed good to the apostles and the elders, with the whole church" (Acts 15:22) to follow this advice, achieved through a process of becoming of one mind

---

[29] See Hans Wolfgang Heidland, ὁμοθυμαδόν, in *Theological Dictionary of the New Testament*, ed. Gerhard Friedrich, trans. Geoffrey W. Bromiley, vol. V (Grand Rapids, MI: Eerdmans, 1967), 185–186; and ὁμοθυμαδόν, ὁμόφρων, in Ceslas Spicq, *Theological Lexicon of the New Testament*, trans. James D. Ernest, vol. 2 (Peabody, MA: Hendrickson, 1994), 580–582.

[30] Luke Timothy Johnson holds that it is "the prophetic witness of Acts 15 as a *narrative* [that] is critical to the theological reflection of the church because it gives the fullest picture in the New Testament of the *process* by which the church reaches decision." See Luke Timothy Johnson, *Scripture and Discernment: Decision Making in the Church* (Nashville, TN: Abingdon, 1996), 78; see also 89–106, for the process of discernment involved in the decision of the Jerusalem assembly.

(*genomenois homothumadon*, Acts 15:25), and as a decision of the Holy Spirit first and themselves second (Acts 15:28).

The crucial point we should note about this episode is that the decision was arrived at through listening, but not just through listening to opinions or arguments. Rather, it was through listening to what God had manifestly done through grace.[31] In this sense it was also "looking." This is how they discerned what the Holy Spirit wished to say to them and were able to speak in the name of the Spirit: "For it has seemed good to the Holy Spirit and to us" (Acts 15:28). One thing we can take from this is the need to listen to contemporary "testimonies" of what the Holy Spirit is doing in the church.

Second, as mentioned, the first three references in the Acts of the Apostles, and the single reference in Romans, are all about *homothumadon* in prayer. This shows us that being *homothumadon* is not just about being one in relations with human persons but also being one in relation to God. Furthermore, it is revealing to see what this prayer is about. In the first instance, after returning to the upper room from the Ascension of Jesus, the 11 remaining apostles together with some women, Mary the mother of Jesus, and his brethren, devote themselves to prayer. In fact, we are told that as many as 120 people so devoted were present, at least at some time, between the Ascension and Pentecost (Acts 1:12–15). Why have these people devoted themselves to prayer? According to both Luke's Gospel and Acts, Jesus had told them to wait in Jerusalem for him to send upon them the promise of his Father, the power of the Holy Spirit, so that they might be his witnesses to the ends of the earth (Luke 24:49, Acts 1:4–8). While they are waiting, they pray. It seems reasonable to me that what they were praying for is that the promise of Jesus, the sending of the Holy Spirit, not be delayed, but fulfilled as soon as possible.

In the second instance we read, "And from day to day, continuing steadfastly with one accord in the temple, and breaking bread from house to house, they shared their food in gladness and simplicity of heart, praising God and having favour with all the people" (Acts 2:46–47). Here we see that their one accord in prayer in the temple is accompanied by other manifestations of unity: the sharing of meals not just joyfully, but with a singleness of heart, and giving praise to God.

In third instance, after Peter and John have been told by the Sanhedrin that they were not to speak or teach in the name of Jesus, and threatened in some unspecified way, they went and reported this to the church. Then we read, "And when they heard it, they lifted up their voices with one accord to God" (Acts 4:24). Their subsequent

---

[31] For recounting and listening to what God had done, and acting upon it, see Johnson, *Scripture and Discernment*, 97–108.

prayer begins by acknowledging who God is and what the Jews and Gentiles did to his holy servant Jesus, followed by a plea that the Lord will "grant to your servants to speak your word with all boldness while you stretch out your hand to heal, and signs and wonders are performed through the name of your holy servant Jesus" (Acts 4:29–30). This prayer for a new empowerment to proclaim the Gospel, and have that proclamation confirmed by God's power is, in essence, a prayer for a renewed manifestation of what occurred at Pentecost, and it is immediately answered.[32]

In the last instance in Romans we read, "And may the God of patience and comfort grant you the same way of thinking among each other according to Christ Jesus, so that with one accord you may with one voice glorify the God and Father of our Lord Jesus Christ" (Rom 15:5–6). Here we see that glorifying the Father in prayer together is the result of having the same way of thinking as Christ, and that this way of thinking is a gift from God. Ultimately, *homothumadon* is a grace from God. When it is *homothumadon* in prayer, we learn that that prayer has two foci: praising and glorifying God and asking to be empowered to evangelise. These should be the foci of common worship in any "synodal process."

Conclusion

This essay began with the assertion that "listening" is not enough if we are to discern what the Spirit is saying to the churches. We also need to be "looking" for what the Holy Spirit is already "doing" in the churches. To do this we must not just attend to the "body" of synodality, the practical details of how to have a synod, or exhort each other to listen to the Holy Spirit. We need to be living in the Holy Spirit if we are to recognise the work of the Holy Spirit. If we do not also attend to this "soul" of synodality we will just end up with a corpse.

Unfortunately, complete consensus is rarely possible.[33] On this point of the near inevitability of some disagreement, Paul offers us a useful perspective. He sought to bring unity to the church in Corinth in the face of serious disputes, divisions, and failures in fraternal charity (1 Cor 1:10–13, 6:1–8, 11:17–22, 14:26–33). In the Corinthian church, as well as great *charismata*, there were also great *schismata* (divisions) and *haireseis* (factions).[34] These will always be present in the church to some degree. Indeed, Paul says that "there must be factions among you so that those who are tried and true may be made

---

[32] See also Johnson, *Scripture and Discernment*, 84–85.
[33] For example, see the voting results, Plenary Council, "Motions and Voting."
[34] The exercise of many charisms does not guarantee *koinonia* and *homothumadon*.

manifest" (1 Cor 11:19). How can we identify factions? It is by their primary focus on "issues," and real or imagined grievances, rather than on personal relationships, that is, *koinonia*, first with the Father, Son, and Holy Spirit, then *ad intra* between believers, then *ad extra* in their relationships with non–believers, seeking to draw them into this *koinonia*.

Vis–à–vis synodality, we need to look at the quality of the relationships within the Body of Christ. Do we see in those who deliberate in a synodal situation "works of the flesh" such as "enmity, strife, jealousy, anger, dissension, party spirit, [and] envy" (Gal 5:20–21), or the "fruit of the Spirit": "love, joy, peace, patience, kindness, goodness, faithfulness, gentleness, [and] self–control" (Gal 5:22–23)? We can identify those "tried and true" by looking for brothers and sisters in Christ who bear this fruit, as well as praising and glorifying God together, praying together for the power of the Holy Spirit, evangelising together, serving each other, forgiving each other, bearing each other's burdens, materially supporting each other, and reaching out in compassion to all who are suffering, or ignorant of the Good News.

The danger is that the deliberations of those who primarily focus on "issues" and grievances will come to dominate, since it is a common human tendency for those who have a grievance to speak up while those who are content remain silent. This is another reason for seeking out "affirmations" of and "testimonies" to the work of the Holy Spirit in the church. To discern what the Holy Spirit wishes to say to the church it is necessary to get a clearer picture of what the Holy Spirit is already doing in the church. In essence, this is what Peter did when he reported to the apostles, elders, and brethren, first in the church in Jerusalem, and then at the first "synod" of the church, about how the Holy Spirit had been given to Gentiles just as he had to Jews (Acts 11:1–18, 15:6–11). Such affirmations and testimonies today should not be limited to those of individuals but should especially be testimonies from bodies of believers living *koinonia* and *homothumadon* in some substantial way. Indeed, testimonies could be drawn from those communities, ministries, initiatives, and institutions that can be affirmed as already building up the body of Christ and participating in its mission.

If we are to discern the work of the Holy Spirit, we need to see not just people in *koinonia* and *homothumadon* with their pastors, and pastors who have the "smell of the sheep," but pastors in *koinonia* and *homothumadon* with each other, even to the extent of being willing to practice fraternal correction for the sake of their corporate ministry (Gal 2:11–14). We must look for "living" *koinonia* and *homothumadon* as the ultimate sign of the fruitful action of the Holy Spirit. We need to look for *koinonia* and *homothumadon* in *leitourgia* (worship), *kerygma* (proclamation), *martyria* (witness), and *diakonia* (service), that is, in the priestly, prophetic, and royal mission.[35] We need to look at those who corporately manifest not just a *sensus fidelium*, but also a *sensus sperantium* and a *sensus amantium*. It is to those corporately living out these gifts from God that we should listen with special attentiveness and openness. Coming back to *syn hodos*, we need to attend to those truly "travelling together" in the Spirit. 🅼

Peter J. McGregor teaches dogmatic theology at the Catholic Institute of Sydney and the University of Notre Dame Australia. He is the author of *Heart to Heart: The Spiritual Christology of Joseph Ratzinger*, and an editor of the *Theology at the Beginning of the Third Millennium* series. His research interests include the theology of Joseph Ratzinger, theological anthropology, fundamental theology, postmodern theology, and missiology. He is a member of the Emmanuel Community (*Communauté de l'Emmanuel*), a community of lay people, priests, and consecrated people within the Catholic Church.

---

[35] See Benedict XVI, *Deus Caritas Est*, no. 25, www.vatican.va/content/benedict-xvi/en/encyclicals/documents/hf_ben-xvi_enc_20051225_deus-caritas-est.html.

Joseph-Albert Cardinal Malula and the "Listening Bishop": An Institution to (Re) Discover

Ignace Ndongala Maduku

Abstract: This article presents the device set up around 1978–1979 by Cardinal Malula in the diocese of Kinshasa (DRC) to promote dialogue and listening, which contribute to the emergence of a "culture of dialogue and encounter." In this respect, the "listening bishop" is an approach, state of mind, and participative device that enables the bishop to listen to his collaborators. A positive ritual and rite that celebrates fraternity, this device unfolds as a path of synodality. In this context, I will attempt to show that the innovative device that builds the *consensus ecclesiae* deserves to be rediscovered and restored, in order to adapt it to the evolution of urban pastoral care.

A Synodal church is a church which listens, which realizes that listening "is more than simply hearing." It is a mutual listening in which everyone has something to learn.[1]

IT IS A COMMONPLACE TO ASSERT THAT THE SECOND VATICAN Council laid the foundations of a synodal church in a perspective adjoining a universalist approach to the church.[2] Anxious to promote collaboration between the baptized, the last council provided for bodies meant to concretize synodality at the local level (diocesan synod, presbyteral council, college of consultors, chapter of canons, and pastoral council), regional (provinces and ecclesiastical regions, particular councils, and episcopal conferences), and universal (ecumenical council and synod of bishops). This article focuses specifically on the context of the Archdiocese of Kinshasa in the Democratic Republic of Congo (DRC). It is a journey as much

---

[1] Pope Francis, "Address Commemorating the 50th Anniversary of the Institution of the Synod of Bishops," October 17, 2015. See also *Evangelii Gaudium*, nos. 16, 32.
[2] Hervé Legrand, "Les évêques, les Églises locales, et l'Église entière. Évolutions institutionnelles depuis Vatican II et chantiers actuels de recherche," *Revue des sciences philosophiques et théologiques* 85, no. 3 (2001): 228.

historical, theological, sociological, and institutional on a participatory collaboration device set up by Cardinal Joseph-Albert Malula. One of its objectives is to report on the synodal process in the diocese of Kinshasa, by highlighting the potential of the "listening bishop" device for the ecclesial commitment of the faithful men and women, the sharing of their responsibilities in a spirit of fraternity, and the emergence of a synodal church.

In this perspective, as a preliminary, I will present some considerations on Malula; then I will briefly develop the pastoral history of the archdiocese of Kinshasa before indicating the articulations of the device of the "listening bishop"; finally, I will situate this device in relation to synodality. By structuring my conclusions around the ecclesiological challenges of this innovation, I will show why, as the title of my article indicates, this device deserves to be revisited and updated. Indeed, as I will attempt to establish, the "listening bishop" was an empirical implementation of synodality which, in line with the last Council, contributed to the emergence in Kinshasa of a dialogical and fraternal church of the children of God open to dialogue and listening, a place of participation and complementarity that enhances baptismal grace, a site for the development of a just partnership and differentiated communion between the baptized.

MALULA, AN AUTHENTIC AND FREE BISHOP IN THE HEART OF THE AFRICAN CONTINENT

Born in 1917, Joseph-Albert Malula died in 1989. Ordained a priest in 1946, he was appointed bishop in 1959 and created Cardinal in 1969.[3] Trained by the Scheut missionaries in four different locations (Léopoldville, Kabwe, Mbata Kiela, Bolongo), Malula made cultural diversity an integral part of his career. As a result, he distinguished himself as much by welcoming difference as by promoting the differentiated equality of God's people. As a mobilizing value of his episcopate, fraternity[4] watered the boldness of his pastoral options,

---

[3] Malula did not attend university. His profile and intellectual influence have earned him two honorary doctorates from the Katholiek Universiteit Leuven (1979) and Boston University (1980) respectively. Among the important responsibilities he assumed are the presidency of the Episcopal Conference of Zaire (1979–1984), the presidency of the Symposium of Episcopal Conferences of Africa and Madagascar SECAM (1984), and the delegated presidency of the Extraordinary Synod (1985). On his biography: Jean-Claude Loba Mkole, "Joseph Malula: 1917 to 1989," *Journal of African Christian Biography* 2, no. 1 (2017): 13–15.

[4] The following brief reflections on fraternity summarize the more extensive developments I have published, notably in Ignace Ndongala Maduku, *Religion et politique en RD Congo. Marche des chrétiens et paroles des évêques catholiques sur les élections* (Paris: Karthala, 2016), 83–97; Ignace Ndongala Maduku, "Des relations

particularly the fight for Congo's independence, Africanization of the church and Christian life,[5] inculturation of liturgy[6] and religious life,[7] structuring of Christian lay militancy,[8] institution of lay ministries,[9] pastoral care of intellectuals,[10] defense of distributive justice, emancipation of women,[11] decentralization of the diocese of Kinshasa,

---

'ndekologiques'. Un néologisme peu connu de l'Abbé J.-A. Malula. Variations autour de la fraternité," *Telema* no. 1 (2016): 23–37, Ignace Ndongala Maduku, "L'Église de Dieu qui est à Kinshasa (1979–1989). Contribution à l'étude de l'image de l'Église-fraternité," in *Théologiens et théologiennes dans l'Afrique d'aujourd'hui*, ed. M. Cheza and G. van't Spijker (Paris-Yaoundé: Karthala-Clé, 2007), 183–202.

[5] Joseph Cardinal Malula, "The Church at the Hour of Africanization," *AFER* 16, no. 3 (1974): 365–371.

[6] The synodality experienced in the diocese of Kinshasa has had an impact on liturgical life, with Malula's *missa cum populo* among the projects that would make up the Roman Missal for the dioceses of Zaire. On the importance of the Zairean rite of Mass for Catholicity, see Rita Mboshu Kongo, *Papa Francesco e il 'Messale Romano per le Diocesi dello Zaire'. Un rito promettente per altre culture* (Vatican: Libreria Editrice Vaticana, 2020); Ignace Ndongala Maduku, Job Mwana-Kitata, Flavien Muzumanga, eds., *Le rite zaïrois de la messe en République démocratique du Congo. Hommage posthume au Révérend Père Laurent Mpongo Mpoto Mamba, cicm* (Paris: L'Harmattan, 2023).

[7] Malula took the initiative of having the nuns of his congregation wear a habit of traditional African dress. The practice has become widespread throughout Congo to the point of affecting all countries of the Black Continent.

[8] Isidore Ndaywel È Nziem, *Nouvelle histoire du Congo. De l'héritage ancien à la République démocratique du Congo* (Bruxelles: De Boeck and Larcier, 1998), 514. See also Jaap van Slageren, "Les laïcs dans une Église d'Afrique: l'œuvre du Cardinal Malula (1917–1989)," *Exchange* 42, no 1 (2013): 118–119.

[9] Although there is a shortage of priests in Kinshasa, Malula justifies the institution of lay ministries by emphasizing baptismal grace and the differentiated equality of God's people. See Joseph Malula, *Œuvres complètes du Cardinal Malula*, ed. Léon de Saint Moulin (Kinshasa: Facultés catholiques de Kinshasa, 1997).

[10] Malula, "Homélie à l'ouverture de la Ve Semaine des intellectuels catholiques," in *Œuvres Complètes*, vol. 6, 269. See J. J. Carney, "The People Bonded Together by Love: Eucharistic Ecclesiology and Small Christian Communities in Africa," *Modern Theology* 30, no 2, (2014): 300–318.

[11] A protagonist of Christian homes as places for the maturing of faith and the emergence of the church, Malula was involved in the emancipation of women. Around 1964, he founded a congregation of diocesan nuns whose mission was to form well-rounded women, first through a fully human formation, then through a fully religious one. Malula, who longed for well-educated, free, and responsible girls of good character, emotionally balanced and capable of leading themselves—in short, authentic girls—created the High school Marie-Thérèse (Motema Mpiko) in 1968 for the training of Congolese women. The project to ensure the official voice of Catholic women through prominent, committed, and democratically elected Christian women from living ecclesial communities led to the creation of the *Mamans catholiques* movement. Malula's vision of this movement was an apostolic organization for women's liberation. It was in his eyes the spearhead of the liberation of Zairean women and a place of complementarity, participating in a synodal approach to the church. See Malula, "La vocation particulière de la Congrégation des sœurs de Sainte Thérèse de l'Enfant Jésus selon l'esprit de son fondateur," in *Œuvres Complètes*, vol.

emergence of a united *presbyterium*, commitment to convening an African synod, and constant crossing of past and present in a prospective perspective.

To illustrate the contribution of fraternity as a mobilizing value with a socializing function, a prelude to synodality, Malula developed a constellation of "adaptive" innovations relating to actors and structures. Under Malula, traditional pastoral care centred on religious catechesis and sacramentalization as necessary elements of individual and private salvation was superseded by detailed action to awaken and animate the laity, mobilized to shoulder ecclesial responsibilities in solidarity with priests. In addition, he initiated a shift in Kinshasa's "hierarchical ethos" of closeness and positive politeness, whose contact culture favored titles and social rank, adopting the designation "*ndeko*" (brother, sister) and the greeting *Boboto, bondeko, esengo* (Peace, brotherhood, joy). This reduced the autonomisation of priests and the asymmetry between priests and laypeople, men and women in the diocese of Kinshasa, encapsulated social learning about a different way of interacting with one another, and promoted a participative model based on the imaginary of the church as fraternal community of the baptized. We also see this in structural innovations undertaken by Malula. Indeed, the Archbishop of Kinshasa modeled his diocese through fraternity as a global, structuring value that informs the system of action of the Kinshasa faithful.[12] To socialize Christians to the values of listening, solidarity, collaboration, dialogue, co-responsibility, and discernment, and consequently to promote places for learning deliberative mechanisms and religious requalification of the laity, Malula promoted the division of parishes according to the yardstick of networked sociability.[13] He divided his diocese into three apostolic regions. The richness of Malula's pastoral innovations reinforces the right and duty of all the baptized to participate actively in ecclesial and liturgical life.

This short biography shows that in his thirty years as bishop Malula acted as a founding bishop of the church, giving pride of place to the church's participatory style "in the same way as the Fathers of the first

---

5, 233; Malula, "Mouvement des mamans catholiques, un appel de l'Église locale," in *Œuvres Complètes*, vol. 6, 274.

[12] Many examples could be given with movements and groups structured around fraternity: Bondeko Group, Bondeko Center, Bilenge ya Mwinda, Kizito-Anuarite. On these groups, see Ndongala, *Religion et politique*, 94–95.

[13] Malula created the Living Ecclesial Communities (CEV) and made the small Christian communities the basic pastoral unit. From then on, a parish in the diocese of Kinshasa meant a multitude of CEVs. Thanks to this instance of primary socialization which favored fraternal relations, the laity took charge of many services, some of which would become ministries. See Carney "The People Bonded Together by Love," 300–318.

centuries of the Church."[14] Perceiving the episcopate as a charge, a responsibility before God and humans with the sole perspective of not betraying Africa,[15] he set himself the objective of bringing about "a Congolese Church in a Congolese State."[16] Hence its ambition: to give a truly Congolese face to the mission and therefore "encourage the emergence of an authentically Black-African Church,"[17] which takes on "a truly Congolese face in its theological and philosophical expression, in evangelization, and also in its liturgy."[18] In his eyes, "All the mystery contained in the universal Church is found in the particular Church headed by the bishop."[19] He understands this direction through the titles of doctor, pontiff, and pastor, like the other bishops spread throughout the world.[20]

Many prejudices circulated about his uninhibited approach to the episcopate. It must be recognized that his approach contrasted with the unreasoned obedience of bishops whom, in the text published on the occasion of his twenty years of episcopate, Malula described as "black-skinned Westerners,"[21] these beings still locked up in the modes of Western Christianity,[22] formed according to "absolute and immutable principles, untouchable and applicable to any realities and situations, serving as a universal postulate for everything, an indisputable, axiomatic postulate."[23] With his shocking sentences and innovative pastoral practice, Malula distinguished himself as a bishop whose conception of the church had distanced itself from the pyramidal approach within which he was born and raised.

Indeed, Malula, who experienced a Congolese church renewing the structures and organization of the churches of the metropolis, grew up in a context where the mission was "an expansion of the cultural, political, and economic borders of Christianity."[24] His approach to the Church was neither pyramidal nor clerical. Invested with episcopal responsibilities, he revised downward the centrality of pre-conciliar structures centered around the parish. Of Tridentine inspiration, these centralized structures concentrated all powers in the priest. In doing

---

[14] Joseph Albert Malula, "L'évêque africain aujourd'hui et demain. Réflexions personnelles et méditations de 20 ans d'épiscopat," in Œuvres Complètes, vol. 3, 99.
[15] Malula, "L'évêque africain," 90.
[16] Malula, "Allocution après l'ordination épiscopale le 20 septembre 1959," in Œuvres Complètes, vol. 2, 49.
[17] Malula, "L'Église à l'heure de l'africanité," in Œuvres Complètes, vol. 3, 51.
[18] Malula, "Allocution après l'ordination épiscopale le 20 septembre 1959," 49.
[19] Malula, "L'évêque africain," 91.
[20] Malula, "L'évêque africain," 92.
[21] Malula, "L'évêque africain," 93.
[22] Malula, "L'évêque africain," 93.
[23] Malula, "L'évêque africain," 93.
[24] Giuseppe Alberigo, "Chrétienté et cultures dans l'histoire de l'Église," in Église et histoire de l'Église en Afrique, ed. G. Ruggieri (Paris: Beauchesne, 1988), XIII.

so, they disqualified the laity and reduced the purpose of pastoral ministry to an enterprise of sacramentalization.

Shortly before the Second Vatican Council, in a context dominated by requests in favor of the Africanization of executives and the church, the sixth assembly of the Congolese episcopate had raised the option in favor of the emergence of living communities, committed laity, and adapted liturgy.[25] This openness of the Congolese bishops that the Second Vatican Council endorsed was positively received by the archbishop of Léopoldville, who included it with great ingenuity and inventiveness in an enterprise both of renovation of ecclesial structures and empowerment of lay people and priests. Hence a significant break with societal ecclesiology and the ideology of *Ecclesia societas inaequalis, hierarchica et perfecta*. Turning his back on any monocratic structure that disqualified the laity and empowered priests—and this, I believe, was the most fruitful insight of his episcopate—Malula gave his diocese the contours of a family supported by fraternity rather than organized according to asymmetrical hierarchical relationships. From this ecclesial sociability emerged a fully African church, creative and truly responsible for itself,[26] which has excelled in the inventive reception of the last Council.

FROM CHANGES IN KINSHASA TO UNPRECEDENTED PASTORAL INNOVATIONS: LISTENING AND DIALOGUE AS PASTORAL REQUIREMENTS

Malula's participation in the Second Vatican Council had fueled in him the project of the Africanization of the church. The young bishop of Léopoldville postulated this Africanization through innovation and the quest for new ways for the work of mission. On a societal level, the transition from semi-rural to urban society characteristic of the Congolese capital, to which is added the extension of the city in its extremities, the rural exodus, and the emergence of an authoritarian state led the archbishop of Kinshasa to integrate into his pastoral projects the changes in the Congolese capital and requirements of its political context. The societal and pastoral challenges of its diocese were met thanks to an organizational culture which promoted, on the one hand, the restructuring of parishes into Living Ecclesial Communities and, on the other hand, the decentralization of the

---

[25] See Épiscopat du Congo, *Actes de la 6e Assemblée plénière de l'Épiscopat du Congo. Léopoldville 1961 (20 novembre–2 décembre)* (Léopoldville: Secrétariat Général de l'Épiscopat, 1961).
[26] Malula, "Communication concernant le projet de confier certaines paroisses à des laïcs," in *Œuvres Complètes,* vol. 6, 182.

diocese into three apostolic regions. This underlay the collaboration of the archbishop of Kinshasa with pastoral agents, particularly lay people and, in passing, promoted of the latter.

Along this line, Malula, who wanted to bring about a brotherly church of the children of God, made dialogue and listening the keywords of the pastoral ministry he promoted in Kinshasa. In his opinion:

> Pastor of his diocese, the bishop must ensure that he promotes and develops a spirit of dialogue with all his collaborators. If we want to dialogue, declared the episcopate of Congo in 1967, we must admit as a basic principle that everything is not done at the top, that the Church is also built at the base through adaptation and initiatives. It is through dialogue that the bishop can be properly made aware of the problems of the different categories of his collaborators, that he can arrive at successful solutions to these problems. These solutions themselves must be, as much as possible, taken together.[27]

To include dialogue in the observable functioning and consolidate proximity with the people of God, Malula worked to find optimal listening methods for his diocese. He also initiated the work of mixed priest-lay teams, one of which produced the document *Présence de l'Église dans le Congo d'aujourd'hui*[28] and the brochure *Visage de Kinshasa et problème de pastorale*.[29] Between January 1968 and 1970, the meetings of the priestly council were devoted to reflection on overall pastoral care. A commission was appointed to develop the basic document for the discussions which resulted in the release of *Mission de l'Église à Kinshasa. Options pastorales*.[30] This important document reflects the awareness of the pastoral implications of the God-world-church articulation.[31] It concludes with a resolute stance in favor of revaluing the role of the laity and the need to decentralize action through the development of small, human-scale communities, the *Communautés ecclesiales vivantes* ("Living Ecclesial Communities" [CEV]).[32] It was within these communities that various services emerged as a precursor to the lay ministries established in 1975.[33] In

---

[27] See Malula, "Place du chrétien dans la société et rôle de la hiérarchie," in *Œuvres Complètes*, vol. 6, 34.

[28] Jean Lefebvre, Félix Vundowe, *Présence de l'Église dans le Congo d'aujourd'hui. Réflexion d'une équipe de prêtres et de laïcs* (Kinshasa: s. e., 1968).

[29] Léon de Saint Moulin, *Visage de Kinshasa et problèmes de pastorale* (Kinshasa: CEP, 1969).

[30] Malula, *Mission de l'Église à Kinshasa. Options pastorales* (Kinshasa, 1970).

[31] Malula, *Mission de l'Église,* 8–14.

[32] Malula, *Mission de l'Église,* 15–18 *passim.*

[33] This innovation alone reflects Malula's desire to think outside the box. Indeed, while the Catholic Church is still governed according to the 1917 *Codex iuris canonici*

1974, the Archbishop of Kinshasa went so far as to collect the opinion of the people of his diocese by initiating an investigation into the type of priest to train and the type of training given to seminarians.[34] In 1986, another consultation took place in the form of a competition to find a name for the Diocesan Pastoral Center.[35] From 1986 to 1988, in order to promote expanded participation of the clergy and laity, Malula advocated large-scale consultation through the synod of his diocese. We can therefore note a diversification of structures which fuel dialogue throughout the life of the diocese: structures for dialogue, consultation, collaboration, and sharing. Léon de Saint Moulin lists a few of them: Pastoral Notes, pastoral animation days (inaugurated in 1969 at the Nganda Center), visits, and meetings at the base which gave rise to the publication of the brochure *L'évêque à l'écoute*.[36]

This explains the link Malula established between mutual listening, dialogue, and one of the great achievements of his episcopate: the institution of the ministry of parish assistant, the ministry of pastoral animator, and the *bakambi* ministry.[37] As he says, "responding to the opening made by Paul VI, we wanted to listen to the Spirit by listening to the pastoral needs of the people of God in Kinshasa, and we believed we could experiment, at the level of our diocese, by creating the lay ministry of parish *mokambi*."[38] This shows how much, in its

---

which recognizes only one type of ministry (priestly) and the parish as the basic pastoral unit, Malula established three new lay ministries in his diocese and made the CEV the basic pastoral unit.

[34] Malula, "Préparation des candidats au presbytérat," in *Œuvres Complètes*, vol. 3, 300.

[35] Archidiocèse de Kinshasa, *Centre Pastoral Diocésain Lindonge* (Kinshasa, 1986), 7.

[36] Léon de Saint Moulin, "Biographie du Cardinal Malula," in *Une vie pleinement donnée à Dieu et aux hommes. Hommage au cardinal Malula* (Kinshasa: Archidiocèse de Kinshasa, 1990), 24.

[37] This is the instituted ministry of the lay parish leader, the *mokambi*. This one collaborates with a priest animator. However, the latter is not in charge of the parish. The valorization of baptismal grace here promotes co-responsibility in a synergy that, beyond listening to lay men and women in the church, institutes lay people as active players in building a listening church. See Malula, "Première annonce du projet de confier des paroisses à des ministres laïcs," in *Œuvres Complètes*, vol. 6, 199–181; Malula, "Communication concernant le projet de confier certaines paroisses à des laïcs," 181–182; Malula,"Impressions du Cardinal après la visite canonique des paroisses confiées à des bakambi," in *Œuvres Complètes*, vol. 6, 196–197; Malula, "Homélie à l'occasion du 10e anniversaire de l'institution des premiers ministres laïcs à Kinshasa," in *Œuvres Complètes*, vol. 6, 212–215.

[38] Malula, "Homélie à l'occasion du 10e anniversaire," 213. The link between the Spirit, the bishop, and the needs of the people of God deserves further development which, in my view, provides a coherent explanation for the institution of lay ministries. In this sense, see the general norms and diocesan directives of the diocesan synod (1986–1988) on the formation and apostolate of the laity and non-ordained ministries. See "Synode diocésain (1986–1988). Options et directives," in *Œuvres Complètes*, vol. 4, 171–174.

genesis as well as in its institution, the lay ministry was a synodal approach favoring listening to the needs of the people of God and promoting collaboration between men and women, laity and clergy.

It appears from the above that to better listen to the needs of his diocese, Malula resolutely advocated dialogue by listening to the Spirit through listening to the Word of God, which depended on listening to the pastoral needs of the people of God in Kinshasa.[39] It insinuated a renewed approach to the articulation of the relationship between Spirit, episcopate, and people of God. It conceives of listening not in an abstract way but from concrete realities, in this case the pastoral needs of the people of God and Congolese society. We see an opening emerging here not by disjunction, but conjunction. It does not proceed from definitions of the hierarchy, but through reception of the needs defined by the people of God, needs received by the hierarchy as motions of the Spirit. We see, by correlating listening to the needs of the people of God with listening to the motions of the Spirit, Malula recognized the ability of the people of God to know their needs and express them.[40] Consequently, he defined the task of the hierarchy as that of listening not to itself, but to the people of God and thus to the Spirit.[41] He invented an institution to match this new articulation of the relationship between Spirit, episcopate, and people of God: the "listening bishop."

THE "LISTENING BISHOP": A DIALOGIC, PARTICIPATORY, AND CONSULTATIVE DEVICE WITH SYNODAL SCOPE

For a good understanding of what will follow, it is appropriate to note that the episcopate of Malula remains marked by his understanding of the differentiated equality of the people of God and propensity to draw effective consequences from it in practice by promoting fraternity. It is in the name of this mobilizing value that Malula takes the opposite view of the conception of a church *societas perfecta, hierarchica et inaequalis*. It goes beyond the distinction between the "sacredness" of ministers and the "secularity" of the laity.[42] He therefore sees the mission of the church as a common work of members of the same family: the people of God (bishops, priests, religious, lay Christians). It is by counting on the collaboration of

---

[39] Here I note the convergence with Pope Francis, who also favors listening to the people of God, the place where, according to him, the voice of Christ resounds through the Spirit. See Pape François, *Un temps pour changer* (Paris: Flammarion, 2020), 126.
[40] Malula, "Lettre à mes collaborateurs et collaboratrices no. 5," 177.
[41] Malula, "Place du chrétien," 34.
[42] On the aporias of the last council concerning this point, see Christoph Theobald, *Un nouveau concile qui ne dit pas son nom ? Le synode sur la synodalité, voie de pacification et de créativité* (Paris: Salvator, 2023).

these different actors that he intends to "promote the emergence of an authentically Black-African Church,"[43] "a fully African Church of Kinshasa: therefore dynamic, creative, and truly responsible for itself."[44] The expressions "authentically Black-African," "fully African," "truly responsible for itself" have all their importance here: in fact, they postulate a renewal of the means of the mission (*leiturgia, martyria, diakonia, oikodomé, koinonia*). Taken up in line with fraternity following the fundamental equality of the people of God, they are accompanied by the pastoral option of:

> Going towards the people of God . . . to bridge the gaps that still separate us from them . . . meet him where he is . . . listen to him to know him, because the Good Shepherd knows his sheep. Go to him to be with him. . . . Be with him to share his joys . . . his sorrows . . . his anxieties . . . clarify his doubts . . . try out his plans . . . appreciate and encourage his efforts. . . . Excuse his weaknesses.[45]

Beyond the inherent predisposition of the episcopal office, the resolute choice of the archbishop of Kinshasa was a prelude to a church on the move, or rather, to a peregrination of the church on the margins. This pilgrimage of the bishop was accompanied by an attitude which placed him in a posture of welcome and listening giving voice to the base. The approach which celebrated fraternity was driven by this conviction encountered above: "The Church is also built from the ground up through adaptation and initiatives."[46] This conviction in turn carried a spirit reflective of the Malula style.[47] It was experienced as a conjunction of views, combination of thoughts, pooling of expertise, and conspiracy of voices. This was what the institution of the "listening bishop" reported from 1978 onwards.[48]

As the name chosen by Malula clearly indicates, the "listening bishop" is at the same time an approach, a state of mind, and an institutional, discursive, and participatory device which places the bishop in the posture of listening to his collaborators, notably the pastoral agents, *bakambi*, priests, and nuns of a deanery. In successive stages Malula specified his expectations and explained the purpose of

---

[43] Malula, "L'Église à l'heure de l'africanité," in *Œuvres Complètes,* vol. 3, 51.

[44] Malula, "Communication concernant le projet de confier certaines paroisses à des laïcs," 182.

[45] Malula, "Lettre à mes collaborateurs," 177.

[46] Malula, "Place du chrétien dans la société et rôle de la hiérarchie," in *Œuvres Complètes,* vol. 6, 34.

[47] I understand style in the sense in which Pope Paul VI uses this term. See *La Documentation catholique,* 1622 (1972): 1104–1105.

[48] The "listening bishop" institution operated in the diocese of Kinshasa from 1978 to 1979.

the bishop's meetings with his collaborators as a way to, on the one hand, keep in touch with the base, the problems specific to each deanery and general problems of the diocese and, on the other hand, seek with them answers in line with the major options of the overall pastoral care of the diocese. It was also the time to establish and strengthen bonds of fraternity with all agents of evangelization and ecclesiastical personnel.[49] The insistence on the "base" made this colloquium a means of "establishing a fruitful dialogue"[50] and collecting news, concerns, orientations, projects, problems, expectations, wishes, and questions from the base. It was also the occasion where the bishop reported on his travels and participation in conferences or symposia.[51]

As a practice of communication, the "listening bishop" is also a material device, a ritual, and a positive rite which celebrates fraternity (*bondeko*) and expresses the "dialogical and fraternal" identity of the Church of Kinshasa. The latter tended to become a fraternity of the children of God.[52] Its normative logic made it a meeting of *bandeko* (brothers and sisters), which unfolded in three sequences: the pre-meeting, meeting, and post-meeting. The deanery which received the bishop prepared for the event.[53] The pastoral agents sharpened their questions in Lingala or French, prepared the themes which would be submitted for debate. Everything was coordinated by the dean priest responsible for welcoming the bishop and his delegation. When the assembly began, after the welcome formalities, the Cardinal addressed a preliminary word, then set out the subject to be debated (retained by the pastoral agents). The bishop or his collaborators answered questions from pastoral agents. At the end of the meeting, the bishop thanked the participants. After the meeting, the device being

---

[49] Malula, "Doyenné de Saint Joseph," in *Œuvres Complètes*, vol. 4, 66. At the deanery of Saint Martin, he specifies the aim of these meetings as being "to allow us to listen to what is happening at the base in order to be able to better guide the entire diocesan pastoral ministry." See Malula, "Doyenné de Saint Martin," in *Œuvres Complètes*, vol. 4, 75.

[50] Malula, "Doyenné de Saint Alphonse," in *Œuvres Complètes*, vol. 4, 78.

[51] Malula "Doyenné de Saint Martin," 76. Malula reports on the symposium of bishops of Africa and Madagascar in which he had just participated.

[52] On this image which I consider characteristic of the ecclesiology of Cardinal Malula, see Ignace Ndongala Maduku, "L'Église de Dieu qui est à Kinshasa (1979–1989). Une *fraternitas quaerens*. Contribution à l'étude de l'image de l'Église-fraternité," in *Épistémologie et théologie. Les Enjeux du dialogue foi-science-éthique pour l'avenir de l'humanité. Mélanges en l'honneur de son Excellence Mgr Tharcisse Tshibangu Tshishiku pour ses 70 ans d'âge et 35 ans d'épiscopat*, ed. L. Santedi Kinkupu and M. Malu (Kinshasa: Facultés catholiques de Kinshasa, 2006), 517–530.

[53] A study of the layout of the premises where the meeting took place, the proxemics deployed, the dramaturgy of the assembly, in short the spatial circumscription of the place and distribution of speech and its exchange remains to be done.

discursive, the bishop began to write down the written transcription of the exchange published in the brochure *L'Évêque à l'écoute*.[54]

The "listening bishop" was therefore at the same time a structure, a device,[55] a time of conviviality, a brochure, a concrete process, a meeting, a structure for dialogue, a moment of communion where the word circulates and allows a revision, a forecast, and a provision of evangelization.[56] It is important to note that this was concretely a dialogic exchange which was neither protocol nor derogation from mutual respect. It mobilized the pastoral agents of a deanery who, using freedom of speech, discussed with their bishop various themes they had previously chosen. With this device, the Congolese Cardinal seized the common interpretation of events with the aim of laying the foundations of the new Congolese Catholic Church.[57] He learned from the *doxa* of his collaborators and retained the common stock of their knowledge and experience. Attentive to the signs of the times, he integrated the sharing of information and debated ideas with pastoral agents in the development of pastoral directives. In this way, an organizational culture was born open to the collaborative construction of consensus on pastoral and societal issues.[58]

---

[54] Here, the bishop commits his authority. Consequently, his function of government is open to the participation of the people of God, with a view to pooling the contributions of lay people and priests. The question of how the personal and collegial exercise of the bishop's authority relates to the synodal exercise of discernment by the ecclesial community remains unanswered. In addition, the written version of the exchanges is not, however, discussed or submitted for assessment by the pastoral agents. No place or time is provided where they can express their dissent or criticism of possible selections, censorship, or reformulations. It nevertheless remains certain that the brochure has a positive impact on pastoral agents and stimulates their participation and commitment to ecclesial living together. A reflection on the popularization of the brochure at the CEV level would have enabled the entire diocese to benefit from the achievements of this device.

[55] With this notion of device, I would like to emphasize the aim of efficiency, optimizing the conditions for realizing communion in a perspective that values baptismal grace and promotes the conjunction of the knowledge and charisms of the people of God.

[56] Malula, "Doyenné de Saint Martin," 75.

[57] Malula, "Doyenné de Saint François," 72.

[58] The themes covered touch on the various areas of mission (*leiturgia, martyria, diakonia, oikodome*, and *koinonia*). Here are just a few of the topics discussed: lay formation, irregular couples, the role of the priest and the nun in covenant schools, appointment of a pastoral coordinator, shortage of priests, church-state relations, overworked priests, lay responsibility in parishes, laxity of Christians for communion, information on the construction of the major seminary, the life of the priest as witness, competence of parish commissions, admission of babies to baptism, admission to first communion, seminary and diocesan sisters, *bakambi* suggestion on the sacrament of the sick, CEV and *bakambi* training, schools and parishes, ecumenism, *Bilenge ya mwinda*, finances, non-geographical base communities, pastoral note on sacraments in Kinshasa, current material situation, family pastoral, school problems, sacraments,

The "listening bishop," however, did not empower the archbishop or establish him as a source of knowledge. The interaction allowed him to discover the practical and discursive performances of pastoral agents. They had the initiative of themes and order of the interactions. They participated in developing the bishop's responses. The posture of the bishop was that of listening in a "collective activity" which opened the space for discussion by granting speech to pastoral agents. According to the issues on the agenda, the skills of the auxiliary bishops and those of the bishop's other immediate collaborators were called upon. Malula gave them the floor to shed light on the problems that fell within their areas of responsibility.[59]

The name "listening bishop" clearly describes the structure of the device whose order, scenography, and grammar were a constructive exchange in a collective debate centered on the church to be built and pastoral care to be developed for a new society.[60] Obviously, thanks to this institution, Malula as a pastor was not disconnected from the reality of his diocese nor its localities. The latter were integrated into the development of pastoral care which now relied on the contribution of those on the ground. The inductive approach favored the interaction of the bishop with priests and lay people in ecclesial responsibility, allowing him to better understand the situation of the evangelizers and those evangelized. With professionalism, the archbishop of Kinshasa expanded the tent of each deanery by opening its horizon to overall pastoral care. The pastoral problems of a deanery were therefore put into perspective in a quest for answers which interests and concerns the entire diocese. The answers to the questions, although detailed and contextualized, were always in line with the overall pastoral care to be promoted.

Devoid of arguments of authority and any display of force or power, avoiding clericalism, the dialogue here was also fraternal. On this subject, we note the emergence of this clear awareness in Malula's eyes that the "listening bishop" is not an answer box nor a divinatory authority. More than once, the Cardinal opened the possibility of a

---

Mama Yemo hospital chaplaincy, river apostolate, school questions, various problems. The range of themes is an invitation to go further in the study of their inclusion in the Pastoral Letters, directives, in short, the doctrinal teaching and pastoral practices of the bishop of Kinshasa.

[59] At the deanery of Saint-François, on January 9, 1979, Msgr. Moke and Mr. Nkuili, diocesan and regional coordinator of Catholic approved schools in Kinshasa, answered questions. See Malula, "Doyenné de Saint Martin," 72. The same happened on January 12, 1979, at the deanery of Saint-Alphonse. See Malula, "Doyenné de Saint Alphonse," 78. At the deanery of Sainte-Anne, he is accompanied by Msgr. Moke and the vicar general, Fr. De Schaetzen. See Malula, "Doyenné de Sainte Anne," 83.

[60] Malula, "Doyenné de Saint Alphonse," 69.

subsequent deepening of the problems posed.[61] Consequently, the exchange constituted the breeding ground for several Pastoral Letters which were either answers to the questions raised, or reflections on the words exchanged. By promoting respect for the authority of the bishop in the distinction and complementarity of skills, this device allowed subsidiarity between laity and priests. As such, it carried what I call a co-construction of pastoral care.[62] This became like a variegated mat woven by all the baptized.

The organizational style and the institutional rite of this device rendered it a convivial ritual of proximity, a true symbolic space-time which allowed participants to experience emotional and effective communion. The time devoted to dialogue, exchange on pastoral questions produced the church as a family and gave substance to ecclesial fraternity. Ultimately, the "listening bishop" participated in the emergence of a "culture of dialogue and encounter" which unfolded as a journey of synodality.

THE "LISTENING BISHOP": A JOURNEY OF SYNODALITY

Since the first millennium, synodality has been seen as a constitutive dimension of the church.[63] The vision of a synodal church developed by Pope Francis refers to a journey that involves lay people, pastors, the bishop of Rome, and believers. According to my analysis, there is a striking convergence between Pope Francis and Cardinal Malula. The two prelates see in the baptized, members of the Body of Christ who participate in the prophetic function of Christ. What is more, they combine communion, participation, and mission.[64] In the eyes of Pope Francis, the synodal path opens by listening to the people and continues by listening to the pastors.[65] To these points of convergence, we can add Malula's option to mobilize pastors to listen to the Spirit's motions through the needs of God's people, and the path he opened with the institution of the "listening bishop."

---

[61] Regarding the problem of irregular couples, the cardinal affirms that "we should therefore wait for the next General Assemblies of SECAM, where we will talk about family life and the Episcopate of Zaire which will deal with marriage and the couple, to know the thought of the bishops." See Malula, "Doyenné de Saint Pierre," 57. The theological problem of the communion of Christians in an irregular situation raised at the Saint-François deanery would give rise to a pastoral letter. The exchange initiated at the Saint Alphonse deanery on the life of the priest as testimony would end with the development of a spiritual directory of the clergy.
[62] I borrow this notion from Michel Foudriat, *La co-construction : une alternative managériale* (Paris: Éditions des Hautes Études en Sciences Politiques, 2019).
[63] Pope Francis, "Discours du 17 octobre 2015," *Documentation catholique* 1521 (2016): 78. See also *Evangelii Gaudium*, nos. 16 and 32.
[64] *Preparatory Document, Synod 2021–2024*, no. 1.
[65] Malula, "Homélie à l'occasion du 10ᵉ anniversaire," 213.

Indeed, through this institution, the church of God which stays in Kinshasa, by concentric and proximal levels (CEV, parishes, deaneries), listens to God to hear the cry of his people, in order to give him a corresponding response. In line with dialogical fraternity, openness to subsidiarity, and respect for the delegation of powers, the construction of pastoral knowledge and reflection on pastoral practice become a co-elaboration, co-construction of meaning, a way of weaving the mat of pastoral care with, by, and in the community. The dialogical fraternity discovered there is a journey of synodality, an ecclesial itinerancy made of learning, which on a few occasions, crosses human roads made of joys, trials, anxieties, and hopes (GS 1). It engages the people of God in a walk together which discovers a different face of the church: a church listening to the Spirit, a church listening to reality and at the forefront of the challenges and opportunities of the hour, a church listening to the cry of the African.[66]

Returning to apprenticeships, it is worth noting that in line with the active participation of the whole people of God and subsidiarity, they are likely to promote, as Hervé Legrand has suggested, "subject Churches and Churches of subjects of rights and initiatives."[67]

The church of Malula did not wander; the path it took was marked out. Well before the diocesan synod he convened from 1986 to 1988, Malula had initiated a synodal dynamic which allowed the people of his diocese to walk together and build a fraternity of the children of God. As we have seen, the synodal road blazed with and by the people of God under the aegis of Malula, the "listening bishop" demonstrated the synodality of the church, built pastoral co-responsibility, and promoted fraternal consensus matched with the *consensus ecclesiae*. The realization of synodality through this device has bequeathed to the Church of Kinshasa "the necessary framework for an authentically African Church: responsible and committed laity, spiritually solid, intellectually strong and pastorally committed priests, . . . authentically African and authentically religious, effective structures (CEVB, deaneries, apostolic regions, Lindonge Pastoral Center, Listening Bishop) and viable institutions (spirituality movements, Catholic action movements)."[68]

---

[66] Jean-Marc Ela, *Le cri de l'homme africain. Questions aux Églises d'Afrique* (Paris: L'Harmattan, 1981).
[67] Hervé Legrand, "Pour une Église synodale et fraternelle," in *Transformer l'Église. Quelques propositions à la lumière de* Fratelli Tutti, ed. M. Camdessus (Paris: Bayard, 2020), 106. See also *Evangelii Gaudium*, no. 120.
[68] Tharcisse Tshibangu Tshishiku, "Préface, " in *Universalité de l'Église catholique et réalisation d'une Église africaine. La pensée et l'œuvre du Cardinal J.-A. Malula. À l'occasion du Centenaire de sa naissance (1917–2017)*, ed. Ignace Ndongala Maduku (Kinshasa: Médiaspaul, 2020), 4.

SOME ECCLESIOLOGICAL REFLECTIONS TO CONCLUDE

The episcopate of Cardinal Malula is suggestive in more than one way. First, there is the Zairian rite of the Mass of which he was one of the instigators, a rite Pope Francis considers promising for other cultures.[69] Then there is the ministry of lay parish leader which remains suggestive for Christian communities. Finally, there is the device of the "listening bishop" here under study.

This paper has highlighted the achievements of the "listening bishop" initiative. The scope of this device has contributed to the emergence in Kinshasa of a church fraternity of God's children, a place of participation and complementarity that enhances the value of baptismal grace, a site for the development of a just partnership and differentiated communion between the baptized: laity and priests, men and women. The overall purpose of this article confirms my initial claim that the "listening bishop" was a concrete expression of synodality that deserves to be reappropriated. Precisely, the scope of this device is important in ecclesiology. First, it illustrates the correlation between ecclesiology and pastoral care and verifies the axiom which attests that "one always has the pastoral care of one's ecclesiology."[70] Then, it poses the need to find inculturated institutions which translate into identifiable functioning the ecclesiology of the last council. As we know, the Second Vatican Council imposed itself on Malula as a source of inspiration he put into dialogue with African traditions.

Broadly speaking, I could say that the "listening bishop" resonates with an understanding of the church's communion perceived and experienced as a fraternity of the children of God. It remains a Congolese way of making the regime promoted by the last council a reality. By building knowledge through the conjunction of voices and pooling of skills, its dialogical, participatory dynamic draws on the tradition of the African palaver. It attenuates the pyramidal aspect of the church and promotes consensus-building by overcoming the top-down approach to relations between pastoral protagonists. Articulated with doctrinal achievements on the baptismal equality of the people of God, this device fulfilled both the mission of the presbyteral and pastoral councils (*Lumen Gentium*, nos. 30, 37; *Apostolicam Actuositatem*, no. 10; *Christus Dominus*, no. 27, can. 495; can. 511–514), who struggled to work in Kinshasa and became bogged down in bureaucracy and legalism. It has become institutionalized as a participation structure matched to overall pastoral care, respectful of

---

[69] Mboshu, *Papa Francesco*, 3–6.
[70] Bernard Lambert, "Orientations nouvelles de la pastorale," in *La nouvelle image de l'Église. Bilan du concile Vatican II*, ed. Bernard Lambert (Paris: Mame, 1967), 335.

the "one-all-some" dialectic[71] and provider of a new organizational culture and ecclesial action based on complementarity and subsidiarity. The "listening bishop" functioned as an ecclesial institution deploying ecclesial synodality and placing the bishop in a posture of listening to his base.

This institution can be said to have been for Malula a permanent reminder favoring the pastoral requirement of "being with" and "going towards" the people of God. The bishop goes to recharge his batteries at the base. He leaves his office to meet people and reality. He is on a quest, he puts himself in a position of investigation and collects requests from the people of his diocese, particularly those on the ground. Embarking on this path of "going forth" defines an epistemological posture which consists of unlearning one's ecclesial culture and learning from the experience of the people of God. The innovative approach which builds the *ecclesiae consensus* also invented a new mode of collaboration which builds overall pastoral care based on the realities of the different deaneries. Even better: it was based on a new form of communication adapted to the changes in the city of Kinshasa. In a sense, one of its major contributions was to deploy the transition from the pyramidal organization to the decentralized circle in a logic which led to the reduction of the autonomisation of the hierarchy. Under these conditions, the people of God saw their status change thanks to a dynamic and interdependent interaction which promoted the development of their skills and pastoral performance against a backdrop of overcoming duality and the priest-laity compartmentalization. By shedding the comfort of authority to open up to a dialogic fraternity, better to "an authority of fraternity," Malula opened himself to subsidiarity and respect for the delegation of powers. He embarked on this path by focusing on the *sensus fidei*,[72] charisma, human potential, and expertise of his collaborators.

---

[71] Omnipresent in the New Testament and the institutions of the early church, the articulation "one, all, some" correlates the personal, collegial, and communitarian modes of leadership in the church. It indicates the interactivity and interdependence of all members in ecclesial responsibility in the line of synodal life. For more on this articulation, see Hervé Legrand, "Les évêques, les Églises locales, et l'Église entière. Évolutions institutionnelles depuis Vatican II et chantiers actuels de recherche," *Revue des sciences philosophiques et théologiques* 85 (2001): 461–509; Hervé Legrand, "Le rôle des communautés locales dans l'appel, l'envoi, la réception, et le soutien des laïcs recevant une charge ecclésiale," *La Maison Dieu* 215, no. 3 (1998): 9–32.

[72] For more on this topic, see International Theological Commission, *Sensus Fidei in the Life of the Church*, no. 2.

The "listening bishop" promoted co-responsibility between the bishop and the faithful of his diocese[73] from a perspective of "participatory democracy." It has contributed to the participation of the laity, especially women, in doctrinal teaching and pastoral decisions, fulfilling one of the normative expectations of the archbishop of Kinshasa, in particular that carried by the articulation of Spirit, episcopate, and people of God: the advent of a church fraternity of the children of God in Kinshasa, in which the equality in principle of the faithful as affirmed is not abstract. It was lived concretely as a request to take advantage of ecclesial subsidiarity in a differentiated way through diversification and complementarity of ministries, and taking into account the participation and needs of God's people and their *sensus fidei*.[74] The synodal vision of the people of God at the root of this device opened to the discovery of pastoral capacities, to the discernment of varied charisms and consolidated mechanisms of interaction and collective dynamics. As such, it constituted an institutional opening in the conciliar vein which Malula, without ignoring the system of councils promoted by Vatican II (presbyteral and pastoral councils), updates, structures and experiments with in the line of a fraternal concertation of the whole people of God.

The institution of the "listening bishop" functioned as an organizational system articulated around pastoral agents (*bakambi*, priests, nuns) and a supra-parochial structure, the deanery. We can immediately see one of its limitations, namely the exclusion of a fringe of the people of God. Here again, we can see how its revival today would include not only other lay people with ecclesial responsibilities at CEV, parish, deanery, and diocesan levels, but also those with no responsibilities at all. If we look closely, such a revival requires the contribution of canonists to determine *de iure condendo* the status of this device devoid of any decision-making power. We must recognize, as Legrand does, that "synodality will remain an intention until Canon Law institutionalizes it."[75] It would also accommodate revisions to its operation. Its rebirth would place the diocese of Kinshasa in a permanent synodal dynamic and make it an outgoing church, a listening church, in short, a synodal church involving the people of God in the *munus propheticum* of Christ. That other local churches can draw inspiration from the experience of the diocese of Kinshasa is obvious and needs no comment. Taking everything into consideration,

---

[73] See in this sense especially, Jean-Paul Durand, "La synodalité des Églises particulières. Fondements théologiques et application juridique," *Teka kom. Praw.-OL PAN* (2014): 21–33.

[74] Christoph Theobald, "*Sensus fidei fidelium*. Enjeux d'avenir d'une notion classique," *Revue de sciences religieuses* 104, no. 2 (2016): 228.

[75] Camdessus, ed., *Transformer l'Église*, 112.

can we not see in the potential of this device a pastoral council that does not speak its name?[76] This would be on the condition of not making it autonomous, but of putting it in complementary connection with other participation devices. ■

Ignace Ndongala Maduku is associate professor at the Institute of Religious Studies of Université de Montréal in Canada and visiting professor at the Centre International Lumen Vitae in Belgium. His current research in theology and religious studies focuses on the episcopate of Cardinal Joseph-Albert Malula, the theological work of Jean-Marc Ela, and the decolonization of theological knowledge and priestly masculinities.

---

[76] I am inspired by the title of the recent book by Christoph Theobald, cited in note 42.

Academic Listening Practices and Synodality: Reflections from a Study of World Youth Days

Charles Mercier

Abstract: In order to analyze the possible contribution of academic listening practices to the synodal process, this article offers a reflexive analysis of two social science studies of World Youth Days. The first investigation is a historical work carried out between 2017 and 2020 on John Paul II's World Youth Days, based on archives and testimonies collected in seven different countries. The second is a sociological and anthropological study carried out in July-August 2023 on the occasion of the WYD in Lisbon: as part of a delegation of pilgrims, the author experienced the pilgrimage in Portugal among the young people and their chaplains, while carrying out research work. At the crossroads of epistemological reflection and life review, the paper presents the opportunities and risks of such empirical research from the viewpoints of the researcher, respondents, and Catholic institution. While highlighting misunderstandings that can arise, the article emphasizes the mutual enrichment academic listening practices in a church setting can bring. If the researcher and researched agree to let go of their rigidities, their companionship can purify both faith and science by desacralizing what should not be sacred.

MOST OF THE PASSENGERS ON THE BUS ARE BETWEEN seventeen and thirty years old. What they have in common is a fifteen-hour journey from Bordeaux (south-western France) to Portugal, where they will participate in the Thirty-Seventh World Youth Day (WYD). As the bus approaches the Spanish border, and after several religious and secular songs have already been sung, one of the young priests accompanying the delegation begins an ice-breaking activity. He asks those studying literature to raise their hands and introduce themselves, then does the same with those studying science, medicine, law, those who already have a job or are looking for one. At the end, he points out that there are two specific individuals on the bus, whom he jokingly refers to as "spies," highly recognizable because they are older than average: a journalist from a Christian radio station, who has come to cover the WYD, and myself. Invited to speak at the microphone, I explain that I am here as a "participant observer," being a professor of modern history at Bordeaux, who has studied John Paul II's WYDs and who would like to analyze those of Pope Francis, through the edition that will take place in Lisbon. I am interested not only in the organization of the event, but also in the identity of its participants; in fact, I would like to interview them. I finish my impromptu speech by thanking the heads of the delegation who agreed to include me in the pilgrimage.

This anecdote illustrates the ambivalence with which academic listening is perceived within Catholicism. In this paper, I would like to analyze the opportunities and risks of social science methods for a synodal church, which Pope Francis defined with these words:

> A synodal Church is a Church which listens, which realizes that listening "is more than simply hearing." It is a mutual listening in which everyone has something to learn. The faithful people, the college of bishops, the Bishop of Rome: all listening to each other, and all listening to the Holy Spirit, the "Spirit of truth," in order to know what he "says to the Churches."[1]

As a result, this article does not present the data collected during my WYDs surveys. The reader will not find detailed information about the preparation and execution of World Youth Days, nor about the profile of the people who organize and participate in it. I invite those interested to refer to my previous publications on WYDs, which deal with three topics concentrically embedded: the first is WYD itself, as a mega-event[2] part of the globalization process[3] and the history of international relations.[4] The second is a study of WYDs as they shed light on the Catholic Church as a system,[5] providing a glimpse of its

---

[1] Pope Francis, "Ceremony Commemorating the 50th Anniversary of the Institution of the Synod of Bishops," October 17, 2015, www.vatican.va/content/francesco/en/speeches/2015/october/documents/papa-francesco_20151017_50-anniversario-sinodo.html.
[2] Charles Mercier, L'Église, les jeunes, et la mondialisation: une histoire des JMJ (Montrouge: Bayard, 2020).
[3] Charles Mercier, "Religion and the Contemporary Phase of Globalization: Insights from a Study of John Paul II's World Youth Days," *Journal of World History* 33, no. 2 (June 2022): 1–30.
[4] Charles Mercier, "Les Journées mondiales de la jeunesse, objet d'une nouvelle histoire diplomatique," *Bulletin de l'Institut Pierre Renouvin* 53, no. 2 (2021): 189–95, doi.org/10.3917/bipr1.053.0189; Charles Mercier, "Un internationalisme catholique à la fin de la guerre froide. Les Journées mondiales de la jeunesse (1984–1991)," *Revue d'histoire* 153, no. 1 (2022): 105–119, doi.org/10.3917/vin.153.0105.
[5] Charles Mercier, "Institution versus Charism? The Emmanuel Community, the Catholic Church, and John Paul II's World Youth Days," *PentecoStudies* 19, no. 2 (November 9, 2020): 152–169, doi.org/10.1558/pent.40169.

protagonists, whether ordinary faithful, bishops,[6] or pope,[7] its concrete workings and adaptations in the face of contemporary issues such as the place of women,[8] inclusion, cultural and religious diversity.[9] The third topic, the broadest, is the changing relationship between youth and religion in a context of globalization and individualization of beliefs. WYDs are an excellent observation post to better grasp these dynamics.[10]

In order to analyze the possible contribution of academic listening practices to the synodal process, this article takes an unusual route for me, out of my academic comfort zone. The aim is not to present the results of research, but reflect on the methods used, going beyond a purely epistemological approach. More than just a critical study of my

---

[6] Charles Mercier, "Les évêques canadiens et la Journée mondiale de la jeunesse de 2002 : essai d'histoire transnationale et politique du catholicisme," *Recherches sociographiques* 58, no. 3 (2017): 603–627, doi.org/10.7202/1043467ar; Charles Mercier, "Les Journées mondiales de la jeunesse de Paris," in *Jean-Marie Lustiger : entre crises et recompositions catholiques, 1954–2007*, ed. Denis Pelletier and Benoît Pellistrandi (Rennes: Presses universitaires de Rennes, 2022), 199–214; Charles Mercier, "La Conférence des évêques de France et les Journées mondiales de la jeunesse de 1997," in *Cent ans de gouvernement de l'Église catholique en France : De l'Assemblée des cardinaux et archevêques à la Conférence des évêques (1919–2019)*, ed. Valentin Favrie, Christian Sorrel, and Charles Mercier (Rennes: Presses universitaires de Rennes, 2022), 239–254, doi.org/10.4000/books.pur.163400.

[7] Charles Mercier, "Jean-Paul II et les Journées mondiales de la jeunesse," *Études* 7–8 (2020): 75–85, doi.org/10.3917/etu.4273.0075; Charles Mercier, "Fenomen Światowych Dni Młodzieży," in *Jan Paweł II—Miara Wielkości Człowieka*, ed. Dominiki Żukowskiej-Gardzińskiej (Varsovie: Narodowe Centrum Kultury, 2020), 309–321.

[8] Charles Mercier, "Breaking through the Stained-Glass Ceiling during John Paul II's Pontificate? Women, Feminism, and World Youth Days," *Journal of Modern and Contemporary Christianity* 2, no. 1 (2023): 115–136, doi.org/10.30687/JoMaCC/2785-6046/2023/01/005.

[9] Charles Mercier, "Les Journées mondiales de la jeunesse de Paris en 1997 : quel rapport avec le catholicisme d'identité ?," in *Catholicisme et Identité. Regards croisés sur le catholicisme français contemporain*, ed. Bruno Dumons and Frédéric Gugelot (Paris: Karthala, 2017), 193–209; Charles Mercier, "La 'religion culturelle' en France et au Québec : quelques réflexions à partir de l'étude des Journées mondiales de la jeunesse," *Studies in Religion/Sciences Religieuses* 52, no. 3 (2023): 340–357, doi.org/10.1177/00084298221122456.

[10] Charles Mercier, "Les papes et les jeunes : un essai de mise en perspective historique," in *Entendre et proposer l'Évangile avec les jeunes. Actes du IXe colloque international de l'ISPC, 12–15 Février 2019*, ed. Isabelle Morel, Enzo Biemmi, and François-Xavier Amherdt (Paris: Cerf, 2020), 137–169; Charles Mercier, "Les Journées mondiales de la jeunesse comme dispositifs de transmission religieuse (1985–2019)," *Histoire de l'éducation* 155 (2021): 47–67; Charles Mercier, Jayeel Cornelio, and Jean-Philippe Warren, "Young People and Religious Actors in a Globalized World. Introduction," *Social Compass* 71, no. 1 (2024): 3–25, doi.org/10.1177/00377686241240693.

scientific approach, this article proceeds from a kind of life review, inspired in particular by Ignatian spirituality, which consists in paying attention to spiritual movements in oneself and others, through a contemplative state of mind.[11] This approach leads me to formulate the thesis that the collaboration between social scientists and the protagonists of the Synod can purify both religion and science, and also open a space for spiritual experiences.

CONTEXT, OBJECTIVES, AND LISTENING PROTOCOL

The academic listening practices discussed in this paper were carried out in the context of two studies on WYDs, held every two or three years since their creation in 1984. The first is a historical study of the eight editions organized during John Paul II's pontificate,[12] conducted between 2015 and 2019. This included the collection of some fifty testimonies in seven different countries. The second study is the above-mentioned sociological and anthropological study carried out in July-August 2023 on the occasion of the Lisbon WYD: as part of a delegation of pilgrims, I experienced the event in Portugal among the young people and their chaplains, to whom I was able to listen in formal interviews as well as when they spoke in public or during group conversations.

In the French public academic context, this state-funded research could not be religiously-oriented. It must use secular methods to produce new scientific knowledge. In order to establish their legitimacy in the academic sphere, French social scientists of religion have clearly marked their independence from their object of study by practicing science for science's sake, not science for pastoral action.[13] That said, a religious motivation implicitly underpinned my work: between the ages of nineteen and twenty-four, I had taken part in three World Youth Days (Paris 1997, Rome 2000, and Toronto 2002). The Paris WYD in particular was a "place of fulfillment," which played a decisive role in the next stage of my life. Looking back on this experience, both personal and collective, and turning it into a story, was one source of motivation for launching my investigation. As a historian, however, I have endeavored to distance myself from this personal interest, in order to listen to the witnesses with a critical ear.

---

[11] Yves Vende, "La relecture de vie, une pratique ancienne. L'examen de vie chez Jésus, Socrate, et Confucius," *Christus* 277, no. 1 (January 2023): 108–116.
[12] Roma (1984), Roma (1985), Buenos Aires (1987), Santiago de Compostela (1989), Czestochowa (1991), Denver (1993), Manila (1995), Paris (1997), Rome (2000), and Toronto (2002).
[13] Émile Poulat, "Aux origines du 'Groupe de sociologie des religions' et de ses archives," *Archives de sciences sociales des religions* 136 (2006): 25–37.

In my research about John Paul II's WYD, the listening protocol was part of what is known as oral history. Oral history is used to collect the life stories of those who do not write down their memories, but also find information not provided by written sources (such as the meaning actors give to their actions or some details of their daily life), approach non-institutional memory, or confirm or refute certain hypotheses.[14] Oral history also aims at grasping the complexity and density of human relationships. The fifty interviews I collected were preceded by documentation work based on the internet, biographical dictionaries and, where possible, publications and archives. As the French historian Philippe Joutard writes, "Having some prior knowledge of what makes up the essence of a life is a first form of respect for one's interlocutor."[15] During the interview, this groundwork makes it possible to reach a certain level of precision more quickly, without the witness needing to retrace his entire itinerary. In this way, he can concentrate on those aspects of his life that left no trace. The fact of arriving with this information, which the witness himself has sometimes forgotten, also enables him to remember the past better. Contact with fragments of archives brings back buried memories. It also helps avoid conscious or unconscious reconstructions, reassuring speeches and the "wooden language" expertly used by some clergymen. The interview is semi-directive, i.e., follows a questionnaire from which it is possible to deviate according to the dynamics of the conversation. The conversation is recorded if the interlocutor has no objections. After the interview, this recording allows me to listen again to key passages, complete my notes, and transcribe certain words that will be used in the scientific publication, according to their relevance to the research question and established plan. The words of the witness are thus reduced to a few extracts, confronted with other words or documents that may confirm or relativize them. Speeches are also interpreted according to conceptual frameworks that are not necessarily those of the witness. For example, I put into perspective the words of Henrietta de Villa, who coordinated the 1995 Manila WYD and later became the Philippine ambassador to the Holy See, with gender studies of women's empowerment strategies in a Catholic context. I also compared her trajectory with that of an American nun,

---

[14] Florence Descamps, *L'historien, l'archiviste, et le magnétophone : de la constitution de la source orale à son exploitation* (Paris: Comité pour l'histoire économique et financière de la France, 2001).
[15] Philippe Joutard, *Ces voix qui nous viennent du passé* (Paris: Hachette, 1983), 228. [Translation, mine]

Sister Mary Ann Walsh, who had been in charge of communications for the 1993 Denver WYD, to identify similarities and differences.[16]

For the Lisbon WYD study, the listening protocol was a little different. Before starting the interview, I knew nothing about the brief lives of the young faithful or priests I was going to interview. Through a poll commissioned from a specialized institute,[17] and other surveys published in the press,[18] I had gathered information on French eighteen- to thirty-year-olds, young Catholics, and WYD participants, but had no precise biographical data. The interviews were therefore more exploratory: I took the time to listen to the childhood and youth stories of the young people I was interviewing, the reasons why they had signed up for WYD, their hopes and fears, how they were living the experience, their view of the world and the church. The long bus journeys, not only from Bordeaux to Lisbon but throughout the entire stay, waits, and walks were ideal opportunities for interviews. I took notes or recorded, depending on the situation. In addition to these formal interviews, I also listened to the words spoken formally (sermons, teachings, speaking into the microphone on the bus), or informally (small talk, conversations in which I found myself involved, or verbalizations of conflicts). Without being in a permanent state of alertness, I tried to be in a receptive state, and in the evening, I took note of all the day's significant facts and remarks.

In both cases, my method was secular. I must admit, however, that as far as the fieldwork in Portugal is concerned, I was inspired by the religious fervor of the event; I had an intense spiritual life because of my participation in the group's religious activities and tried to create links between my scientific research and faith during personal times of prayer. However, I did not explicitly integrate spiritual practices such as *Lectio Divina* into my research, as Catherine Sexton did in her study of elderly nuns.[19]

---

[16] Mercier, "Breaking through the Stained-Glass Ceiling?"
[17] Kantar Public poll for LACES (University of Bordeaux) and GSRL with the support of the Institut universitaire de France, conducted from June 14 to 16, 2023 among a sample of 1,000 young people aged between 18 and 30, representative of the 18–30 age group in France, veriangroup.com/hubfs/FR/Rapport-des-jeunes-%C3%A0-la-la%C3%AFcit%C3%A9.pdf?hsLang=fr.
[18] Including a survey of WYD participants in the French Catholic daily newspaper *La Croix*. See www.la-croix.com/Religion/JMJ-jeunes-catholiques-fervents-contre-courant-notre-sondage-exclusif-2023-05-25-1201268810.
[19] Catherine Sexton, "Practical Theology Method as Contemplative Enquiry: From Holy Listening to Sacred Reading and Shared Horizons," *Practical Theology* 12, no. 1 (2019): 44–57 doi.org/10.1080/1756073X.2019.1575042.

REACTIONS OF INDIVIDUALS INTERVIEWED

I would now like to turn to the reactions of the interviewees to this academic listening approach, which took different forms, ranging from mistrust and incomprehension to recognition and gratitude. Some of the interviewees' reactions changed over the course of the research process.

For my historical research, most of the players seemed happy to be asked for an interview, sometimes seeing it as an opportunity to recount memories important to them, which could be passed on via a publication. Some confided in me that they had not yet found an attentive ear ready to listen to their experience. For example, one of the local organizers of the 1993 Denver WYD wrote to me: "You are the first person in 25 years to ask me about my experience or reflections on the event, although the diocese has done print and video retrospectives since." After the event, he had been rather abruptly dismissed by the archdiocese of Denver and felt he had not been thanked for the immense energy expended in setting up the event: "Was there professional reward for my participation or recognition of the role I played? No." In his case, the listening I offered him a posteriori had a substitute function, remedying the feeling of not being listened to by the Catholic institution. On the other hand, some of the people I approached declined or did not follow up my interview proposals. Not everyone involved in WYD wants to be listened to by an academic, especially those for whom the experience was painful, ended badly, or was insignificant.

I encountered less of this kind of resistance during my sociological research at WYD 2023. Almost all the young people, priests, and nuns I approached agreed to talk to me; the fact that I was immersed in the event with them gradually helped to break down any resistance or fears. Some of them, however, checked whether I was Catholic before telling me about their experience. From a "spy" who aroused a certain mistrust, and in whose presence you had to be on your guard, I gradually became a pilgrim among others you could talk to and confide in. I heard several young pilgrims, who had set off without any friends, tell me with great simplicity about their fear of not being able to form bonds because they were introverts, and of finding themselves isolated as a result. Others confided in me their fear of breaking down because of fatigue and lack of sleep. Some priests confessed to me that they were distraught by the turn of events: having come to supervise young people, who were in fact living their lives on their own, in groups that came and went without regulation, they found themselves unable to play their role as chaplains as they had imagined it. Another priest told me that WYD was a physical and psychological test for him. A nun told me about the subaltern experiences she had had at previous WYDs, where the young seminarians and priests monopolized the floor, without giving her a chance to be heard by the young people. In a festive event, at times swirling and noisy, my proposal to lend an attentive ear to everyone's stories seems to have met a need, as if there was an expectation of listening not fully taken care of by the organization.

What about the reaction of interviewees when they discovered the scientific publication in which their words were used and interpreted? Out of ethical consideration, participants whom I quoted were sent copies of book chapters or articles ahead of publication. Most of the time, I received no response; perhaps because, for the reasons mentioned above, they did not fully recognize themselves in the final write-up, in which their words were segmented and confronted with other sources of information. A French priest involved in the organization of the 1997 Paris WYD told me how interesting it had been to read my "well-documented" book on the WYD,[20] while at the same time disputing certain phrases concerning his role in the organization chart. The traces available in the archives, and the conclusions I arrived at after cross-checking and confronting the various testimonies gathered, did not match his memories. Here we see the tension between memory and history, as highlighted by Paul Ricoeur:

> Memory has the advantage of recognizing the past as having been, even though it is no longer; history has the power to widen the gaze in space and time, the strength of criticism in terms of testimony, explanation, and understanding, the rhetorical mastery of the text, and above all, the exercise of fairness with regard to the competing claims of memories that are wounded and sometimes blind to the misfortune of others.[21]

REACTIONS OF INSTITUTIONAL ACTORS

Having discussed the reactions of the interviewees, I would now like to turn to the reaction of members of the Catholic hierarchy to the publications resulting from these academic listening practices. In France, following the publication of my book, I received several very positive letters from bishops involved in the permanent council of the French Bishops' Conference. One of them wrote:

---

[20] Mercier, *L'Église, les jeunes, et la mondialisation*.
[21] Paul Ricœur, "L'écriture de l'histoire et la représentation du passé," *Annales* 55, no. 4 (2000): 747, doi.org/10.3406/ahess.2000.279877. [Translation mine]

> It is fascinating to see an event you have lived through analyzed by the varied methods of contemporary history. It is nice to be able, at certain moments, for no other reason than to come together for the Kingdom, since it is there nearby, but it is important to be aware that such events involve human relationships, social and ecclesial constructs, requiring the dedication of a few not always paid back![22]

Following the publication of a specific study on the role of the French Bishops' Conference in the organization of the 1997 Paris World Youth Day,[23] Father Bernard Ardura, President of the Pontifical Committee for Historical Sciences from 2009 to 2023, also gave a favorable assessment:

> A peaceful and balanced analysis of the Paris WYD showed how a personal initiative by the Archbishop of Paris, which may initially have offended some of his confreres, could be welcomed by the CEF [*Conférence des évêques de France*—French Bishops' Conference] and implemented thanks to a joint effort in which the episcopal collegiality was clearly involved.[24]

By contrast, in the Vatican my publications received a cooler reception. After I sent in one of my articles comparing the preparation and running of the World Youth Days in Toronto (2002) and Paris (1997), I was criticized for evoking conflicts and interpreting them in terms of power, whereas in the church "only service exists." I was invited to a discussion in Rome, where my interlocutors expressed their incomprehension, while at the same time finding me an extenuating circumstance: I was French, and therefore imbued with a secular vision of the world forged by *laïcité*. I replied that, in my opinion, it was not credible to present the preparation of the WYDs as a harmonious process, in which the views of the many protagonists would immediately converge towards the common goal: this idealized story was not faithful to the complexity of reality, nor did it help the protagonists understand the stakes involved in organizing an event of this dimension. Pope Francis himself had said: "Human life is structured on oppositions. This is something that also happens in the Church. Tensions don't necessarily have to be resolved or

---

[22] [Translation mine].
[23] Mercier, "La Conférence des évêques de France et les Journées mondiales de la jeunesse de 1997."
[24] Bernard Ardura, "Conclusion," in *Cent ans de gouvernement de l'Église catholique en France*, 255–265, doi.org/10.4000/books.pur.163400.

homologated."[25] At the end of my Roman sojourn, my interlocutors and I tried to take a step toward each other, in an attempt to understand our respective viewpoints, rooted in cultures having different relationships to religion.

RISKS AND OPPORTUNITIES

This Roman discussion raises questions about the opportunities and risks of scientific listening in a church setting. Beyond research on the WYDs, these questions are also raised by investigations carried out by academics and experts who have sought to understand the dynamics of abusive behavior within Catholicism, sometimes at the request of the Catholic hierarchy itself.[26] As part of their investigations, commissions on historical sexual abuse have engaged in listening exercises with victims, offenders, and those in positions of authority, and these commissions employed secular frameworks to analyze and interpret the testimonies collected. In such investigations, the church is treated as an institution like any other, with its internal power dynamics and conflicts, organizational strengths and weaknesses.

It seems to me that this approach raises no ecclesiological problems. Within Catholicism, it has become mainstream to distinguish between "the person of the Church and its personnel,"[27] between what the church is called to be and the reality of the morals of its members. Vatican II recognized the complex nature of the church as both a hierarchically organized society and mystical body. From a theological perspective, the relativizing dynamics of the social sciences make it possible to "desacralize" what does not need to be holy, fight against the essentialization of cultural elements, and "flush out a few deceptions," to use the words of historian Alain Cabantous.[28] Critical and empirical approaches also make it possible to take the Incarnation seriously: the organization of WYD is based on human beings, with their qualities and flaws, and is part of dynamics that concern the whole social body and from which the church is not exempt, even if it may have conceived itself as a "perfect society" with

---

[25] Interview with Antonio Spadaro, quoted by Sandro Magister on his blog (November 14, 2016), chiesa.espresso.repubblica.it/articolo/1351414.html. [Translation mine]

[26] For example, for France, the report of the Independent Commission on Sexual Abuse in the Church, set up in February 2019 by the Bishops of France, and whose final report is available online (www.ciase.fr/rapport-final/). This report has caused some misunderstanding in the Vatican, and its authors have still not been received by Pope Francis.

[27] Jacques Maritain, *De l'Église du Christ : la personne de l'Église et son personnel* (Paris: Desclée De Brouwer, 1970).

[28] Alain Cabantous, "Le vent souffle où il veut," in *L'historien et la foi*, ed. Jean Delumeau (Paris: Fayard, 1996), 34.

specific rules.[29] Awareness of this fact can lead to greater realism and pastoral effectiveness.

What is more problematic from a faith perspective is the sociological treatment of religious experience as expressed by the participants. To study spiritual emotion secularly, a fortiori when it underpins a way of seeing the world, is it not to saw off the branch on which we are looking at the stars? By putting the experience of WYD pilgrims through the mill of the social sciences, do we not run the risk of trading in a feeling of fulfillment for a rational pleasure that is rewarding, but ultimately desiccating? For example, the experience of jubilation expressed by WYD participants when they find themselves immersed in a large crowd, at once multicultural and united by the same faith, can be analyzed in the same way Émile Durkheim wrote about the gatherings of traditional Australian societies, after long periods of dispersion.[30] For both aborigines and WYD pilgrims, joy can be explained as a physical phenomenon caused by the coalescence of individuals and as a psychological consequence of the reunion of an ordinarily dispersed group. On this view, the Pope is the totemic figure who makes the gathering and its emotional consequences possible. This narrative gives rise to the intellectual pleasure of explanation, yet it is not entirely satisfactory for the believer, or the pilgrim, because it is reductionist. As Gabriel Le Bras, a pioneer of the sociology of religion in France, once wrote: "One must have the loyalty, the intelligence, when one claims to be a member of a religious society, to exclude a natural explanation of the supranatural."[31] Critical listening to religious phenomena can lead a researcher to develop an instrumental relationship with what has constituted a space of gratuity in his own existence and that of millions of other people.

ENTERING INTO CONVERSATION

It seems to me that this challenge can be overcome. The way Canadian sociologist Raymond Lemieux analyzes John Paul II's trip to Canada in 1985 is inspiring from this point of view. His mobilization of concepts from the social sciences enables him to

---

[29] Roland Minnerath, "Face à l'État, réémergence de l'Église 'société parfaite,'" *Société, droit, et religion* 6, no. 1 (2016): 9–19, doi.org/10.3917/sdr.006.0009.
[30] Émile Durkheim, *Les formes élémentaires de la vie religieuse. Le système totémique en Australie* (Paris: Presses universitaires de France, 1994), 308–312.
[31] Gabriel Le Bras, "Réflexions sur les différences entre sociologie scientifique et sociologie pastorale," *Archives de sociologie des religions* 8 (1959): 17–18. [Translation mine]

distance himself from the emotional discourse of the participants. But at the same time, Lemieux is aware of the limits of "rational tools, insofar as these tools do not themselves include their own critique."[32] Scientific discourse need not be sacralized, since it is socially constructed too.[33] Taking the believers' experience of communion seriously, and to some extent participating in it, opens up a new type of understanding initially closed to Lemieux. This approach can be found in certain currents in the psychology of religion, which apprehend spiritual experience as a legitimate means of exploring existence, rather than an illusion to be conquered by triumphant reason: "It's a passive, receptive mode of knowledge, without desire, that is to say, one that doesn't strive but lets it happen. Contemplative, not active knowledge."[34]

This approach is also present in anthropology, when facts are interpreted within the framework in which they are experienced. This requires the ethnologist to question his or her "rationality" in order to take "beliefs" seriously, even if it means finding himself or herself transformed and putting himself or herself in uncomfortable situations.[35] Edith (1921–2016) and Victor (1920–1983) Turner are two typical figures of anthropologists "contaminated" by their object of study. For this couple of British Marxist academics, observing African ritual experience provoked a spiritual transformation that led them to convert to Catholicism, and include their religious experience in their anthropological work. In the field of practical theology, this experience of displacement and "conversion" of social science methods was recounted by Catherine Sexton, who finds herself evangelized by the elderly nuns she interviews as part of an empirical research project:

> I experienced the sisters as ministering to me at the heart of the research process, . . . through their word and their gift. The sisters, as participants, made at least two specific contributions to the research process, as opposed to the research content: to the "conversion" of my

---

[32] Raymond Lemieux, "Charisme, Mass-Media, et religion populaire: le voyage du pape au Canada," *Social Compass* 34, no. 1 (1987): 29.
[33] An idea also put forward by American sociologist Robert Wuthnow in "Science and the Sacred," in *The Sacred in a Secular Age*, ed. Phillip E. Hammond (Berkeley: University of California Press, 1985), 194.
[34] Réginald Richard, *Religion de l'adolescence, adolescence de la religion : vers une psychologie de la religion de l'adolescence* (Québec: Presses de l'Université Laval, 1985), 75. [Translation mine]
[35] See, in particular, Abdellah Hammoudi's account of his pilgrimage to Mecca as he sought to emancipate himself from the Muslim religion in which he had been raised (*Une saison à La Mecque : récit de pèlerinage* [Paris: Seuil, 2005]).

method to the service of God and secondly to my own journey of conversion.[36]

I have experienced the same kind of dynamic in my investigations of WYDs, especially the one in Lisbon. The young people I interviewed transformed me. The simplicity and depth of the way they bore witness to God's action in their lives lifted me spiritually and awakened an inner dynamism. They gave me great joy and a sense of fulfillment. It seemed to me that grace was at work in this academic listening activity. Whereas, before leaving for Lisbon, I had been afraid of being like an old bull in a China shop, I discovered I could find a tailored position in the group.

Beyond this personal experience, I also discovered that scientific studies of WYD did not have a disenchanting effect, as I had first feared, but could, on the contrary, be an opportunity for the believer who listens carefully to hear the breath of the Spirit. First of all, it is striking to note the gap between the relative poverty of the means mobilized during the preparations, the limitations and problems of the organizers, and the extraordinarily positive impact of the event on the lives of many people. In a historical or sociological account of the WYDs, one can find a "background music" which sounds like the Gospel passage of the "five loaves and two fishes." With limited resources, and disciples who were "poor guys," the Lord managed to feed a large crowd. Contrary to Gabriel Le Bras's assertion, it does not seem to me that the secular explanation of a phenomenon prevents a supernatural reading of events.

Because it has been conducted on a global scale, the WYD survey also reveals regularities, regardless of cultural context or time, which can be understood as signs of the action of a God who transcends borders. Listening to testimonies from the four corners of the globe, I was struck by the convergence of discourses describing similar spiritual experiences even though cultural contexts differed profoundly and people did not know each other: for example, young people from different countries expressed the same feeling of experiencing a comforting anticipation of the afterlife, a kind of "transfiguration" that fleetingly unveiled something which could be called the "Kingdom of God." I heard or read very similar words from a young Pole who attended the Czestochowa WYD in 1991, a young Quebecer who attended the Toronto WYD in 2002, and a French Jesuit who attended the Lisbon WYD in 2023. In each of their discourses, I found a feeling of connection with transcendence, a perception of the beauty of the world, the experience of profound peace and joy, the

---

[36] Sexton, "Practical Theology Method as Contemplative Enquiry," 51.

feeling of being integrated into a harmonious whole that transcended them without crushing their singularity. This universality was not uniformity, but was expressed in different words according to each person's particular cultural roots and personality.

CONCLUSION

At the end of this reflection, it seems to me that academic listening practices can enable the Catholic Church to take a step back from the synodal exercise. Indeed, the social sciences reveal power relations and processes of domination the faithful and clergy often deny. But just because there is a process of consultation that begins at the grassroots does not mean that the question of power does not arise. Religious listening practices can be instrumentalized to promote, more or less consciously, a conservative or liberal agenda or to assert one's own views. Ensuring the conditions for genuine deliberation whose outcome is not known in advance, requires a real letting go, which is not at all obvious in a cultural context that favors control. The social sciences can help not only to move away from a somewhat romantic vision of the synodal process,[37] but also moderate the hopes that a new, more horizontal and inclusive style of governance would make the Catholic Church desirable again. By situating religious attitudes within broader social dynamics, the social sciences can increase Catholic leaders' awareness of the importance of external causes: the church's ability to attract people is far from dependent on its organization, policies, or communications alone. Cultural, political, and economic factors also matter, and over these the church has little control. In short, the social sciences can protect the Catholic Church from a form of self-referentiality in which God's place is taken by ideologies, strategies, or methodologies.

If social science practices can enrich the synodal church, the reverse is also true. By calling into question the distinction between the faithful people and the magisterium, synodality has something to offer academics, reminding them that they do not hold a monopoly on knowledge, built through the confrontation of viewpoints and experiences. To quote the French philosopher Bruno Latour, social scientists cannot "sit on high" or "occupy the viewpoint of nowhere, that of God."[38] Synodality invites epistemological humility. It leans more on the side of interdisciplinarity, in which each person studies the same object from his or her specific roots before comparing the

---

[37] *Métamorphoses de la synodalité : de Vatican II au pape François* (Paris: Artège, 2023).
[38] Bruno Latour, *Changer de société, refaire de la sociologie* (Paris: La Découverte, 2014), 49.

results, than on the side of transdisciplinarity or metadisciplinarity, in which various roles are played by the same person, rising above the usual categories. To paraphrase the Apostle Paul,[39] the theologian cannot say to the sociologist, "I do not need you," and the historian cannot say to the witnesses, "I do not need you."

To conclude this paper, I would like to emphasize the mutual enrichment that academic listening practices in a church setting can bring. If those conducting the survey and those being surveyed agree to let go of their rigidities, and listen to each other in depth, putting aside their ready-made interpretation keys, these practices can be an opportunity to experience a form of "overflow,"[40] or "pilgrimage," to use words frequently used by Pope Francis, notably during his meeting with young academics in Lisbon on August 3, 2023:

> To be a pilgrim literally means to put aside our daily routine and choose to set out on a different path, moving away from our comfort zone towards a new horizon of meaning. The notion of "pilgrimage" nicely describes our human condition for, like pilgrims, we find ourselves facing great questions that have no simple or immediate answers, but challenge us to continue the journey, to rise above ourselves and to press beyond the here and now.[41]

It seems to me that the Catholic Church should not be afraid of being studied and listened to in secular ways. Non-theologian academics are not spies, but human beings on their own journey. This kind of companionship can purify both faith and science, desacralizing what should not be sacred, and allowing us to be surprised by the action of the Spirit.[42] 𝕄

Charles Mercier, PhD, is professor of modern history at the University of Bordeaux and a former member of the Institut universitaire de France. He is also associate researcher at the Groupe Sociétés Religions Laïcités (EPHE/CNRS) in Paris. He was a Georgetown University Berkley Center visiting researcher from February to June 2018. Mercier has written or edited twelve books,

---

[39] 1 Cor 12:21.
[40] François and Austen Ivereigh, *Un temps pour changer* (Paris: Flammarion, 2020), 120–121.
[41] Available at www.vatican.va/content/francesco/en/speeches/2023/august/documents/20230803-portogallo-universitari.html.
[42] I would like to thank Alexis Artaud de la Ferrière, Anna Rowlands, and all the participants in the "Listening Practices in Global Catholicism" conference for providing constructive feedback on the first draft of this paper and encouraging me to deepen my reflection thanks to their own presentations.

including *L'Église, les jeunes, et la mondialisation : une histoire des JMJ* (2020). Mercier received his PhD in history from Paris 1-Panthéon Sorbonne University in 2011.

Two "Fires" of Leadership: Is it Possible to Listen and Lead Parish Cultural Change?

Hannah Vaughan-Spruce

Abstract: Pope Francis has claimed that "we are living through a change of epoch, the deepest level of which is cultural." "A change of epoch" entails much change in Catholic parishes especially across the Western world. Change can be chosen or unchosen. Actively chosen change is explored in this paper. Examples include parishes self-consciously adapting to become more mission-focused or purposefully adopting more traditional liturgical styles. Drawing on empirical case studies of British parishes undertaken in the course of my doctoral research in 2017 and 2018, this paper explores two different styles of leadership using Pope Francis's metaphor of two "fires." While "powerful flame" stands for bold, visionary leadership, "charcoal fire" represents more mild and tender listening. I consider questions such as: what is the cultural impact on a community when listening is engaged in, and when it is not? How might listening impact a parish's direction of travel if intentional change is pursued? And what limitations to change might a listening approach entail?

POPE FRANCIS HAS CLAIMED THAT "WE ARE LIVING THROUGH a change of epoch, the deepest level of which is cultural."[1] Sociologically, this "change of epoch" has had profound implications on the Catholic Church in Britain. In the fifteen years up to 2022, Mass attendance in Britain decreased by more than half, to 594,000.[2] To place this figure in stark comparison, the average weekly live attendance at a football match is 830,000.[3] Such decline is reflected in the radical and pressing decisions dioceses find them-

---

[1] Jorge Bergoglio, *The Aparecida Document*, Latin American Episcopal Conference (CELAM, 2007), 44.

[2] In 1999, typical weekly Mass attendance across England, Wales, and Scotland was 1,264,000. While 2022 Mass attendance data for Scotland is not available, if the "Covid hit" is similar there to England and Wales, the average weekly Mass attendance across Britain in 2022 was 594,000. T. Kinnear, "Statistical Appendices," in *The Oxford History of British and Irish Catholicism*, Vol. 5: *Recapturing the Apostolate of the Laity, 1914–2021*, ed. A. Harris (Oxford: Oxford University Press, 2023), 357–376.

[3] In 2021–2022, the average attendance at a live football match from one of England's top six tiers was 834,724.

selves forced to make. One diocese is restructuring from 111 parishes to 52 in the next two years. Another is reducing from 87 down to 25. Every local church faces much upheaval and change in the coming decade. Few Catholics will be untouched either by the closure of their parish or amalgamation with another.

This sociological "change of epoch"—extraordinary decline in the Western church, which some claim is catalysed by the forces of secularism—is experienced by each of us. Yet there is a parallel "change of epoch" taking place, less visible, but surely more powerful, originating not from secularism but, I would argue, the Holy Spirit. I want to call this the pneumatological "change of epoch." It is a return to forms of community life and leadership characteristic of the New Testament and early church.[4] The sociological "change of epoch" converges with the pneumatological "change of epoch" in a new apostolic age.

In this new apostolic age, the church's visible, sociological transformation once again into a humble, afflicted minority is deeply complementary to her invisible, pneumatological transformation into a synodal, missional church. While her visible, sociological form in the west increasingly reflects the form of the early church, the Holy Spirit calls the church to inner renewal, a pastoral conversion. In this pneumatological transformation, the new apostolic church is called to recapture not only the synodal ways of living and leading of the early church, but also her apostolic fire, the "fiery mission," in Pope Francis's words.[5] "Synodality is ordered to mission,"[6] we are consistently reminded and, "Synodality has its origin and ultimate purpose in mission: it is born of mission and directed to mission."[7] In other words, this pneumatological renewal of the church is ordered towards going out, to counter the "self-referential," "atrophied" sickness that led to the sociological decline in the first place.[8]

---

[4] Synod of Bishops, Synthesis Report, "A Synodal Church in Mission," 2023, Part 1, 1a, www.synod.va/en/news/a-synodal-church-in-mission.html.

[5] Pope Francis, "Homily, Ordinary Consistory for the Creation of New Cardinals," August 27, 2022, www.vatican.va/content/francesco/en/homilies/2022/documents/20220827-omelia-concistoro.html.

[6] "A Synodal Church in Mission," Part 1, 2e.

[7] Pope Francis, "Address to Participants in the Conference Organised by the Dicastery for Laity, Family, and Life," February 18, 2023, www.vatican.va/content/francesco/en/speeches/2023/february/documents/20230218-convegno.html.

[8] One of many examples: "The community of disciples of Jesus was born apostolic and missionary. The Holy Spirit moulds her outwardly—a Church which goes forth, which goes out—so that she is not closed in on herself but outgoing, a contagious witness of Jesus." Pope Francis, General Audience, January 11, 2023, www.vatican.va/content/francesco/en/audiences/2023/documents/20230111-udienza-generale.html#:~:text=Today%20we%20begin%20a%20new,%2C%20born%20missionary%2C%20not%20proselytizing.

In this article, I explore the role of leadership in the context of these parallel "changes of epoch" we are experiencing. Specifically, I explore leadership at the parish level, in keeping with my experience coaching and witnessing change in over one hundred parishes across Britain through the Catholic ministry Divine Renovation.[9] Even more specifically, I home in on the question of listening in leadership. A "change of epoch" calls for visionary and courageous leadership at the parish level. Is it possible to couple listening to diverse voices with bold leadership? I ask whether there are tensions between the two. What practical steps might be taken to mitigate these tensions?

My data originates from empirical research undertaken in two British and one Canadian parishes in 2017–2018, preceding the global synodal process.[10] While the parishes had not encountered the concept of "synodality" and, therefore, did not explicitly refer to "synodal" ways of leading or listening, the realities are present or absent, while not being named as such.

ACTIVE AND PASSIVE RESPONSES TO THE "CHANGE OF EPOCH"

As with any period of change, in the context of the two parallel "changes of epoch"—the sociological and pneumatological—parishes may respond differently. Broadly, they may respond actively by choosing intentional adaptation which may take myriad different forms, or they may respond passively by choosing not to adapt. The sociological evidence indicates that those who respond passively, maintaining their current forms, will likely wither, closing or amalgamating with another parish.[11]

---

[9] See www.divinerenovation.org.

[10] My empirical methods consisted of three successive weeks spent in each parish. My primary method was one of participant observation, being immersed in the daily life, activities, and liturgies of the parish. I conducted formal, semi-structured interviews with six parishioners, one of whom was the parish priest. From these interviews, certain espoused values and beliefs of the parishioners emerged, and I presented these back to three representative focus groups. These focus groups were intentionally drawn from highly engaged through to highly disengaged populations of parishioners, in order to understand a range of outlooks and experiences. The methods received written approval from Prof. Conor Gissane, Chair of the Ethics Sub-Committee, St. Mary's University, Twickenham, on September 8, 2017. Written agreements were signed between each parish and me as researcher, as well as with each interviewee and focus group participant.

[11] These parishes display the reality that, in Pope Francis's words, "When Christian life loses sight of the horizon of evangelization, the horizon of proclamation, it grows sick: it closes in on itself, it becomes self-referential, it becomes atrophied" (General Audience, January 11, 2023).

I focus here on those parishes that respond actively.[12] In the work of our ministry, we observe that there as many ways of responding actively as there are personalities and leadership styles. I do not want to be prescriptive, but rather highlight one or two types of response—pointing to the interplay between leadership and listening—and indicating the characteristics, advantages, and disadvantages of each.

To do this, I propose a metaphor from Pope Francis's homily at the 2022 Consistory. Drawing on Jesus's image of fire in Luke 12:79—"I came to bring fire to the earth, and how I wish it were already kindled!"—Pope Francis indicates two images for "bringing fire to the earth" we surely need in this "change of epoch." The first image is the "powerful flame" or "consuming fire" of the Holy Spirit—the "fiery mission . . . not only for *what* he came to accomplish but also for *how* he accomplished it." This fire is "apostolic courage," "zeal for the salvation of every human being," and "magnanimity," Jesus' "boundless and unconditional love, for his heart is afire with the mercy of the Father." The Holy Father comments that, "This is the same powerful fire that impelled the Apostle Paul in his tireless service to the Gospel, in his "race," his missionary zeal constantly inspired by the Spirit and the Word."[13]

As well as this "powerful flame," there is another type of fire: the charcoal fire of the post-Resurrection breakfast (John 21:9). "The Lord also wants to share this fire with us, so that like him, with *meekness, fidelity, closeness*, and *tenderness*—this is God's style: closeness, compassion, and tenderness—we can lead many people to savour the presence of Jesus alive in our midst." It is the "mild kind of fire," "kept aflame by simple, 'homemade' prayers, gestures, and tender gazes, and by the love that patiently accompanies their children on their journey of growth."

I want to propose these two types of fire as images expressing something of the types of leadership that are proving fruitful in the "change of epoch." The "powerful flame" of "fiery mission" stands

---

[12] I want to briefly introduce the reasons behind the choice of three parishes and their sociological characteristics, while recognising the impossibility of doing full justice in the context of a short article. The suburban Canadian parish was chosen for its surprising flourishing in a context in which Christianity was otherwise declining. Importantly, its sociodemographic realities were not dissimiliar from the two British parishes which were, on the contrary, seeing normal levels of decline. The level of Catholic disaffiliation and the percentage of Nones in the wider population of each of the three parishes were roughly similar (all were located in areas where the percentage of Nones was between 24.5 percent and 29.7 percent). Immigration did not affect the Canadian parish significantly at the time of the study and the population was majority white and Canadian.

[13] Pope Francis, Ordinary Consistory, August 27, 2022, www.vatican.va/content/francesco/en/homilies/2022/documents/20220827-omelia-concistoro.html.

for the bold, visionary, and sometimes uncomfortable leadership that corresponds to the powerful movement of the Holy Spirit. It might (crudely) be classified as "top-down" leadership. The mild, charcoal fire stands for compassionate and tender listening corresponding to the intimate closeness of the Holy Spirit: perhaps classified as "bottom-up" leadership. Where the first style stands for the "mission" aim of the global synodal process, I propose that the second style stands for "communion" and "participation." All three are needed. While one style of leadership might cause tensions in the other, they are not mutually exclusive, and both are needed for the pneumatological transformation of parishes at this "change of epoch."

"POWERFUL FLAME" LEADERSHIP

In the context of late secularisation in which we find ourselves in Britain, distinctiveness from the wider culture is a characteristic of small religious subcultures that tend to survive. Sociologist Christian Smith developed "subcultural identity theory" to indicate the social reality where minorities find their drive for meaning and belonging satisfied by locating themselves within "social groups (or subcultures) that sustain distinctive, morally orienting collective identities."[14] Smith's theory makes sense of the trend in Catholic parishes to develop a distinctive vision: a picture of the future of the parish that inspires passion and gives a direction of travel. One parishioner whose parish priest had shared a vision with the parish said, "I feel like [Father X] has a vision—I'm in a business environment and no one will do anything without a vision." He commented that when there is no vision, "it's so discouraging sometimes for us Catholics . . . we think, 'okay, it's no point' whereas I feel here, there is a vision."[15]

It is perhaps unsurprising that, in a time of much societal and cultural upheaval, a clearly outlined vision is welcomed by parishioners for whom it reinforces the "distinctive, morally orienting collective identity" of which Smith speaks. A parishioner from another parish commented that the leadership team had "been really good at fostering 'you're a part of it.' It's not just a responsibility. 'You're a part of the mission.' We have a clear vision and get excited about doing missionary work because the vision's so clear."[16]

---

[14] C. Smith, M. Emerson, S. Gallagher, P. Kennedy, and D. Sikkink, *American Evangelicalism: Embattled and Thriving* (Chicago: The University of Chicago Press, 1998), 90.
[15] Hannah Vaughan-Spruce, "From Sacred Canopy to Sacred Umbrellas: Cultural Characteristics of Parishes that Thrive," (PhD Thesis, Liverpool Hope University, 2021), research.stmarys.ac.uk/id/eprint/6447.
[16] Vaughan-Spruce, "From Sacred Canopy to Sacred Umbrellas."

Yet a parish's adoption of a distinctive vision also carries risks. Faced with sociological decline and passionate for change, a visionary leader can do damage through leading change too abruptly, non-collaboratively, or towards a vision that is extreme in its distinctiveness. In these situations, rather than promote "collective identity," any sense of identity can be destabilised. At the end of 2018, I was a participant observer in a British suburban parish across several months as a newly-arrived parish priest shared his vision.[17] Already he had galvanised some sense of outward-looking mission among parishioners, and I joined a group of around twenty of them one freezing cold evening a few days before Christmas. Led by the parish priest wearing a black cape and biretta, parishioners sang carols around a new estate near the church. As we stopped on street corners to sing, faces appeared at lit, upstairs windows. A few people bravely opened their front doors to the cold to hear more clearly. When they asked if we were collecting money, the response was always no, but a card with Christmas Mass times was handed out.

Over the course of Advent, the new parish priest passionately introduced a vision for the parish that centred around traditional liturgy, a form of liturgical expression that was unknown to most parishioners. The unfolding scenario in this parish displayed how extreme distinctiveness has advantages (parishioners travelled from further afield and the number of new people grew) and disadvantages (current parishioners experienced alienation). Some parishioners tried to embrace the changes. One lady said that she had been at an event outside the parish where they had sung the Salve Regina. She said, "Twelve months ago I would have rolled my eyes and gone, 'Oh, I'm not singing this, I don't know Latin, I don't care about this.' But because I've learnt a lot this year, it's opened my ability to participate prayerfully in some of the more traditional services."[18]

For many, though, that Advent season was an experience of destabilisation and bewilderment. A catechist shared the words of a parishioner in her twenties: "'You never taught any of this to us when we were doing our Confirmation.'" The catechist said, "So she's struggling even more than me."[19] Other parishioners commented, "I've felt very troubled this year,"[20] and, "[The] spirit of the church has gone."[21] An exchange between two parishioners epitomises the

---

[17] This parish is suburban, founded in the mid-1950s, and lying to the west of a large, southern English town. Average weekly Mass attendance in the year I studied the parish was 250, and 31 percent of households in the parish were counted as deprived.
[18] Vaughan-Spruce, "From Sacred Canopy to Sacred Umbrellas."
[19] Vaughan-Spruce, "From Sacred Canopy to Sacred Umbrellas."
[20] Vaughan-Spruce, "From Sacred Canopy to Sacred Umbrellas."
[21] Vaughan-Spruce, "From Sacred Canopy to Sacred Umbrellas."

experience. The first parishioner said, "I might be the only one in church who doesn't like it but I'm being honest that's all." "You're not the only one," the second replied. "I don't understand it and to me it's a dead language," said the first parishioner.[22]

The parish priest experienced the outcomes of his abrupt changes when he tried to raise parishioner commitment levels. He told me, "I've said to them that, really, everyone in the parish should have at least one thing that they're doing, that they're involved with, a group they're committed to, or a programme they're working with, or some catechesis they're helping with, that indicates a level of commitment beyond Sunday Mass."[23] But the response was resistant, parishioners mentioned "nagging" and "Catholic guilt" tactics.[24] A catechist commented, "A lot of them went, 'woah!' [pulls back] A lot of them felt they couldn't respond, and some said, 'We're just here for the First Communion programme.'"[25]

We see here the pitfalls of "fiery mission." Leaders can lean towards a "coercive style" of leadership suitable in a crisis or emergency scenario but not in a community setting seeking to respond to the "change of epoch."[26]

We might contrast this example to the Canadian parish that displayed leadership with vision but with greater appreciation for a listening approach. The parish priest said, "As a pastor, [there is a] real art of leading change in a parish. . . . The point is it's got to be gradual." He uses the metaphor of houses built on stilts in Louisiana. He said, "when a leg is beginning to rot out they put a new one in beside the old one, and let the old one just disintegrate and wash away. They don't take a sledgehammer to knock it out. And I think that's an important image of how culture shift works. Because it's often very slow, it happens slowly. And if you take a sledgehammer to it, people get hurt."[27]

---

[22] Vaughan-Spruce, "From Sacred Canopy to Sacred Umbrellas."
[23] Vaughan-Spruce, "From Sacred Canopy to Sacred Umbrellas."
[24] Vaughan-Spruce, "From Sacred Canopy to Sacred Umbrellas."
[25] Vaughan-Spruce, "From Sacred Canopy to Sacred Umbrellas."
[26] See Daniel Goleman, "Leadership that Gets Results," *Harvard Business Review*, March–April 2000, hbr.org/2000/03/leadership-that-gets-results.
[27] Vaughan-Spruce, "From Sacred Canopy to Sacred Umbrellas." More recently, a South African parish priest shared about the synodal process his parish undertook to develop vision, displaying the possibility of developing a vision and clear direction of travel through consultative means. During a homily, he reminded his parishioners of the five areas of direction for the parish over the coming years that emerged from synodal consultation: to be a parish that worked in teams, to focus on young people, to increase faith formation, to build community with the marginalised more intentionally, to assist the poor and unemployed. See Fr. Brett Williams, "How Synodal Listening Transformed this Preacher's Homilies and Faith Community,"

This parish experienced little of the resistance experienced by the British parish to promote commitment. On the contrary, the parishioners' language reflected a sense of their belonging coupled with responsibility. Typical phrases heard from parishioners included: "a sense of belonging to something that's bigger than us," "We're equipped to go and do the same that was done for us," "You're a part of the mission" and, "You feel loved within the mission, because we feel like we're a part of it." Strikingly, the global synodal themes of "communion" and "participation" are heard in these comments, complementing the drive towards greater mission.[28]

Fascinatingly, a parishioner who admitted she was not supportive of the vision said, "I think part of why we've adapted or able to change is that there's often a good sales pitch that goes with it. [Laughter.] There's preparation, and things are intentionally done. Whether you agree with them or not, you know that someone has probably intended to make the changes, it's not haphazard and they're going to prepare you. Whether you agree with it or not."[29] Her comments are an encouraging indication that intentional leadership need not alienate, that there is room "on the bus" even for those who are not enthusiastic about the direction in which it is heading.

"CHARCOAL FIRE" LEADERSHIP

I am using the "charcoal fire" image as shorthand to express leadership that is "bottom-up," and collaborative, and fostering inclusive listening. It is a style embodied in the Canadian parish thanks to a period of upheaval caused by an overplaying of the "powerful flame" leadership. The parish suffered some chaos through an overabundance of activity and difficulties caused by the parish priest's entrepreneurial leadership style and frequent travel. One staff member remembered, "There was gossip behind people's backs, . . . and arguments, and . . . you tried to avoid certain people. Nobody knew what each other's ministry was doing, you know. . . . There was no support for each other."[30]

America, October 2, 2023, www.americamagazine.org/faith/2023/10/02/podcast-synod-synodality-listening-homily-246182.

[28] The parish undertook a social scientific assessment that indicated the level of engagement of parishioners. Within two years, the parish's engaged:disengaged ratio rose from 0.83:1 to a high of 2.93:1. That is, the number of engaged parishioners (described as having a strong psychological connection to their parish) to every one actively disengaged parishioner (who rarely shows up or is otherwise hostile about the parish). While perhaps a crude tool, it is an indication of the parish's success towards achieving greater "communion" and "participation."

[29] Vaughan-Spruce, "From Sacred Canopy to Sacred Umbrellas."

[30] Vaughan-Spruce, "From Sacred Canopy to Sacred Umbrellas."

Everything came to a head, triggering a crisis team meeting. At this meeting, the parish priest, seeing the chaos and confusion he had caused, profusely apologised. The staff member recalled, "He said, 'I'm so sorry I have allowed this to happen . . . I'm going to change.'"[31] Subsequently, the parish developed a focus on healthy conflict, being able to disagree with one another and talk through the disagreement. A parishioner said, "We call them critical conversations, or crucial conversations . . . what we want to work towards is a solution together."[32] Arrived at through crisis, we see a demonstration of "powerful flame" leadership being corrected through the vulnerability and humility of the "charcoal fire," allowing parishioners' experiences and voices to shape direction of travel. Not only did this episode result in change for the parish priest, it also modelled for parishioners how to build close and trusting relationships that bore fruit for the mission.

In a second, British, suburban parish, "charcoal fire" leadership has been promoted for decades. It is evidenced in the vast lay involvement, with 88 parish activities listed on their organisational chart, and over 200 parish volunteers.[33]

One Sunday afternoon in early February 2018, I travelled with the parish priest to a scout hut in a nearby neighbourhood. We dropped in on one of the parish's twelve small communities that meet regularly. Inside the scout hut, around 30 people enjoyed a buffet lunch, almost all families with children. Children ran around, while adults chatted at the sides of the rooms. Some knew each other quite well already while others were new. Others were busy in the kitchen. This particular small community did not experience too much emphasis on faith formation. The parishioner coordinating small communities told me that the approach of this group is, "We don't do prayers outside of Mass—that kind of thing!—fine. I don't mind meeting people but none of that. So [they] do more social type activities."[34]

It became evident that this small community, in marginalising reference to faith in their meetings, was misaligned with the Pastoral Council's desire to see a greater emphasis on growth in faith through these small communities. Yet, in the Pastoral Council's reluctance explicitly to offer visionary or bold leadership, and out of a desire to honour the "bottom-up" approach, highly valued across the parish, their presence in the parish unintentionally came to be experienced as

---

[31] Vaughan-Spruce, "From Sacred Canopy to Sacred Umbrellas."
[32] Vaughan-Spruce, "From Sacred Canopy to Sacred Umbrellas."
[33] This is a large southern urban parish with four churches. The average weekly Mass attendance in the year I studied the parish was 1071. The parish was more affluent with a large proportion of the population being white British (92 percent).
[34] Vaughan-Spruce, "From Sacred Canopy to Sacred Umbrellas."

one of benign neglect. One parishioner, very active in leading groups and events, remarked, "They seem to do thinking upstairs somewhere but there's not much engagement. . . . We're all getting on with what we're doing. Each of them in theory has a role, but there's not much contact between the two. . . . There's no real kind of engagement with 'what does this mean,' or where it's going."[35]

For parishioners who highly prized their autonomy and empowerment, a perhaps surprising wistfulness was expressed for more explicit (we could say "top-down") leadership. Repeatedly, parishioners spoke to me of the confusion that was rife: poor communication, blurred lines, silo mentalities. One parishioner referred to "meetings for the sake of meetings." The parish priest, fairly new to the parish, perceived the manifold difficulties and commented, "Everybody is willing, everybody's kind and everybody's wanting to do things . . . I don't think there's a clearly articulated vision of where the parish is moving towards. . . . There's lots of energy . . . to move things forward . . . [but] there's not always a great harnessing of that energy to go in the same direction. I mean sometimes you're going here, there, and everywhere."[36] He added, "One of my primary objectives . . . [is] to start to get some . . . structures in place so that people know who's making decisions and how those decisions are communicated." In other words, he proposed to correct the overplayed "charcoal fire" leadership with more directional, "powerful flame" leadership.

The example of this second British parish arguably confirms Smith's theory about the need for "distinctiveness" for religious subcultures to survive. The scout hut community, resisting distinctiveness through reluctance to incorporate the faith dimension, bore little resemblance to the self-consciously "distinctively" Catholic parishioners singing carols and handing out Christmas Mass cards on the new estate. Yet, in articulating a desire for clearer direction (to know "'what does this mean,' or where it's going"), parishioners at the second British parish seemed to express a desire for greater distinctiveness or "collective identity."

CHARACTERISTICS OF PNEUMATOLOGICAL TRANSFORMATION

I commented at the outset that a parish in the declining western church will be forced to undergo unchosen adaptation thanks to sociological forces beyond its control. The question is whether it will embrace the pneumatological transformation prompted at this "change of epoch" in a new apostolic age. Our brief survey has indicated

---

[35] Vaughan-Spruce, "From Sacred Canopy to Sacred Umbrellas."
[36] Vaughan-Spruce, "From Sacred Canopy to Sacred Umbrellas."

characteristics of parishes that are intentionally undergoing an invisible, cultural transformation that complements the visible, sociological one. This inner transformation is marked by a distinctiveness: a parish that knows what it offers that is different from the wider neighbourhood in which it is situated and expresses this by sharing vision. This vision might be bold, and yet it is most fruitfully brought about slowly, with humility and vulnerability where needed, and yet with persevering direction that offers unity and purpose. These characteristics seem to be summarised in the global Synod's keywords: communion, participation, mission.

At this "change of epoch," it is possible to overplay both "powerful flame," intentional leadership and "charcoal fire," inclusive leadership. My examples from British and Canadian parishes demonstrate that both extremes can be corrected. I propose that bold, visionary leadership is required to foster communities marked by a "distinctiveness" that contributes towards their survival in a late secular environment. Yet, without the softening of inclusive, listening approaches, a bold leader can unwittingly alienate and destabilise a parish community. Likewise, an inclusive, listening leadership approach—with no strengthening from a courageous and explicit vision—can leave parishioners directionless, lacking the distinctive, "collective identity" they likely seek in a bewildering time of change. Both dimensions of leadership can be combined to ensure that the pneumatological "change of epoch" accompanies the sociological one: both are critical for our new apostolic age. M

Hannah Vaughan-Spruce is executive director of global mission at Divine Renovation, a Catholic ministry inspiring and equipping parishes around the world to become mission-focused. She read theology at Cambridge and was awarded her PhD from St. Mary's University, Twickenham in the area of sociology of religion and theology in 2021. She has published a number of books, including co-authoring, *Why Catholics Leave, What They Miss, and How They Might Return* (Paulist, 2019), *Handbook for Catechists* (CTS, 2018), and the forthcoming *After Secularisation: The Present and Future of British Catholicism* (CTS, 2025). She is a consecrated virgin based in the Diocese of Plymouth, UK.

Sabbath, Contemplative Time, and Liturgical Listening

Claire E. Wolfteich

Abstract: As we explore listening practices in global Catholicism, we have an opportunity to learn from spiritual traditions and their wisdom about stillness, receptivity, rest, and attention. This article focuses on Sabbath in dialogue with Jewish and Christian writings, particularly with regard to the dignity of work, sacred time, and receptive relationship to God and all of creation. Considering Catholic teachings on Sunday and Sabbath, I develop the idea of liturgical listening, arguing that the Eucharistic assembly can be a formative space for cultivating practices of listening together.

FOR WENDELL BERRY (1934–), AMERICAN AUTHOR, CULTURAL critic, farmer, and environmentalist, Sunday morning walks in the woods of rural Kentucky were Sabbath practices, time to be still, to quiet. As he writes in his collection of "Sabbath poems":

> I go among trees and sit still.
> All my stirring becomes quiet
> around me like circles on water.
> My tasks lie in their places where I left them, asleep like cattle.

In the stillness and in this place, tasks slumbering, Berry is able to hear. Silence opens the sounds of what has not been heard—internal fear, but also his own voice, his long muted but quietly emerging "song": *"I hear my song at last, and I sing it."*[1] Berry spends many Sunday mornings at church, but when the weather is good he is drawn to the sloping woodlands and finds the outdoors to be a particularly powerful space to practice Sabbath: "The idea of the sabbath gains in meaning as it is brought out-of-doors and into a place where nature's principles of self-sustaining wholeness and health are still evident."

---

[1] Wendell Berry, *This Day: Collected & New Sabbath Poems* (New York: Counterpoint, 2014), 7.

Walks in solitude enable him to perceive the organic weave of the "one fabric of creation."[2]

Howard Thurman (1899–1981), African American mystic, preacher, and mentor to civil rights leader Martin Luther King, Jr., also loved trees. "The signature of God is all around me," Thurman writes, "in the rocks, in the trees, in the minds of men."[3] In "Mysticism and Social Change," Thurman recounts: "When I was a boy I was always driven to worship when I saw a storm come up on the shores of the Atlantic Ocean on the Florida coast. A stillness pervaded everything. The tall sea grass stood at attention."[4] That sense of stillness and attention imbedded in nature remained an important part of Thurman's spirituality. Amidst his public ministry and leadership, Thurman found it important to "center down," to "come to a point of rest, a place of pause."[5] In that place of pause, Thurman writes, we begin to listen and hear at a deeper level. Thurman describes this listening as a form of discernment, a sonic sifting among a multitude of competing sounds:

> The streets of our minds seethe with endless traffic;
> Our spirits resound with clashing, with noisy silences,
> While something deep within hungers and thirsts for the still moment and the resting lull . . .
> As we listen, floating up through all the jangling echoes of our turbulence, there is a sound of another kind—
> A deeper note which only the stillness of the heart makes clear.[6]

Like Berry, Thurman seeks an inner stillness that opens space to hear. It is not only external noise that crowds out the deeper note but also interior spiritual cacophony and restlessness. The natural world helped Thurman to listen, center down, and hear the deeper note. This listening required prayer and practice, as Thurman reflected: "Give me the listening ear. I seek this day the disciplined mind, the disciplined heart, the disciplined life that makes my ear the focus of attention."[7]

As the synodal process seeks to cultivate listening and dialogue among Catholics for the renewal of the church, we have an opportunity to learn from rich traditions of spirituality and their wisdom about listening, stillness, time, our relationship with the natural world, and

---

[2] Berry, *This Day*, xxii.
[3] Lerita Coleman Brown, *What Makes You Come Alive: A Spiritual Walk with Howard Thurman* (Minneapolis, MN: Broadleaf, 2023), 45.
[4] Brown, *What Makes You Come Alive*, 44.
[5] Howard Thurman, *Meditations of the Heart* (Boston, MA: Beacon, 2014), 29.
[6] Thurman, *Meditations of the Heart*, 28–29.
[7] Thurman, *Meditations of the Heart*, 208.

cultivating attention. There is something about being still that opens us to the world, enables us to perceive reality—ourselves, others, even God—more fully. There are many spiritual practices that develop a capacity to be still, pay attention, listen. Here I explore Sabbath in dialogue with Jewish and Christian writings, unpacking some of the many-layered meanings of Sabbath, particularly with regard to the dignity of work, sacred time, and receptive relationship to God and all of creation. Considering Catholic teachings on Sunday and Sabbath, I develop the idea of liturgical listening, with the Eucharistic gathering a central practice of listening together.

SABBATH, CREATION, AND DIGNIFIED WORK

Sabbath keeping is an ancient practice with complex layers of meaning and debates about theology and practice in different communities. There is no single meaning of Sabbath; thus, this brief exploration picks up key themes without aiming to flatten the complexity and diversity. Two biblical motifs stand out when considering Sabbath: creation and liberation. In six days, God creates the world and then rests: "On the seventh day God finished the work that he had done, and he rested on the seventh day from all the work that he had done. So God blessed the seventh day and hallowed it" (Gen 2:2–3). The biblical imperative to "remember the Sabbath day and keep it holy" is a call to keep alive the memory of God's creation of the world (Gen 1–2:3, Exod 20:8–11). In his 1998 apostolic letter *Dies Domini* ("The Day of the Lord"), John Paul II sought to reanimate Sunday as a sacred day of rest and worship. Key to recovering the doctrinal foundations of Sunday is, for John Paul II, the creation story in Genesis 2:3 and an understanding of the Sabbath: "In order to grasp fully the meaning of Sunday . . . we must re-read the great story of creation and deepen our understanding of the theology of the 'Sabbath.'"[8] This word "re-reading" brings to mind the ancient spiritual practice of *lectio divina*, repetitive reading or hearing the Word, meditation on it, prayer, and contemplation. One could say that Sabbath keeping is an invitation to do *lectio* with the biblical stories of creation.

So too, keeping Sabbath recalls the divine gift of freedom: "Remember that you were a slave in the land of Egypt, and the LORD your God brought you out from there with a mighty hand and an outstretched arm; therefore the LORD your God commanded you to keep the sabbath day" (Deut 5:12–15). Sabbath observance recalls that divine act of liberation; obedience to the Sabbath command

---

[8] John Paul II, *Dies Domini* ("The Day of the Lord"), no. 8, www.vatican.va/content/john-paul-ii/en/apost_letters/1998/documents/hf_jp-ii_apl_05071998_dies-domini.html.

is ironically a mark of freedom. This is why Walter Brueggemann argues for Sabbath as "resistance and alternative" to economism, consumerism, anxiety, and coercion—a "new social reality."[9]

The seventh day does not undermine the value and meaning of the other six but rather opens space for freedom, celebration of what has been created and given, and rest from work. Sabbath is a day set apart, a respite from toil and human manipulation of the world, from ceaseless productivity, or what Josef Pieper called "total work."[10] Work is still good—but when work dominates the human person, leaving little time for rest, recreation, stillness, and other aspects of life, humanity is depleted and the capacity for attention diminished. There must be time when, in Berry's words, we can let tasks lie, when we can come to Thurman's place of pause. "Leisure is a form of that stillness that is the necessary preparation for accepting reality," Pieper writes, for "only the person who is still can hear."[11] Sabbath is a complement to a theology of good work, where labor is part of a human calling but never the sum total. As Jewish theologian and mystic Abraham Joshua Heschel writes: "The Sabbath as a day of abstaining from work is not a depreciation but an affirmation of labor, a divine exaltation of its dignity."[12]

Here there is resonance with Catholic social teaching in its emphasis on the dignity of the worker. In his 1981 encyclical *Laborem Exercens* ("On Human Work"), John Paul II advances a high theology of work as a human calling and participation in God's creative activity. At the same time, he asserts that both work and rest are part of God's creativity and so too human life. Human beings naturally need—and have a right to—rest, time for worship, family, and recreation.[13] Jewish and Catholic teachings, then, both affirm the dignity of labor in juxtaposing work with rhythms of pause and restoration, important in their own right, not as tools to increase the efficiency of labor.

So too work must be seen in relationship to the natural world, to nonhuman creatures. As Berry laments, human work too often has destructive impact on the natural environment. Sabbath rest is needed not only to restore human beings but to give respite to the land and orient human beings again and again to the gift that is the earth and all

---

[9] Walter Brueggemann, *Sabbath as Resistance: Saying No to the Culture of Now* (Louisville, KY: Westminster John Knox, 2014), xiv, 43.

[10] Josef Pieper, *Leisure, the Basis of Culture* (South Bend, IN: St. Augustine's, 1998), 4.

[11] Pieper, *Leisure*, 31.

[12] Abraham Joshua Heschel, *The Sabbath* (New York: Farrar, Straus, and Giroux, 1951), 28.

[13] John Paul II, *Laborem Exercens* ("On Human Work"), nos. 9, 25: www.vatican.va/content/john-paul-ii/en/encyclicals/documents/hf_jp-ii_enc_14091981_laborem-exercens.html.

its creatures. As Berry's Sabbath walks cultivated his attention to the wholeness and damage of the land, so Sabbath rest deepens awareness of divine providence and the creative labors of the natural world. Berry writes: "We are to rest on the sabbath . . . in order to understand that the providence or the productivity of the living world, the most essential work, continues while we rest. This work . . . is far more complex and wonderful than any work we have done or ever will do."[14]

Sabbath theology and Catholic social teaching converge to contest systemic patterns of overwork and exploitation and environmental destruction, envisioning instead a more just, spacious, and relational way of life.[15] According to biblical texts, Sabbath rest, release, and renewal is to be extended to the poor, foreigner, animals, and the land (Exod 20:8–11, Exod 23:10–12, Lev 25:1–7). Sabbath is not seen here as a luxury but a principle of justice. In keeping Sabbath, we gain a measure of freedom from toil and recognize that need for rest and restoration in others. We learn how to pause and pay attention, listen to one another and the natural world. Jewish environmental scholar David Mevorach Seiden describes weekly Shabbat observance as a "rehearsal for living sustainably and justly in relation to the Earth and all her species."[16] In the word "rehearsal," there is the sense of practice, training, done over time to hone skills and create embodied memory. So too, Pope Francis's 2015 encyclical *Laudato Si'* notes the importance of the Sabbath—and its extension in the sabbatical year and Jubilee—as a practice of relational justice with others and the land.[17] Across Jewish and Christian traditions, the Sabbath can be seen as a liberative practice that cultivates attention, gratitude for the gifts of creation, and just relationship with other human beings and the natural world.

CONTEMPLATIVE TIME

Sabbath keeping also embodies a theology of time as sacred gift, countering the commodification and compression of time. David

---

[14] Berry, *This Day*, xxii.
[15] See Claire E. Wolfteich, "Sabbath Theology and Practice: Implications for Ecological Spirituality and Ethics," in *An Anthology of Contemporary Ecotheology, Philosophy, and Eco-Justice Practices*, ed. Nadja Furlan, Ecothee, vol. 7 (Ljubljana, Slovenia: Poligrafi, 2024), 75–84.
[16] David Mevorach Seidenberg, *Kabbalah and Ecology: God's Image in the More-Than-Human World* (Cambridge: Cambridge University Press, 2015), 322, footnote 1039.
[17] Pope Francis, *Laudato Si'*, no. 71, www.vatican.va/content/francesco/en/encyclicals/documents/papa-francesco_20150524_enciclica-laudato-si.html.

Maume describes the "overpaced American,"[18] while other scholars describe a "cult of speed,"[19] and the impact of "time poverty."[20] Our language also reflects a commodification of time, seen as capital; we "spend time," "waste time," and "save time." In this culture of speed and time scarcity, moments of nonproductive pause can seem impossible, and sitting still among trees—well, a bit sentimental. Describing Sabbath keeping as a kind of cultural and political resistance, Ana Levy-Lyons outlines the sharp counter-cultural choice before us: "As sweet and gentle as the Sabbath may be, its arrival collides violently with the secular world. It forces us to choose every week: will I surrender to a deeper principle of joy and meaning or will I embezzle time from God?"[21]

In contrast with a compressed, scarce, and anxious sense of time, writers on Sabbath describe time as sacred and spacious. For Heschel, Sabbath is a "palace in time" that brings "adjacency to eternity."[22] Sabbath keeping is an art that imbues time with holiness and vivid color, "the art of painting on the canvas of time the mysterious grandeur of the climax of creation. . . . Our keeping of the Sabbath day is a paraphrase of His sanctification of the seventh day."[23] Time is a sacred gift to be shared with mutual generosity and receptivity. Dorothy Bass describes Sabbath keeping as "receiving the gift of time."[24] John Paul II encourages Christians to "give their time to Christ."[25] Even God squanders time freely with us, lingering with the good creation on the seventh day, according to John Paul II's poetic description: "The divine rest of the seventh day . . . speaks, as it were, of God's lingering before the 'very good' work (Gen 1:31) which his hand has wrought, in order to cast upon it *a gaze full of joyous delight.* This is a 'contemplative' gaze which does not look to new accomplishments but enjoys the beauty of what has already been

---

[18] David J. Maume, "The 'Over-Paced' American: Recent Trends in the Intensification of Work," in *Research in the Sociology of Work,* vol. 17: Workplace Temporalities, ed. B. Rubin (Leeds: Emerald, 2007), 251–283.
[19] Carl Honoré, *In Praise of Slowness: How a Worldwide Movement is Challenging the Cult of Speed*, 1st ed. (San Francisco: HarperSanFrancisco, 2004). See also Heather Menzies, *No Time: Stress and the Crisis of Modern Life* (Madeira Park, BC: Douglas and McIntyre, 2005).
[20] On this point and its relationship to Sabbath, see Claire E. Wolfteich, "Time Poverty, Women's Labor, and Catholic Social Teaching: A Practical Theological Exploration," *Journal of Moral Theology* 2, no. 2 (June 2013): 40–59.
[21] Ana Levy-Lyons, "Sabbath Practice as Political Resistance," *Tikkun* 27 (2012): 18.
[22] Heschel, *The Sabbath*, 15, 14.
[23] Heschel, *The Sabbath*, 16.
[24] Dorothy C. Bass, *Receiving the Day: Christian Practices for Opening the Gift of Time* (Hoboken, NJ: Jossey Bass, 2000).
[25] John Paul II, *Dies Domini*, no. 7.

achieved."[26] The practice of Sabbath keeping imitates this contemplative God who takes time to see, pay attention to, all that is. The image of a lingering God in joyful relationship with creation suggests a way of being that is relational, grateful, attentive, contemplative, spacious.

Still, inviting images of contemplative time do collide against the realities of time poverty and the fact that gender, race, and class all impact how time, work, and leisure are experienced. We should avoid an overly romanticized vision of Sabbath. Some are unable to access Sabbath time. And, while slowing can open us to listen, it is also the case that many people practice listening in choppy fragments of time, multitasking, stretching attention and energy to triage what most needs to be heard. We can embrace the contemplative invitation of Sabbath while retaining a spirit of flexibility in practice and recognition of interstitial forms of practice—the few moments of rest a parent might gain huddled in a bathroom or car, the quick prayer by an exhausted worker, the effort to pause tasks when someone unexpectedly needs a listening ear.

We need to engage holistically with these lived realities along with the beautiful theology of time that emerges in writing on Sabbath and Sunday. From a Christian perspective, writes John Paul II, Sunday is "the day which reveals the meaning of time."[27] The Lord's Day is the "eighth day"; every Sunday is a little Easter. John Paul II does not want Sabbath or Sunday to be conflated simply with leisure and its contemporary packaging in the notion of the "weekend." He critiques a cultural weakening of the meaning of Sunday, too often undermined by all-consuming work, decreasing religious affiliation, and Sunday morning youth soccer. While the concept of the "weekend" addresses our human need for rest and relaxation, "when Sunday loses its fundamental meaning and becomes merely part of a 'weekend,' it can happen that people stay locked within a horizon so limited."[28] According to John Paul II, the mystery of Christ's life, death, and resurrection fundamentally changes time. We live into this mystery particularly in setting aside Sunday as a day of worship together.

LITURGICAL LISTENING

Liturgy is by no means the only space for cultivating listening. Everyday communities of family, workplace, schools, and neighbor-

---

[26] John Paul II, *Dies Domini*, no. 11. I have developed the theme of contemplative lingering in Claire E. Wolfteich, "Sabbath Stillness: Thoughts of a Lingering God," *Spiritus* 24, no. 1 (2024): 146–159, doi.org/10.1353/scs.2024.a924578.
[27] John Paul II, *Dies Domini*, no. 75.
[28] John Paul II, *Dies Domini*, no. 4.

hood are training grounds for the practice of listening. And as Berry, Thurman, and many others have attested, solitude in nature can open the ear and heart in profound ways.

However, the Eucharistic liturgy is a formative practice of ecclesial listening. In dialogue with Jewish understandings of Sabbath, John Paul II seeks to reanimate Sunday as a time of contemplative rest and communal listening in the Eucharistic assembly. Together, the church listens to the Holy Spirit: "The Spirit is unfailingly present to every one of the Church's days, appearing unpredictably and lavishly with the wealth of his gifts. But it is in the Sunday gathering for the weekly celebration of Easter that the Church listens to the Spirit in a special way and reaches out with him to Christ." Listening to the Word, attentive to the Spirit, also is the foundation of the *sense of the faithful*: "Authentic participation in the *sensus fidei* relies necessarily on a profound and attentive listening to the word of God"; "What is required is an attentive and receptive listening to the Scriptures in the liturgy, and a heartfelt response."[29] John Paul II describes this contemplative listening to the Word as an imitation of Mary's "pondering": the people listen to the Word proclaimed and, like Mary the mother of Jesus, "ponder" what they hear in their hearts.[30]

As the Eucharistic liturgy is a special space for listening to the Holy Spirit and the Word, it also reflects and cultivates the community's attentiveness to the needs of others and the natural world. This listening is expressed in the prayers of the faithful, in the passing of the peace, in gratitude for the gifts of bread and wine, "fruit of the vine and work of human hands." As Pope Francis states in *Laudato Si'*: "And so the day of rest, centred on the Eucharist, sheds its light on the whole week, and motivates us to greater concern for nature and the poor."[31]

Liturgical listening has potential to form a pondering people who can hear and respond to the Holy Spirit and one another, who delight in creation and the Creator. The ability to listen to the Holy Spirit as we listen to one another is a key dimension of a synodal church, states Pope Francis in his opening address: "Without the Holy Spirit, this will be a kind of diocesan parliament, but not a Synod. We are not holding a diocesan parliament, examining this or that question, but making a journey of listening to one another and the Holy Spirit, discussing yes, but discussing with the Holy Spirit, which is a way of

---

[29] International Theological Commission, *Sensus Fidei in the Life of the Church*, nos. 92, 93, 99, www.vatican.va/roman_curia/congregations/cfaith/cti_documents/rc_cti_20140610_sensus-fidei_en.html.
[30] John Paul II, *Dies Domini*, nos. 85, 86.
[31] Pope Francis, *Laudato Si'*, no. 237.

praying."[32] Liturgical listening cultivates habits of prayerful discernment and attention essential for the synodal church. For this reason, it is not surprising that the synthesis report on the synod described the Eucharist as "the source and summit of synodality."[33]

LISTENING WITH THE EAR OF THE HEART

Summer mist settles in around the mountains surrounding Weston Priory, a Benedictine monastery in southern Vermont. Mass was being held in the converted barn, walls open to the wet green grass outside. Brother Michael, guitar still slung around his shoulders, shares his homily with the circle of his fellow monks and the rows of folks gathered on this Sunday morning. In the early morning quiet set aside for *lectio divina*, he said, the song of the small brown hermit thrush deepens the silence and sustains him. Noting that the Green Mountains form the monastery's back yard, and the Okemo Mountains its front yard, Brother Michael paints a picture of a community deeply attentive to the beauty of creation, the monks' silence and song blending with the sounds of creatures all around. From my seat at Mass, I look out at the trees and the edges of the labyrinth, paths curving in between tall grasses that host darting butterflies and a dragonfly or two.

The opening line of the prologue of the *Rule of Saint Benedict* counsels: "Listen with the ear of your heart." Listening is a central practice for Benedictine spirituality, a form of obedience, presence, and attentiveness. That listening is embodied in the personal and communal practices of *lectio divina*: "Let us hear with attentive ears what the divine voice cries out to us daily."[34] Listening to the Word, listening for the Spirit, are essential daily practices; so too is listening for God's voice in one another and all of creation. Known for its liturgical music, the Weston Priory monks produced an original song entitled "Listen," drawing from the importance of the practice in Benedictine spirituality: "Listen and gentle be present to all you've ever close kept in your loving heart! . . . Often look up and see the splendor of life suspended in your heart and mind so longing to be forever alive in this moment's stillness: the thrush echoes your delight."[35]

---

[32] Francis, "Address to the Faithful of the Diocese of Rome," September 28, 2021, www.vatican.va/content/francesco/en/speeches/2021/september/documents/20210918-fedeli-diocesiroma.html.

[33] XVI Ordinary General Assembly of the Synod of Bishops, "A Synodal Church in Mission: Synthesis Report," October 28, 2023, 5.

[34] Judith Sutera, *St. Benedict's Rule: An Inclusive Translation* (Collegeville, MN: Liturgical Press, 2021).

[35] The Benedictine Foundation of the State of Vermont, "Listen," (1973, 1994): www.westonpriory.org/esales/lyrics/Listen.pdf.

Most Sunday liturgies take place in churches and chapels with solid walls, without the open view to the Green Mountains and the porous openness to the song of the thrush mingling with prayer. More likely there are children being hustled to crying rooms, people half-listening as they mull to-do lists, and cell phones buzzing at uncomfortable points in the Eucharistic prayer. Still, we can draw much from this image of a liturgical, listening community. Liturgy perhaps can train the ear to hear, re-read the stories of creation and liberation, ponder the Word, listen for the Spirit, listen to the needs and hearts of a community and the world around us. Liturgy perhaps can reflect "the reality of time" as divine gift, confounding productive and consumerist frameworks of time, patterning us to the mystery of sacred time.

LISTENING AND SABBATH

In reflecting on Sabbath, we are led to ask: What do our patterns of work and time use occlude from our hearing? What "deeper note" might we hear if we could "center down"? Are we locked in limited horizons, missing a more fundamental mystery that has reshaped the meaning of time? And, especially in light of the call to be a synodal church, how do we as a faith community learn to listen better together?

Sabbath is a powerful theology and practice—a "resistance and alternative" to oppressive systems of work that deny human beings space for rest and relationship. Sabbath invites a regular rhythm of renewal. It affirms time not as productive capital to be spent and saved but rather as a lavish divine gift, made holy. Sabbath turns us towards the whole of the created world—the trees, storms, and tall sea grass—to notice and care for all creatures and the land. This is a posture of attention, receptivity, and relationship, all qualities essential to the practice of listening. And in the Sunday Eucharistic gathering, the church has a foundational practice of communal, contemplative listening.

From Wendell Berry's Kentucky trees to Howard Thurman's deeper note, from Benedict's ear of the heart to John Paul II's liturgical pondering: listening is a spiritual practice. It is a contemplative and relational practice of attention and receptivity. Traditions of spirituality bring wisdom about how we learn this practice. Sabbath theology and practice opens an alternative vision of work and time and a dialogical space for listening together with all of creation to God's own creative and liberative spirit. ∎

Claire E. Wolfteich, PhD, is professor of practical theology and spirituality studies at Boston University School of Theology, where she also co-directs the Center for Practical Theology. She is project director of the Creative Callings research and innovation hub, funded by the Lilly Endowment. Dr. Wolfteich's book publications include *Motherwork, Public Leadership, and Women's Life Writing: Explorations in Spirituality Studies and Practical Theology* (Brill, 2017); *Catholic Approaches in Practical Theology: International and Interdisciplinary Perspectives* (Peeters, 2016), co-edited with Annemie Dillen; the edited volume *Invitation to Practical Theology: Catholic Voices and Visions* (Paulist, 2014); and *Sabbath in the City: Sustaining Urban Pastoral Excellence* (Westminster John Knox, 2008), co-authored with Bryan P. Stone.

Listening in Stereo and Communicating in Semaphore: Child Sexual Abuse Survivor-Led Strategies for Culture Change in the Catholic Church

Alana Harris

Abstract: This expository piece, focusing on a grassroots movement called LOUDfence to address child sexual abuse in religious settings, explores the ways in which the symbolic activity of tying ribbons to church fences offers an active and adaptable listening strategy for giving visibility and voice to survivors and survivor-allies. Working through signs, symbols, embodied actions, and ecclesial metaphors, it offers a methodology and mode for creative, trauma-informed, and lay-led cultural change in Catholic and Anglican church contexts.

A kitchen table in Cumbria (in the north of England and on the border with Scotland) might seem like an unlikely place to start a global movement, but we know there is sound precedent across history for surprises from the peripheries. *LOUDfence UK* originated in the small village of Kirkbampton in October 2021 as a response to a local child sexual abuse revelation centred around the bishop of Carlisle.[1] It was a simple act of solidarity deployed by Antonia Sobocki, a Catholic survivor of family abuse, to support her neighbour and give everyone in the church, survivors and survivor-allies, a voice. That first LOUDfence three years ago, and the more than twenty that have followed since, pivoted around tying ribbons of all colours and styles to railings, suspended wires, around trees, and as internal displays within churches.[2] In these liminal

---

[1] Maddy Fry, "Bishop of Carlisle admits 'Error of Judgement,'" *Church Times*, October 9, 2020, www.churchtimes.co.uk/articles/2020/9-october/news/uk/bishop-of-carlisle-admits-error-of-judgement.

[2] Phil Coleman, "Church Abuse Activist: 'These Ribbons are a Cry for Change,'" *News & Star, The Cumberland News*, October 11, 2020, www.newsandstar.co.uk/news/18781342.church-abuse-activist-these-ribbons-cry-change/, and "Pioneering Carlisle 'Loudfence' Campaign to Beat Clerical Abuse Looks Set to Go National," *News & Star, The Cumberland News*, October 30, 2021, www.newsandstar.co.uk/news/19683333.pioneering-loudfence-campaign-beat-clerical-abuse-looks-set-go-

settings, the ribbons and handwritten messages symbolically enable people to send and receive messages of care, compassion, and support. In giving visibility and voice to the eviscerating effects of Child Sexual Abuse (CSA), LOUDfence aims to foster honesty and truth telling, seeking to break cultures of silence, taboo, and containment. It is a form of "deep" listening, trauma-informed theology, and feminist pastoral praxis in which we hear (and see) the "speaking wound."[3]

LOUDfence installations across Britain have been mostly ecumenical, involving Catholic and Anglican parishes, and often over multiple days. In September 2023, two representatives of LOUDfence UK addressed the Pontifical Commission for the Protection of Minors and met Pope Francis, who offered prayers and blessings to the work, alongside expressing hope that their informal ministry would spread to other places.[4] Following an invitation to hold a LOUDfence at Lourdes (and in Paris at the Plenary Assembly of the Conference of Catholic Bishops of France) in March 2023, a sister movement, *Rubans contre l'oubli*, has started.[5] In April 2024, a LOUDfence (curated by the UK volunteer team, in consultation with the US bishop and local survivors), was held at St Joseph's Cathedral, Diocese of Wheeling-Charleston in West Virginia.[6]

These diocesan-focused events have brought together local survivor groups and CSA safeguarding teams, working with bishops and priests, men and women religious, and hundreds of concerned people within, but *also estranged from or outside* the churches, to grieve, remember, and recognise abuse in communities. A LOUDfence may be likened to those "spontaneous shrines" that spring up on the roadside to commemorate trauma, or flowers placed outside

---

national/#:~:text=It%20encourages%20those%20affected%20by,42%20of%20the%20country's%20cathedrals.

[3] Margaret D. Stetz, "Listening 'With Serious Intent': Feminist Pedagogical Practice and Social Transformation," *Transformations* 12, no. 1 (2001): 7–27; Cathy Caruth, *Unclaimed Experience—Trauma, Narrative, and History* (Baltimore, MD: Johns Hopkins University Press, 1996), 9.

[4] Vatican News, "Protection of Minors: Pope Meets with Two Women from LOUDfence during Plenary," September 23, 2023, www.vaticannews.va/en/vatican-city/news/2023-09/protection-minors-plenary-annual-report-audience-loudfence.html.

[5] See rubanscontreloubli.fr and x.com/ContreLoubli.

[6] Chris Altieri, "UK Abuse Survivors Campaign Seeks Cultural Change in the Church," *Crux*, April 8, 2024, cruxnow.com/church-in-the-usa/2024/04/uk-abuse-survivors-campaign-seeks-culture-change-in-the-church; Coleen Rowan, "West Virginia Diocese Welcomes LOUDfence Campaign of Awareness, Support for Abuse Victims," *Catholic Review,* April 13, 2024 catholicreview.org/west-virginia-diocese-welcomes-loudfence-campaign-of-awareness-support-for-abuse-victims/.

places associated with loss and suffering[7]—a pop-up public memorial that has the capacity to surface and re-sound the pain, festering hurt, and profound damage suppressed and often hidden in our communities.

In its DIY methodology and symbolic mode, a LOUDfence ranges well beyond most procedural, church-based safeguarding or CSA institutional actions, reaching from the liminal site of a church boundary fence to dialogue, potentially, with the passing public. One such occurrence was recollected by Antonia, flowing from the LOUDfence in Plymouth in February 2023:

> A teenage girl passed by and noted the ribbons. She was on her way to collect her grandfather for his dinner from the pub further along the road near to the church.
>   A little while later she returned with her grandfather, and he stopped to look at the ribbons. He asked what they were for. . . . He looked at the ribbons with his granddaughter. He asked if he too could tie a ribbon. His granddaughter looked at him and asked "Why granddad? We don't know anyone who has been abused?" He answered: "Yes you do. This was me. I was raped as a child. I don't know why I'm talking about it. I've never spoken of it until now." . . . They had a very open conversation then and there.[8]

As a lay movement of volunteers outside institutional structures but in conversation and collaboration with church authorities, the LOUDfence movement, as experienced and enacted across England, Wales, and Scotland, offers a suggestive model for active listening in a synodal church.

This short expository piece, focusing as a case study on a recent LOUDfence held at the Catholic and Anglican cathedrals in Newcastle (in the north of England) in March 2024,[9] seeks to expound two interrelated facets of LOUDfence as a flexible, adaptive, and lay-attuned listening practice with potentially global application in responding to the scourge of CSA in our churches but also, and perhaps especially, in wider society too.

I contend that a LOUDfence might be thought of not only as an *event,* but also a *methodology* and *mode* for survivor-led cultural change through its capacity to communicate in semaphore by using

---

[7] Jack Santino, "Performative Commemoratives, the Personal, and the Public: Spontaneous Shrines, Emergent Ritual, and the Field of Folklore," *Journal of American Folklore* 117, no. 466 (2004): 363–372.

[8] Oral history interview with Antonia Sobocki, June 5, 2024, with Ethics Clearance from King's College London, HR/DP-23/24-40771.

[9] See newcastle.anglican.org/news/survivors-of-church-based-abuse-host-special-loudfence-service-at-newcastle-cath.php.

universal signs and sacramental symbols. Its coloured ribbons and displayed Christian images and objects communicate messages without a flurry of words and deploy a visual register to "speak" across emotional and institutional distances, like coded flags held aloft. These listening practices require "ears attuned" to the rite and rote evoked by the material and visual installations of a LOUDfence. Nevertheless, for those with "eyes to see and ears to hear" there is an opportunity for attentive listening in stereo—as multi-modal, multi-channel meanings are differentially conveyed to survivors, survivor allies, institutional stakeholders, members of the public passing by, the media, and indeed past and future LOUDfence participants (as the symbolic registers grow, diversify, and acquire accretions).

In the discussion that follows, examples are offered to demonstrate the creative and performative rituals, and liturgical and sacramental actions assembled, to give often non-verbal, embodied "voice" to pain, trauma, damage, and unhealed individual and collective wounds within the church. A LOUDfence makes recourse to longstanding, but over the last few decades somewhat dormant, symbolic tools and folk or vernacular vocabularies drawn from the traditional "Catholic" imaginary to make the *sensus fidelium* heard.[10] The LOUDfence movement promises a form of grassroots, polyvalent "synodal listening in the spirit" as a portable, temporary, and potentially iterative sounding board that surfaces, amplifies, and sends out messages of sorrow and support to nameless survivors and their suppressed experiences in a form of active memorialisation. It can be differentiated from the more formal, official, and permanent public memorials to CSA survivors planned in Australia and France following the Royal Commission into Institutional Responses to Child Sexual Abuse and the Independent Commission on Sexual Abuse in the Catholic Church (CIASE).[11] Nevertheless, it also finds itself in a continuum with these other forms and formats of listening, speaking, testifying, lamenting, repenting, and witnessing.

---

[10] Colleen McDannell, *Material Christianity—Religion and Popular Culture in America* (New Haven, CT: Yale University Press, 1998); Andrew Greeley, *The Catholic Imaginary* (Berkeley: University of California Press, 2001); David Morgan, *The Embodied Eye: Religious Visual Culture and the Social Life of Feeling* (Berkeley: University of California Press, 2012); Gaëlle Bargain-Darrigues and Gustavo Morello, "Lived Religion Beyond Words: A Denotive Analysis of Participant-Produced Photos of Meaningful Objects," *Sociological Review* 71, no. 5 (2023): 1037–1057.

[11] See www.dss.gov.au/families-and-children-programs-services-children/national-memorial-for-victims-and-survivors-of-institutional-child-sexual-abuse.

Trauma-Informed and Creative Methods to Give Visibility and Voice to CSA

The practice of tying ribbons to cathedral fences in commemoration of victim-survivors of CSA started in Ballarat (Country Victoria, Australia—another periphery) in 2015, while the Royal Commission held hearings in that highly traumatised community designated as the epicenter of the nation's abuse crisis.[12] Several Australian academics have written independently about the ways in which LOUDfences in that setting speak and act as a form of protest and accountability—a confronting installation to speak truth to power.[13] These acts of defiance and contested memorialization sound in the context of a "traumascape" and function as a "work of acknowledgement" to the continuing pain of survivors and their cry for institutional transformative justice. One of the most poignant LOUDfences in Australia was the one hastily assembled, without permission, at St. Mary's Cathedral in Sydney in January 2023 when Ballarat-resident Paul Auchettl tied ribbons for his deceased brother during Cardinal George Pell's memorial mass.[14]

There is, however, a different origin story that wraps around the LOUDfences held in the UK—Antonia Sobocki was prompted to her act of tying ribbons to an Anglican church fence by a diocesan scandal, her appreciation of women's collective agency, and ecumenical solidarity in a small rural village.[15] The LOUDfence events that have followed over the last three years are hard to define and describe simply and concisely. LOUDfence is a word that acts as a "brand" as well as a descriptor, a collective noun, a programme, and sometimes even a verb. A LOUDfence might span a single day (or multiple days or even months, as in one parish). They are mostly curated by Antonia and a core team but are also crowd-sourced, with attendees adding coloured ribbons and fabric to the fences, writing messages, and

---

[12] Kathleen McPhillips, "'Unbearable Knowledge': Managing Cultural Trauma at the Royal Commission," *Psychoanalytic Dialogues* 27, no. 2 (2017): 130–146.

[13] Dave McDonald, "The Work of Acknowledgement: 'Loud Fence' as a Community-Level Response to Institutional Child Sexual Abuse Testimony," *Social and Legal Studies* 33, no. 2 (2024): 213–235; Megan Deas, Kerry McCallum, and Kerry Martin, "Mediating via Materiality: Continuing Critical Conversations about Child Sexual Abuse in Australia," *Difficult Conversations* (London: British Council, 2023), doi.org/10.57884/6P72-TZ16.

[14] Christopher Knaus, "'Unfinished Business': Ballarat Abuse Survivor to Tie a Ribbon at St. Mary's before George Pell Funeral," *The Guardian*, January 23, 2023, www.theguardian.com/australia-news/2023/jan/26/unfinished-business-ballarat-abuse-survivor-to-tie-a-ribbon-at-st-marys-before-george-pell-funeral.

[15] Jane Chevous, Alana Harris, and Antonia Sobocki, "'A Solidarity Dance': Feminist Approaches to Abuse," in *Feminist Theologies: A Companion*, ed. Kerrie Handasyde, Katharine Massam, and Sean Burns (London: SCM, 2024), 135–148.

participating in planned prayers and activities. A LOUDfence might be a stand-alone day event (with a Mass) or folded into a scheduled series of actions over several days encompassing processions, customized liturgies, acts of reparation, and bidding prayers. Participants are invited through institutional safeguarding networks (and diocesan survivor representative bodies), through word of mouth and advance notification of an event on social media, and there is always also an element of serendipity—the curious passerby or two who sees the ribbons fluttering in the breeze and stops to engage. In the UK, the ribbons and messages are usually displayed for an agreed and fixed period, but as will be discussed below, varied diocesan conventions are evolving to preserve—or symbolically transform—the ribbons afterwards. As will become apparent, while a LOUDfence is an *event*, it is also a *method* or *mode of modelling culture change* through creative repertoires and rich cultural symbols. It uses images, metaphors, and a devotional and sacramental imaginary (including *ex votos* and icons) to speak through multiple registers when words fail or are inadequate. Survivors can surface their story or signal their presence—by tying a ribbon or writing a message (outside church grounds) or through partaking in ritual activities within the buildings—without having to fully disclose (and risk re-traumatisation or instrumentalization). Survivor-allies like me, processing our anger, shame, and sense of collective complicity and responsibility, can show our support, solidarity, and compassion by typing a ribbon cipher, encountering the written fragments of traumatic experiences (and lifelong wounds) arrayed on the cathedral or parish church fences, and offering a supportive shoulder or listening ear (if invited to do so). Drawing on the foundational semiotics and modifying them upon their migration to Britain and movement around England, Scotland, and Wales, a diversified form of performative communication has emerged drawing upon the particularities of places and locations "storied" over the centuries.[16]

Thus far in Britain a LOUDfence has always been held with the permission of, and in close consultation (though with varying degrees of enthusiasm) with diocesan authorities, following extensive preparation and multiple planning meetings with the bishop and cathedral/church officials, safeguarding staff, and local survivors and survivor-allies. The ecumenical cast of a LOUDfence, characteristic of almost every installation over the last three years, has also been critical as the synchronisation of a display at *both* Anglican and Catholic cathedrals spreads the framework and focus for surfacing CSA in religious settings. This approach is in line with the

---

[16] Marion Bowman, "Arthur and Bridget in Avalon: Celtic Myth, Vernacular Religion, and Contemporary Spirituality in Glastonbury," *Fabula* 48 (2007): 16–32.

methodology of the 2022 UK Independent Inquiry into Child Sexual Abuse, which highlighted serious child protection and safeguarding failings in *all* religious organisations—and many other child-focused institutions too—so that the Catholic Church alone as a minority church in multi-religious Britain has not been the sole focus of publicised survivor anger and societal opprobrium.[17]

The UK LOUDfences held have also illuminated the widely-known but little discussed fact that the family, as a site for physical and sexual abuse, is the most dangerous place for children and, as a consequence, religious organisations have, until now, mostly shirked their responsibility to minister to these victim-survivors as part of their transformation into a safe and survivor-sensitive institution.[18] In charting the ways in which a LOUDfence offers an opportunity to convey trauma and give voice to pain and solidarity—through visual signalling including colour, material objects, spatial arrangements, and ritual—a recent ecumenical installation serves as an illuminating case study.

COMMUNICATING IN SEMAPHORE: ANGELS, STRAWBERRIES, AND RIBBONS BLOWING IN THE WIND

From March 3–5, 2024, the iron railings of the Norman-style St. Nicholas Cathedral (Church of England) and Pugin-designed St. Mary's Catholic Cathedral, both in the centre of Newcastle, were festooned with coloured ribbons. Nestled amongst the riot of colour were formal well-wishes from Fr. Hans Zollner (laminated, to protect the letter from the weather),[19] longer endorsements (on coat of arms letterhead) from bishops of other English dioceses, and personalised and hand-written tags and one-sentence *memoria* notes (and black ribbons) for named individuals (many of whom are no longer alive through suicide). Participants at the event added their own ribbons and wrote messages—on diocesan-designed postcards, the back of an Antony Gormley "Angel of the North" cardboard *ex voto*,[20]

---

[17] Alexis Jay, Malcolm Evans, Ivor Frank, and Drusilla Sharpling, *The Report of the Independent Inquiry into Child Sexual Abuse* (London: House of Commons, 2022), www.iicsa.org.uk/final-report.html.

[18] Tanja Repič Slavič, "Relations, Roles, and Dynamics within Incestuous Families," *The Person and the Challenges: The Journal of Theology, Education, Canon Law, and Social Studies Inspired by John Paul II* 10 (2020): 177–191.

[19] Hans Zollner is a Jesuit priest, psychologist, professor at the Gregorian University, and former member of the Vatican's Pontifical Commission for the Protection of Minors.

[20] Antony Gormley is an acclaimed sculptor, who attended a nearby Benedictine Catholic school in the north of England and erected this metal angel in Gateshead (7 miles from Newcastle) in 1998. For more information about the once controversial,

or unadorned luggage tags. Inside the Catholic cathedral, arranged on the steps leading up to the altar, was a display of shoes—adult sizes and some very small, some painted in gold leaf (and with an explanatory sign that they commemorated the women religious victims of Marko Rupnik)[21]—each with a note commanding the viewer: "see me."

Half a mile away at the Anglican cathedral, adorning one of their fourteen-century perpendicular columns, was a "strawberry field"—little red gems knitted, crocheted, or fashioned in cardboard by parishioners across the diocese. This co-participatory craft project was designed by survivor-artists and pivoted around their insight that

---

now iconic sculpture, see www.gateshead.gov.uk/article/5303/The-history-of-the-Angel-of-the-North.

[21] Elise Ann Allen, "Former Nuns in Rupnick Abuse Case Reveal Identities while Calling for 'Complete Transparency,'" *Catholic Herald*, February 22, 2024, catholicherald.co.uk/former-nuns-in-rupnik-abuse-case-reveal-identities-while-calling-for-complete-transparency/.

sometimes something beautiful can grow, with time and nurturing, out of "muck."[22] There are fascinating lessons to be drawn here about craft, community, mission, and connection which Rev. Dr. Steve Taylor is exploring with his "ordinary knitters" project.[23]

There was also the opportunity to engage with Sarah Troughton's "Transformation" series—ten linocut angels ("like the angel that liberated Peter in Acts," she says)—bridging heaven and earth and traversing emotions such as shame, betrayal, and despair, alongside justice, dignity, and honour.[24] Reproduced on postcards (and evoking the brass rubbings she did in churches as a child), they were available to take as a memento of the event or use as a gentle visual prompt to conversation with others. When the Catholic bishop of Hexham and Newcastle preached at the opening LOUDfence Sunday Mass (March

---

[22] "LOUDfence Strawberry Craft Project," Safeguarding: www.newcastle.anglican.org/safeguarding/if-i-told-you-what-would-you-do-/loudfence-strawberry-craft-project/ and "If I Told You, What Would You Do?" Project, Safeguarding: newcastle.anglican.org/safeguarding/if-i-told-you-what-would-you-do-/.

[23] See "Ordinary Knitters," www.facebook.com/ordinaryknitters/.

[24] "Angels Creative Project," Safeguarding: newcastle.anglican.org/safeguarding/if-i-told-you-what-would-you-do-/angels-creative-project/.

226 *Listening in Stereo and Communicating in Semaphore*

3, 2024), he tailored his sermon around one of these postcards, performatively linking both cathedrals as a powerful signal of Christian unity through prayer, penitence, and advocacy.[25]

Outside the Catholic cathedral, facing the main road and opposite the busy central train station, pink and green ribbons were tied to the open hand of a life-size statue of Cardinal Basil Hume, a locally-born former archbishop of Westminster but also a Benedictine, a religious congregation whose prestigious schools (Downside and the nearby Ampleforth) were the subject of a separate ICCSA Investigation Report.[26] Inside St. Mary's, during an opening liturgy of remembrance and repentance, Bishop Stephen Wright reiterated the apology to victim-survivors he made at his recent installation and pledged to make his diocese safe and supportive of those hurt by abuse within the church or indeed elsewhere.[27] At the closing liturgy on the evening of Wednesday, May 5, his Anglican counterpart Right Rev. Dr. Helen-Ann Hartley tied a LOUDfence "pledge ribbon" (another new development, printed by LOUDfence organisers initially to give to Pope Francis) around the statue of the cathedral's patron, St. Nicholas—thereby committing the diocese into which she has newly arrived to be a haven for survivors and hub for survivor-focused art therapy.

From this qualitative, ethnographic, and visual survey, it is possible to discern the culturally-coded and locally-specific semiotics activated by this LOUDfence—for example St. Mary's Cathedral's *ex votos* reference its nineteenth-century heritage encompassing Gateshead (where the steel sculpture The Angel of the North is located, in contrast to the differing Anglican diocesan borders) as well as tacitly signalling Gormley's education at Ampleforth and the region's industrial past. The ribbons tied to the open hand of the much-loved but equally administratively accountable Dom Basil, OSB, were visually arresting for passersby but also underlined a veiled but pointed reference to the current primate of the Catholic Church in England and Wales (and his immediate predecessor, too) in their handling of perpetrator priests and failures in compassionate ministry

---

[25] "The Third Sunday of Lent, Sunday March 3, 2024, St. Mary's RC Cathedral," www.youtube.com/watch?v=NmAyJKd4qqo, at 33.45.
[26] Alexis Jay, Malcom Evans, Ivor Frank, and Drusilla Sharpling, *Ampleforth and Downside: English Benedictine Congregation Case Study* (London: House of Commons, 2018), www.iicsa.org.uk/reports-recommendations/publications/investigation/ampleforth-downside.html.
[27] Christopher Lamb, "English Catholic Bishop's Installation Models Synodality with Abuse Victims," *National Catholic Reporter,* August 8, 2023, www.ncronline.org/news/english-catholic-bishops-installation-models-synodality-abuse-victims.

to victim-survivors.[28] This can be contrasted with the desire of parishioner-survivors at St. Nicholas to supplement the more generic coloured ribbons with diocesan-sourced (through the Women's Institute network), individualized hand-knitted strawberries—linking the LOUDfence event to their broader "If I Told You What Would You Do?" programme and other local, survivor-led artistic initiatives. In an embrace of active co-production and "craftvism" (activism through crafting),[29] the distinctive bureaucratic structure of the Anglican Church and its embrace of "established church" parochial reach was given tangible expression.

As an *event, methodology*, and *model* for culture change, LOUDfence deploys a variety of creative repertoires and a rich palette of cultural symbols. In analysing the ways in which LOUDfence promotes voice, performatively speaks, and ritually acts, it is helpful to draw upon Leonard Norman Primiano's concept of "vernacular religion." This concept enables a recognition of LOUDfence as a democratic listening practice, a grassroots initiative to give experiential expression to belief (and grief), flexible, adaptable, and a powerfully multi-vocal mechanism for "calling out" the abuses of power, scandalous hypocrisy, and cultures of deflection and denial.[30] LOUDfence draws upon a deep cultural reservoir of symbolism and creative praxis to deploy similar imaginative strategies to those interrogated by Marion Bowman and Ulo Valk in their ethnographic survey of vernacular religion across different Christian and spiritual traditions.[31] As Molly Farneth has argued within a US context, attention to the rituals people create, maintain, and transform offers insight into dynamic and accessible strategies available to forge community, rebalance power, and heal breaches of trust and faith.[32] LOUDfence's aspirations to "depth sound" the abuse crisis in the Catholic and Anglican Churches are "encoded" in the ribbons fluttering on fences—and the rituals devised to complement their

---

[28] "Catholic Church Abuse: Cardinal Vincent Nichols Criticised over Leadership," *BBC News*, November 10, 2020, www.bbc.co.uk/news/uk-54889033; Christopher Lamb, "Claims against Cardinal Cormac Murphy-O'Connor 'Lacked Credibility,'" *The Tablet*, September 29, 2018, www.thetablet.co.uk/news/10798/claims-against-cardinal-cormac-murphy-o-connor-lacked-credibility-.
[29] Sarah Corbett and Sarah Housley, "The Craftivist Collective Guide to Craftivism," *Utopian Studies* 22, no. 2 (2011): 344–351.
[30] Deborah Dash Moore, ed., *Vernacular Religion: Collected Essays of Leonard Norman Primiano* (New York: New York University Press, 2022).
[31] Marion Bowman and Ulo Valk, *Vernacular Religion in Everyday Life: Expressions of Belief* (London: Routledge, 2012).
[32] Molly Farneth, *The Politics of Ritual* (Princeton, NJ: Princeton University Press, 2023).

installation—yet this seemingly simple and abstract visual signalling is readily decipherable and symbolically powerful.

LISTENING IN STEREO: AMPLIFYING DIVERGENT AND DISCORDANT VOICES

As will be apparent from this case study, a LOUDfence is an intentionally temporary and ephemeral memorialization—often a temporary fence or guy line will be erected to display ribbons (as at Liverpool Catholic Cathedral on March 9, 2024)[33]—and like a performance, this makes the commemorative process a living, organic, customisable, and potentially iterative occurrence. The Anglican diocese of Carlisle, for example is preparing for its fourth LOUDfence, as part of a designated "safeguarding season" or annual period of lamentation (for perpetrators and bystanders), and within his pastoral message in October 2023, the bishop of Penrith gave thanks for this period of focused listening and learning, implicitly referencing earlier LOUDfence events as staging posts in the diocese's learning about praxis-oriented actions to make the church a safer environment.[34]

These more ephemeral approaches might be contrasted with recommendation 17.6 of the Australian Royal Commission into Institutional Responses to CSA, which suggested the building of a national and permanent memorial for victims and survivors in the vein of holocaust memorials or the National September 11 Memorial Museum.[35] An initial design of glass archways, called *Transparency and Truth*, won an artistic competition in 2021, with construction timetabled to begin this year.[36] However, insurmountable structural difficulties have required the Australian government to reopen the competition design for a new tender, and the costs for the planned 2026 launch have spiralled to $7.9 million Australian dollars.[37] An academic involved in the French equivalent investigation, CIASE, has

---

[33] "LOUDfence: Catholics and Anglicans Stand Together against Abuse," www.liverpoolcatholic.org.uk/news/loudfence-catholic-and-anglican-churches-stand-together-against-abuse.

[34] "Diocese of Carlisle, Safeguarding Season October 15—November 3, 2023," www.youtube.com/watch?v=6DEHQhBkMRY.

[35] Stephanie N. Arel, *Bearing Witness: The Wounds of Mass Trauma at Memorial Museums* (Minneapolis, MN: Fortress, 2023).

[36] "National Memorial for Victims and Survivors of Institutional Child Sexual Abuse," www.dss.gov.au/families-and-children-programs-services-children/national-memorial-for-victims-and-survivors-of-institutional-child-sexual-abuse.

[37] ABC News, www.dailymotion.com/video/x8yv2jm.

also recommended a permanent memorial,[38] but the focus of attention in that national jurisdiction presently seems to be redress and legal compensation.[39]

The danger of aiming for a more permanent memorial—in the vein of the "sites of conscience" movement[40]—is that whatever is created or erected needs to be recognisable and meaningful to a broad range of victim-survivors and must not signal completion, "turning of the page," or "moving on" with undue identification with (or containment to) one site and constituency. Community-engagement workers and trauma-informed artists are acutely aware of and wrestling with these complexities and ambiguities. In Ballarat, the in-progress CSA memorial (sponsored by the Council and part-funded by the Australian government) is called "Continuous Voices" in recognition that any commemoration needs to be backward-facing *and* forward looking, resonating with the many CSA experiences gathered in and offering opportunities for spatial (and ritual) amplification.[41]

The LOUDfence movement in the UK—if we can call it that—implicitly recognises that an iterative, incremental, and evolving redress, annexed to a healing and reparative process—needs to be part of any memorialization plan. Scholars analysing the interpersonal dynamics of the Truth and Reconciliation Commission in South Africa, or community reintegration actions after "the Troubles" in Northern Ireland, have devised a "staircase model of intergroup apologies," which analyses and conceptualises the sequencing and deepening of a pathway to reconciliation and transitional justice.[42] A LOUDfence is a *moving* memorial—emotionally and literally. It is a mobile, portable, pop-up, and simple display—requiring minimal financial outlay and relatively little time to assemble. It relocates to

---

[38] Alice d'Oléon, "A Memorial for Clergy Abuse Victims is a Must, Says Advocate," *La Croix International*, November 6, 2023, international.la-croix.com/news/ethics/a-memorial-for-clergy-abuse-victims-is-a-must-says-advocate/18645.

[39] Christophe Henning, "Nearly 1,400 Sex Abuse Victims Seek Compensation from the Catholic Church in France," *La Croix International*, March 15, 2024, international.la-croix.com/religion/nearly-1400-sex-abuse-victims-seek-compensation-from-catholic-church-in-france.

[40] See www.sitesofconscience.org/?gad_source=1&gclid=CjwKCAjw7NmzBhBLEiwAxrHQ-aob2vQSSB1d4U1-4or_AY7ulQHN29M3TsdyNwRzWe03RJAGNcB0DxoC_KMQAvD_BwE.

[41] "Compassion through Creative Art, Continuous Voices," www.creativeballarat.com.au/continuousvoices.

[42] Michael J. A. Wohl, Matthew J. Hornsey, and Catherine R. Philpot, "A Critical Review of Official Public Apologies: Aims, Pitfalls, and a Staircase Model of Effectiveness," *Social Issues and Policy Review* 5, no. 1 (2011): 70–100; Samuel J. Nunney and Antony S. R. Manstead, "Step by Step: Testing the Staircase Model of Intergroup Apologies," *European Journal of Social Psychology* 51, no. 3 (2021): 538–550.

the places it is called and modulates slightly with each move. The Cardiff Cathedral LOUDfence (October 21, 2023) featured "love spoons" (carved wooden tokens of love) *ex votos* for messages. Similarly, the LOUDfence staged in Oban (June 30–July 1, 2024) was co-hosted by the Church of Scotland and Catholic diocese of Argyll and the Isles featuring tartan ribbons, a bagpipe lament, and messaging in both English and Scots Gaelic. This form of "listening memorial," co-produced and evolving as attendees participate in its creation, is cumulative, stepped, and staggered, but also increasingly symphonic.

The "listening" is also reciprocal and dialogical—victim survivor groups in a LOUDfence location work with (lay) church safeguarding officers and are brought into structured, focused, and purposeful conversations with the clergy and bishop. In Newcastle, some of those who attended the LOUDfence and disclosed their abuse there to a clergy or safeguarding staff member have now initiated investigations and are accessing support structures, alongside functioning as an informal advisory group. Dialogue that is opened out, often for the first time around the event preparation, continues after a LOUDfence formally "ends" with new initiatives (clergy training, pastoral reviews) and often preparations for another LOUDfence as an annual event.

One powerful example of a follow-up activity from a LOUDfence held in Birmingham across May 7–13, 2023, is the "Love in the Heart of the Church" initiative. Ribbons from St. Chad's Catholic Cathedral fence were added to the LOUDfence ribbons collected from St. Philip's Anglican Cathedral LOUDfence (October 3–9, 2022) as a mark of ecumenical acknowledgement of CSA survivors in the Catholic and Anglican dioceses. On September 9, 2023, fibre artist Mahawa Keita and an ecumenical group of survivors took part in a workshop to weave the ribbons,[43] symbolising connection, compassion, and care, into an altar piece. The textile "icon" situated deliberately behind the altar and between two candles, is permanently displayed in St. Philip's Cathedral in Birmingham and will travel, as a peripatetic memorial object, to a suburban parish in the diocese this September 2024.

Green shoots are emerging from this intense activity over nearly three years in parish churches and cathedral across Britain, sparking new conversations, rippling waves of effect/affect, and even some signs of thaw, *rapprochement*, and *metanoia*. Some of this culture change emerges merely from the initial planning and execution stages,

---

[43] "LOUDfence Ribbons Make Artwork to Recognise Abuse Victims and Survivors," www.birminghamdiocese.org.uk/news/loudfence-ribbons-make-artwork-to-recognise-abuse-victims-and-survivors.

with clergy confessing they have "never met a survivor" and were therefore initially fearful of "saying the wrong thing" or "not knowing what to do." Usually there is a great deal of anxiety and reticence in the lead-up to a LOUDfence, swinging paradoxically between the emotional extremes of disengagement and scepticism (wondering whether something so simple will make help or have any impact at all) to the other emotional dial of extreme fear and trepidation of "opening Pandora's box" with risk of reinjury, offence, and protest, or escalated litigation. The nearly two dozen LOUDfences held have required time, patience, and trust to surmount these fears, dissociation tactics, and silencing cultural taboos.

From in-progress research on the effect of a LOUDfence after its staging, it appears that those actively involved in these occasions report an increase in *understanding* trauma and *emotional intelligence*. This is most acute for supportive clergy, who speak of the humility and vulnerability of listening to survivors' testimonies and reassuring people that they are seen, believed, and will be helped (where the professional safeguarding team then step in). Bishops who have held a LOUDfence have welcomed addressing "the elephant in the room" and, realized that the church needs to "own" this dark and shameful history and the toxic cultures that have incubated the abuse, draw lessons, and work proactively (rather than defensively and evasively). In one diocese, following their first LOUDfence, refreshed "professional development" courses were initiated in the seminary, with compulsory retraining instated for existing clergy. In another diocese, a consultancy organization has been started by victim-survivor trainers (one of whom is a priest) who are leading practical, candid, and child-centred conversations about CSA disclosures, sex education, and safeguarding practises in Catholic schools.[44]

The visual and sonic power of a LOUDfence, with its ribbons blowing on a church railing and communicative repertoires for sounding out spaces profoundly damaged by abuse, is well testified by the Day of Prayer for Victims and Survivors held at St. Anne's parish church in Buxton, diocese of Nottingham on April 24, 2024. This was a particularly poignant and powerful occasion that brought together a hurt and grieving community following the jailing in 2012 of their former parish priest, Paul Cullen, for abuse of three young children in the 1980s. He died in prison in 2018 while serving a custodial sentence. Alongside a powerful photo of Bishop Patrick and clergy prostrating themselves before the altar which circulated widely on social media, the parishioner-designed installations throughout the church included a prayer tree for handwritten messages and a painting

---

[44] See "Survivor Training—Beyond Just Words," survivortraining.org.uk/category/who-we-are/.

in the Lady Chapel, evocative of the #metoo movement, urging people to overcome silence. The LOUDfence in that parish is still "up" five months later, as the continuing presence of the ribbons and installations in the church function as a prompt for conversations and ongoing recovery work.

It remains to be seen what other cultural semiotics will be harnessed to a LOUDfence when it moves beyond a UK setting. The French sister movement *Rubans contre l'oubli* often uses heart-shaped tag cards and (ribbon-laden) temporary fencing in their transportable LOUDfence events. In one sense, LOUDfence already operates transnationally through the digital space, with extensive use of Twitter/X to send, receive, and post messages of testimony, compassion, and support. The first American LOUDfence held on Sunday April 7, 2024 in Wheeling drew survivors from outside West Virginia through the reach of social media, and in the days following a CSA survivor retweeted a photo of a tag written for him (anonymously) and hung on the cathedral fence: "For Greg M., survivor of sexual abuse and trafficking, we see you and hear you and love you. We are sorry!" His accompanying tweet commentary read: "Someone DM'd me this photo and message earlier today. I was moved to tears that someone would think to include me. And on D[ivine] M[ercy] S[unday], I feel seen and cared for."[45] Here is a form of speaking and listening circulating and recirculating, on a loop and amplified through social media, which mixes images and text, church devotionals (Divine Mercy Sunday) with extemporised, crowd-sourced rituals. Sometimes this speaking and listening is immediate and embodied, such as volunteer Patricia's compassionate care—survivor to survivor—in offering comfort, privacy, and tissues at the Newcastle LOUDfence.[46] Conversations, exchanges, and disclosures often happen at a fence when ribbons are being tied and messages affixed, such as the survivor who evocatively communicated to me the personal impact of a LOUDfence for her:

> I have had a public institutional apology for the first time [alongside the legal processes I have negotiated] and I now feel like my abuse has been taken into the heart of the institution, ingested like an antibiotic into the wounded body of Christ.

---

[45] "Me Name is Greg, @ElCaminoGreg," x.com/HTH_Now/status/1778581547920277554.
[46] Patricia Debney and Alana Harris, "'Praying for No More Empty Shoes' alongside Survivors of Child Sexual Abuse," *The Tablet*, April 25, 2024, www.thetablet.co.uk/blogs/1/2770/praying-for-no-more-empty-shoes-alongside-survivors-of-child-sexual-abuse.

Drawing powerfully on suggestive ecclesiological framings of the church as the Mystical Body of Christ, this survivor's insights chime with other reanimations of this ecclesial analogy, offering richly suggestive and queered theological analogies into the various wounds under which the contemporary church labours, including misogyny and homophobia, HIV/AIDS, and the destruction and injustices of the global ecological crisis.[47]

Conclusion

A LOUDfence is not intended to be a substitute for legal, financial, and personal redress for victim-survivors, and care needs to be taken to ensure that this trauma-informed, creative, and highly adaptive mode of memorialization is not captured or co-opted by religious authorities as a form of virtue signalling or evasion of criminal and remedial responsibility. Nevertheless, when deployed as a

---

[47] Samuel Ernest, "HIV/AIDS Ecclesiology and Ruptures of the Body," *The Polyphony*, June 21, 2021, thepolyphony.org/2021/06/21/hiv-aids-ecclesiology-ruptures/.

complement to more individualized and formal accountability, its methodology can speak to the deeper, relational, and readily internalized healing and restitution envisaged through a "transitional justice" conceptual framework. The movement is also currently powered by a mostly feminized and voluntary labour force, which raises pertinent questions about women's leadership and pastoral contributions within institutional Catholicism. If a specific and trained "survivor listening ministry" was to be launched, given the early stages of a serious exploration of this possibility in one English diocese, what would this skilled pastoral work mean for laywomen, with potential extension into a more formal diaconate ministry?

This article has explored the ways in which the LOUDfence movement is an example of an imaginative, survivor-led action for culture change in the church, through foregrounding its symbolic, even sacramental repertoire for speaking about violence, pain, and brokenness that resonates profoundly with a cruciform-shaped understanding of the church as the Mystical Body. It is unsurprising, therefore, that there is a deep seam of devotional tradition reanimated by the LOUDfence movement, including recourse to the Blessed Virgin Mary, with emerging vernacular theologies re-welcoming Mary as "the first safeguarder."

Alongside this highly flexible and adaptable vocabulary—which communicates materially and metaphorically—a LOUDfence fosters new places for listening from its liminal place betwixt and between the inside-outside of the church and the slippage between the public and private spheres. This active listening, and the circulation of these messages of love, support, belief, and acceptance through physical and digital landscapes prompt us to venture forth and enlarge the space of our tent.[48] LOUDfences are models for active listening in a synodal church—avenues for survivors and survivor-allies to lament, speak truth to power, and demonstrate the experiences and insights of the *sensus fidelium*. They are excellent case studies for a synodal church needing to find ways to embrace "lived religion" and an "ordinary theology"—the affective, embodied, prosaic, and intensely practical theologizing of Christians (often women) who have received scant formal theological education but are drawing on profound faith resources and experiential insights at what Jeff Astley calls "the church's front line."[49]

---

[48] "Working Document for the Continental Stage 2022," www.synod.va/content/dam/synod/common/phases/continental-stage/dcs/Documento-Tappa-Continentale-EN.pdf.
[49] Jeff Astley, *Ordinary Theology: Looking, Listening, and Learning in Theology* (London: Routledge, 2022). See also Nancy Tatom Ammerman, *Studying Lived Religion: Contexts and Practices* (New York: New York University Press, 2021).

Material and embodied ways of listening and atoning are foregrounded in this movement, so it is little wonder that the next stage in its development is the inauguration of a National Pilgrimage of Reparation from October 18–20, 2024. Bringing together the Anglican and Catholic Archbishops of Wales, pilgrims gathered at St. Winefride's Holy Well in Flintshire and pray for healing and rebirth at a medieval site (1115 CE) recently dedicated to CSA survivors, given the saint's experience of sexual violence.[50] Tapping into a deep Catholic past and subterranean Celtic spirituality that embraced clootie wells, rag trees, holy wells, and powerful saints' shrines, there is an ancient and indigenous spiritual repertoire in the UK—with potential appeal to places beyond—being reanimated with synodal-like praxis to address a global epidemic[51] acknowledged as "the Cross of the Moment."[52]

Alana Harris is a trained theologian and historian of religion who works at King's College London. She has published extensively in the field of "lived religion," and her interdisciplinary research focuses broadly on oral history testimony, gender and embodiment, materiality, and Catholic devotional cultures.

---

[50] "News Briefing: Britain and Ireland," *The Tablet*, May 6, 2024, www.thetablet.co.uk/news/18704/news-briefing-britain-and-ireland.

[51] Massimo Faggioli and Alana Harris, "Pursuing the Long Shadow over the 'Domestic Church': Toward a Global History of Abuse in Catholic Settings," *Catholic Historical Review* 110, no. 2 (2024): 339–368.

[52] Pat Jones, Marcus Pound, and Catherine Sexton, *The Cross of the Moment: A Report from the Boundary Breaking Project* (Durham: University of Durham, 2024), www.durham.ac.uk/media/durham-university/research-/research-centres/catholic-studies-centre-for-ccs/The-Cross-of-the-Moment_digital.pdf.

Asking to Listen:
Engaging Social Scientific Methods as a Listening Practice in Global Catholicism

Tricia C. Bruce

Abstract: Asking enables listening. This paper explores how the practice of asking, when enacted as an intentional social scientific process, can facilitate the synodal value of listening across the global Catholic Church. Drawing upon social science methodologies and evidence, it demonstrates that effective listening is not merely passive reception but proactive invitation to engage diverse or silenced perspectives. Systematic asking incorporates everyday people and experiences otherwise overlooked and creates space for difficult topics. Seeing listening as a practice of asking underscores the value of setting rules for engagement that promote a posture of reception that fosters trust and openness through humility, curiosity, and willingness to step into worlds different from one's own. Embracing this mutual approach can prompt a more inclusive synodal process, enhancing the church's ability to engage meaningfully with all in its midst.

The multi-year journey of the Synod on Synodality in the global Catholic Church reverberates at its core a foundational principle: *listening*. The value of listening—and listening to *all*—undergirds Pope Francis's call for a more synodal church, attentive to a plurality of voices whose formal status in the church does not lend itself to involvement in decision-making. Listening yields voice. Access. Perspective. Challenge. Change.

So, too, is listening foundational to the work of sociologists, including myself—whose deep investment in studying diverse manifestations of Catholicism in everyday lives, identities, and structures requires adequate tools to surface idiosyncratic perspectives. Sociologically, listening well lends credibility, depth, a careful balance of representativeness, distinctiveness, and built-in accountability such that studies are done not in isolation but in dialogue through a shared process of growing knowledge.

Here, I name a central difference between the stated *value* of listening (as extolled through the multi-year Synodal process) and the intentional *practice* of listening (as reified in the work of empirical social scientists): *asking*. Systematic listening, it turns out, requires asking. Drawing upon decades of study touching upon myriad facets of lived Catholicism, I outlay fifteen dimensions to listening that center a more active and invitational posture of *asking*, methodically. Where listening is the desired end, asking is a means to that end. Social science lends a methodology for asking.

ASKING TO HEAR

But first: a story. Among my many quests to listen, sociologically, I led a team of sociologists in asking how US residents think about the issue of abortion.[1] It is a topic that dominates headlines and for which statistics abound. It is also a topic that, it turns out, not many people talk about in-depth. Mostly because no one asks them. Or because talking—and asking—about the issue feels risky. Listening does not happen without the asking.

One of our interviewees was Ricardo (a pseudonym). Dawning a denim jacket and hair combed into a wave, 48-year-old Ricardo first told us his name was "Richard." "When I started getting into the job market, I used 'Richard'" so I wouldn't be stuck working in, like, some factory or whatever, you know?" While at the car shop a day prior, the second-generation Colombian Californian was told he did not "look like a Ricardo"—"What does that even mean?" Discrimination, for Ricardo, feels commonplace.

Being "positive" and "nice to people" feels foundational to Ricardo, as does family and concern for the environment. His dad—a "very proud American"—migrated to flee violence, secure a better job, and "find a new life." Growing up in an immigrant family meant "tr[ying] to be as American as we could":

> I played baseball—Little League—and all that kind of stuff. My parents tried to understand baseball. I remember one instance, we went to a California Angels game and my dad was like, "Oh, they just scored a touchdown!" and I'm like "No, they hit a homerun." So, you know, they tried.[2]

Attending Catholic Mass as a kid was more of a bribe-based exchange, rewarded with ice cream from Dad because "Mom was into it." Ricardo is agnostic today, seeing souls as "energy" but uncertain where they go once they leave their bodies. He is "pretty open-

---

[1] Tricia C. Bruce, *How Americans Understand Abortion* (Notre Dame, IN: McGrath Institute, 2020).
[2] Ricardo is one of 217 interviewees included in the 2020 National Study of Abortion Attitudes. See Bruce, *How Americans Understand Abortion*.

minded" and wants people to "just live their lives, you know, not based on some type of religious doctrine type of thing."

Asking about abortion, "It's kind of dividing people," Ricardo says. He is put off by politicians who "try to push their religious doctrine on people." Prayer is "good"; to "force prayer" is not. Attempts to regulate behavior, in general, feel "scary." "People have different viewpoints.... I think it's just ignorance, that's all."

But it is not that he—or anyone, Ricardo says—would "want" abortion or "enjoy getting it done." "It's a traumatic thing." Such was the case for himself, when his former girlfriend sought an abortion two decades ago. Her epilepsy "was something that could have carried on ... that's what the doctors had told her at the time—so it was better not to have the child. And so, we got an abortion." "I don't think [anyone's] like 'Yeah, I want to get an abortion!'" He bristles at the false assumptions of a "pro-choice" label:

> Of course I'm pro-choice. But I'm also pro-life. Like, I'm not anti-life! So, I think that's—I don't know, I don't know the word to use. But saying you're "pro-choice" doesn't mean you're not pro-life. It just doesn't make sense to me. It's just the wrong wording. And I get it—it's a political thing to make people think, like, "Oh, if you're pro-choice, you're not for life." Which is not true.

Ricardo was one of 217 Americans whom we asked to think out loud about the issue of abortion. What did the word itself conjure? What earliest memories of an encounter with it come to mind? Who and what connects with some of the different associations and meanings abortion introduces? None of this is captured well in happenstance conversations. First and foremost: "happenstance" conversations about many topics—especially contentious ones—do not tend to happen. People have learned not to ask and not to share, including many Catholics and others connected with the Catholic Church.

What becomes evident from the practice of social science is that thorough "listening" is preconditioned on asking. Listening is in fact a *practice of asking*: it is not merely a passive act of waiting for information or receiving it once it does. Listening compels a more dynamic, active, and interactive process of invitation, query, and reciprocity.

By asking, social scientific approaches to listening, moreover, do something other forms of listening do not: invite an empirical look at a full range of viewpoints, surfacing potential disagreement and moral positions that challenge those emerging from other sources. Put another way: listening in social science can bring the "is" into conversation with the "ought." The facts are the same, either way; social science surfaces and shares them.

ASKING AS A "STRANGER"

Many needed forms of listening rely upon established, trusted relationships. People are more inclined to share and be vulnerable when they perceive the person with whom they speak to also be willing to share and be vulnerable.

With the exception of some social scientific methodologies (such as ethnography), however, this is *not* the kind of listening and relationship upon which social science relies. This positions it uniquely and distinctively as less relationship-conditioned and relationship-building and more about the specific moment of interaction. That interaction, furthermore, may be the only exchange the researcher and research participant have—quite literally, a once-in-a-lifetime, fleeting exchange.

For this reason, the kind of intentional listening amplified by social science is in some ways akin to classic social theorist Georg Simmel's concept of "The Stranger."[3] Known for his use of dyads and character prototypes by which to understand the world and people in it, Simmel speaks of "the stranger" as occupying a special kind of position in society. The stranger is both in and out, near and far, part of "us" and part of "them." As Simmel writes:

> In spite of being inorganically appended to it, the stranger is yet an organic member of the group. Its uniform life includes the specific conditions of this element. Only we do not know how to designate the peculiar unity of this position other than by saying that it is composed of certain measures of nearness and distance. Although some quantities of them characterize all relationships, a special proportion and reciprocal tension produce the particular, formal relation to the "stranger."[4]

Simmel posits that "to be a stranger is naturally a very positive relation; it is a specific form of interaction."[5] An interaction with a stranger lends a reflection on what makes us distinctively us and another distinctively another. An interaction with a stranger, too, puts up a natural barrier: we do not "know" them, and they do not "know" us.

An interview—such as that with Ricardo and so many across other projects—positions a social scientist as stranger in interaction with a research participant as stranger: self as other and other as self. Social scientists carry a responsibility to recognize themselves in what they

---

[3] Georg Simmel, "The Stranger," in *The Sociology of Georg Simmel*, trans. Kurt H. Wolff (New York: Free Press, 1950), 402–408.
[4] Simmel, "The Stranger," 408.
[5] Simmel, "The Stranger," 402.

do, while also creating distance from self by a focus on an unknown other.

Simmel's idea of the stranger also rings true in the social scientific goal of listening to ordinary people. It is not merely those voices at the margins that are too often exempted from a broader understanding of social issues and social life: *it's the vast majority of everyday voices*. "Stranger" connotes not the famous, appointed, or spokesperson but, quite simply, a person whose merit in the conversation takes root in their very humanity as themselves, whoever and whatever that might be. All are—or can be—strangers.

Toward this end, the promise of confidentiality is key. Unlike public interactions or formal pronouncements or even informal conversations among family, colleagues, and friends, social science methodologies prioritize the ability to share freely, in confidence. Ideas do not even need to be fully thought out; this form of listening captures people where and how they are in that moment. It is designed to avoid performative dialogue, public accountability, or the norms of other types of listening linked back to one's own name and identity.

The duality exemplified in Simmel's construct of the stranger is not wholly unlike what the global Catholic Church positions itself to do via the synodal process: invite and ask ordinary people to speak and share within the vast global expanse of a shared faith tradition.[6]

A synodal approach to listening positions the church to welcome and integrate diverse voices of "strangers" who, together, form its common community. Organic, grassroots initiatives necessarily balance with structured intentionality and deliberate frameworks to facilitate meaningful listening.

THE PRACTICE OF ASKING

What does this look like in practice? The remainder of this paper draws upon examples excerpted from confidential interviews across a variety of topical arena touching the experience of Catholicism locally and globally. It highlights how ordinary people—positioned as "strangers"—speak about listening in the course of being asked about another social issue. It gleans from this fifteen characteristics of listening predicated on asking. I name and illustrate each with one or more confidential interview excerpts.[7]

---

[6] In contrast to Simmel's notion of "the stranger," however, a theological perspective would affirm the baptized as "all members of one body" and therefore *not* strangers.

[7] Interview excerpts are compiled from a variety of sociological projects I and my teams have led, including: Tricia C. Bruce, *How Americans Understand Abortion*; Tricia C. Bruce, *Called to Contribute* (www.calledtocontribute.org); Tricia C. Bruce, *The National Study of Catholic Priests: Insights from In-Depth Interviews* (Washington,

The practice of asking assumes a posture of humility and withholds judgment. It is curious and seeks to learn. It enters as a guest, open to different experiences and perspectives without leaping to evaluation. It welcomes the risk of discomfort and embodies humility, recognizing limitations, and valuing different perspectives. We hear this in confidential interviews with priests, for example, who share their own experiences of authentic listening through asking, vulnerability, and non-judgment:

> When I'm assigned to a new parish, within the first year I set up home gatherings where people can invite others, and we sit down and share. And I hear some of their stories. And I do a lot of listening. Get to know their situations, their stories. . . . I'll usually ask them, "What do they want me to pay attention to?" And not depend upon somebody that comes at you right away and sizes up every situation . . . but to really come at it as a learner. . . . I'm not presumptuous that I know where I should lead them.

> I honestly think it has to be authentic listening across the board. And when you are who you are and you're real about yourself, your gifts, but also your brokenness. Again, whether you're a bishop, priest, or laity, and people realize that you're striving to do your best, to be your best, to help them find God—I think that that's the key to it all. People are willing to listen when they know that you really are trying to be yourself and care and you just want what's best for others and your own journey, you know? I think that that's it—the authenticity and the true, compassionate listening, even if you can't fix it.

> I think sometimes people just want to be heard and really seen. The model for me is the story of the woman caught in adultery where Jesus . . . and this is what I try to do as a priest . . . Jesus entered her circle of pain, right? And he didn't automatically point a finger and say, "No, you shouldn't." At first, he turned to everybody else and made them, kind of like, "Hey look at yourself, be real to yourself first before you throw any stones." And then he went to that woman and got to her level and let her know his love first. And then once she felt it and knew it was real, then she was able to be lifted up to where he wanted her to be. And she could hear, "Go and sin no more." Whereas if it first started out with, "You're a sinner, stop it." It's not going to change anybody. It's going to close them off to church. But I think if they know they're loved and listened to, respected for who they are, broken and all, then they'll be able to rise to where God wants them to be. And I think that's what the priest should do.

DC: Catholic University of America, 2023); Springtide Research Institute, 2024 Study of Young People and Civic Life.

The practice of asking sees another as person first. It recognizes the humanity in each person, prioritizing raw humanness over agendas. It knows people by name, inviting validation by acknowledging individuals' unique identities and experiences. An interviewee speaks here to the need for validation as a precondition to asking and listening about the topic of abortion:

> It's so toxic. I can't even imagine, like, "Hey, let's get together and have a picnic and bring both sides together, and everybody bring a potluck!" . . . People use that as an opportunity to come with agendas. They can't help it. It's frustrating to me that you can't just have an open mind, you know? I'd be willing to listen. . . . I would hope that that could happen . . . where both sides can openly share their stories around a campfire. . . . And when you have that thought, you can either hold up a card and say, "I never thought about it." . . . I'm actually gonna think about that.

The practice of asking takes people seriously. It values others' perspectives and experiences, treating them with seriousness and respect, even when they differ. Two women speak to this in confidential interviews, reasserting the need to respect different backgrounds and vantage points:

> I pray the church just believes women. You know, not to co-opt that #MeToo movement. It's kind of this similar vein, like, believe women, believe survivors. Listen to their stories, and take them seriously. I would say that.

> I think it's time for us to step back and listen to what our sisters have to say. Not that they think with one voice on it. I mean, women obviously have a wide range of opinions, but I think their opinions are formed from a different place and I think that is something to which men need to listen.

The practice of asking invites radical honesty. It fosters rapport through directness and sincerity. It is not afraid of the unknown and does not take the easy way out. It embraces the potential discomfort of honesty. Here, a priest discloses in a confidential interview his desire to share more openly with his bishop:

> I think just by listening, if [bishops] would just listen to us, you know, I mean there's a lot of experience. And, you know, coming with an open mind, rather than just having your mind made up already. That would help a lot. And the bishop being honest with his clergy about stuff. . . . But also trying to trust that the spirit is present in the whole community.

The practice of asking acknowledges vantage point and positionality. It recognizes and anticipates different perspectives and positions—in those asked and those asking. It holds and values unique viewpoints and experiences. It values and validates the perspectives of those marginalized or dismissed, recognizing the richness of what they add. A confidential interview with a young person captures this sentiment, referring to their interactions with older adults:

> I get that a lot—like, "Oh, you're young ... what do you know about this? You don't know anything." And it's like, yes, I understand you're older. That does not mean that you know everything. It just means that you have a bit more experience, which is fine. Claim your experience. You are older, but I'm younger, which means I'm also open. Have a more open mind than you. Cause you've been stuck in your traditional values for so long. I'm more open to seeing things differently.

The practice of asking enters worlds different from one's own. It steps into experiences and beliefs that differ, bridging to empathy and connection. It sees value in the perspective of the "other." Here, a young interviewee speaks to the value of listening to those in a "different world":

> I think just listening, and being open to hearing beliefs that are completely different from your own—but also hearing about why people have those beliefs. Because I feel like a lot of the times ... like for gay rights, like, a lot of my friends are gay. And it's like for you, you may not know a gay person period. And so you have this completely different world. We're living in completely different worlds. And I think just understanding that and us giving them grace and them giving us grace.

The practice of asking invites experiential accounts—including those not usually (or perhaps ever) shared. It encourages sharing personal stories apart from judgment, recognizing the importance of lived experience in understanding complex issues. It makes space for secrets and controversy. Several interviewees reiterate the value of sharing lived experiences with others:

> I think they really just need to sit with us, and, and no one is doing that yet. . . . Can you just bring women—and just hear their stories, or, you know, study it? . . . If anyone really just sat and listened. . . . Please hear us; the Spirit is moving. . . . Sure, I'm one little person, but within a group of people, just being able to share that.

> It's good for somebody to listen to you about some things that you have concerns about. Especially because I've been through it.

I do think it's like, feeling listened to, I mean, it's like . . . It's been a hard, hard journey. . . . I've spent a lot of time not saying my piece because of the strictures of my position.

The practice of asking requires a deliberate pause. It makes time for reflection and space for meaningful consideration. It necessarily stops all else to ask and hear. It makes time. A confidential interview with a priest illustrates this as a dynamic of bishops' willingness to listen:

I know some priests in this diocese who have said that [our bishop] has listened. . . . Anybody who calls and says, "Can I speak with the bishop?" He'll make time. So that encourages me. . . . I mean, it may never be an informal, like, "Bishop, can I talk to you for a minute, because I'm just going through a hard time type of thing." . . . But I think if you called and said, "I need to talk to you," I believe that he would do so. . . . I think that he does seem to say, "I'll listen."

The practice of asking walks alongside people in a moment of accompaniment. It joins—ever so temporarily—another on their journey, attentive to what that journey looks and feels like. It sits with both the oppressed and the oppressor. The theme of accompaniment arises in confidential interviews with priests:

Accompaniment is much more of a sense of your arm around somebody's shoulder, you know, and quite physically walking with them. . . . Too many people experience it: there's somebody waving their finger at you telling you what to do, or what you didn't do. And there's a big difference—in the challenges with the pastor who's waving his finger. And that's how people experience it. They don't experience the arm around the shoulder. . . . There's a sense of just kind of listening and being with that is often missing.

It's having spoken to victims, and to listen to the painful. Listen, and be present. Expressing sorrow and regret and assistance. And then also having to sit down with perpetrators. Both.

The practice of asking leads with respect and welcome more than shame and exclusion. It does not belittle but sees dignity in another. Interviewees point to this characteristic of welcome and respect in authentic listening:

It's really easy to belittle young people and be very patronizing. So I think just listening, hearing what young people have to say. I feel like it's easy for older people to like not just take with a grain of salt but completely overlook what young people say. So I think listening honestly and candidly are very important. And just like leaving, leaving your premonitions at the door.

> Father came up, and I told him that I was very upset about, you know, I can't have kids now. Father's approach, because he is an older priest, he sits down and he talks to you. You could tell that, it's like you were being scolded, you know, because you're not supposed to have birth control or anything like that. . . . So I just kinda felt like I was being scolded the entire time that Father was sitting up there. I mean he may have been listening to me, but his eyes were telling a different story, so that—it was hurtful, because I wanted to have kids, but I couldn't, and it still hurts.

The practice of asking rebuilds a foundation for trust and credibility. It lays the groundwork for trust through authentic listening. It lets people be heard. It fosters a more cohesive and resilient community. An interview with a priest reiterates asking and listening as foundational to trust:

> I find myself having to defend more and more the hierarchy and making those distinctions and a variety of things because it's gotten to the point where nobody wants to listen to a hierarchy at all. They've lost that credibility . . . I don't think it's affected the way people have seen me as a priest. I think more and more do see me as an agent of healing. But I had to earn that trust first.

The practice of asking opens pathways for silence, apology, and healing. It rethinks and reconstructs meanings and relationships. It attends to wounds otherwise unspoken and unattended. Priests speak to this as a dynamic of moving through crisis and healing:

> I think the church, when we are in crisis, we tend to want to respond and say many words. And I will tell you that—at least this victim—he does not want many words. He wants to have a place where he feels like he can be loved by God . . . an open line of communication. I make sure that he knows that he can speak to me at any time. And I think we just have to love them, acknowledge that this was horrible. In many times, it's enough to even just listen.

> Just listening to them. Listening is part of what they feel like they—nobody listened to their story. And because nobody listened to their story, they don't trust anyone anymore. . . . Healing has been listening to their story every time they talk about it. . . . You just listen to them even though—painful as it may be, because some words are very . . . Even though those conversations are very difficult, and painful as it may be, I've always been—just listening has been part of my conversation with them.

We just basically need a healer right now. Just somebody to come in and listen to us. Somebody to say, hey, I get that, you know, you guys are hurting. And I'm just here to just kind of help everybody heal. . . . That healing is going to be a long process by its nature, and he's not going to be performing miracles, but he's not going to be doing anything to prevent the healing from happening.

The practice of asking listens more than it speaks—because not asking risks harm. So, too, does asking and then *not* listening. Confidential interviews surface how disagreement and polarization can disrupt listening:

I don't say anything because there's no point. If you're gonna blurt that out to me and not even consider that maybe I have a different point of view then there's no point in engaging because I already know you're not gonna listen.

I used to think there was some overlap but I feel like the polarization is just so extreme now, I just can't even like, again it's really people are not listening and have a conversation they just want to scream . . . I just feel like it's just a waste of . . . I mean all of the protests, I just see what comes out of it, like, nothing came out of it, okay? I don't see any talking or solutions or help.

I am just a priest that really believes we need this listening. That's what's going to help heal. That's what's going to restore the credibility. But if you're not even willing to meet with these people? And sit down to acknowledge their pain? Well, you're only adding to their trauma! You're not helping to heal it! Now granted, some are so angry because of what has happened. It's hard to hear. But at the same time, we gotta listen. We gotta do that. And so that's why in accompanying people—I'm walking with the people, [asking:] What do you need? How can we support you? But again, it was also practice. How do we put this into practice?

The practice of asking has tolerance for ambiguity. It offers the opportunity to complicate and contradict. It explores along the spectrum rather than only at the edges. Asking and listening picks up on contradictions and change, as heard from interviewees:

I guess my perspective has matured, as I've talked to people and as I've learned and explored and read.

As I got older and I met other types of people and I was exposed to other people who didn't have a family like I had, and how their life in their circumstances led them down different roads that really made it more difficult for them. And I just understood how and why people could choose that route and I made the commitment not to make a judgement against it. So the first step—so, to not judge someone for that and keeping an open mind. And once I was able to have an open mind and to listen to their experiences and ideas then my ideas changed.

The practice of asking listens to hear. It does not listen merely to respond. A young person speaks to this in a confidential interview:

> I feel like if they're listening, they're not listening to respond, they're listening to hear. . . . Like they let me talk. And like maybe they'll ask questions more or like ask for clarification on something or ask me to, to expand on something if they don't understand what I'm saying. . . . To me, that shows like they're actually willing to have a conversation because one, they're letting me talk, but two, they're actively engaging in the conversation and they're letting, they're showing—they're trying to understand what I'm saying. And three, like actually giving the media that I consume a chance to maybe help them understand the topic better.

Through all examples and empirical insights is a common chorus of appreciation for being asked as a road to listening, echoed in this interviewee's words: "Thank you for listening to me. To be listened to—that alone is a gift."

CONCLUSION

Social science offers valuable tools for enacting listening as a practice of asking, a skill that can aid the global Catholic Church through the synod process and beyond. Listening is not passive, but active: invited and attained with intentionality such as that exemplified in the tools of social science.

Such a practice bridges "stranger" to "knowledge" by eliciting and valuing the everyday person and everyday experience. It facilitates listening to difficult topics people typically avoid. It provides for plurality as much as representation, extending beyond the loudest voices. It leads with a posture of reception, listening with the intent to understand rather than respond. This approach, akin to the concept of "welcome" without instant affirmation, can create spaces where all feel heard and valued, fostering trust and openness.

Ultimately, effective listening necessitates the practice of asking. Listening is not only receptive; the invitation to listen compels the responsibility to ask. It involves a proactive stance, recognizing the transformative potential of listening and committing to share or act upon insights gained. A responsibility to listen goes beyond hearing and into responding, validating, and integrating diverse experiences and perspectives. Listening can heal, validate, and build trust.

By embracing listening as a dynamic and transformative practice informed by social science, the Catholic Church can better navigate the challenges of the contemporary world, fostering a more inclusive, compassionate, and resilient community. The insights from social science and the voices of everyday individuals within the church are essential to understanding and enhancing the practice of asking in global Catholicism. M

Tricia C. Bruce, PhD, is a sociologist of religion and author or editor of several books and high-impact reports including *Parish and Place*, *Faithful Revolution*, and *How Americans Understand Abortion*. Her work appears in *The Wall Street Journal, Time Magazine, Science Advances*, and more, and has been awarded by the Catholic Press Association, American Sociological Association Religion Section, and Religious Research Association. She is currently director of Springtide Research Institute, president of the Association for the Sociology of Religion, consultor to the Vatican's General Secretariat of the Synod, and faculty fellow of the University of Southern California's Institute for Advanced Catholic Studies.

Research-Backed Practices to Engage Youth in a Vibrant Catholic Church: The Case for Implementing Sacred Listening Practices

Josh Packard and Megan Bissell

Abstract: This article explores the theological and practical implications of Sacred Listening, a concept developed in response to the Synod on Synodality initiated by Pope Francis. The Synod emphasizes the church's call to a more relational and participatory ecclesial life, rooted in listening, dialogue, and accompaniment. Sacred Listening is proposed as a theologically grounded practice designed to rebuild trust and foster deeper connections within the faith community, particularly in a low-trust environment. Drawing on the theological principles of *Imago Dei*, as well as contemporary social science research, the article presents Sacred Listening as a means to move beyond traditional modes of institutional authority toward relational trust and authentic engagement. The article further introduces practical tools that operationalize these principles, providing concrete strategies for religious leaders to engage with their communities more effectively. This work contributes to the ongoing theological discourse on synodality and offers a framework for creating a more inclusive and responsive church in today's complex social landscape.

The Synod on Synodality, as initiated by Pope Francis, represents a pivotal moment in the life of the church, calling for a renewed emphasis on listening, dialogue, and participatory engagement. Synodality is not merely an administrative or structural innovation but embodies a profound theological shift towards a church that listens deeply to the voices of all its members, especially those traditionally marginalized or overlooked.[1] This theological shift is grounded in the recognition of the inherent dignity of every person, as articulated in the doctrine of *Imago Dei*, and demands a corresponding transformation in how the

---

[1] See International Theological Commission, *Synodality in the Life and Mission of the Church*.

church interacts with the faithful.²

This article introduces and develops a theory of "Sacred Listening," a concept constructed in response to the ecclesial and societal challenges highlighted by the synodal process. Sacred Listening, as theorized here, is rooted in the theological imperatives of synodality and informed by contemporary research in social science. It proposes a model of relational engagement that seeks to rebuild trust and foster deeper connections within the faith community. By synthesizing theological insights with empirical findings, this theory offers a framework for creating practical tools—referred to as Sacred Listening Tools—designed to facilitate more effective and empathetic pastoral care.

The theory of Sacred Listening is predicated on the need for the church to move beyond solely using traditional modes of authority and communication, which often rely only or mainly on institutional credibility, and embrace instead approaches that prioritize relational trust and authentic engagement.³ In a context where institutional trust is increasingly fragile, particularly among younger generations, Sacred Listening offers a means to re-establish meaningful relationships and ensure that the church's pastoral outreach is both theologically sound and responsive to contemporary realities.⁴

This essay will explore the theoretical underpinnings of Sacred Listening, drawing on key theological principles such as *Imago Dei*, as well as insights from social science research on trust, authority, and relational dynamics. It will further demonstrate how this theory can be operationalized through the development of Sacred Listening Tools, which are practical applications intended to enhance the church's capacity to engage with its members in a manner consistent with the synodal vision. By doing so, this work aims to contribute to the ongoing theological discourse on synodality and offer concrete strategies for pastoral leaders seeking to navigate the complexities of ministry in a low-trust environment.

LOW-TRUST TOOLS: A RELATIONAL APPROACH TO MINISTRY

In the context of the church's synodal journey, the need for effective ministry strategies that resonate with contemporary

---

[2] See Vatican II, *Pastoral Constitution on the Church in the Modern* World (*Gaudium et Spes*), nos. 40–44.
[3] Bradford E. Hinze, *Prophetic Obedience: Ecclesiology for a Dialogical Church* (Maryknoll, NY: Orbis Books, 2016).
[4] Lydia Saad, "Historically Low Faith in US Institutions Continues," *Gallup*, July 6, 2023; *2021 Edelman Trust Barometer*, www.edelman.com/trust/2021-trust-barometer.

challenges is increasingly evident. Pope Francis has underscored the significance of accompaniment—engaging with the faithful in their spiritual journeys—as a core element of the church's pastoral mission. This emphasis on accompaniment—deeply rooted in the principles of listening, dialogue, and participation—compels the church to reconsider and adopt more relational and less hierarchical modes of engagement.

The pervasive decline in trust toward institutional entities, including religious institutions, necessitates a paradigmatic shift from traditional models of authority toward approaches that prioritize authentic, interpersonal relationships. Empirical research indicates that younger generations, in particular, exhibit a preference for leaders who engage relationally rather than those who rely predominantly on institutional authority.[5] This trend highlights the critical importance of developing "low-trust tools"—strategies that build trust through relational engagement rather than the exertion of institutional power.

The efficacy of these low-trust tools is underpinned by frameworks such as the Developmental Relationships Framework from Search Institute[6] and the concept of Relational Authority developed by the co-authors at Springtide Research Institute.[7] The Developmental Relationships Framework delineates essential elements that contribute to trust-building and individual growth, including the expression of care, the challenge to grow, the provision of support, the sharing of power, and the expansion of possibilities.[8] Concurrently, the concept of Relational Authority, as explored in the research conducted by the co-authors at Springtide Research Institute, posits that authority within ministry contexts for young people in the 21st century is not merely conferred by position but must be earned through consistent and

---

[5] Pew Research Center, *The Age Gap in Religion Around the World* (Research Report, Pew Research Center, June 13, 2018); *2021 Edelman Trust Barometer*.

[6] Founded in 1958, Search Institute is a nonprofit organization dedicated to providing research-based insights and resources to foster positive youth development and strengthen communities. It focuses on identifying and promoting developmental assets that help young people succeed in school, work, and life. Its widely recognized and published framework of 40 Developmental Assets has been instrumental in guiding communities, schools, and organizations in creating supportive environments that enhance young people's growth and resilience.

[7] Springtide Research Institute is a nonpartisan, nonprofit organization founded by Lasallian Educational and Research Initiatives in Minnesota as an expression of the Christian Brothers of De La Salle. Their mission is to provide social scientific research to better understand the experiences of young people.

[8] Kent Pekel, Eugene C. Roehlkepartain, Amy K. Syvertsen, Peter C. Scales, Theresa K. Sullivan, and Jenna Sethi, "Finding the Fluoride: Examining How and Why Developmental Relationships Are the Active Ingredient in Interventions That Work," *American Journal of Orthopsychiatry* 88, no. 5 (2018): 493–504, doi.org/10.1037/ort0000333.

authentic relational engagement.⁹

As we proceed to examine these frameworks, it becomes evident that the church can equip itself with methodologies that not only address the current deficit in trust but also actively cultivate genuine engagement and participation. These relational tools are indispensable for fostering within the church a culture congruent with the principles of synodality and Pope Francis's vision for a more inclusive and dialogical church.

The subsequent section will explore the theoretical foundations that underlie these relational approaches, analyzing how they can be systematically integrated into the church's ministry to effectively address challenges posed by the contemporary context.

The Need for Relational Trust

Distinct from institutional trust, relational trust is built through personal interactions where consistency, empathy, and transparency are evident. Studies show that when young people perceive leaders as genuinely caring and relatable, they are more likely to engage meaningfully with them.[10] This shift towards relational trust over institutional trust reflects the broader societal trend away from hierarchical structures and towards more horizontal, community-oriented relationships.[11]

The growing emphasis on relational trust as a cornerstone of effective ministry in the twenty-first century is not just a theoretical shift but is supported by concrete frameworks that provide actionable guidance for building and maintaining such trust. One of the most robust and applicable of these frameworks is the Developmental Relationships Framework, which offers a detailed approach to fostering relational trust within the church. This framework not only aligns with the broader societal shift towards more personal and community-oriented relationships but also provides the church with

---

[9] Springtide Research Institute, *The State of Religion and Young People 2020: Relational Authority* (Springtide Research Institute, 2020).

[10] Steven C. Argue and Tyler S. Greenway, "Empathy with Emerging Generations as a Foundation for Ministry," *Christian Education Journal* 17, no. 1 (2020): 110–129, doi.org/10.1177/0739891319899666; Richard E. Boyatzis, Terry Brizz, and Lindsey N. Godwin, "The Effect of Religious Leaders' Emotional and Social Competencies on Improving Parish Vibrancy," *Journal of Leadership and Organizational Studies* 18, no. 2 (2010): 192–206, doi.org/10.1177/1548051810369676; Jodi G. Hunt, "And Then There Was Zoom: A Catholic Theological Examination on the Development of Digital Youth Ministry," *Religions* 11, no. 11 (2020): 565–565, doi.org/10.3390/rel11110565.

[11] Zygmunt Bauman, *Community: Seeking Safety in an Insecure World* (Cambridge: Polity, 2001); Hartmut Rosa, *Uncontrollability of the World* (Cambridge: Polity, 2020).

practical tools to implement in its mission to engage meaningfully with young people.

The Developmental Relationships Framework

Developed by the Search Institute, the Developmental Relationships Framework provides a well-researched foundation for understanding how to build relational trust. This framework identifies five essential elements that contribute to the well-being and growth of young people: expressing care, challenging growth, providing support, sharing power, and expanding possibilities. These elements are crucial for rebuilding trust with young people, as they demonstrate that their voices and experiences are valued within the faith community.[12]

The principles of the Developmental Relationships Framework can be effectively applied within the church context to create an environment where young people feel valued, supported, and empowered. In a special issue of *Religions* focused on Catholic Youth and Young Adult Ministry, Chris Miller, a Catholic educator and psychologist, argues that Developmental Relationships is one of the most promising pathways forward for the Catholic Church, writing that "the most essential element to effective ministry is the development of relationships or what is referred to as relational ministry."[13]

This framework's emphasis on mutual respect and shared power aligns with Catholic social teaching, particularly the church's commitment to the dignity of every person and the preferential option for the poor, as highlighted in *Gaudium et Spes*.

Relational Authority: Building Trust through Authentic Engagement

Alongside the Developmental Relationships Framework, the concept of Relational Authority, developed through research at Springtide Research Institute, plays a crucial role in Sacred Listening Practices. Relational Authority shifts the focus from traditional hierarchical authority to authority earned through consistent, authentic relationships.

---

[12] Pekel, Roehlkepartain, Syvertsen, Scales, Sullivan, and Sethi, "Finding the Fluoride"; Junlei Li and Megan M. Julian, "Developmental Relationships as the Active Ingredient: A Unifying Working Hypothesis of 'What Works' Across Intervention Settings," *American Journal of Orthopsychiatry* 82, no. 2 (2012): 157–166.

[13] C. Miller, "The Sexual Abuse Crisis in the US, Its Effect on Catholic Youth Ministry, and a Way Forward Through Relational Ministry Utilizing the Developmental Relationships Framework," *Religions* 11, no. 11 (2020): 572, doi.org/10.3390/rel11110572.

This concept is built on several key components. Deep, active listening forms the foundation, showing that leaders genuinely value the voices and experiences of young people, aligning with the church's call for accompaniment. Transparency in interactions, particularly around the complexities of faith, helps demystify leadership, making it more accessible and relatable. Integrity is essential, as young people are more likely to trust leaders who consistently align their actions with their words, thereby reinforcing their credibility. Demonstrating genuine care for individuals as unique persons deepens relational bonds, reflecting the Catholic emphasis on the inherent dignity of every person. Finally, while expertise remains important, it is shared humbly and used to empower rather than dominate, further strengthening relational authority.

In the contemporary Catholic landscape, there is a growing recognition of the vital role accompaniment plays in fostering meaningful engagement and trust with young people. As the youth of today distrust social institutions, the church is challenged to rethink its approaches to ministry, moving beyond traditional models of instruction and catechesis towards a more relational, dialogical, and accompaniment-centered approach.[14]

Recent research has highlighted the need for a spirituality of youth ministry that emphasizes not just the transmission of doctrine, but the creation of sacred spaces where young people can encounter the divine in a profound and transformative way.[15] The principles of Relational Authority align closely with the US Conference of Catholic Bishops' (USCCB) framework in *Listen, Teach, Send*, which emphasizes the church's mission of accompaniment through deep listening, teaching, and guiding young people on their faith journey.[16] The focus on active listening within Relational Authority directly supports the *Listen, Teach, Send* framework's call for a ministry rooted in authentic engagement and empathy, ensuring that the voices of young people are not only heard but valued.

Transparency, integrity, and care, as outlined in Relational Authority, resonate with the church's broader teachings on human dignity and the need for pastoral leaders to embody Christ-like compassion in all their interactions. The framework's emphasis on humble expertise aligns with the church's call for a servant leadership

---

[14] Tracey Lamont, "Ministry with Young Adults: Toward a New Ecclesiological Imagination," *Religions* 11, no. 11 (2020): 570, doi.org/10.3390/rel11110570.
[15] Michael Hryniuk, "Creating Space for God: Toward a Spirituality of Youth Ministry," *Religious Education* 100, no. 2 (2005): 139–156, doi.org/10.1080/00344080590932445.
[16] USCCB, *National Pastoral Framework for Youth and Young Adult Ministry: Listen, Teach, Send* (United States Conference of Catholic Bishops, 2020).

model, where authority is exercised not through domination but service and empowerment of the faithful. Together, these elements reinforce the church's mission to foster a community of trust, where young people are supported in their spiritual growth and feel genuinely connected to the church's life and mission.

Integrating Frameworks for Effective Ministry

The combination of the Developmental Relationships Framework and Relational Authority offers a robust approach to ministry in a low-trust world. While the Developmental Relationships Framework provides the structural elements needed to build trust, Relational Authority ensures that this trust is rooted in authentic, consistent, and empathetic engagement. For example, when a youth minister uses practices informed by both frameworks, they might begin by actively listening to the concerns of a young person, thereby establishing relational trust. Through this process, the minister expresses care and provides support (Developmental Relationships Framework), while also demonstrating transparency and integrity (Relational Authority). This integrated approach not only fosters trust but also empowers young people to take an active role in their spiritual journey.

Catholic Perspectives on Relational Ministry

The importance of relational ministry is deeply embedded in Catholic teaching. The *Catechism of the Catholic Church* underscores the dignity of every person and the church's role in fostering community through authentic relationships.[17] The Synod on Synodality further emphasizes the church's commitment to listening, dialogue, and participation, essential components of both the Developmental Relationships Framework and Relational Authority. By integrating these frameworks, the church can more effectively engage with young people in a way that is both relationally and theologically sound. This approach not only addresses the immediate challenges of ministering in a low-trust environment but also aligns with the broader mission of the church to accompany individuals on their faith journeys with empathy, respect, and care.

In the following sections, we will explore how these frameworks and a theological underpinning can be applied in practice through Sacred Listening, offering concrete examples and strategies for religious leaders seeking to rebuild trust in their communities. However, before we get to practical application it is important to

---

[17] *Catechism of the Catholic Church*, no. 1878.

understand the corresponding theological foundations of listening that can help guide a relational ministerial response through the development and utilization of low-trust tools in a Catholic context.

Theological Foundations of Listening: A Synodal Approach

As the church seeks to engage more effectively with young people and navigate the challenges of ministering in a low-trust environment, it is essential to ground these efforts in a robust theological framework. The previous discussion highlighted the importance of relational ministry, drawing on the Developmental Relationships Framework and the concept of Relational Authority to build trust and foster authentic connections. However, to fully realize the potential of these frameworks within a Catholic context, it is crucial to explore the corresponding theological foundations of listening.

As a theological practice, listening is not merely a tool for effective ministry but a profound expression of the church's mission to uphold the dignity of every person and accompany individuals on their spiritual journeys. The Synod on Synodality places listening at the heart of the church's life, emphasizing dialogue and participation as key elements of a more relational and participatory ecclesial community. This section will delve into the moral and theological significance of listening within the church, examining how it aligns with Catholic teachings on human dignity, justice, and communal discernment.

Moral Theology and the Dignity of the Person

Moral theology within the Catholic tradition upholds the inherent dignity of every human being, rooted in the theological doctrine of *Imago Dei*—the belief that all individuals are created in the image and likeness of God.[18] This core tenet affirms that every person deserves to be treated with respect, empathy, and care, which are essential elements of authentic Christian ministry. In this context, listening is more than a practical skill; it is a theological act that acknowledges and honors the divine image in each individual.

The *Catechism of the Catholic Church* emphasizes that respect for human dignity is foundational to all social and moral teaching, calling the church to be attentive to the needs and concerns of the faithful.[19] This theological grounding compels the church to create spaces where individuals feel valued and heard, fostering an environment of mutual

---

[18] Charles E. Curran, *The Catholic Moral Tradition Today: A Synthesis* (Washington, DC: Georgetown University Press, 1999).
[19] *Catechism of the Catholic Church*, no. 1700.

respect and understanding. Listening becomes a means of manifesting the church's commitment to the dignity of every person, as it allows for the voices of the marginalized, disenfranchised, and youth to be recognized and affirmed within the faith community.

Listening as a Moral Practice in Synodality

The concept of synodality, as articulated by Pope Francis, extends beyond structural reforms within the church and represents a deeper moral practice rooted in communal discernment and the collective pursuit of truth. The International Theological Commission defines synodality as "the action of the Spirit in the communion of the Body of Christ and in the missionary journey of the People of God."[20] Central to this journey is the practice of listening, which enables the church to discern God's will through the lived experiences of the faithful.

In this synodal context, listening is an essential component of moral theology because it facilitates genuine dialogue and participation within the church. It requires an openness to the perspectives and experiences of others, particularly those who have been marginalized or whose voices have been historically silenced. By engaging in deep and intentional listening, the church not only fulfills its moral obligation to accompany the faithful but also strengthens its communal bonds and fosters a more inclusive ecclesial life.

This approach aligns with the teachings of the Second Vatican Council, which called for the church to be attentive to "the joys and the hopes, the griefs and the anxieties" of all people, especially those who are poor or in any way afflicted.[21] Listening, therefore, is integral to the church's mission of solidarity and justice, as it ensures that every member of the community is heard and their experiences inform the church's moral and pastoral responses.

Theological Implications of Listening for Justice and Participation

Moral theology also emphasizes the virtue of justice, which involves giving each person their due—not only in material terms but also in ensuring that their spiritual and emotional needs are met. Within the church, justice requires that individuals are not only heard but that their voices contribute meaningfully to the life of the community. Listening, therefore, becomes an act of justice, as it

---

[20] International Theological Commission, *Synodality in the Life and Mission of the Church*, no. 46.
[21] Second Vatican Council, *Gaudium et Spes*, no. 1.

provides individuals the opportunity to share their experiences, challenges, and hopes, and participate actively in the church's mission.

The Synod on Synodality's focus on listening as a form of participation reflects the church's broader commitment to justice. Listening prioritizes every person's contribution to the church's moral and spiritual life, recognizing that true justice within the church involves a relational dynamic where all members are engaged and their voices respected. This perspective reinforces the idea that listening is not just a pastoral tool but a moral imperative that enables the church to live out its commitment to justice and solidarity.

The theological foundations of listening, as explored in this section, align closely with the broader vision of the Synod on Synodality for a more inclusive and participatory church. By framing listening as a practice that embodies the principles of *Imago Dei* and justice, the church can more effectively engage with young people and those who feel alienated or unheard. This approach revitalizes the church's moral witness and ensures that its pastoral practices are grounded in the rich tradition of moral theology.

In this context, listening is not merely a passive act but an active engagement that reflects the church's commitment to accompaniment, solidarity, and justice. By embracing the theological principles of listening, the church can create a more vibrant and inclusive faith community that truly reflects the divine love and compassion at the heart of the Gospel.

As we move forward in this discussion, the next section will introduce a theory of sacred listening, building on these theological foundations to offer a practical framework for ministry in a low-trust world. By understanding and applying the theology of listening, religious leaders can develop strategies that not only address the challenges of the contemporary church but also foster deeper, more meaningful relationships within their communities.

TOWARD A THEORY OF SACRED LISTENING

Building on the foundations established in the previous discussions, this section proposes a theory of Sacred Listening as an essential component of relational ministry. As emphasized in previous sections, relational trust is critical, and the church should consider adopting tools that resonate with contemporary challenges, particularly in the context of synodality. Sacred Listening emerges as a pivotal practice within this framework, transcending mere conversation to embody a profound commitment to valuing and engaging with each person's spiritual journey.

Sacred Listening is not simply a psychological technique or a communication strategy; it is a theologically-grounded practice that reflects the church's mission of accompaniment, as outlined by Pope Francis in *Evangelii Gaudium*. This document calls the church to proclaim the Gospel through accompaniment and encounter which is deeply personal, a call that resonates with the principles of Sacred Listening. Further, Pope Francis calls for an accompaniment rooted in listening and dialogue not bound by time. By integrating theological principles with insights from psychology, communication, and sociology, Sacred Listening fosters the deep, empathetic connections necessary for building trust and facilitating the kind of spiritual growth called for in the context of a listening church. This practice is framed through three key components—*Imago Dei*, Alignment, and Pattern Recognition—which together form the bedrock of relational ministry in a low-trust environment.

Imago Dei

The concept of *Imago Dei* serves as the theological foundation for Sacred Listening.[22] This doctrine compels the church to approach every interaction with reverence and respect, recognizing the divine presence in each person. As Pope John Paul II emphasized in *Redemptor Hominis*, the recognition of humanity's dignity as created in the image of God is fundamental to the mission of the church.[23] Sacred Listening, therefore, involves more than just hearing words; it requires an intentional commitment to understanding the deeper spiritual and emotional dimensions of the individual's experience.

This theological grounding is essential for fostering a sense of belonging within faith communities. This recognition that runs throughout Catholic teaching, but particularly expressed in the works of Pope Francis, necessitates that the church actively engage the faith narratives of individuals, affirming their identity and place within the community. In this context, Sacred Listening becomes a crucial element in faith formation, where being truly heard can lead to moments of profound spiritual insight and transformation, fulfilling the church's mission of accompaniment.

The psychological and sociological literature further supports this approach. Research shows that when individuals feel their identity and

---

[22] While a full exploration of *Imago Dei* is beyond the scope of this article, the authors have found the foundational concept informative for the development of Sacred Listening in part because of its ability to transcend denominational contexts. For more information, see Ryan S. Peterson, *The* Imago Dei *as Human Identity: A Theological Interpretation* (University Park, PA: Penn State University Press, 2016).

[23] See John Paul II, *Redemptor Hominis* (Encyclical Letter on the Redeemer of Man), no. 7.

experiences are valued, it significantly enhances their relational satisfaction and well-being.[24] By grounding Sacred Listening in *Imago Dei*, the church not only affirms the individual's dignity but also fosters the relational trust essential for effective ministry.

Alignment

The concept of Alignment, which involves harmonizing with the speaker both emotionally and cognitively, draws from both theological and psychological foundations. In the context of pastoral care, alignment is about entering into the experiences of the other, reflecting Christ's empathetic engagement with humanity. Saint Thomas Aquinas's principle of synderesis—the innate ability to align with the good and true—provides a theological basis for this practice.[25] This principle underscores the importance of aligning our actions and thoughts with God's will, which in pastoral care translates to aligning ourselves with the needs and experiences of those we serve.

From a psychological perspective, alignment is supported by theories of perceived responsiveness and active listening. Studies demonstrate that when listeners respond in ways that make the speaker feel understood and valued, it enhances relational satisfaction and fosters deeper connections.[26] This body of research emphasizes the importance of active listening as a means of creating an empathetic and non-judgmental environment, which is crucial for effective pastoral care in a modern context.

In Sacred Listening, alignment is not just a psychological tool but a sacred practice. By aligning with the speaker's emotional and spiritual state, the listener embodies the church's call to be a compassionate presence in the lives of others, as modeled by Christ. This approach enhances the relational bonds necessary for community building and spiritual growth, as discussed in the "Low-Trust Tools"

---

[24] Harry T. Reis, Margaret S. Clark, and John G. Holmes, "Perceived Partner Responsiveness as an Organizing Construct in the Study of Intimacy and Closeness," in *Handbook of Closeness and Intimacy*, ed. D. J. Mashek and A. P. Aron (Mahwah, NJ: Lawrence Erlbaum, 2004), 201–225.
[25] Thomas Aquinas, *Summa Theologiae*, I–II, q. 94, a. 1.
[26] Hiroaki Kawamichi, Kazufumi Yoshihara, Akihiro T. Sasaki, Sho K. Sugawara, Hiroki C. Tanabe, Ryoji Shinohara, Yuka Sugisawa, Kentaro Tokutake, Yukiko Mochizuki, Tokie Anme, and Norihiro Sadato, "Perceiving Active Listening Activates the Reward System and Improves the Impression of Relevant Experiences," *Social Neuroscience* 10, no. 1 (2015): 16–26, doi.org/10.1080/17470919.2014.954732; Carl R. Rogers and Richard E. Farson, *Active Listening* (Boston, MA: Houghton Mifflin, 1957); Harry Weger, Gina Castle Bell, Elizabeth M. Minei, and Melissa C. Robinson, "The Relative Effectiveness of Active Listening in Initial Interactions," *International Journal of Listening* 28, no. 1 (2014): 13–31, doi:10.1080/10904018.2013.813234.

section. Pope Francis highlights this in *Evangelii Gaudium*, where he calls for a church that is "bruised, hurting, and dirty because it has been out on the streets," fully engaging with the realities of those it serves.[27]

Pattern Recognition

Pattern recognition in Sacred Listening involves identifying recurring themes and dynamics within conversations, which can provide deeper insights into the individual's spiritual journey and the broader cultural context influencing their beliefs and behaviors. This component is crucial for understanding how personal experiences are shaped by larger social, cultural, and historical forces.

Theologically, this practice is rooted in the Catholic tradition of discernment. Saint Ignatius of Loyola's *Spiritual Exercises* emphasize the importance of recognizing patterns of consolation and desolation in the spiritual life, guiding individuals toward a deeper understanding of God's will,[28] In Sacred Listening, pattern recognition helps the listener discern underlying spiritual currents in a person's narrative, allowing for more meaningful and empathetic engagement.

Sociologically, pattern recognition aligns with the use of narrative therapy and social learning theory, where understanding the broader context of an individual's story can lead to more effective pastoral care. Recognizing patterns in conversations enables the listener to provide appropriate support and guidance, enhancing the individual's ability to navigate their faith journey.[29] This approach is essential for the church's mission, as it helps identify not only individual needs but also broader trends that may be affecting the faith community as a whole.

This holistic approach, which integrates theological discernment with sociological and psychological tools, allows for a deeper engagement with the speaker's experiences. By understanding the patterns in an individual's life, the church can better accompany them on their spiritual journey, reinforcing the themes explored in both the "Low-Trust Tools" and "Sacred Listening and Moral Theology" sections.

---

[27] Francis, *Evangelii Gaudium*, no. 49.
[28] Ignatius of Loyola, *The Spiritual Exercises and Selected Works*, ed. George E. Ganss, The Classics of Western Spirituality (Mahwah, NJ: Paulist, 1991).
[29] Mark H. Butler, Jacob D. Gossner, Connor C. Barham, Madeline C. Hansen-Bethea, and Misha D. Crawford, "Discerning Motivational Interviewing through a Spiritual Lens: Discovering a Christian MI Archetype and Native MI Language," *Journal of Marital and Family Therapy* 47, no. 3 (2021): 767–784, doi.org/10.1111/jmft.12472.

Faith Formation and Sacred Listening

Faith formation is deeply rooted in human experience and profoundly influenced by interactions within the community. Sacred Listening, when grounded in the principles of *Imago Dei*, Alignment, and Pattern Recognition, becomes a powerful tool for nurturing faith and facilitating spiritual growth. This practice not only affirms the dignity of the individual but also fosters the deep, empathetic connections essential for building a trusting and inclusive church community.

Pope Francis has emphasized the need for the church to be a place where every person feels heard, respected, and valued—where their stories are taken seriously, and the community is committed to walking with them on their spiritual journey.[30] Sacred Listening, therefore, is not merely a pastoral tool but a theological imperative. It calls the church to be fully present to the needs and experiences of its members, fulfilling its mission of accompaniment and embodying the principles of synodality. As the church moves forward in its synodal journey, Sacred Listening practices offer a concrete way to operationalize the vision of a more inclusive and participatory church, where every voice is valued, and every person's dignity is upheld.

Sacred Listening practices can play a crucial role in faith formation. By integrating theological principles with psychological, communication, and sociological insights, these practices demonstrate their transformative power in nurturing faith, enhancing spiritual well-being, and strengthening communal bonds. Through such meaningful interaction, the church can effectively engage with its members, creating a community that truly reflects the divine love and compassion that lies at the heart of the Gospel.

SACRED LISTENING IN PRACTICE

In an era marked by growing skepticism toward institutions, particularly among younger generations, the church faces the critical challenge of fostering meaningful connections that resonate with contemporary spiritual needs. The Synod on Synodality calls the church to a renewed commitment to listening, dialogue, and accompaniment—key elements that require more than superficial engagement. In response to this challenge, we have developed the theory of Sacred Listening above. In this section, we explore what Sacred Listening Theory looks like in practice.

Unlike traditional "high-trust tools" that rely on presumed

---

[30] Pope Francis, *Amoris Laetitia*, nos. 136–138.

institutional authority, these practices acknowledge and address the prevailing skepticism, particularly among younger generations, who seek authenticity and relational depth. By employing these "low-trust tools," pastoral leaders can facilitate focused and impartial listening, encouraging individuals to share their stories and experiences in ways that lead to deeper spiritual growth and a renewed sense of belonging within the church.

Through Sacred Listening Practices, the church can effectively operate within a low-trust environment, rebuilding trust and fostering deeper connections within its communities. These tools are not merely functional; they are a concrete manifestation of the church's theological mission, bridging the gap between theological reflection and actionable ministry. They ensure that the church's mission remains relevant and impactful in today's world by embodying the principles of synodality—listening, accompanying, and discerning together in a spirit of communion.

In the sections that follow, we will take a deep look at one specific Sacred Listening Practice—Mapping Trusted Relationships—to illustrate how these principles come together in a practical example. This exploration will demonstrate how the theoretical components of Sacred Listening are operationalized, offering a tangible model for how the church can engage meaningfully with individuals in a low-trust context, thus living out the call to be a more listening and responsive church.

Mapping Trusted Relationships

The "Mapping Trusted Relationships" exercise provides a concrete example of how the theoretical components of Sacred Listening—*Imago Dei*, alignment, and pattern recognition—can be operationalized in a pastoral context.[31] This tool is especially relevant in the context of the Synod on Synodality, as it embodies the church's commitment to becoming a more listening, responsive community, particularly in environments where trust in institutions is fragile.

Furthermore, the exercise is an embodiment of the church's mission of justice, as it ensures that all voices, especially those of the young and marginalized, are given due attention. Pope Benedict XVI's encyclical *Caritas in Veritate* reminds us that justice requires listening to one another as a fundamental aspect of our commitment to the common good.[32] This exercise operationalizes this commitment by

---

[31] This activity will be described briefly in these pages. The full exercise can be accessed at www.futureoffaith.org/sacredlisteningtools.
[32] Pope Benedict XVI, *Caritas in Veritate* (Encyclical Letter on Integral Human Development in Charity and Truth), no. 54.

creating a structured process through which young people can articulate their trusted relationships and spiritual experiences, offering the church a tangible means of fulfilling its mission of justice.

Overview

The "Mapping Trusted Relationships" exercise is an interactive activity designed with three phases to help participants identify and reflect on the key individuals in their lives who play significant roles in their daily interactions, trust circles, and faith conversations. By using simple shapes and prompts, participants map out their social and spiritual connections, providing a visual representation of their relational landscape. This exercise not only fosters self-awareness and personal reflection but also encourages open dialogue about the integration of faith in everyday relationships. Through guided discussions and follow-up, the activity aims to deepen connections, build a supportive community, and empower participants to explore and expand their spiritual lives within a trusted network.

The exercise begins with the "Intentions" phase. Here the facilitator begins by establishing a sacred space, acknowledging each participant as inherently sacred and a reflection of the divine, setting the stage for deep, respectful engagement. This sacred space is not just a physical environment but a relational one, grounded in the understanding that each person's voice deserves to be heard with empathy and reverence. The purpose of the exercise is then shared, emphasizing that it involves mapping significant relationships and spiritual interactions through simple shapes and words. To deepen the sense of sacredness, the facilitator may introduce a ritual, such as a poem, meditation, or prayer, that resonates with the group's cultural or spiritual background.

Second, in the "Ask and Record" phase, participants are provided with materials like index cards and writing utensils. They are instructed to draw shapes on the cards—circles for people they talk to daily, squares for those they trust with secrets, and triangles for those they discuss faith with. Numeric and textual prompts are added to capture details about their relationships and spiritual practices. Participants then flip the card to write down a faith-related conversation topic they would like to explore. Finally, they are encouraged to reflect on the exercise and note any insights or feelings about their relationships.

Lastly, in the "Explore and Follow-Up" phase, participants engage in a group discussion or individual reflection to share insights from the exercise, guided by questions about their relationships and faith life. The facilitator collects and organizes the responses to identify patterns and plan follow-up interactions. Regular check-ins are scheduled to reinforce Sacred Listening practices and track any changes in participants' conversations about faith. Additionally, efforts are made to scale relationships by connecting participants with others who can help them grow spiritually, potentially through events, new groups, or personal introductions based on shared interests.

The "Mapping Trusted Relationships" tool translates the abstract components of Sacred Listening into a practical exercise designed to build trust in a low-trust environment. Here's how each component is operationalized:

***Imago Dei*:** This component is woven throughout the exercise as it establishes that every participant is valued, and their experiences are sacred. By framing the activity within the understanding that each individual is made in the image of God, the exercise fosters an environment where participants feel their voices are respected and their dignity is upheld. This theological grounding ensures that the act of listening is not merely a procedural task but a sacred responsibility.

Alignment: The exercise involves guiding participants to map out their trusted relationships, using simple shapes on notecards to represent different types of connections (e.g., daily interactions, those trusted with secrets, and those with whom they discuss faith). This step aligns the participants' internal experiences with external expressions, creating a visual representation of their social and spiritual networks. By doing so, the exercise helps participants and pastoral leaders align their understanding of these relationships with the broader context of the participant's faith journey. The act of mapping is not just about categorization; it is about aligning the participants' inner worlds with the church's pastoral outreach, ensuring that pastoral care is tailored to the actual lived experiences of individuals.

Pattern Recognition: Once the relationships are mapped, the exercise moves into a phase of guided reflection, where patterns and themes within the participants' relational networks are identified and explored. This is where the concept of Pattern Recognition becomes crucial. By analyzing these patterns, pastoral leaders can discern commonalities in the types of relationships most influential in the participants' spiritual lives. This understanding allows the church to respond more effectively to the needs of young people, recognizing the broader social contexts that shape their faith journeys. Pattern Recognition in this context also allows ministry leaders to identify areas where trust is strong and where it may need to be rebuilt, providing actionable insights that go beyond individual encounters.

The "Mapping Trusted Relationships" exercise is not just a tool for pastoral care; it is a response to Pope Francis's call for a synodal church—one that listens, engages, and responds to the faithful, particularly in a world where trust in institutions is diminishing. This tool exemplifies how the church can move beyond traditional, high-trust methods of engagement and adopt practices better suited to the current context of skepticism and disaffiliation. By focusing on the relational dynamics within a young person's life, the exercise helps the church accompany its members more effectively, ensuring that pastoral care is rooted in genuine understanding and respect for individual experiences.

Moreover, this practice aligns with the broader goals of the Synod on Synodality, which seeks to transform the church into a community more attentive to the voices of all its members, especially those who feel disconnected or marginalized. The exercise provides a practical example of how the church can operationalize its commitment to listening, not just as a temporary measure during the synodal process but as an ongoing practice that sustains its mission in a low-trust environment.

CONCLUSION

The Sacred Listening Theory and exercise outlined in this article are not just a response to the declining trust in religious institutions; they are a direct and practical extension of the vision set forth by the Synod on Synodality. This synodal journey, called forth by Pope Francis, challenges the church to engage more deeply with its members through listening, dialogue, and a commitment to accompaniment. Sacred Listening Practices operationalize this call, providing concrete tools that translate the theological principles of synodality into actionable ministry practices.

In the context of the Synod on Synodality, the church is invited to move beyond traditional methods of engagement, which often rely on institutional authority, and adopt a more relational approach that meets the needs of contemporary society. Sacred Listening Practices are designed to build trust in a low-trust environment by prioritizing authentic, empathetic engagement over institutional power. They embody the church's mission to accompany all its members, especially the young and those who feel marginalized or disconnected.

These practices are deeply rooted in the theological principles of *Imago Dei* and justice, reflecting the church's commitment to recognizing the inherent dignity of every person. By integrating these principles into its pastoral practices, the church not only enhances its moral witness but also ensures that it remains relevant and responsive to the needs of its members. Sacred Listening thus becomes a vital means by which the church can fulfill its synodal mission of becoming a more inclusive and participatory community.

Moreover, Sacred Listening Practices represent a dynamic and evolving approach to ministry, that requires continuous adaptation and responsiveness. As the church listens more deeply to the voices of its members, it must also be prepared to act on what it hears, fostering a cycle of listening, learning, and growth. This reciprocal model is essential for rebuilding trust and fostering a deeper sense of belonging within the faith community.

Sacred Listening is not just a tool for ministry; but a tangible expression of the synodal church that Pope Francis envisions—a church that listens, accompanies, and engages with the realities of its people. By embracing these practices, the church can more effectively carry out its mission in today's world, fostering meaningful relationships that reflect the true essence of the Gospel. Through Sacred Listening, the church becomes a living embodiment of the synodal path, journeying together with its members in faith, hope, and love. M

Josh Packard, PhD, is the co-founder of Future of Faith, a non-profit dedicated to helping support relational ministry approaches through research and resources centered in listening. He was previously the founding executive director of Springtide Research Institute and the executive president of Strategy and Operations at the National Catholic Educational Association. Prior to working in the non-profit sector, Dr. Packard was a professor of sociology specializing in the sociology of religion. He has numerous academic and professional publications. He holds a PhD in Sociology from Vanderbilt University and a BA from Texas Lutheran University.

Megan Bissell, MA, is the executive director of Future of Faith. She has previously worked as the head of research at Springtide Research Institute, vice president of research at the National Catholic Educational Association, and deputy director of the Social Research Lab. She is one of the foremost applied sociologists in the field of religion, having constructed the largest dataset about young people and faith and coordinated dozens of research projects in the field. She holds her MA in Sociology from the University of Northern Colorado.

Epilogue: Listening and the Moral Life

Alexis Artaud de La Ferrière

Abstract: The Synod on Synodality placed the concept of "listening" at its core. Throughout the four-year process of the synod, people have agonized over who was listening to whom, on what terms, and to what end. The aim of this epilogue is to reflect on the moral implications of listening. I argue that we have the capacity to engage in listening at various levels of depth—that is, the degree to which the listener is decentered from him or herself, entering into a relationship with the other, and ultimately with Christ. I describe three gradually deepening levels of listening: *intentional listening*, which constitutes a simple act of acknowledging and curiously learning about the other; *recognitive listening*, wherein understanding of the other occurs; and *caritative listening*, a practice of free self-giving in a kenotic move which transforms listening into an authentically Christian practice.

Whatever else was at stake over the course of the Synod on Synodality, one central issue was the notion of "listening." Throughout the four-year process of the Synod, people agonized over who was listening to whom, on what terms, and to what end. Proponents of synodality argued that it should be received as "an authentic ethic of listening which seeks to learn from and engage all of the members of the community in honesty and charity."[1] Critics, however, were skeptical, especially when it came to the preparatory "listening phase" of the synod. They were concerned that the focus on "horizontal" listening within the church should not undermine its capacity for "vertical" listening. Thus, for example, Tracey Rowlands warned that "one can so hypostasize the Church as separate from Christ—as, perhaps, a 'people of God' made transparent through sociological analysis—that she degrades into a voluntary and even purely human association with a merely historical connection to a putative founder."[2] The articles in

---

[1] Mario Cardinal Grech, "Message to the United States Conference of Catholic Bishops," November 18, 2021, www.usccb.org/resources/ENG_Video-Message%20to%20the%20USCCB.pdf.
[2] Angela Franks, "Christ as the Way of Synodality," *The Thomist* 87, no. 2 (2023): 257, doi.org/10.1353/tho.2023.0008.

this special issue deal with specific aspects of this debate: the place of the Holy Spirit in synodal listening and discernment, the efficacy of "conversation in the spirit" methodology, the relationship between sociology and theology, the theological relevance of listening to people at the margins, as well as practical reflections on experiences of listening practices at all levels of the church. All of these contribute to a richer understanding of the potential risks and rewards of becoming a more synodal church.

My aim in this epilogue is to offer an initial reflection on the moral implications of listening as a practice and disposition. Starting from a basic sensory account, I argue that we have the capacity to engage in listening at various levels of depth—that is, the degree to which the listener is decentered from him or herself, entering into a relationship with the other, and ultimately with Christ. I describe three gradually deepening levels of listening: *intentional listening*, which constitutes a simple act of acknowledging and curiously learning about the other; *recognitive listening*, wherein understanding of the other occurs; and *caritative listening*, a practice of free self-giving in a kenotic move which transforms listening into an authentically Christian practice.

What follows is not meant to constitute a theology of synodal listening; my immediate concern in these pages is restricted to "listening" as horizontal and intersubjective relationship between human persons. I do not venture so far as to consider "the relationship between listening to the Word of God attested to in Scripture, the reception of Tradition and the Magisterium of the Church, and the prophetic reading of the signs of the times,"[3] questions at the heart of the synodal process and treated in various ways by the preceding articles. This choice of focus is not to diminish the importance of such thicker theological questions or of vertical listening in general.[4] Rather, I want to articulate why we should also consider the simple act of horizontal listening as a legitimate topic of Christian inquiry into the moral life.

THREE LEVELS OF LISTENING

Listening is closely associated with sense-perception, and yet richer and more complex than the mere fact of acquiring information about the external world through sensory organs. Listening is not equivalent to what occurs during a hearing test, where a patient wears

---

[3] *Synthesis Report of the First Session of the XVI Ordinary General Assembly of the Synod of Bishops*, no. I.2.f.
[4] See Thomas G. Dalzell, "Eucharist, Communion, and Orthopraxis in the Theology of Joseph Ratzinger," *Irish Theological Quarterly* 78, no. 2 (2013): 103–122, doi.org/10.1177/00211400124726.

headphones and is instructed to push a button when they hear an auditory stimulus. At the same time, I do not mean by "listening" something so broad that it is synonymous with acquiring knowledge about the world.

In everyday language, "listening" evokes auditory sense-perception. Listening is done by means of hearing and is usually distinguished as a specific type of the latter when we hear purposefully or with intent, commit our attention closely to something with the express purpose of hearing that thing. Let us call this *intentional listening*, both in the sense that it is done deliberately and corresponds to a mental state with intentionality, i.e., a mental state with content, or is about something. To illustrate this first, basic notion of listening, imagine the following example. I am sitting on my terrace on a sunny afternoon reading a book, completely unaware of the soundscape constantly resonating against my eardrums. In some real physical sense, I am hearing all sorts of sounds, but not listening to any of them. Then, something changes. At some point, perhaps because my mind wanders momentarily from the words on the page, I notice a particular sound that may have been present all the while or have suddenly appeared—say a chaffinch's song. Now I am *listening* to that song, heeding it, appreciating it, perhaps getting up to look out for a small spot of orange-pink breast feathers in the dark green of the hedgerow. Like Samuel in the temple, my consciousness and actions are now awake and directed outwardly towards the source of that sound.

This sort of intentional listening describes a very basic capacity, easily recognizable in ourselves and certain other, non-human animals. It evokes both our embodiedness and ability to be attentive to and curious about the world. But it falls short of a moral practice in the sense of an activity through which we embody a virtue. "Listening" can also mean something more morally profound: a deeper notion we might call *recognitive listening*. On this account, the act of listening is associated with our capacity to learn about and understand something or someone external to ourselves. This assumes a capacity for deliberately paying heed to something through our auditory sense-perception, as in intentional listening. However, something additional is also taking place: I am not only externally focusing my attention on a particular sound, but mentally recognizing that thing or person, either because I have some pre-existing knowledge which allows me to pick it out of its environment and understand something of its essence. Or perhaps because, through the act of listening, I am able to learn something about it that gives rise to understanding. Alternatively, both may be present: pre-existing knowledge may be complemented by new knowledge learnt through listening, which gives rise to a deeper level of understanding.

To return to our birdsong example: perhaps when my mind drifts away from my book and I first notice the chaffinch song, I was not previously aware of what a chaffinch sounds like. I notice a series of notes, but do not recognize the song and do not know what kind of bird sings like that. So, I focus on the song—maybe I notice that the notes are descending, then I perceive a flourish at the end of each phrase. If I were very perceptive, the song might evoke in me the image of a bowler running to deliver a cricket ball, as some ornithologists describe it. During this time, I am also looking out for the source of the song—and suddenly I catch a glimpse of the chaffinch in the hedge. I am no longer just focused on an external noise in the air. I have come to understand that this song is of a particular bird, and my mind has recognized the chaffinch's being, perhaps not profoundly, but certainly in such a way that I am now listening to *that* bird and understand something about *that* creature of which I was previously ignorant.

How much we can understand (or what kind of understanding we can expect) through listening will depend on what or whom we are listening to. My understanding of the chaffinch by listening to its song will penetrate deeper than my understanding of a quartz watch by listening to it tick. My understanding of another person will potentially be much greater still, assuming certain conditions for recognitive listening are met. Joseph Beatty, for example, argues that the "fundamental project [of listening] is *understanding* the other and so achieving a kind of fidelity to the meaning or intention of the other."[5] This is possible with another human person in a way that is not with a quartz watch because the latter expresses neither meaning nor intention (although it arguably conveys or reflects a limited range of meaning and intention from the person who designed it). In some sense, the chaffinch does express meaning or intention not readily accessible to my understanding in the way another person's meanings and intentions are. Recognitive listening is most fully present when it occurs intersubjectively, between two persons who share a common language.

A third notion is one I will call *caritative listening*. This describes the act of listening to another person with the deliberate intent that the other person might be heard and feel they are listened to. For example, say that my wife comes home one day visibly upset. As she is someone I love, this is distressing for me, and I will want to know what upset her. Wanting to gain this knowledge leads me down the path to intentional listening; I want to direct my attention towards my wife. Perhaps, this will also lead me to a form of recognitive listening; I do

---

[5] Joseph Beatty, "Good Listening," *Educational Theory* 49, no. 3 (1999): 282.

not merely want to extract information from my wife, I want to understand her subjective experience of the supposed event. Note that these two instances of listening are both directed toward myself as an end. *I* want to know so that *I* will understand. In the case of recognitive listening, I am somewhat displaced in the sense that I am seeking understanding of another person's inner life, but this is still directed toward an end within myself. This is not to say that these are necessarily ignoble or selfish intentions. It may be that I genuinely want to understand what happened out of love for my wife; one of love's manifestations is a desire to know and understand the beloved better. I may intend my act of listening as an instrumental means to helping my wife; maybe I have previous knowledge about an existing dispute with a neighbor and judge I would be well positioned to pre-empt further distress to my wife if I can learn about the most recent incident and discuss it with the neighbor (of course, my judgement regarding the helpfulness of my action might be mistaken!). Regardless, the point is that these intentions will not be sufficient to lead me to caritative listening.

In order for that to occur, my intention must be to give my wife an opportunity to be listened to. Whereas the crux of intentional and recognitive listening lies in the internal experience of the listener who notices, learns, and understands something about the thing or person to which/whom they are listening, the constitutive end of caritative listening is centered on the other's experience. This implies a more radical decentering of the self—the aim is not to effect a change in oneself but to participate in a change in the other (although the listener is also necessarily changed by the very act of decentering). Even though caritative listening is sustained by the listener, its salient experience belongs to the other, who feels they are being properly recognized through the listening act, where their meaning or intention is being understood by the listener. In that sense, caritative listening is a gift freely given by the listener—a kenosis wherein the listener empties him or herself for the sake of the other.

At the beginning of my text, I wrote that the act of listening ultimately brings us into a deeper relationship with Christ. This Christological dimension of listening was also highlighted by the authors of the *Synthesis Report* following the first session of the synod: "Placing Jesus at the center of our lives requires some degree of self-emptying. In this perspective, providing a listening ear means being willing to 'decenter' oneself in order to leave space for the other."[6] Charlotte Brontë expresses this in other terms through the voice of Rochester when her brooding hero confesses to Jane Eyre that

---

[6] *Synthesis Report*, no. III.16.c.

he can speak to her "almost as freely as if I were writing my thoughts in a diary" because he feels Jane listens to him "with no malevolent scorn of indiscretion, but with a kind of innate sympathy; not the less comforting and encouraging because it is very unobtrusive in its manifestations."[7] What Rochester perceives here is no mere passive receptiveness in Jane. It is a disposition, which develops in her and gradually comes to characterize her identity in the novel. Here and elsewhere, Jane actively practices a form of surrender and self-denial through which she ultimately gains freedom and mastery over her world, thereby reconciling any apparent tension between her Christ-like and proto-feminist qualities.

As with other kinds of gift-giving, caritative listening does not always succeed. It can go wrong in several ways. First, the listening party may engage someone in a listening relation but not genuinely intend or have the capacity to properly recognize the other person. The most obvious way in which this could happen is where the listening party is insincere in their intent and wanting to deceive the person to whom they are listening. For example, a seducer may want to lull the object of their desire into a false sense of intimacy by posing as someone with whom secrets can be shared, "and then in the course of the telling to fool them" as admits the amoral Johannes in Kierkegaard's examination of the aesthetic stage preceding the ethical stage of life.[8] In such a scenario, caritative listening is a sham; the listening act is not intended for the benefit of the other but as a means of gaining dominancy over the other and extracting pleasure from them. Importantly in such a scenario, the seduced party may feel as though they have been listened to and genuinely recognized by the seducer, but in fact they are mistaken. A less obvious way in which caritative listening can fail is where the listener is not intentionally deceitful but mistaken about their own intentions or capacities. There is a passage in chapter III of *Emma* in which the eponymous heroine feels she can show "no greater kindness than in listening" to her young protégée, Harriet. However, throughout much of the novel, Emma is ever misunderstanding and ignoring Harriet's true character and wishes, preferring to impose her own ill-conceived match-making schemes rather than to recognize the young woman's true love for the tenant farmer Robert Martin, of whom Emma disapproves. Again, in this instance Harriet may well feel she is being listened to by Emma (and probably is to a greater degree than in the previous scenario involving the deceitful seducer) but, unbeknownst to her, Emma

---

[7] Charlotte Brontë, *Jane Eyre: An Autobiography*, Project Gutenberg, March, 1998, www.gutenberg.org/files/1260/1260-h/1260-h.htm.
[8] Søren Kierkegaard, *Either/Or*, trans. Howard and Edna Hong (Princeton, NJ: Princeton University Press), 370.

cannot at this stage in the novel truly listen to Harriet because she is so focused on her own schemes and fancies. Importantly, both of these instances of infelicitous caritative listening can be described as moral failings in which the listener is either unwilling or unable to decenter themselves in a kenotic move for the good of the other.

Thus, we have identified three levels of listening: *intentional*, *recognitive*, and *caritative*. In each case, the listener engages in the same basic act of paying heed to something or someone in the external world—they all require conscious externalization of one's attention and decentering of the self. What differentiates the three types of listening is the degree of decentering they imply and the specific end towards which they are oriented. Intentional listening implies a greater degree of decentering than recognitive listening because in the latter, one is not only conscious of an external phenomenon, but makes a deliberate effort to understand the other. When that other is a person with whom we share a common language, that understanding can potentially be much deeper so that recognitive listening is really only fully accomplished as an intersubjective act. In turn, caritative listening implies a greater degree of decentering than recognitive listening because caritative listening is oriented towards an end situated within the other person (in this case it can only be another human person): they might know they are heard, and have the experience of being listened to.

These levels of listening should be thought of as ideal-types or mental images. I do not suppose real people go about their day, assessing their environment and choosing to "switch on" a particular type of listening according to what the situation demands. The fact that one of these types of listening may be engaged at a particular time does not necessarily preclude that another is also concomitantly engaged—and people need not consciously be aware of different types of listening, nor think explicitly about the concept of listening at all to successfully perform a listening act. We do make a conscious effort in the direction and manner in which we listen; but to a large extent, if listening is genuinely occurring, we will not be thinking about the act itself but that thing or person to which we are paying heed. Indeed, if I am overly concerned about *whether* I am in fact listening and *what sort* of listening I am doing, then I am probably so caught up in my own interiority that I am not really listening at all. As ever, the risk of engaging in moral theory is that it could displace rather than sustain moral action. M

Alexis Artaud de La Ferrière is lecturer in sociology at Royal Holloway College, University of London and associate researcher at the *Groupe Sociétés Religions Laïcités* (EPHE/CNRS) in Paris.